IN DEFENSE
OF THE INDIANS

The Defense of the Most Reverend Lord,
Don Fray Bartolomé de Las Casas,
of the Order of Preachers,
Late Bishop of Chiapa, Against
the Persecutors and Slanderers
of the Peoples of the New World
Discovered Across the Seas

Don Barthélemi de Las Casas, Évêque de Chiapa,
Protecteur des naturels de l'Amérique. From the
Paris, 1822, edition by J. A. Llorente,
Oeuvres de don Barthélemi de Las Casas.

IN DEFENSE
OF THE INDIANS

*The Defense of the Most Reverend Lord, Don Fray
Bartolomé de Las Casas, of the Order of Preachers,
Late Bishop of Chiapa, Against the Persecutors
and Slanderers of the Peoples of the New World
Discovered Across the Seas*

Bartolomé de Las Casas

Translated and Edited by STAFFORD POOLE, C.M.

Foreword by Martin E. Marty

ffi NORTHERN ILLINOIS UNIVERSITY PRESS · DeKalb

We wish to thank the University of New Mexico Press for permission to use the information relating to the dating of this treatise taken from Henry Raup Wagner, *The Life and Writings of Bartolomé de las Casas* (© 1967) p. 279.

We also wish to thank the trustees of the Newberry Library for permission to use the following from the Edward E. Ayer collection:

Mexican calendar motif on half-title page, collected by Waldeck, Ayer Ms. 1271;

Don Barthélemi de Las Casas portrait from J. A. Llorente, *Oeuvres de don Barthélemi de Las Casas* 1822;

Ornamental letters used on openings, from Las Casas, *Brevissima Relación de la Destruyción de las Indias,* Seville, 1552;

Entire set of previously unpublished Indian drawings from the Codex Zempoala (Ayer Ms. 1472) and Codex Tepotzotlan (Ayer Ms. 1479).

Library of Congress Cataloging in Publication Data

Casas, Bartolomé de las, Bp. of Chiapa, 1474-1566.
In defense of the Indians/ Bartolomé de las Casas; translated and edited by Stafford Poole; new foreword by Martin E. Marty

Translation of a ca. 1552 Latin ms. in the Bibliothéque nationale, Paris (Nouveaux fonds Latins, no. 12926)
      Includes bibliographical references.
      1. Indians, Treatment of. 2. Sepúlveda, Juan Ginés de, 1490-1573.
3. Catholic Church in America—Missions. 4. Spain—Colonies—Administration.
I. Poole, Stafford, ed. II. Title
ISBN 0-87580-556-6 (pbk.: acid-free paper)   92—60321
Copyright © 1992 by Northern Illinois University Press

  3rd impression, 1999

Published by the Northern Illinois University Press, DeKalb, Illinois 60115
Manufactured in the United States using acid-free paper

To

John Francis Bannon, S.J.

Sacerdos, Magister, Amicus

Contents

II. THE *DEFENSE*

x   *Contents*

Foreword

HALF a millennium after the event, historians and the general public have learned to say not that Columbus *discovered* America but that with his voyages he *encountered* a world that was new to Europeans. It also should long ago have been noticed that Columbus never really did "discover" the Native Americans whom he called Indians. The adventurer brought stereotypes into which these people had to fit: we Europeans, he deduced, might both "save" them and "enslave" them.

Bartolome de Las Casas, a Dominican priest, might more properly have been described all along as the one who *discovered* these Americans. Now we might also change that to say he *encountered* them. Las Casas smashed his own stereotypes and came to know these as the "others" who were not simply objects for salvation, certainly not subjects for slavery, nor mere pagans or heathen, enemies or permanent strangers. They were full fellow human beings, possessing valid traditions, dignity, and rights.

Not every one in his day thought so. For decades Las Casas, officially named to be the protector of the Indians, pleaded their case in two hemispheres. He did so at risk to reputation and even life, but he never tired. The priest denounced slaveholders in America and defended their slaves in Spain. Las Casas created trouble for conquistadores while he spoke up for their conquered victims—most of whom were dying as a result of imported European diseases against which they had no immunity, the Europeans' cruel disregard for Native American life, or formal and constant warfare against them.

The slaveholders and killers had their defenders in high places, especially among those who profited from slavery, whether in America or Spain. The most notable advocate was Juan Gines de Sepulveda, a Cordoban theologian, who—as readers of this defense of the Indians against Sepulveda will learn—argued on Aristotelian grounds that war against the Native Americans was just. Why? Because they were inferior to the Spaniards, just as children were to adults, women to men, and even as apes were to humans. Almost sixty years after Columbus's first encounters and fifty after Las Casas first sailed to America, Sepulveda and Las Casas squared off in the face of distinguished theologians at the Council of Valladolid. Las Casas's review of his case is in the book before you.

This is not the place to review the history of the text or the translations; Stafford Poole, who completed work undertaken by Dominican Father Christopher Lehner, leaves us in his debt for this translation. Poole admirably introduces it, in all technical senses and with a page-by-page supply of valuable and necessary footnotes. Nor is this the place to thicken a volume that occupies space among whole shelves full if not whole libraries full of Lascasiana. As a long-time reader of and about Las Casas, I want instead figuratively to sit at the side of new readers and engage them in the discovery of, or at least encounter with, the "New World" represented by the author of this defense.

The world of Bartolome de Las Casas, like that of all past worlds, will be alien. The past, we keep being reminded, is a foreign country: they do things differently there. Count on finding alienating expressions on almost every page. The *Lascasistas* who have tried to present the author as a simply heroic figure who would "fit" in a modern liberal culture do him, history, the truth, the imagination, and his Indians no good.

To begin with, the genre of the *Defense* can be offputting, unless and until one lets the book's character work its effects on the modern consciousness. The vehemence of his *ad hominem* argument and the emotional language used seem more appropriate for stagy television programs rather than a literary and legal search for truth. The reader must understand that, for Las Casas, profound and vital truths were at stake in his debates. (And he was right.) Stating these truths demanded acts of passion, and they were forthcoming. We are forewarned of excesses and extremes by editor Poole, who by his devotion has to come across as some sort of champion, but who also admits that Las Casas circles around and then spirals back to revisit Sepulvedan arguments he has already successfully demolished. The empathic reader sees that at once. When I read Las Casas's explosive and repetitive passages, however, I learned not to be put off but to be enthralled: they have a kind of ritual, incantatory power that does not take away from the argument but reinforces it. Indeed, thinking of the paragraphs as musical themes a composer keeps developing is an appropriate way to be drawn into the still compelling case of the old Dominican.

Along with the overwhelming argument, the over-defense of the Indians, and the overkill of Sepulveda (who may not have felt a thing!), there are other alienating features. Not only is the world of Las Casas past and thus foreign; it issues from a world view few will share today. I would like to think that not a single reader would approve his defense of the natives on the grounds that they were not Catholic heretics, against whom war would be just. Also, one hopes that even the most ardent Catholic missionaries have a hard time endorsing the thought world of Las Casas and his kind. These late medieval figures pictured the struggle for Indian souls to be desperate: policies that cut short the life of the unredeemed or that drove the Indian into hostility against Spain and Christianity threatened to send precious souls to eternal fires of hell. Sepulveda seemed not to care; the Indians were pagan, savage, apelike, worthy of death and hell. Las Casas, in return, fairly shrieks: the natives are citizens, capable of nobility, often to be admired and never to be killed or enslaved. Failure to understand the cosmic backdrop of the issues will mean keeping Las Casas only at a distance, when he belongs up close in a world where "rights" remain at stake even where "mission" often fades.

Third, get ready not only for a world that is distant because it is past and because it exposes a cosmic backdrop that is hard to recover today, but also for a world that sets before us a very imperfect human being. Don't get me wrong. While not eligible to be a *Lascasista*, whether on linguistic, cultural, or religious grounds, I am in the company of those who regard him as heroic and in a way saintly.

To certify credentials: eight years before the Columbus quincentennial that brought Las Casas to the fore once again, I began my own history, titled *Pilgrims in Their Own Land: 500 Years of Religion in America*, not with the Virginians and Puritans of 1607 and 1620/1630, as historians of my kind used to do, but with a chapter on "The Conqueror Versus the Missionary." In it is a picture of Las Casas that we captioned as if it were a *Who's Who* entry: "Known as the Protector of the Indians, Bartolome de Las Casas (1474–1566) never set foot on what is today the United States. Paradoxically, he is remembered widely as the first great figure to speak up for the rights of minorities in the New World, even though he played a brief part in legitimizing black slavery. His portrayals of Spanish cruelties in the Americas gave rise to a 'Black Legend' about Spaniards, which the English happily exploited to show themselves in a more favorable light" (24).

Such a portrait caption was a protection against contemporaries who expect our ancestors to be as virtuous, indeed as perfect as we—we of the generations of genocide and Holocaust, prejudices and racisms and two World Wars. It was also an anticipation of a Lascasian reference I must reenter into the record:

> Las Casas did the Indians no favor when he overadvertised their virtues; it would be unwise to misrepresent him here. A man of his own day, a day that took human slavery for granted, he made a tragic proposal back in 1516—one that had enormous consequences. While outlining his communal system [he was also the hemisphere's pioneer European utopian experimenter] for the New World he added a fatal line: "If necessary white and black slaves can be brought from Castile." Two years later he shortened this proposal simply to "Negro slaves." Like other early protectors of the Indians, Las Casas thought them superior to black Africans, but because he was already the voice of conscience to thoughtful people in church and court, his word meant more than the word of others. In 1518 Charles V first authorized the purchase of slaves for use in the Indies. Years later Las Casas vehemently reversed his stand. In his *Historia* he, almost alone in his time, said that "the same law applies equally to the Negro as to the Indians," but by then it was too late to do much good. (35)

Reprinting that paragraph serves as a reminder that even the most ardent *Lascasista* has to qualify claims for his heroism or sainthood. At our house whenever, yes whenever—for the occasions are frequent—one reads an honest biography, there comes a moment when that reader gasps or gulps or sighs. His or her mate then is trained to ask, by now by instinct, "What was *his* [or *her*] cosmic flaw?" Las Casas had a cosmic flaw, or at least offered a cosmically flawed proposal in 1518, and the reader of this *Defense* centuries later has to reckon with it in any effort to create a balance sheet on the author.

Balance is the last and least thing Las Casas sought. He was for justice, truth, and the rights of the Indians, and would stay around as long as it took to make his point. He would shout as loud as he thought necessary. He would cry not in sentimentality but in rage and sympathy as often as the tears would naturally well up, and he would plead even at the expense of his own dignity. And while writing at white heat, he could also keep cool enough to cite classic theologians and philosophers who were as vivid to his hearers at Valladolid and his readers everywhere as most of them are obscure—and thus in need of the footnote identifications Poole provides—to most of us in our time.

Calling attention to both the cosmic flaw and the lesser irritations in Las Casas and his world is a woeful way to end a Foreword to a book which its editors, publishers, and foreword-writer believe to be a necessary book for our own times. Las Casas, as I mentioned above, "came back" during the Columbus quincentennial of 1992. This time, much of the public who are of European descent, eager to repent for the sins of foreparents five centuries ago, sometimes ready to make some redress, and willing to make Columbus and the Spaniards their own verbal victims mindlessly wrote off all Europeans of five centuries ago as dehumanizers who plotted genocide and were almost apelike exploiters. Those of our contemporaries who stayed around long enough to do their own examining found that matters were then, as they always are, more complicated than stereotypers let them be. There were countervoices among the explorers, among them some missionaries, all of whose assumptions none of us share but some of whose expressions all of us might share.

Among them, as the stock of Columbus has turned bearish, that of Las Casas has gone bullish. He strikes many as worthy of investment: investment of time and energy, of a second look for some, and a first look for many. If *In Defense of the Indians* is the text that serves as that first look, its readers have chosen well. By letting us move around firsthand in an alien world, those who make it available have also exposed to view a profound and impassioned soul who helps make some issues of the 500-year-old events seem current, still demanding, still urgent.

MARTIN E. MARTY
The University of Chicago

Preface

T H I S edition of Las Casas's *Defense* was originally intended for publication in 1966 as part of the international Las Casas year, commemorating the four-hundredth anniversary of the great Bishop's death. The project was initiated by Doctor Lewis Hanke, then of Columbia University, now of the University of Massachusetts (Amherst), an internationally known *Lascasista*. The actual work of translation was to have been done by the Dominican Fathers in Washington, D.C., under the direction of Father William Hinnebusch, O.P., and the first draft of a translation was undertaken by Father Christopher Lehner, O.P., who did yeoman's work on the entire Latin treatise. However, the Dominican Fathers were reassigned to work on a new critical edition of the works of Thomas Aquinas, and Father Hinnebusch had to begin writing an English history of the Dominican Order. It was at this point, in 1966, that Doctor Hanke asked me to finish the task.

And so, at the beginning, credit and acknowledgment must be given to Father Lehner for his work. Without it, this translation would have been many more years in preparation.

My translation is based on Father Lehner's. I went through the Latin and compared his translation with the original, and then either made a new one, altered his, or did some other type of editorial work. The result is a substantially different translation, but it is impossible to say for sure in any passage which is his work and which is mine. However, I must bear final responsibility for the completed translation and for any inaccuracies or infelicities.

The Manuscript

There are no known copies of the Spanish original of Las Casas's *Defense,* and the only surviving copy of the Latin text is the Bibliothèque Nationale, Paris, Nouveaux Fonds Latins, no. 12926.[1] The provenance of the Latin manuscript is impossible to reconstruct. At one time it belonged to the library of the Abbey of St. Germain des Près. It is mentioned in the catalogue of that library that was written about the year 1740, but it is not mentioned in the catalogue of 1677. Where it was throughout the seventeenth century, and how it came to St. Germain and from there to the Bibliothèque Nationale, is not known.

Henry Raup Wagner is of the opinion that the original Spanish manuscript was written between 1548 and 1550 and that it had about one hundred folio leaves (Millares Carlo says about ninety *pliegos*).[2] Wagner adds, "From these two accounts I infer that: (1) Casas originally wrote his *Apologia* perhaps the year after his return to court, as he twice says that some time elapsed before the Emperor convoked the junta. (2) The *Apologia* that Casas read to the judges in 1550 was probably expanded from the first draft, for Sepúlveda was not prepared for it, and requested a copy of the official resumé in order to reply. I conclude that the Latin translation was made later."[3]

There is no external evidence for dating the Latin translation, and internal evidence offers only approximations. Millares Carlo says that the handwriting is of the sixteenth century (though rather more legible than most handwriting of that time). On the other hand, the *Inventaire* of Delisle dates the manuscript from the seventeenth century, but this hardly seems possible.[4] That the Latin translation dates from some time after the Valladolid dispute has been generally accepted and is proved

1. A microfilm of the manuscript is in the Library of Congress, Manuscript Division, filed under "Paris, Bibliothèque Nationale." Positive copies are available, but the Library's copy lacks the first seventeen folios.
2. Agustín Millares Carlo, "Una Obra Inédita de Fray Bartolomé de Las Casas," *Investigaciones Bibliográficas Iberoamericanas* (Mexico, 1950), p. 43.
3. Henry Raup Wagner, *The Life and Writings of Bartolomé de las Casas* (Albuquerque, 1967), p. 279.
4. Millares Carlo, p. 43. L. V. Delisle, *Inventaire des Mss. Latins conservés à la Bibliothèque Nationale sous les Numéros 8823–18613 et faisant suite à la serie dont le catalogue á été publié en 1744.* (Paris, 1870), par. 12926.

by its reference to this junta's having convened in the past (conclusion of chapter 41). The only reference to a specific event that can be dated is in a marginal note on folio 38, which says, apropos of the Church's power to pass judgment on unbelievers, "Sic Modo in Concilio Tridentino, Sessione 14a, #2." Inasmuch as Session 14 of the Council of Trent was promulgated (given the force of law) on 25 November 1551, this is the earliest possible dating. The introductory letter of Bartolomé de La Vega speaks of the Indian problem as seventy years old, a fact which would date his letter around 1562, and this would be the latest possible date for the manuscript.

Better evidence for a cut-off date is provided by Las Casas's introductory letter to Philip II, who was then ruling Spain as regent for Charles V. Philip had returned from Germany to Spain in June of 1551, and he remained there until May 1553, when he left for England and his marriage to Mary Tudor. He did not return to Spain until 1559. If we presume that the letter was actually intended for Philip's reading and was not some sort of formality, the latest possible date would be mid-1553.

In light of these clues and the furious energy shown by Las Casas even at this late stage of his life, together with his desire to have his work known throughout the scholarly world and the many indications of hasty writing and copying within the text, it is probably safe to say that the Latin translation dates from within one or two years of the Valladolid dispute: that is, sometime in 1552 or early 1553.

The manuscript consists of 253 folios divided into sixty-three chapters without headings or summaries. The Vega letter, unpaginated, is appended at the end though it is clearly intended as an introduction and is so treated in this translation. The *Defense* is preceded by two summaries, the first of Las Casas's position, the second of Sepúlveda's, as expressed in his *Democrates Alter*. There are numerous corrections (which are of uneven value) in the text of the *Defense* and many marginal notations. Millares Carlo is of the opinion that it was copied by the same scribe who transcribed the *De Unico Vocationis Modo*.[5] He also thinks that some of the marginal notations are in the Bishop's own hand. However, Dr. Raymond Marcus of the University of Rouen and Mme. Marthe Dulong of the Bibliothèque Nationale, both of whom

5. Millares Carlo, p. 43.

have closely studied the original, believe that only one marginal note is in the Bishop's handwriting.[6]

There are five distinct handwritings in the manuscript, which are referred to under the following designations:

Hand A. This is the hand of a corrector, similar to that of the scribe but not the same. He made most of the corrections.

Hand B. Las Casas's own hand which, in the opinion of the experts cited, appears only on folio 1.

Hand C. A marginal annotator whose hand appears on folios 2 and 3 only. He makes a rather harsh judgment on the summary of Las Casas's position.

Hand D. The hand of the scribe who made a few marginal notations and corrections.

Hand E. A marginal annotator (using a semi-cursive hand) who made most of the marginal notations.

Las Casas's Citations

Like all scholastics before and after him, Las Casas relied very heavily on the use of authority to prove his points, and as a good dialectician he tried to overwhelm his adversary with a wealth of citations, all designed to bolster his own arguments and smother those of his opponent. Las Casas appealed to four principal sources: the Bible, theologians (especially the Fathers of the Church), canon and Roman civil law, and Aristotle.

Of the Fathers and theologians of the Church, Las Casas relied most heavily on his fellow Dominican Thomas Aquinas; the great doctor is cited twice as often as any other authority. Second only to him is Saint Augustine. After these two and before any other individual authority comes Aristotle. Some of the authorities cited by Las Casas were contemporary with his youth, such as Torquemada, Prierias, and Cajetan. Of the great Spanish scholastics and jurists of the sixteenth century, only Vitoria is cited and that but four times—probably the largest number of references that Las Casas made to Vitoria in any single work. There is no mention of Cano, and Soto is mentioned only once in a

6. Mme. Dulong to Father Hinnebusch, 22 April 1964.

marginal note. The one favorable reference to Erasmus is very unusual so late in sixteenth-century Spanish thought.

There is no denying that Las Casas's theological learning was both broad and deep, though he clearly concentrated on those areas of both theology and law which would bolster his crusade in favor of the Indians. He is at home in the law, both civil and canon, but here he tends to be more repetitious; that is, he cites the same sources again and again. He seems interested only in those areas of law that support his stand. It would be difficult to say, on the evidence of the *Defense* alone, how truly complete his legal knowledge was.

Las Casas's ordinary method of citation is simply to include his authorities in the body of the text, but to continue this in the translation would be awkward and tiresome and would interrupt the flow of the narrative; hence I have taken the liberty of modernizing this method by using footnotes. Further specifications or clarifications of his citations are enclosed in brackets.

All biblical passages in this translation are taken from the Jerusalem Bible and are used with the permission of the publisher, Doubleday and Company. This means that the proper names, which have customarily undergone a variety of spellings in transliteration from Greek and Hebrew, follow the usage of the Jerusalem Bible. In some cases Las Casas's arguments depend on the wording of the Latin Vulgate (the fifth-century translation by Saint Jerome and still the official Latin Bible of the Catholic Church). In these cases the quotations have been altered somewhat to keep the sense of the argument.

There is a special problem in citations of the psalms, which for the most part are enumerated differently in Catholic and non-Catholic editions of the Old Testament. The Jerusalem Bible follows the usages of most non-Catholic versions whereas Las Casas follows the enumeration of the Vulgate. Las Casas's enumeration has been kept in this translation.

In the case of patristic citations, all of Las Casas's quotations have been compared with the collection of J. P. Migne. This vast assortment of Christian writing is embodied in two collections, the *Cursus Patrologiae Graecae* and the *Cursus Patrologiae Latinae* (abbreviated to *PG* and *PL* respectively). The ordinary method of citation is to give the abbreviation with the number of the volume and the column. Migne's collection is not always critical and, in his Latin translation of the Greek Fathers, great variations are to be found. These have usually been indicated only in a general way.

For citations from the works of Saint Thomas Aquinas, especially his *Summa Theologiae,* it is not necessary to refer to any specific edition because the method of citation is uniform. The *Summa* is divided into four parts, which are usually signified by I, I–II, II–II, and III. These parts are divided into questions (*q*) and the questions into articles (*a*). Within the articles a thesis is stated, together with objections to it, and then the answer is given, together with an exposition (the body of the article, designated *c* or *in corpore*), which is followed by rebuttals to the objections (indicated by the preposition *ad* and a number, e.g., ad 2um). Thus, a typical *Summa* citation would be I–II, q. 90, a. 4, ad 3um, et a. 5 in corpore. This means: the first part of the second part, question 90, article 4, in the reply to the third objection and in the body of article 5. Although apparently complex, it works quite well in practice.

The citations of civil and canon law are more complicated. Roman civil law was codified in the sixth century under the Emperor Justinian, and this codification, called the *Corpus Iuris Civilis* (Body of Civil Law), consisted of four parts:

The *Codex,* which contains the laws properly so called.

The *Digests,* which contain excerpts from the principal jurists.

The *Institutes,* which are textbooks of law.

The *Novellae,* which Las Casas usually calls by another name (*Authenticae*), consists of later laws and decrees. A later version, called the *Authenticum,* also was considered to have the force of law. Because the latter two titles are frequently abbreviated, it is sometimes difficult to know just which collection Las Casas is citing.

Canon law is somewhat more complex, both in its history and its citation. There are six principal components of the *Corpus Iuris Canonici* (Body of Canon Law). These are: Gratian's Decree, the Decretals of Gregory IX, the Liber Sextus (Sixth Book), the Clementines, the Extravagantes Communes, and the Extravagantes Ioannis XXII. Because of indiscriminate citation, the latter two are often considered as one book.

Gratian in the translation refers to the *Decretum Gratiani* (Gratian's Decree), a collection and systematization of Church legislation that was put together about the year 1140 by an Italian canonist named Graziano. At first it was unofficial (though it had great prestige), and eventually it came to have official standing. Gratian's Decree is divided into three parts. The first part is subdivided into distinctions (*D*) and canons (*c*). A typical citation in the older form used by Las Casas is c. *Veritate,* D. 8 (modern form D. 8, c. 4), which means Part I, distinction 8, the canon beginning with the word *Veritate.* The second part is divided into causes (*C*), questions (*q*), and canons (*c*). A typical citation in the older form is Si quo, 23, q. 4, and in the modern is c. 47, C. 23, q. 4. In this second part, a citation of question 3 of cause 23 usually has the introductory words *De Poenitentia.* The third part of Gratian's Decree has the generic title of *De Consecratione.*

The *Decretals of Gregory IX* were the first official collection of Church laws, drawn up by the Dominican Raymond of Péñafort and promulgated in the year 1234 by the Pope for whom they are named. Because it was distinct from Gratian's Decree, it was indicated by the sign *extra,* which Las Casas occasionally used. The Decretals are divided into books, titles, and chapters. In Las Casas's method of citation the books are not mentioned; instead, the titles and chapters are given by their opening words. Thus one of his commonest citations is *Quod Super His: De Voto,* that is, the title *De Voto* (On the Vow) and the chapter beginning with the words *Quod super his.* In modern citation this would be Decretals 3, 24, 8 (that is, Book 3, title 24, chapter 8).

The *Liber Sextus,* an addition to the five books of the Decretals, was issued in 1298 by Boniface VIII. Las Casas uses the sign *In VIo* or *in sexto* to refer to it.

The *Clementines,* a body of laws promulgated in 1317 by Pope John XXII and taken for the most part from the constitutions of Pope Clement V at the Council of Vienne (1311–1312). They are usually designated by *Clementinis* or its abbreviation.

The *Extravagantes Communes* and the *Extravagantes Ioannis XXII* contain additional laws from the time of Boniface VIII (d. 1303) to Sixtus IV (d. 1484).

Notes on the Translation

Las Casas's *Defense* is not an easy work to translate. Its Latin is a combination of the Medieval, Classical, and Renaissance elements. The great variations of meaning that individual words underwent from the

Classical period to the sixteenth century often makes the precise sense of a passage unclear. This can be seen in the many possible translations of *ratio*. Other terms, such as *irascibile*, took on technical meanings in scholastic philosophy.[7]

The difficulty is compounded by the fact that the *Defense* was written in haste and the manuscript has been frequently corrected. Spelling and grammatical errors are not uncommon, despite the work of an anonymous corrector. Hispanisms abound, and at one point, in the case of Queen Isabella's will, it reverts to Spanish altogether. As in other Latin works of the period, the sentences flow on and on, forming long paragraphs held together by connectives. There is an excess of superlatives and synonyms. Though Classical Latin used superlatives more often than modern English, Las Casas fairly revels in them. He thinks in extremes, even in his grammar; he rarely uses one noun when two or three will serve the same task.

This translation, it is hoped, will be free of archaism, as Las Casas was writing for a contemporary, scholarly audience. But a translation that would be too readable and too clear would be unfaithful to the original, which is repetitive, verbose, technical, and often filled with close scholastic reasoning. Footnotes have been deliberately kept to a minimum. All the citations in the text are an integral part of the original Latin. For the sake of smooth reading, they have been placed in footnotes at the bottom of the page, whereas the translator's notes and comments have been added at the end of the volume.

The final value of this translation will depend on how well it communicates to the modern reader the thought and outlook of Bartolomé de Las Casas. If it succeeds in any way in renewing his spirit in our times, it will be well worth the effort that has gone into it.

7. My standard reference has been Charles Dufresne DuCange, *Glossarium Mediae et Infimae Latinitatis.* 7 vols (Paris, 1840). See also W. H. Maigne d'Arnis, *Lexicon Manuale ad Scriptores Mediae et Infimae Latinitatis.* 2 vols (Paris, 1890).

IN DEFENSE OF THE INDIANS

The Defense of the Most Reverend Lord, Don Fray
Bartolomé de Las Casas, of the Order of Preachers, Late
Bishop of Chiapa, Against the Persecutors and Slanderers
of the Peoples of the New World Discovered Across the Seas

Introductory Letter by Bartolomé de la Vega

*Fray Bartolomé de Vega, of the Order
of Preachers, to the Supreme Royal
Council of the Indies,
Eternal Happiness*

Illustrious Judges of the Royal Council:

 T is hardly possible to say how much the author of this work [Las Casas and his *Defense*] deserves from the kingdoms of Spain. He was the first to discover the truth in Indian affairs, affairs which are not only extremely complicated but above all are closely connected with the salvation of the peoples of Spain, not to speak of all the Indies. How very important it is, in Indian affairs, to learn the truth, to know the cases, to understand all the legislation, can be plainly seen from the unheard-of plundering and thievery, from the devastation of that New World, and from the loss of so many thousands of souls, all brought about through ignorance of this matter.

The ancient Romans and the founders of other ancient kingdoms whose states were ruled by just laws used to honor those who attacked some outstanding abuse or who were benefactors of the state by having their likenesses carved in stone. To these images, erected in temples and elsewhere, they paid the highest reverence in order that death might not blot out the memory of men whose lives had been of such great advantage to the state. For these reasons there is no doubt that if those ancient times had had the good fortune to possess the author of the present book, mortal men would have venerated his image. They would have decreed that he be recognized, honored, and loved by all as the discoverer of truth in Indian affairs and as the father of all the inhabitants of that New World.

The highest honor is due to teachers of sacred theology and all those learned in law who have enlightened the world through their teaching by devoting careful attention to the writing of books. Those among them are to be the more highly esteemed who, borrowing their light from no other human being, have themselves been the first to spread the rays of truth and light over the whole world. For this reason the Most Reverend Bishop of Chiapa, deserves well of the Spanish people. He was not just the first to show the way toward understanding the justice of the Indians' cause. By his work and labor in this important and difficult matter the truth has come to shine all over Spain. But he also, for a great many years, has waged a crusade by debating and examining this matter with certain doctors who have attempted with all their energy to defend what is the exact opposite to every truth and who to this very day refuse to retreat from their insane opinions. If they had not been defied and defeated by the all-out effort of this Bishop, they would have infected nearly all of Spain with their utterly false dogma.

Because these men are found everywhere and are blind to justice to the Indians and their concerns, they are unashamed of teaching their death-dealing methods and errors regarding the Indies, errors by which many have been taken in even to the present moment. With the greatest assurance they assert that they are battling for the truth, upholding the just cause of our Spanish people. (On the contrary, as they are bound to defend the cause of God and of the Indian peoples who have been redeemed by the blood of Christ, I do not doubt that many thousands of their souls have been consumed by everlasting flames because of this widespread teaching, so unholy and so unjust.)

Therefore this ignorance so harmful to many, this darkness, I say, so deep among the peoples of Spain, is dispelled by the present work. In it, by many arguments from nature itself and by a large number of the clearest testimonies from Sacred Scripture and the holy doctors and, in addition, from decrees of both councils and Popes, there is clear proof of what is true and just in the affairs of the Indies.

This work also teaches a large number of points that are new but are extremely necessary for all to know. We know that these points have escaped the above-mentioned doctors who in other areas are men of more than ordinary eloquence. In it is taught the method of preaching the gospel of Jesus Christ. In it, too, is shown the way unbelievers are to be converted to the faith. In it the tyrannies of the Indies are exposed. Unbelievable robberies are revealed. Godless massacres are condemned. The way is opened to make reparation for injuries. All doubts are cleared up. And far more remarkable is the fact that the Indian problem, which for the past seventy years has remained so obscure, so chaotic and confused, is now presented in an orderly way, is now clearer than daylight, now escapes no one, is now known by all. This book is the means by which the darkness is driven from Spain, the fog is raised, men are aroused from their slumber, the misguided come back to a truer judgment, those who were wise in their own eyes are put to rout. At last there is enlightenment for all of Spain, which up to the present has remained in ignorance of the great question of the Indies (which is beyond all doubt the most important in the world).

Unless I am mistaken, there is certainly no other matter that can surpass this business of the Indies in magnitude. For what is at stake is nothing less than the salvation or loss of both the bodies and souls of all the inhabitants of that recently discovered world. Rightly, then, is this work to be regarded as supremely important, for it is vitally necessary for the whole world. On it the author has spent so much labor. He has grown old from many anxieties and sleepless nights. He has read through many books, as anyone can easily see for himself in the result. His zeal and labors will be repaid by him who promises a reward to those who bring to light the truth and wisdom which is God. "They that explain me shall have life everlasting."

And since such a great work is evidently to the advantage of all Spain, may Your Highness be pleased to command that it be published with the royal approval and agreement. As ruler and protector of all the Indies, it is your special office to search for the truth about this extremely difficult and necessary affair lest, through want of knowledge of the truth, that New World be torn up by the roots and everlasting fire consume the souls that still remain. But if this work is printed by your order so that the truth of this matter may be made known to all, many things (in my judgment) will be restored to their earlier condition. And it is impossible to say how great will be the increase to be added to the dominions of Spain. To [Spain] I am myself most closely bound, and I pray for its daily temporal progress as I do for its eternal happiness.

Summary of the Defense of the Most Reverend Lord, Fray Bartolomé de Las Casas, Late Bishop of Chiapa, against Ginés Sepúlveda, Theologian of Córdoba

N the year of Our Lord 1542, the Emperor Charles, King of Spain, who is deserving of everlasting memory in the hearts of men, was informed that Spaniards were roving far and wide with massacres, violence, and oppression, and that they were enslaving and inflicting the worst burdens on the Indians who live near the Ocean Sea, who by decree of the Roman Pontiff belong to the supreme empire of Castile and León. As a result, he convoked at Valladolid a solemn assembly. Having summoned men from every expert and learned council, he charged them to determine as far as they could whether the atrocities reported to him were true and to recommend a suitable plan by which such evils might be avoided, so that the Indians might be returned to their former freedom, and by which, at the same time, that New World, once it had been calmed by advantageous laws and careful instructions, might be governed in the future. For many days this matter was argued in great debates, and at last certain laws were enacted by which the military expeditions of the Spaniards against the Indians, called in Spanish *conquistas*, were forbidden. At the same time orders were given that all the Indians who had been reduced to slavery by those to whom they had been unjustly given when the land was divided, that is, in *repartimiento* or *encomienda* (a satanic invention, never before heard of), should be restored to freedom, and furthermore that all the Indians should be placed under the authority of the kings of Spain in all matters and their natural rulers and lords should retain their power and jurisdiction.

This incensed the Spaniards for whom the Indians were rich prey and whose wealth was growing through their acts of violence, their robberies, and their plundering of the Indians. Filled with indignation and roaring with outrage, they complained that the Emperor was robbing them of their property, as if he were not depriving plunderers of their sacrilegious loot but lawful owners of their rightful possessions. The result was that some of them, leaving no stone unturned in providing for their own advantage, shamelessly turned away from and rebelled against the Emperor. Others fled to men with a reputation for learning who could attack the imperial laws with solid legal arguments in order that the Emperor might be convinced of the injustice of the laws and eventually either abolish them or at least suspend their application. This has happened with some of [the laws], not because they were not absolutely right and just but because, having learned of the rebellion by those traitors, he [Charles] feared a greater evil and a more violent insurrection.

These men found a defender of their opinion in a certain learned man who, surely in this case, has shown himself to be not learned enough. This man was a certain Ginés Sepúlveda, the royal historian, who composed a little work, embellished with flowers of eloquence, to which he gave the title *On the Just Causes of War.* In it he attacks these New Laws with all his might, though never making express mention of them in any way, but defends the past and future wars and expeditions of the Spaniards against the Indians and approves slavery (that is, the allotment or encomienda), under which the Indians, oppressed by the Spaniards, either die or lead a life harsher than death. They have been split into shares as if they were herds of cattle or sheep; that is, allotted among the Spaniards and assigned by a specified number to each to become their slaves.

From the very day that the New World was first opened to us, the Spaniards have always seen to it that there would first be conquistas or invasions, then divisions and allotments of a certain number of Indians, which were carried out region by region throughout that entire land. Sepúlveda brings forward certain counterfeit arguments that favor the greediest cravings of tyrants by twisting texts from the sacred books and the doctrines of the holiest and wisest fathers and philosophers. Citing the crimes and native vices of the Indians and informed, to be sure, by the Spaniards, those bitterest foes of the Indians, and relying on their false accusations, he falsely defames the larger part of the human race whom the providence of God has scattered abroad in the vast expanses of the Indies.

When he had learned that such a booklet had been written by Ginés and a Spanish summary of the work had come into his hands (for at that time he could not obtain a Latin copy of the work), the Bishop of Chiapa, understanding what Ginés's opinion was and wanting to protect and defend the Indians against every injustice, wrote the following *Defense* for the Indians (who lived peacefully without injury to any other nation) against those invaders and oppressors who hold them in slavery and work them to death. He dedicated the *Defense* to our Most Serene Prince Philip, who at that time had been appointed by the unvanquished Emperor Charles, his father, to govern this kingdom. The *Defense* included the reply to the four arguments by which Sepúlveda defended those expeditions of the Spaniards and the allotments under whose title they enslaved the Indians. When the Bishop had refuted Sepúlveda at Alcalá de Henares and that whole distinguished university had condemned Sepúlveda's opinion as unsound, and for this very reason had forbidden the work to be published, the dispute between the Bishop and Sepúlveda reached the ears of the Emperor, who was then busy in Germany. In the year 1551 of our salvation he commanded that notable theologians and jurists should meet with the members of the Council of the Indies to hear both the Bishop and Sepúlveda and decide what would be best for the public interest.

First, Sepúlveda had an opportunity to speak for one day. Then they heard the Bishop speak for five days. He read through this entire *Defense* chapter by chapter. Finally, after much debate, the [commission] judged that the expeditions, which in Spanish we call conquistas, are evil, unlawful, and unjust and, therefore, ought to be altogether outlawed in the future. However, concerning the allotments, which are called repartimientos in Spanish, they made no decision because there was still rebellion by some of the oppressors in the kingdoms of Peru and other provinces were in a state of confusion.

Summary of Sepúlveda's Position

HE work that Sepúlveda, the theologian and royal historian, wrote against the Indians can be summarized in the following arguments by which he defended armed expeditions against the Indians as justified so long as the war is carried on lawfully and according to rules, as the Kings of Spain have thus far commanded that it be waged.

He argues first that those people are barbaric, uninstructed in letters and the art of government, and completely ignorant, unreasoning, and totally incapable of learning anything but the mechanical arts; that they are sunk in vice, are cruel, and are of such character that, as nature teaches, they are to be governed by the will of others. This, at various times, many reliable men who have [known] them and lived in close association with them have asserted under oath. This is clear also from the sixth chapter of the third book of [Oviedo's] *General History of the Indies,* which was examined and approved by the Supreme Council of the Indies.

But, for their own welfare, people of this kind are held by natural law to submit to the control of those who are wiser and superior in virtue and learning, as are the Spaniards (especially the nobility), the learned, the clergy, the religious, and, finally, all those who have been properly educated and trained. Such persons must be considered when a judgment is to be made about the morals and character of any people, for in them especially shine forth natural ability, uprightness, training, and the best morals of any nation. Both in Spain and among the Indians, spiritual and temporal government is entrusted to these people rather than to soldiers, who, for the most part, are unprincipled and, under cover of military license, inflict many injuries.

The conclusion drawn from this is that the Indians are obliged by the natural law to obey those who are outstanding in virtue and character in the same way that matter yields to form, body to soul, sense to reason, animals to human beings, women to men, children to adults, and, finally, the imperfect to the more perfect, the worse to the better, the cheaper to the more precious and excellent, to the advantage of both. This is the natural order, which the eternal and divine law commands be observed, according to Augustine.[1]

Therefore, if the Indians, once warned, refuse to obey this legitimate sovereignty, they can be forced to do so for their own welfare by recourse to the terrors of war. And this war will be just both by civil and natural law, according to the second, third, and fifth chapters of the *Politics* of Aristotle, the most perceptive commentator on justice and the wisest interpreter of the other moral virtues, as well as of nature and nature's laws. Philosophers and great theologians alike follow him as a master. The wise man in the book of Proverbs approves Aristotle's teaching that the fool ought to be slave to the wise.[2] Saint Thomas, too, teaches the same thing, and Thomas holds first place among scholastic theologians, always following, as he does, Aristotle's opinion in the explanation of natural laws.[3] Finally, all political philosophers, basing themselves on this reason alone, teach that in cities, kingdoms, and states those who excel in prudence and virtue should preside with sovereignty over the government so that government may be just according to the natural law.

Everywhere in the world we see that the best kings and rightly organized states appoint their wiser and more excellent men for the administration of the government. This universal custom is considered to be a law of nature, and all natural laws are divine inasmuch as they flow from the eternal law. Saint Augustine considers this to be God's will, determining that the natural order be observed and forbidding it to be overturned. Hence Augustine often says that if someone is unwilling to do what is good for himself and he is obliged to act for his own welfare, it is just to force him to do it even though he is unwilling and resists. This agrees with what Augustine teaches in different parts of *The City of God,* which Saint Thomas cites when he upholds the same opinion that the Romans justly subjugated the other nations of the

1. *De Libero Arbitrio,* Lib. 2.
2. 11 [29].
3. *De Regimine Principum* [Lib. 2, c. 10].

world.[4] God wanted the greater part of the world to come under their dominion so that it might be ruled more justly under the government of a wise people who cherished justice. But even if these barbarians (that is, the Indians) do not lack capacity, with still more reason they must obey and heed the commands of those who can teach them to live like human beings and do the things that are beneficial for both their present and future life.

In the second place, Sepúlveda proves that the Indians, even though unwilling, must accept the Spanish yoke so that they may be corrected and be punished for the sins and crimes against the divine and natural laws by which they have been contaminated, especially their idolatry and the impious custom of human sacrifice. Indeed, it is proved in various passages of Holy Scripture that the Amorites and the Perizzites and other inhabitants of the Promised Land were exterminated by the Children of Israel because of these two sins, and also that the Hebrews themselves were punished for the same sins by the destruction of large numbers of their people and by the enslavement of their nation and exile from the Promised Land, their fatherland. From this it is evident that the law by which both the former and the latter were condemned is natural and divine and, as a consequence, is to be observed always. This is what that learned bishop and holy martyr Cyprian teaches. Further, it is the more common opinion among all the doctors that pagans who do not observe the natural law may be punished by Christians. Those people are considered not to be keeping the natural law among whom some mortal sins go unpunished or are not judged to be against the natural law. Thus Cajetan's tenet that war cannot be waged against a nation by reason of its lack of faith is to be understood of those who are guilty of unbelief alone. The case is different when the sins about which we spoke above accompany the unbelief.

Thirdly, Sepúlveda argues that the injuries and extreme misery which the Indians used to inflict and which those who have not yet been subdued still inflict today on a great number of innocent persons, whom they used to sacrifice each year to the evil spirit, should be stopped. All who can do so are held by the natural and divine law to defend any and all persons from such injuries, for all men are neighbors to one another

---

4. *De Regimine Principum* [Lib. 3, c. 4].

and brothers, as the theologians teach. That all, if they can, are bound to ward off danger from their neighbor is proved from these words of the wise man: "Rescue those being led away to death,"[5] and again, in the same book: God "gave each one a commandment concerning his neighbor."[6] The above-mentioned evil, however, cannot be avoided unless these barbarians are tamed and subjugated.

Fourthly, he advances the gain in bringing about the spread and growth of the Christian religion. This will be accomplished if, once those regions have been brought under control, the gospel of Christ can be preached by consecrated men safely and without any danger, so that they will not be massacred by either [pagan] rulers or priests, as they have already done three or four times. He supports this by the authority of Augustine, who writes that Christ wanted men to be drawn to the faith by meekness and gentleness during the first period of the infant Church.[7] However, after the Church grew in power and numbers, Christ wanted men to be compelled, even when unwilling, to accept the Christian religion. This he shows in the parable of the banquet to which the first persons were invited, whereas the rest were compelled and forced. Violence was resorted to in order to bring them to the banquet because, as Augustine says, the following prophecy had not yet been fulfilled: "All kings will do him homage; all nations become his servants!"[8] The more this is realized, the more the Church uses its powers, not only by inviting but also by compelling [unbelievers] to the faith.

Lest anyone think that the arguments Augustine uses against heretics do not apply to pagans, Sepúlveda strengthens [the arguments] by citing the law of the God-fearing Emperor Constantine against the pagans. Having closed the pagan temples and prohibited shameful auguries, immolations, and sacrifices, Constantine forbade the worship of idols under penalty of death and confiscation of property. The holy Fathers Ambrose and Augustine, as well as other Christian men, praised this law as fair and just. Nevertheless, Sepúlveda declares that he does not want the unwilling to be baptized. This is forbidden by divine law, and no law can oblige anyone to be baptized against his will. But he says

---

5. [Proverbs 24:11]. Citations in brackets have been supplied by the translator.
6. [Ecclesiasticus 17:12].
7. *Epistola ad Donatum.*
8. [Psalm 71:11].

that violent measures and whatever is probably helpful should be tried, so that heretics and pagans may acknowledge their error, come to their senses, and thus ask for baptism of their own accord, as many of these Indians did when moved by violence and force of war.

This is similar to the methods used by Constantine and employed also by Genandius, Exarch of Africa, whom Saint Gregory praised exceedingly for waging war on the pagans to extend the limits of the Christian religion. Nor is it valid, says Sepúlveda, for someone to object that this can be admitted only when the war is waged on subjects, because those against whom Genandius drew the sword were not subjects of the Roman people, for had they been subjects of the Roman people he would not have waged war on them.

Sepúlveda concludes his work by saying that it is totally just, as well as most beneficial to these barbarians, that they be conquered and brought under the rule of the Spaniards, who are worshipers of Christ. This is the easiest way for them to embrace the Christian religion, as experience has clearly taught. This is especially true when this can be accomplished with minimum bloodshed. In fact, every year they used to sacrifice many more men to their gods than will perish when the terrors of warfare are launched against them, to the immeasurable benefit of both the living and those who will come after them.

Furthermore, he asserts that the Roman Pontiff, Alexander VI, in a decree to the College of Cardinals declared armed expeditions against the Indians to be just, that he allowed the Kings of Castile the right to conquer them and add them to their empire, and expressly forbade, for just reasons, other rulers to take up arms against them. Therefore, just as no one can deny that wars undertaken by God's command are just, no one will deny that a war is just that God's Vicar, after mature deliberation and in the exercise of his pontifical authority, declares to be justified.

Everything in his little work, says Sepúlveda, is proved most thoroughly by various citations from the sacred books of the Old and New Testaments, from the natural law, and also from the authority of theologians who teach that when war is just (that is, when it is carried on against those upon whom it has been declared, as this one was), soldiers are not bound to make restitution of things acquired by right of war. This is true even though they may have taken up arms not so much from a love of establishing truth and justice as from greed to despoil the enemy and gain possessions, although, if they wage war in this spirit, they sin gravely. However, those who inflict injuries and steal property contrary to the laws of war and justice, as many have done, are held to restitution and commit a very serious crime, and the ruler who tolerates such actions, or does not forbid them when he can, is guilty of the same crime and is held to give an account to God.

Preface to the Defense of the Most Reverend Fray Bartolomé de Las Casas, of the Order of Saint Dominic, Late Bishop of Chiapa, to Philip, Great Prince of Spain

Fray Bartolomé de Las Casas,
of the Order of Saint Dominic,
Late Bishop of Chiapa, to
Philip, Great Prince of Spain

Illustrious Prince:

 T is right that matters which concern the safety and peace of the great empire placed in your keeping by the divine goodness be reported to you, for you rule Spain and that marvelous New World in the name of the great Charles, your father, and you strive for immortal glory, not just with the imperial power but especially with the generous spirit and with the wisdom implanted in you by Christ. Therefore I have thought it advisable to bring to the attention of Your Highness that there has come into my hands a certain brief synopsis in Spanish of a work that Ginés de Sepúlveda is reported to have written in Latin. In it he gives four reasons, each of which, in his opinion, proves beyond refutation that war against the Indians is justified, provided that it be waged properly and the laws of war be observed, just as, up to the present, the kings of Spain have commanded that it be waged and carried out.

I hear that it is this man's intention to demonstrate the title by which the Kings of Spain possess the empire of the Indies and to bolster his position with arguments and laws, so that from now on no one will be able to slander you even tacitly on this point. I have read and reread this work carefully. And it is said that Sepúlveda drives home various other points at greater length in his Latin work (which I have not yet had the chance to see). What impression it has made on others I do not know. I certainly have detected in it poisons disguised with honey. Under pretext of pleasing his prince, a man who is a theologian offers honey-coated poison. In place of bread, he offers a stone. Great Prince, unless this deadly poison is stopped by your wisdom, so that it will not become widespread, it will infect the minds of readers, deceive the unwary, and arm and incite tyrants to injustice. Believe me, that little book will bring ruin to the minds of many.

In the first place, while claiming that he wants to vindicate your jurisdiction over the Indies, he tears to pieces and reduces your rights by presenting arguments that are partly foolish, partly false, partly of the kind that have the least force. Furthermore, if this man's judgment in this matter should be printed, [and] sanctioned with the royal license and privilege, there can be no doubt that within a short time the empire of the Indies will be entirely overthrown and destroyed.

Indeed, if so many laws already issued, so many decrees, so many harsh threats, and so many statutes conscientiously enacted by the Emperor Charles and his predecessors have been ineffective in prevent-ing so many thousands of innocent men from perishing by sword, hunger, and all the misfortunes of total war, and extensive areas of their highly civilized kingdoms and most fertile provinces from being sav-agely devastated; if the fear of God and the dread of hell have not even moderated (I shall not say curbed) the utterly ruthless and cruel spirits of the Spaniards; if the outcries of preachers and holy men that they were barred from the sacraments of the Church and were not forgiven in sacramental confession were of no avail, what will happen when evil men (for whom, according to the old proverb, nothing is wanting except the opportunity) read that a scholar, a doctor of theology, and the royal historian has published books approving those criminal wars and hellish campaigns and, by supporting arguments, confirms and defends the unheard-of crime whereby Christian men, forgetting Christian virtue, hold in slavery those people, the most unfortunate of all, who appear to have escaped the ferocity of that most cruel race by chance rather than by the mercy of the Spaniards? Furthermore, [what will happen when they read] that he teaches that soldiers may lawfully keep every-thing they take in these wars, even though they undertook the cam-paign with the evil intention of looting, that is, of pillaging by fire, sword, murder, plunder and violence, upsetting, overturning, and throwing into confusion all laws, divine and human, and that they are not bound to restore such goods because the Spaniards who do these things and shed the blood of the innocent consecrate their hands to God (as I hear Sepúlveda has written) and merit Christ's grace because they prevent the worship of idols?

Whom will they spare? What blood will they not shed? What cruelty will they not commit, these brutal men who are hardened to seeing fields bathed in human blood, who make no distinction of sex or age, who do not spare infants at their mothers' breasts, pregnant women, the great, the lowly, or even men of feeble and gray old age for whom the weight of years usually awakens reverence or mercy? What will they not do if they hear that there is a man teaching that they are consecrating their hands to God when they crush the Indians with massacres, pillaging, and tyranny—that they are doing the same as those who killed the Children of Israel who were adoring the calf? They will give more trust to him, as to someone who tells them what they want to hear, than they would to the son of God himself if he were face to face before us and teaching something different.

If, then, the Indians are being brought to the point of extermination, if as many peoples are being destroyed as widespread kingdoms are being overthrown, what sane man would doubt that the most flourishing empire of the New World, once its native inhabitants have been destroyed, will become a wilderness, and nothing but dominion over tigers, lions, and wild beasts for the Kings of Spain? When the all-wise God commanded certain nations to be overthrown, he did not want them completely destroyed at once, lest the empty lands without human beings become the lair of wild animals which might harm the few Jews who were the new inhabitants.[1]

Therefore when Sepúlveda, by word or in his published works, teaches that campaigns against the Indians are lawful, what does he do except encourage oppressors and provide an opportunity for as many crimes and lamentable evils as these [men] commit, more than anyone would find it possible to believe? In the meantime, with most certain harm to his own soul, he is the reason why countless human beings, suffering brutal massacres, perish forever, that is, men who, through the

1. So we read in the seventh chapter of Deuteronomy.

inhuman brutality of the Spaniards, breathe their last before they hear the word of God, [or] are fed by Christ's gentle doctrine, [or] are strengthened by the Christian sacraments. What more horrible or unjust occurrence can be imagined than this?

Therefore, if Sepúlveda's opinion (that campaigns against the Indians are lawful) is approved, the most holy faith of Christ, to the reproach of the name Christian, will be hateful and detestable to all the peoples of that world to whom the word will come of the inhuman crimes that the Spaniards inflict on that unhappy race, so that neither in our lifetime nor in the future will they want to accept our faith under any condition, for they see that its first heralds are not pastors but plunderers, not fathers but tyrants, and that those who profess it are ungodly, cruel, and without pity in their merciless savagery.

Furthermore, since Sepúlveda's book is polished, painstaking, persuasive, and carefully built up throughout with many tricky kinds of argument, it will permanently deceive these thieves, these enemies of the human race, so that they will never come to their senses nor, admitting their crimes, flee to the mercy of God, who, in his unutterable love, is perhaps calling them to penance, nor will they implore his help. Under the pretext of religion, [Sepúlveda] excuses the criminal wickedness of these men, which carries with it all the evils to be found anywhere in the lives of mortal men. He praises with lofty language these plunderers who loot with utmost savagery, and he commends their warlike virtue.

Finally, it is intolerable that a man to whom has been entrusted the duty of writing the imperial history should publish a destructive error that is in total disagreement with the words of the gospel and the meekness and kindness of which all Christ's teaching is redolent and which the Church, imitating its master, exercises toward those who do not know Christ. For men of the future will, with good reason, decide that a man who has gone wrong so disgracefully in a matter so clear has taken no account of the truth when writing history, a fact that, no matter how learnedly and gracefully that history will have been written, will tarnish the most celebrated victories of the Emperor.

Therefore I considered the many misfortunes, the great harvest of evils so deserving of rebuke, and the severest punishment which will arise from his teaching: offense against God, ill repute and hatred for our most holy religion, irreparable damage, the loss of so many believing souls, and the loss of the right of the kings of Spain to the empire of the New World. I considered also that these opinions of his will spread through all the nations of the world the savage and firmly rooted practice of seizing what belongs to others and increasing one's property by shedding human blood (an evil reproach under which the Spanish people have labored for so long), which, Sepúlveda claims, are for the power and glory of Spain.

I could not contain myself. Mindful that I am a Christian, a religious, a bishop, a Spaniard, and a subject of the King of Spain, I cannot but unsheathe the sword of my pen for the defense of the truth, the honor of God's house, and the spreading of the revered gospel of Our Lord Jesus Christ so that, according to the measure of the grace given to me, I might wipe the stain from the Christian name, take away the obstacles and stumbling blocks hindering the spread of belief in the gospel, and proclaim the truth which I have vowed in baptism, have learned in the religious life, and finally, however unworthy, have professed when consecrated bishop. For by all these titles I am bound to set myself up as a wall against the wicked for the defense of a completely innocent people, soon to be grafted onto the true house of Israel, whom the ravening wolves unceasingly pursue. I am also obliged to block the road along which so many thousands of men are lured to their eternal destruction and to defend with my life my sheep, whom I promised by a solemn oath to protect against every wolf, ecclesiastical or lay, who breaks into my sheepfold.

Finally, I want to set forth the true right of my prince, that is, the title by which he may possess the New World, and to hide [*sic*] the frightful and disgraceful crimes that my own people, the Spaniards, have inflicted in violation of justice and right during these last few years on the Indians, who have been ruined by terrible butchery, and to wash away the shame brought upon that name among all the nations.

Four things, therefore, that I must give a full account of are to be treated here.

First, I shall refute Sepúlveda's opinion claiming that war against the Indians is justified because they are barbarous, uncivilized, unteachable, and lacking civil government.

Second, I shall show that, to the most definite ruin of his own soul, Sepúlveda is wrong when he teaches that war against the Indians is justified as punishment for their crimes against the natural law, especially the crimes of idolatry and human sacrifice.

Third, we shall attack his third argument, on the basis of which Sepúlveda teaches that war can be waged unconditionally and indiscriminately against those peoples in order to free the innocent.

Fourth, I shall discuss how foreign to the teaching of the gospel and Christian mercy is his fourth proposition, maintaining that war against the Indians is justified as a means of extending the boundaries of the Christian religion and of opening the way for those who proclaim and preach the gospel.

When I have finished, the truth of this case and the magnitude of the crime committed by those who have maltreated the Indians by robberies, massacres, and other incredible misfortunes of war, and continue to do so, will be clear; and at the same time how groundless are the arguments of a man who is wrong both in law and in fact, by what design he was led to write that dangerous book, in what way he has distorted the teachings of philosophers and theologians, falsified the words of Sacred Scripture, of divine and human laws, and how no less destructively he has quoted statements of Pope Alexander VI to favor the success of his wicked cause. Finally, the true title by which the Kings of Spain hold their rule over the New World will be shown.

For this reason, Most Excellent Prince, I beg Your Highness to order this work, which I have written at the cost of much sweat and [many] sleepless nights, to be weighed and examined by learned men. If anything is found to be stated improperly or badly, I shall be most pleased to have my sleepless nights perfected by their charity. If, however, anything is found to be expressed well, I look for no other human reward except that Your Highness command Sepúlveda to give me a copy of the Latin work he wrote on this subject so that, when I have refuted his falsehoods more completely, the truth may shine forth and rule the consciences of all men.

Farewell!

In Defense of the Indians

Chapter One

HEY who teach, either in word or in writing, that the natives of the New World, whom we commonly call Indians, ought to be conquered and subjugated by war before the gospel is proclaimed and preached to them so that, after they have finally been subjugated, they may be instructed and hear the word of God, make two disgraceful mistakes. First, in connection with divine and human law they abuse God's words and do violence to the Scriptures, to papal decrees, and to the teaching handed down from the holy fathers. And they go wrong again by quoting histories that are nothing but sheer fables and shameless nonsense. By means of these, men who are totally hostile to the poor Indians and who are their utterly deceitful

enemies betray them. Second, they mistake the meaning of the decree or bull of the Supreme Pontiff Alexander VI, whose words they corrupt and twist in support of their opinions, as will be clear from all that follows.

Their error and ignorance are also convincingly substantiated by the fact that they draw conclusions on matters which concern a countless number of men and vast areas of extensive provinces. Since they do not fully understand all these things, it is the height of effrontery and rashness for them to attribute publicly to the Indians the gravest failings both of nature and conduct, condemning *en masse* so many thousands of people, while, as a matter of fact, the greater number of them are free from these faults. All this drags innumerable souls to ruin and blocks the service of spreading the Christian religion by closing the eyes of those who, crazed by blind ambition, bend all their energies of mind and body to the one purpose of gaining wealth, power, honors, and dignities. For the sake of these things they kill and destroy with inhuman cruelty people who are completely innocent, meek, harmless, temperate, and quite ready and willing to receive and embrace the word of God.

Who is there possessed of only a sound mind, not to say a little knowledge of theology, who has dared to pronounce a judgment and opinion so un-Christian that it spawns so many cruel wars, so many massacres, so many bereavements, and so many deplorable evils? Do we not have Christ's words: "See that you never despise any of these little ones," "Alas for the man who provides obstacles," "He who is not with me is against me; and he who does not gather with me scatters," and "Each day has trouble enough of its own"?[1] Who is so godless that he would want to incite men who are savage, ambitious, proud, greedy, uncontrolled, and everlastingly lazy to pillage their brothers and destroy their souls as well as their possessions, even though war is never lawful except when it is waged because of unavoidable necessity?

And so what man of sound mind will approve a war against men who are harmless, ignorant, gentle, temperate, unarmed, and destitute of every human defense? For the results of such a war are very surely the loss of the souls of that people who perish without knowing God and without the support of the sacraments, and, for the survivors, hatred and loathing of the Christian religion. Hence the purpose God

1. [Matthew 18:10 and 18:7. Luke 11:23. Matthew 6:34].

intends, and for the attainment of which he suffered so much, may be frustrated by the evil and cruelty that our men wreak on them with inhuman barbarity. What will these people think of Christ, the true God of the Christians, when they see Christians venting their rage against them with so many massacres, so much bloodshed without any just cause, at any rate without any just cause that they know of (nor can one even be imagined), and without any fault committed on their [the Indians] part against the Christians?

What good can come from these military campaigns that would, in the eyes of God, who evaluates all things with unutterable love, compensate for so many evils, so many injuries, and so many unaccustomed misfortunes? Furthermore, how will that nation love us, how will they become our friends (which is necessary if they are to accept our religion), when children see themselves deprived of parents, wives of husbands, and fathers of children and friends? When they see those they love wounded, imprisoned, plundered, and reduced from an immense number to a few? When they see their rulers stripped of their authority, crushed, and afflicted with a wretched slavery? All these things flow necessarily from war. Who is there who would want the gospel preached to himself in such a fashion? Does not this negative precept apply to all men in general: "See that you do not do to another what you would not have done to you by another"?[2] And the same for the affirmative command: "So always treat others as you would like them to treat you."[3] This is something that every man knows, grasps, and understands by the natural light that has been imparted to our minds.

It is obvious from all this that they who teach that these gentlest of sheep must be tamed by ravening wolves in a savage war before they are to be fed with the word of God are wrong about matters that are totally clear and are opposed to the natural law. Moreover, they commit an ungodly error when they say that these wars are just if they are waged as they should be. They mean, I suppose, if they are waged with restraint, by killing only those who have to be killed in order to subjugate the rest. It is as if they held all the peoples of the New World shut up in cages or slave pens and would want to cut off as many human heads as are usually sold each day in the markets for the feeding and

2. [Tobit 2:16].
3. [Matthew 7:12].

nourishment of the populace. (I suggest this as a comparison.) But if they would consider that war and the massacre of this timid race has lasted, not for one day or a hundred days, but for ten or twenty years, to the incredible harm of the natives; that, as they wander about, hidden and scattered through woods and forests, unarmed, naked, deprived of every human help, they are slaughtered by the Spaniards; that, stripped of their wealth and wretched, they are driven from their homes, stunned and frightened by the unbelievable terror with which their oppressors have filled them through the monstrous crimes they have committed. If those who say such things would only consider that the hearts of this unfortunate people are so shattered with fear that they want to hurl themselves headlong into the deepest caverns of the earth to escape the clutches of these plunderers, I have no doubt that they would say things that are more temperate and more wise.

To come to the point, then, this *Defense* will contain two main topics. First, I shall show that the Reverend Doctor Sepúlveda, together with his followers, is wrong in law in everything he alleges against the Indians. While doing this, I shall provide an answer to all his arguments and to the authorities he violently distorts. Second, I shall show how wrong they are in fact, with great harm to their own souls. For the Creator of every being has not so despised these peoples of the New World that he willed them to lack reason and made them like brute animals, so that they should be called barbarians, savages, wild men, and brutes, as they [Sepúlveda et al.] think or imagine. On the contrary, they [the Indians] are of such gentleness and decency that they are, more than the other nations of the entire world, supremely fitted and prepared to abandon the worship of idols and to accept, province by province and people by people, the word of God and the preaching of the truth.

As to the first point, which we have discussed elsewhere at greater length and in general against all those infected with errors of this kind about the question of unbelievers; for now, as a sort of assault on the first argument for Sepúlveda's position, we should recognize that there are four kinds of barbarians, according to the Philosopher in Books 1 and 3 of the *Politics* and in Book 7 of the *Ethics,* and according to Saint Thomas and other doctors in various places.

First, barbarian in the loose and broad sense of the word means any cruel, inhuman, wild, and merciless man acting against human reason out of anger or native disposition, so that, putting aside decency, meekness, and humane moderation, he becomes hard, severe, quarrelsome, unbearable, cruel, and plunges blindly into crimes that only the wildest beasts of the forest would commit. Speaking of this kind of barbarian, the Philosopher says in the *Politics* that just as the man who obeys right reason and excellent laws is superior to all the animals, so too, if he leaves the path of right reason and law, he is the wickedest, worst, and most inhuman of all animals.[4]

Boethius also speaks of these when he refers to the courtiers of the tyrant Theodoric as barbarians because of their savage and insatiable greed. "How often," he asks, "have I protected, by putting my authority in danger, such poor wretches as the unpunished greed of the barbarians abused with uncounted false accusations?"[5]

The Second Book of Maccabees also mentions this kind of barbarian. For when Nicanor, a ruthless and savage despot, wanted to join battle with Judas Maccabaeus in Samaria on the Sabbath, some of the Jews who were with him said to him: "You must not massacre them in such a savage, barbarous way," that is, savagely and inhumanly.[6] Both the Greeks and the Latins, and any others who live even in the most highly developed states, can be called barbarians if, by the savagery of their behavior, they are anything like the Scythians, whose country was regarded as singularly barbaric, as Isidore notes, because of the savage and inhuman practices of this race.[7]

Indeed, our Spaniards are not unacquainted with a number of these practices. On the contrary, in the absolutely inhuman things they have done to those nations they have surpassed all other barbarians.

To this class of barbarian belong all those who, aroused by anger, hatred, or some other strong feeling, violently defend something, completely forgetful of reason and virtue. Gregory speaks of this in his *Letters,*[8] and Gratian, when speaking of the uprising that occurred at

---

4. Book 1, chap. 2.
5. *De Consolatione* [*Philosophiae*], Lib. 1, prosa 4.
6. 15 [1–2].
7. *Etymologiae,* 14, 4.
8. 2, 69.

Milan over the election of one of the bishops, says: "Many of the Milanese, driven by barbaric fury, come together."[9] In his *Ethics,* the Philosopher calls this type of barbarian brutish when he writes: "It is found chiefly among barbarians, but some brutish qualities are also produced by disease or deformity; and we also call by this evil name those men who go beyond all ordinary standards by reason of vice."[10]

9. c. 10, D. 63.
10. Book 7, chap. 1.

Chapter Two

The second kind of barbarian includes those who do not have a written language that corresponds to the spoken one, as the Latin language does with ours, and therefore they do not know how to express in it what they mean. For this reason they are considered to be uncultured and ignorant of letters and learning. Hence, so that his own people, the English, might not be regarded as barbarians, the Venerable Bede wrote in English on all the branches of the liberal arts, as we read in his life and as Saint Thomas notes.[1] Likewise, Saint Gregory speaks in his *Moralia* as John Gerson quotes him:

See how the tongue of Britain, which knew only how to grind out barbaric sounds, has long since begun to resound with Hebrew words in praise of God. See how the ocean, which before was swelling, is now calmed beneath the feet of the saints and is subject to them. Its barbarous motions, which the princes of the earth had not been able to control with the sword, the mouths of priests now bind with simple words through the fear of God.[2]

In this sense he is called a barbarian who, because of the difference of his language, does not understand another speaking to him. Thus Paul, speaking of himself, says: "If I am ignorant of what the sound means, I am a barbarian to the man who is speaking and he is a barbarian to me."[3] Saint John Chrysostom often calls the holy kings, the Magi, barbarians in this sense: "Indeed, because a star called the wise men from the east and barbarous men underwent the fatigue of so long a pilgrimage."[4]

Barbarians of this kind are not called barbarians in the absolute but in a restricted sense; that is, they are not barbarians literally but by circumstance, as Chrysostom indicates in the same passage when he says: "The star which had gone before them only to desert them, leads to his worship not just any barbarians, but those among them who were indeed outstanding in the dignity of wisdom."[5]

From these words of Chrysostom it is obvious that a people can be called barbarians and still be wise, courageous, prudent, and lead a settled life. So, in ancient times, the Greeks called the Romans barbarians, and, in turn, the Romans called the Greeks and other nations of the world barbarians. It is quite clear that in the first book of the *Politics* the Philosopher is not talking about this category when he writes that barbarians are by nature slaves and do not have the ability to govern themselves or others.[6] However, he speaks of this kind of barbarian in

1. *In Libros Politicorum Aristotelis Expositio* [Liber 1us], lectio 1^a [par. 22].
2. *Moralia,* Liber 27us, cap. 11um [no. 21, ad v. 30].
3. 1 Corinthians 14 [11].
4. *Homilia 7^a in Matthaeum,* cap. 2um. [This is a paraphrase.]
5. *Homilia 7^a in Matthaeum,* in the complete work, cap. 2um.
6. Book 1.

the third book of the *Politics,* where, discussing the four kinds of kings and kingdoms, he places barbarian kingdoms in the second place. Although he says their rulers are rather like tyrants, nevertheless he holds that they are legal and hereditary rulers according to the usage of their country. Their subjects are so virtuous that they bear the exactions, taxes, burdens, and labors their rulers demand from them, even though they are burdensome. He also writes that these kingdoms are more stable and secure than others, for their subjects love and protect the ruler who governs them according to the practices of the country and who is the natural ruler whose children will inherit his kingdom.

This is what Aristotle says:

There is another sort of monarchy not uncommon among barbarians, which closely resembles tyranny. But this is both legal and hereditary. For barbarians, being more servile in character than Greeks, and Asiatics than Europeans, do not rebel against a despotic government. Such royalties have the nature of tyrannies but there is no danger of their being overthrown, for they are hereditary and legal. For this reason also, their guards are such as a king and not such as a tyrant would employ. For kings are guarded by citizen-soldiers, tyrants, however, by mercenaries. For kings rule according to law over voluntary subjects, but tyrants over involuntary [subjects]; and the ones are guarded by their fellow-citizens, the others are guarded against them.[7]

The third kind of barbarian, in the proper and strict meaning of the word, are those who, either because of their evil and wicked character or the barrenness of the region in which they live, are cruel, savage, sottish, stupid, and strangers to reason. They are not governed by law or right, do not cultivate friendships, and have no state or politically organized community. Rather, they are without ruler, laws, and institutions. They do not contract marriage according to any set forms and, finally, they do not engage in civilized commerce. They do not buy, they do not sell, they do not hire, they do not lease, they do not make contracts, they do not deposit, they do not borrow, they do not lend. Finally, they enter into none of the contracts regulated by the law of nations.[8] Indeed, they live spread out and scattered, dwelling in the forests and in the mountains, being content with their mates only, just as do animals, both domestic and wild.

7. *Politics,* Book 3.
8. This is treated in the Digests, 1, 1, 5, 10.

These are barbarians in the absolute and strict sense of the word, such as were perhaps living in the country that has been named Barbary. They lack the reasoning and way of life suited to human beings and those things which all men habitually accept. The Philosopher discusses these barbarians and calls them slaves by nature since they have no natural government, no political institutions (for there is no order among them), and they are not subject to anyone, nor do they have a ruler. Certainly, no one among such men has the skill needed for government, nor is there among them quickness of mind or correctness of judgment. As a result, they do not want to choose a ruler for themselves who would bind them to virtue under political rule. They have no laws which they fear or by which all their affairs are regulated. There is no one to evaluate good deeds, promote virtue, or restrain vice by penalties. Finally, caring nothing for life in a society, they lead a life very much like that of brute animals. Since they fall so far short of other men in intellectual capacity and behavior, they are inclined to harm others. They are quick to fight, quarrelsome, eager for war, and inclined to every kind of savagery. They live on their prey like wild beasts and birds. Hence they are not naturally free except at home, since they have no one to rule them.

Against these, the Philosopher cites Homer's reproach of a certain person whom he calls unsociable, because of his evil disposition, and isolated without anyone living nearby, because he has such traits that he would be unable to establish or continue any friendship or close association. He calls him lawless because he did not submit to the rule of law. He calls him restless and factious and, finally, wicked and criminal, since he cannot bring his acts into line with the dictates of reason, and hence, avid for battles and brawls, he became ready for and swift to every evil. We see all this in birds of prey that do not fly together in a flock. The saying of the Philosopher applied to these men:

He who is without a state is either above humanity or a beast, so that he is contemptuously denounced by Homer as "the tribeless, lawless, homeless one"; for he is so by nature, craving war like one who is not restrained by any yoke, like vultures.[9]

Barbarians of this kind (or better, wild men) are rarely found in any

9. [*Politics*], Book 1, chap. 2.

part of the world and are few in number when compared with the rest of mankind, as Aristotle notes at the beginning of the seventh book of the *Ethics*. So, too, men endowed with heroic virtue, whom we call heroes and demigods, are also quite rare.

The Philosopher makes the same point in his *On Heaven and Earth*, where he writes: "Nature always follows the best course possible," and somewhat further on: "Nature lavishes greater care on the nobler things,"[10] and again, in his work *On Old Age and Youth*, he says: "Nature makes the best of possible things."[11] Furthermore, in the *Rhetoric* he states: "Things which happen by nature have a fixed and intrinsic cause, since they occur uniformly, either always or in most cases."[12] Therefore, for the most part, nature brings forth and produces what is best and perfect. Rarely do natural causes fail to produce the effects which follow from their natures. Seldom is a man born lame, crippled, blind, or one eyed, or with the soles on top of the feet, as some were in Africa, according to the testimony of Augustine and others. Generally, fire generates fire; oil, oil; man, another man. Finally, every creature brings forth and generates perfectly what is like itself and is of the same species, and all men naturally understand and admit first principles.

The only reason for this, of course, is that the works of nature are the works of the Supreme Intellect who is God, as is stated in the *Book on Causes*.[13] For this reason it is in accord with divine providence and goodness that nature should always or for the most part produce the best and the perfect, [and] rarely and exceptionally the imperfect and the very bad.[14]

Therefore this kind of barbarian is savage, imperfect, and the worst of men, and they are mistakes of nature or freaks in a rational nature, as the Commentator on *The Soul* says in the following words: "What intellectual error and false opinion are in relation to the thinking process, so is the freak to bodily nature."[15] And since a rational nature is

10. *De Caelo et Mundo*, Book 2 [chap. 5, tr. by J. L. Stocks (Oxford, 1922), 288ᵃ].
11. *De Iuventute et Senectute.* [Apparently chap. 1 of a work attributed to Aristotle. Cf. *De Iuventute et Senectute*, in *Aristotelis Opera cum Averrois Commentariis* (Venice, 1562–1574), VI, 149ff.]
12. Book 1, chap. 10. [*Rhetorica*, tr. by W. R. Robert (Oxford, 1924), par. 1369a.]
13. *De Causis.* [In all probability, chap. 16 of this pseudo-Aristotelian work. Cf. the commentary on this chapter.]
14. Saint Thomas treats of this in *In Librum Secundum Sententiarum*, dist. 34, q. [1], a. 8, in corpore, and in the reply to the second objection and in many other places.
15. Book 3.

provided for and guided by divine providence for its own sake in a way superior to that of other creatures, not only in what concerns the species but also each individual, it evidently follows that it would be impossible to find in a rational nature such a freak or mistake of nature, that is, one that does not fit the common notion of man, except very rarely and in far fewer instances than in other creatures. For the good and all-powerful God, in his love for mankind, has created all things for man's use and protects him whom he has endowed with so many qualities by a singular affection and care (as we have said), and guides his actions and enlightens each one's mind and disposes him for virtue in accordance with the ability given to him. Hence it necessarily follows that a rational nature, receiving its power from the Creator alone, should include men who, as a rule, are endowed with the best gifts of their nature and are rarely slow witted or barbarous. For if nature does this for beasts, why will it not do the same for man, whom God willed to stand above all other animals, chosen for himself and wonderfully endowed? And we must hold that nature makes man more perfect in no other way than by his intellect, by which he most specially stands above the other animals.

Who, therefore, except one who is irreverent toward God and contemptuous of nature, has dared to write that countless numbers of natives across the ocean are barbarous, savage, uncivilized, and slow witted when, if they are evaluated by an accurate judgment, they completely outnumber all other men? This is consistent with what Saint Thomas writes: "The good which is proportionate to the common state of nature is to be found in most men and is lacking only in a few. . . . Thus it is clear that the majority of men have sufficient knowledge to guide their lives, and the few who do not have this knowledge are said to be half-witted or fools."[16] Therefore, since barbarians of that kind, as Saint Thomas says, lack that good of the intellect which is knowledge of the truth, a good proportionate to the common condition of rational nature, it is evident that in each part of the world, or anywhere among the nations, barbarians of this sort or freaks of rational nature can only be quite rare.[17] For since God's love of mankind is so great and it is his will to save all men, it is in accord with his wisdom that in the whole

16. [*Summa Theologiae*], 1, q. 28, a. 3, ad 3um. [Apparently an erroneous citation.] This is a summary of Saint Thomas.
17. *De Veritate*, q. 18, a. 6.

universe, which is perfect in all its parts, his supreme wisdom should shine more and more in the most perfect thing: rational nature. Therefore, the barbarians of the kind we have placed in the third category are most rare, because with such natural endowments they cannot seek God, know him, call upon him, or love him. They do not have a capacity for doctrine or for performing the acts of faith or love.

Again, if we believe that such a huge part of mankind is barbaric, it would follow that God's design has for the most part been ineffective, with so many thousands of men deprived of the natural light that is common to all peoples. And so there would be a great reduction in the perfection of the entire universe—something that is unacceptable and unthinkable for any Christian. Saint Thomas says that for this reason God created immense numbers of angels, many more than material beings. He offers as the reason "that since it is the perfection of the universe which God chiefly intends in the creation of things, the more perfect some things are, in so much greater abundance were they created by God."[18] We can also cite on this point the teaching of the holy doctor that many more angels remained in heaven than fell. Saint Thomas is moved by the consideration that "sin is contrary to natural inclination. Those things which are against the natural order happen with less frequency. For nature attains its effects either always or more often than not."[19]

18. [*Summa Theologiae*], 1, q. 50, a. 3 [in corpore]. *In Librum Secundum Sententiarum,* dist. 3, q. 1, a. 3. *Summa Contra Gentiles,* Lib. 2, cap. 92.
19. [*Summa Theologiae*], 1, q. 63, a. 9 in corpore.

Chapter Three

Our thesis is not contradicted by the fact that we see that most men are morally corrupt and that, according to Solomon, "the number of fools is beyond counting."[1] But this results from the fact that men, from their early years, are reared in the midst of goods of the body and senses, the source of corrupt behavior, and, because they constantly deal with them, know them better. But spiritual things, the goods of reason, and things intellectual, which are far removed from the senses, they do not know as well. Because they understand and are always dealing with material things, but spiritual things are not so readily evident, it happens that men, for the most part, are plunged into sinful conduct. Yet this does not happen among the angels because they are all entirely intellectual beings to whom sensible goods are unable to bring difficulty or disturbance.

Rational nature, after the angelic, is nobler and more perfect than all other created things, and thus is the best and noblest part of the whole universe, to the extent that it has a greater resemblance to God. Thus

1. Ecclesiastes 1 [15].

if the majority of men were freaks, even in their bodies—for example, having their eyes in their foreheads or being deaf-mutes—the conclusion would be that the perfection of the universe (which, as we have said above, is God's principal intention in the act of creation) would lack something in one of its nobler parts. It would, in the majority of cases, be suffering evil or a mistake of nature or abnormalities, something that does not occur in other creatures. Thus the plan of God, who wills the universe to be as beautiful and perfect as possible, would be in great part frustrated. But this is entirely unfitting and quite false. Therefore it is impossible that dullness in natural power and in the higher faculties, as well as in the internal senses that serve the higher faculties for understanding well, will be found in the majority of men. Rather, we find that for the most part men are intelligent, far sighted, diligent, and talented, so that it is impossible for a whole region or country to be slow witted and stupid, moronic, or suffering from similar natural defects or abnormalities. We have discussed this more fully in our treatise *On the Only Method of Attracting All Peoples to the True Faith,*[2] where we made this conclusion evident by arguments and citations; that is, that it would be impossible to find one whole race, nation, region, or country anywhere in the world that is slow-witted, moronic, foolish, or stupid, or even not having for the most part sufficient natural knowledge and ability to rule and govern itself.

To those who are barbarians in this absolute, strict, and proper sense we should apply what the Philosopher says in the *Politics,*[3] that they ought to be governed by the Greeks, that is, by those who are wiser, for nature makes them slaves because of the dullness and brutality of their disposition. Since they are far removed from what is best in human nature, they ought to be ruled by others so that they can be taught how to live in a civilized and human way. In turn, because they are generally strong, they should perform services for their masters. Thus both master and slave benefit.

The Philosopher adds that it is lawful to catch or hunt barbarians of this type like wild beasts so that they might be led to the right way of life. Two points must be noted here. First, to force barbarians to live in a civilized and human way is not lawful for anyone and everyone, but

2. 1, 5.
3. Book 1 [chap. 1].

only for monarchs and the rulers of states. Second, it must be borne in mind that barbarians must not be compelled harshly in the manner described by the Philosopher, but are to be gently persuaded and lovingly drawn to accept the best way of life. For we are commanded by divine law to love our neighbor as ourselves, and since we want our own vices to be corrected and uprooted gently, we should do the same to our brothers, even if they are barbarians. This is what we are taught by Paul: "We who are strong have a duty to put up with the qualms of the weak without thinking of ourselves. Each of us should think of his neighbors and help them to become stronger Christians. Christ did not think of himself." And, a little further along: "It can only be to God's glory, then, for you to treat each other in the same friendly way as Christ treated you."[4]

Again, if we want to be sons of Christ and followers of the truth of the gospel, we should consider that, even though these peoples may be completely barbaric, they are nevertheless created in God's image. They are not so forsaken by divine providence that they are incapable of attaining Christ's kingdom. They are our brothers, redeemed by Christ's most precious blood, no less than the wisest and most learned men in the whole world. Finally, we must consider it possible that some of them are predestined to become renowned and glorious in Christ's kingdom. Consequently, to these men who are wild and ignorant in their barbarism we owe the right which is theirs, that is, brotherly kindness and Christian love, according to Paul: "I owe a duty to Greeks just as much as to barbarians, to the educated just as much as to the uneducated, and it is this that makes me want to bring the Good News to you too in Rome."[5] Christ wanted love to be called his single commandment. This we owe to all men. Nobody is excepted. "There is no room for distinction between Greek and Jew, between the circumcised and the uncircumcised, or between barbarian and Scythian, slave and free man. There is only Christ: he is everything and he is in everything."[6]

Therefore, although the Philosopher, who was ignorant of Christian truth and love, writes that the wise may hunt down barbarians in the same way as they would wild animals, let no one conclude from this that barbarians are to be killed or loaded like beasts of burden with

4. Romans 15 [1–2, 7].
5. Romans 1 [14–15].
6. [Colossians 3:17].

excessive, cruel, hard, and harsh labor and that, for this purpose, they can be hunted and captured by wiser men. Good-bye, Aristotle! From Christ, the eternal truth, we have the command "You must love your neighbor as yourself."[7] And again Paul says "Love is not selfish,"[8] but seeks the things of Jesus Christ. Christ seeks souls, not property. He who alone is the immortal king of kings thirsts not for riches, not for ease and pleasures, but for the salvation of mankind, for which, fastened to the wood of the cross, he offered his life. He who wants a large part of mankind to be such that, following Aristotle's teachings, he may act like a ferocious executioner toward them, press them into slavery, and through them grow rich, is a despotic master, not a Christian; a son of Satan, not of God; a plunderer, not a shepherd; a person who is led by the spirit of the devil, not heaven. If you seek Indians so that gently, mildly, quietly, humanely, and in a Christian manner you may instruct them in the word of God and by your labor bring them to Christ's flock, imprinting the gentle Christ on their minds, you perform the work of an apostle and will receive an imperishable crown of glory from our sacrificed lamb. But if it be in order that by sword, fire, massacre, trickery, violence, tyranny, cruelty, and an inhumanity that is worse than barbaric you may destroy and plunder utterly harmless peoples who are ready to renounce evil and receive the word of God, you are children of the devil and the most horrible plunderers of all. "My yoke," says Christ, "is easy and my burden light."[9] You impose intolerable burdens and destroy the creatures of God, you who ought to be life to the blind and light to the ignorant. Listen to Dionysius: "One should teach the ignorant, not torture them, just as we do not crucify the blind but lead them by the hand"; and a little later: "It is extremely shocking, therefore, that the one whom Christ, the highest goodness, seeks when lost in the mountains, calls back when he strays, and, no sooner found, carries back on his sacred shoulders, is tormented, rejected, and cast aside by you."[10]

This is the way the Apostles spread the gospel and brought the whole world to the feet of Christ, as is clear from the Acts of the Apostles. In the *Roman Lectionary* we read of Blessed Jude Thaddeus:

7. Matthew 22 [40].
8. 1 Corinthians 13 [5].
9. [Matthew 11:30].
10. *Epistola ad Demophilum Monachum.*

Sent by divine inspiration to the city of Edessa as an evangelist and preacher of the word of God, the blessed Apostle came into Mesopotamia and the southern districts of Pontus, spreading the gospel. With sacred doctrine he tamed fierce and unconquered peoples with, as it were, their beast-like character, and brought them under the yoke of the faith of the Lord.

This chase was different from the one Aristotle taught. Although he was a profound philosopher, he was not worthy to be captured in the chase so that he could come to God through knowledge of the true faith.[11]

11. The three kinds of barbarians we have discussed are drawn from Saint Thomas, *In Libros Politicorum Aristotelis Expositio,* Lib. 1 et 3; *Super Epistolam Ad Romanos Lectura,* lectio 1; *Super Primam Epistolam ad Corinthios* lectura, cap. 14, lectio 2; *Super Epistolam ad Colossenses Lectura,* cap. 3, lectio 2.

Chapter Four

As a result of the points we have proved and made clear, the distinction the Philosopher makes between the two above-mentioned kinds of barbarian is evident. For those he deals with in the first book of the *Politics,* and whom we have just discussed, are barbarians without qualification, in the proper and strict sense of the word, that is, dull witted and lacking in the reasoning powers necessary for self-government. They are without laws, without king, etc. For this reason they are by nature unfitted for rule.

However, he admits, and proves, that the barbarians he deals with in the third book of the same work have a lawful, just, and natural government. Even though they lack the art and use of writing, they are not wanting in the capacity and skill to rule and govern themselves, both publicly and privately. Thus they have kingdoms, communities, and cities that they govern wisely according to their laws and customs. Thus their government is legitimate and natural, even though it has some resemblance to tyranny. From these statements we have no choice but to conclude that the rulers of such nations enjoy the use of reason and that their people and the inhabitants of their provinces do not lack peace and justice. Otherwise they could not be established or preserved as political entities for long. This is made clear by the Philosopher and Augustine.[1] Therefore not all barbarians are irrational or natural slaves or unfit for government. Some barbarians, then, in accord with justice and nature, have kingdoms, royal dignities, jurisdiction, and good laws, and there is among them lawful government.

Now if we shall have shown that among our Indians of the western and southern shores (granting that we call them barbarians and that they are barbarians) there are important kingdoms, large numbers of people who live settled lives in a society, great cities, kings, judges and laws, persons who engage in commerce, buying, selling, lending, and the other contracts of the law of nations, will it not stand proved that the Reverend Doctor Sepúlveda has spoken wrongly and viciously against peoples like these, either out of malice or ignorance of Aristotle's teaching, and, therefore, has falsely and perhaps irreparably slandered them before the entire world? From the fact that the Indians are barbarians it does not necessarily follow that they are incapable of government and have to be ruled by others, except to be taught about the Catholic faith and to be admitted to the holy sacraments. They are not ignorant, inhuman, or bestial. Rather, long before they had heard the word Spaniard they had properly organized states, wisely ordered by excellent laws, religion, and custom. They cultivated friendship and, bound to-

---

1. *Politics,* Book 3, chap. 8, and Book 5, chap. 7 [Las Casas seems to be citing these sources rather loosely]. *De Civitate Dei,* Lib. 2, cap. 21.

gether in common fellowship, lived in populous cities in which they wisely administered the affairs of both peace and war justly and equitably, truly governed by laws that at very many points surpass ours, and could have won the admiration of the sages of Athens, as I will show in the second part of this *Defense.*

Now if they are to be subjugated by war because they are ignorant of polished literature, let Sepúlveda hear Trogus Pompey:

Nor could the Spaniards submit to the yoke of a conquered province until Caesar Augustus, after he had conquered the world, turned his victorious armies against them and organized that barbaric and wild people as a province, once he had led them by law to a more civilized way of life.[2]

Now see how he called the Spanish people barbaric and wild. I would like to hear Sepúlveda, in his cleverness, answer this question: Does he think that the war of the Romans against the Spanish was justified in order to free them from barbarism? And this question also: Did the Spanish wage an unjust war when they vigorously defended themselves against them?

Next, I call the Spaniards who plunder that unhappy people torturers. Do you think that the Romans, once they had subjugated the wild and barbaric peoples of Spain, could with secure right divide all of you among themselves, handing over so many head of both males and females as allotments to individuals? And do you then conclude that the Romans could have stripped your rulers of their authority and consigned all of you, after you had been deprived of your liberty, to wretched labors, especially in searching for gold and silver lodes and mining and refining the metals? And if the Romans finally did that, as is evident from Diodorus,[3] [would you not judge] that you also have the right to defend your freedom, indeed your very life, by war? Sepúlveda, would you have permitted Saint James to evangelize your own people of Córdoba in that way? For God's sake and man's faith in him, is this the way to impose the yoke of Christ on Christian men? Is this the way to remove wild barbarism from the minds of barbarians? Is it not, rather, to act like thieves, cut-throats, and cruel plunderers and to drive the gentlest of people headlong into despair? The Indian race is not that

2. Book 44, near the end.
3. [*Bibliotheca Universalis*], Book 6, chap. 9. [This is probably Book 5, chap. 36.]

barbaric, nor are they dull witted or stupid, but they are easy to teach and very talented in learning all the liberal arts, and very ready to accept, honor, and observe the Christian religion and correct their sins (as experience has taught) once priests have introduced them to the sacred mysteries and taught them the word of God. They have been endowed with excellent conduct, and before the coming of the Spaniards, as we have said, they had political states that were well founded on beneficial laws.

Furthermore, they are so skilled in every mechanical art that with every right they should be set ahead of all the nations of the known world on this score, so very beautiful in their skill and artistry are the things this people produces in the grace of its architecture, its painting, and its needlework. But Sepúlveda despises these mechanical arts, as if these things do not reflect inventiveness, ingenuity, industry, and right reason. For a mechanical art is an operative habit of the intellect that is usually defined as "the right way to make things, directing the acts of the reason, through which the artisan proceeds in orderly fashion, easily, and unerringly in the very act of reason."[4] So these men are not stupid, Reverend Doctor. Their skillfully fashioned works of superior refinement awaken the admiration of all nations, because works proclaim a man's talent, for, as the poet says, the work commends the craftsman. Also, Prosper [of Aquitaine] says: "See, the maker is proclaimed by the wonderful signs of his works and the effects, too, sing of their author."[5]

In the liberal arts that they have been taught up to now, such as grammar and logic, they are remarkably adept. With every kind of music they charm the ears of their audience with wonderful sweetness. They write skillfully and quite elegantly, so that most often we are at a loss to know whether the characters are handwritten or printed. I shall explain this at greater length in the second part of this *Defense,* not by quoting the totally groundless lies of the worst [deceivers] in the histories published so far but the truth itself and what I have seen with my eyes, felt with my hands, and heard with my own ears while living a great many years among those peoples.

4. See the Philosopher, *Posterior Analytics,* Book 1. [Either a very free or an erroneous citation.]
5. [*Divi Prosperi Aquitanici Episcopi Regiensis Opera* (Lyons, 1539), p. 144].

Now if Sepúlveda had wanted, as a serious man should, to know the full truth before he sat down to write with his mind corrupted by the lies of tyrants, he should have consulted the honest religious who have lived among those peoples for many years and know their endowments of character and industry, as well as the progress they have made in religion and morality. Indeed, Rome is far from Spain, yet in that city the talent of these people and their aptitude and capacity for grasping the liberal arts have been recognized. Here is Paolo Giovio, Bishop of Nocera, in praise of those peoples whom you call dull witted and stupid. In his *History of His Times* he has left this testimony for later generations to read:

Hernán Cortés, hurrying overland to the kingdoms of Mexico after defeating the Indians, occupied the city of Tenochtitlán, after he had conquered in many battles, using boats which he had built, that city set upon a salt lagoon— wonderful like the city of Venice in its buildings and the size of its population.[6]

As you see, he declares that the Indian city is worthy of admiration because of its buildings, which are like those of Venice.

As to the terrible crime of human sacrifice, which you exaggerate, see what Giovio adds in the same place. "The rulers of the Mexicans have a right to sacrifice living men to their gods, provided they have been condemned for a crime." Concerning the natural gifts of that people, what does he assert? "Thus it was not altogether difficult for Cortés to lead a gifted and teachable people, once they had abandoned their superstitious idolatry, to the worship of Christ. For they learn our writing with pleasure and with admiration, now that they have given up the hieroglyphics by which they used to record their annals, enshrining for posterity in various symbols the memory of their kings."

This is what you, a man of such great scholarship, should have done in ascertaining the truth, instead of writing, with the sharp edge of your pen poised for the whispers of irresponsible men, your little book that slanders the Indian inhabitants of such a large part of the earth. Do you quote to us Oviedo's *History*, which bears the approval of the Royal Council, as though Oviedo, as he himself testifies,[7] was not a despotic master who kept unfortunate Indians oppressed by slavery like cattle

6. *Historiae Sui Temporis*, Lib. 34.
7. Book 6, chap. 8.

and, in imitation of the other thieves, ruined a great part of the continent, or as though the Council, when it approves a book, appears to approve also all the lies it contains, or as if, when the Council approves a book, it knows whether its contents are true? To this enemy you give your belief, as also to the one who is an interested party. For he possessed an allotment of Indians, as did the other tyrannical masters.

From this it is clear that the basis for Sepúlveda's teaching that these people are uncivilized and ignorant is worse than false. Yet even if we were to grant that this race has no keenness of mind or artistic ability, certainly they are not, in consequence, obliged to submit themselves to those who are more intelligent and to adopt their ways, so that, if they refuse, they may be subdued by having war waged against them and be enslaved, as happens today. For men are obliged by the natural law to do many things they cannot be forced to do against their will. We are bound by the natural law to embrace virtue and imitate the uprightness of good men. No one, however, is punished for being bad unless he is guilty of rebellion. Where the Catholic faith has been preached in a Christian manner and as it ought to be, all men are bound by the natural law to accept it, yet no one is forced to accept the faith of Christ. No one is punished because he is sunk in vice, unless he is rebellious or harms the property and persons of others. No one is forced to embrace virtue and show himself as a good man. One who receives a favor is bound by the natural law to return the favor by what we call antidotal obligation. Yet no one is forced to this, nor is he punished if he omits it, according to the common interpretation of the jurists.[8]

To relieve the need of a brother is a work of mercy to which nature inclines and obliges men, yet no one is forced to give alms. But for these points see the fuller discussion below in chapter [probably intended 27]. Therefore, not even a truly wise man may force an ignorant barbarian to submit to him, especially by yielding his liberty, without doing him an injustice. This the poor Indians suffer, with extreme injustice, against all the laws of God and of men and against the law of nature itself. For evil must not be done that good may come of it, for example, if someone were to castrate another against his will. For although eunuchs are freed from the lust that drives human minds forward in its mad rush, yet he who castrates another is most severely punished.[9]

8. See the Digests, 1, 1, 5, 10, and 5, 3, 25, 12.
9. See the Digests, 48, 8; 48, 8, 3, 4; and 48, 8, 4.

Now if, on the basis of this utterly absurd argument, war against the Indians were lawful, one nation might rise up against another and one man against another man, and on the pretext of superior wisdom, might strive to bring the other into subjection. On this basis the Turks, and the Moors—the truly barbaric scum of the nations—with complete right and in accord with the law of nature could carry on war, which, as it seems to some, is permitted to us by a lawful decree of the state. If we admit this, will not everything high and low, divine and human, be thrown into confusion? What can be proposed more contrary to the eternal law than what Sepúlveda often declares? What plague deserves more to be loathed? I am of the opinion that Sepúlveda, in his modesty, thinks Spain regards other nations as wiser than herself. Therefore she must be forced to submit to them according to the eternal law! And, indeed, the eternal law has arranged and determined all things in admirable proportion and order. It separated kingdom from kingdom and people from people "when the Most High gave the nations their inheritance, when he divided the sons of men."[10] Also, each nation placed over itself, under divine guidance, a king and rulers: "Over each nation he has set a governor."[11] For all kings or rulers, even among the barbarians, are servants of God, as divine wisdom teaches: "By me monarchs rule and princes issue just laws; by me rulers govern and the great impose justice on the world."[12] And all kings and governors who fail to rule their subjects rightly, barbarians or not, believers or not, are violators of the eternal law and face God, who is the avenging judge of that transgression. Since, therefore, every nation by the eternal law has a ruler or prince, it is wrong for one nation to attack another under pretext of being superior in wisdom or to overthrow other kingdoms. For it acts contrary to the eternal law, as we read in Proverbs: "Do not displace the ancient landmark, set up by your ancestors."[13] This is not an act of wisdom, but of great injustice and a lying excuse for plundering others. Hence every nation, no matter how barbaric, has the right to defend itself against a more civilized one that wants to conquer it and take away its freedom. And, moreover, it can lawfully punish with death the more civilized as a savage and cruel aggressor against the law

10. According to the text of Deuteronomy 32 [8].
11. According to Ecclesiasticus 17 [14].
12. Chap. 8 [15–16].
13. Proverbs 22 [28].

of nature. And this war is certainly more just than the one that, under pretext of wisdom, is waged against them.

Sepúlveda advances another argument: The less perfect yield naturally to the more perfect as matter does to form, body to soul, sense to reason. I do not deny this at all. Nevertheless, this is true only when two elements are joined by nature in first act, as when matter and the form that gives being to the thing unite in one composite, [for example] when body and soul are joined to each other and make an animal, and when the senses and reason exist in the same subject. But if the perfect and the imperfect are separated and inhere in different subjects, then imperfect things do not yield to the more perfect, but they are not yet joined in first act.

According to this distinction, if the wise and the unwise live in one and the same political community or under the same prince or ruler, then the unwise ought to submit themselves willingly to the wiser man who governs the state, for example, the king or his laws or his governors. If they refuse to do this, it is lawful to use force against them and they can be punished, since the law of nature demands this. On the other hand, no free person, and much less a free people, is bound to submit to anyone, whether king or nation, no matter how much better the latter may be and no matter how advantageous he may think it will be to himself [sic]. Augustine of Ancona teaches this conclusion in this very form, that is, when the imperfect yield to the more perfect.[14] No free nation, therefore, can be compelled to submit itself to a wiser one, even if such submission could lead to [its] great advantage. When the Philosopher advances the argument that matter yields to form, he intends to assert only that nature has produced men fitted by an inborn talent for governing others who have not been endowed with so great a natural ability.[15] And so he teaches that such wiser men are to be entrusted with the helm of government for its preservation and welfare. Others ought to be subject to them as matter is subject to form and the body to the soul.

Sepúlveda's final argument that everyone can be compelled, even when unwilling, to do those things that are beneficial to him, if taken without qualification, is false in the extreme. For Augustine, whom he

14. *Liber de Potestate Papae,* q. 22, a. 7. See also Egidio of Rome, *Super Secundum Sententiarum,* dist. 44, a. 2.
15. *Politics,* Book 1.

cites, is speaking of those who had promised something useful for themselves and did not keep their promise, with damage or injury to others. Specifically, he is discussing heretics whom the Church compels to keep their baptismal vows, not only because they are useful for themselves but especially *because they have promised and vowed them to God and, from the promise, they are bound by a certain special obligation.* For it would not be enough to argue that the vows are beneficial to them. For we see that no unbeliever is forced to receive baptism. From the teaching of the above-mentioned Augustine the doctors conclude that one can and should be forced to do a good he has promised, but not one he has not promised. But many things will have to be discussed later concerning this.

Chapter Five

There is a fourth kind of barbarian, which includes all those who do not acknowledge Christ. For no matter how well governed a people may be or how philosophical a man, they are subject to complete barbarism, specifically, the barbarism of vice, if they are not imbued with the mysteries of Christian philosophy. Now these vices can be cleansed only by the sacraments and the power of the Christian law, which is the only unspotted law that "converts souls" and frees and cleanses the hearts of men from every vice and superstition of idolatry, from which springs the source of all the evils that make both private and public life miserable and unhappy. "For the beginning of immorality is in seeking idols and the corruption of life is in finding them."[1]

The Christian faith brings the grace of the Holy Spirit, which wipes away all wickedness, filth, and foolishness from human hearts. This is clear in the case of the Roman people, who sought to enact laws for all other nations in order to dominate them and who were, at one time, highly praised for their reputation for political skill and wisdom. Now this people itself was ruled by heinous vices and detestable practices, especially in its shameful games and hateful sacrifices, as in the games and plays held in the circus and in the obscene sacrifices to Priapus and Bacchus. In these everything was so disgraceful, ugly, and repugnant to sound reason that they far outdistanced all other nations in insensitivity of mind and barbarism. This is explained clearly and at length by Saint Augustine[2] and by Lactantius when he speaks about the religion of the Romans and Greeks, who wanted to be considered wiser than all the other nations of the world. He [Lactantius] writes that they habitually worshiped and offered homage to their gods by prostituting their children in the *gymnasia* so that anyone could abuse them at his pleasure. And he adds: "Is there anything astonishing in the fact that all disgraceful practices have come down from this people for whom these vices were religious acts, things which not only were not avoided but were even encouraged?"[3]

These are they who called all other nations barbarians, though no true barbarians could do anything more absurd or foolish. Perhaps the Romans excelled in quickness of judgment and mental expertise, so that they could make themselves tyrants over mankind and subdue foreign territories amid great destruction. But even if the Greeks and Romans did refrain from these horrible crimes and foul vices, where is the credit due if not to the splendor of the gospel, which, once it had spread throughout all the nations of the world, came to the notice even of that

---

1. Wisdom 14 [12].
2. *De Civitate Dei* [books 2–7]. Saint Cyprian in his fourth treatise, *Ad Demetrianum Idolatram et Christianorum Persecutorem*.
3. *Divinarum Institutionum*, Book 1, chap. 20.

[*sic*] ambitious nation? Since, therefore, through their foul and corrupt way of life and the other detestable acts practiced by unbelievers (which arise especially from and follow on superstitious opinions about divine matters) they became like animals,[4] certainly anyone who has not been initiated into the Christian mysteries is considered barbarous and unfortunate. And so note that the fourth kind of barbarian has been indicated.

The Turks and the Arabs are a people said to be well versed in political affairs. But how can they be honored with this reputation for uprightness when they are an effeminate and luxury-loving people, given to every sort of sexual immorality? The Turks, in particular, do not consider impure and horrible vices worthy of punishment.

Furthermore, neither the Greeks nor the Romans nor the Turks nor the Moors should be said to be exercising justice, since neither prudence nor justice can be found in a people that does not recognize Christ, as Augustine proves.[5]

When, therefore, those who are devoid of Christian truth have sunk into vices and crimes and have strayed from reason in many ways, no matter how well versed they may be in the skills of government, and certainly all those who do not worship Christ, either because they have not heard his words even by hearsay or because, once they have heard them, reject them, all these are true barbarians.

This is obvious from the Acts of the Apostles, where, after telling about the Apostle Paul's shipwreck on Malta, Saint Luke adds: "The barbarians showed us no small courtesy."[6] Malta is a port on the island of Lesbos, which gave us the lyric poets Alcaeus and Sappho, as well as Pittacus (called "the Maltese"), who was one of the seven sages of Greece, and Theophrastus, a disciple of Aristotle.[7] Because of this reputation it is praised by Horace: "Others will praise famous Rhodes or

4. As Saint Paul says in his Epistle to the Romans, chap. 1, as does Saint Thomas in his commentary on this section, lectio 1 [*Super Epistolam ad Romanos Lectura*, cap. 1, lectura 7], and in his [*Summa Theologiae*], 11–11, q. 94, a. 3, ad 3[um].
5. *De Civitate Dei*, Book 2, chap. 21, and as we read in Gratian, c. 29, C. 24, q. 1, and c. 29, D. 2, *De Poenitentia*. And that is what [Augustine] asserts when speaking of the Roman state in the work cited, Book 19, chap. 21. And Lactantius proves the same point quite thoroughly in his *Institutionum*, Book 1, chap. 20.
6. 28 [1].
7. According to Aulus Gaelius [*Noctes Atticae*, Book 13, chap. 5].

Malta."[8] Yet the Apostle calls the people barbarians, not because they were slow witted or wild but because they did not acknowledge Christ, although Lyra writes in this regard that they were called barbarians because they did not know Hebrew, Greek, or Latin. This is how Saint Jerome speaks. Speaking about barbarous nations, he says: "For Africa, Persia, the Orient, India, and all barbarous nations adore one Christ. They observe one law and rule of truth."[9]

Now on Good Friday the Church prays against these barbarians, who are enemies of the Church, in these words: "Let us pray for the Most Christian Emperor, so that our God and Lord may make all barbarian peoples subject to him for our lasting peace," and later: "May all the barbarian peoples who put their trust in their fierceness be restrained by the right hand of your power." However, with regard to the barbarians who do not bother Christian people the Church does not pray that they be restrained but that iniquity be removed from their hearts so that they might abandon their idols and be converted to the one true God. And so, a little later:

Almighty and Eternal God, you seek not the death of sinners but you always seek that they may live; graciously accept our prayer and free them from the worship of idols and bring them into the flock of your holy Church, for the praise and glory of your name.

Here there is a clear recognition of some distinction among barbarians, as the Church suggests in rather precise terms. Moreover, from everything that was brought forth above it is clear that there are four

---

8. [*Odes*, Book 1, ode 7].

9. *Epistola ad Evandrum seu Eugenium Episcopum* [also called *ad Evangelum, PL,* 22: 1194, letter 146]. See also Gratian, c. 24, D. 93, and c. 12, C. 32, q. 7. Jerome repeats this in his letters to Heliodorus and Laeta, in the same volume, p. 68, and the laws of Gratian's Decree generally say the same thing, for example, c. 44, C. 7, q. 1, for it also speaks of the Turks or the Saracens in the same place. See also c. 1, C. 23, q. 3, and c. 5, C. 23, q. 3. Also in the laws, Codex, 1, 37: "And he spoke of the Vandals who had usurped the whole province of Africa by their tyranny." And the same point is repeated in the section on military matters in the Digests, 49, 5, 6, as well as in the introduction to the Institutes: "And indeed they acknowledge that the last exertions of a barbaric people have been brought under our yoke." The gloss on this section states: "Barbarians are those who are outside the universal limits of the Roman Empire, that is, the Church," as if outside it there is no Empire. This will be made clear later in chapter [probably 10]. The gloss adds: "especially enemies."

classes of barbarians and that the first, second, and fourth classes are based in some way on certain fierce practices and especially on their lack of faith. Now the first class can include even Christian men if, in some way, they manifest fierceness, wildness, savagery, and cruelty. It is on this basis that the Spaniards who have maltreated the Indians—harmless peoples who are far gentler than all others—with so many horrible defeats, so many massacres, and evils worse than hell itself are barbarians and worse than barbarians. They also showed that they are barbarians when they insolently took up arms and rebelled against the Emperor. Now the fourth kind of barbarian refers to those who are outside the faith of Christ, and this includes all unbelievers.

Barbarians in the strict sense of the term, however, are those about whom we spoke in the third class, that is, those who are sunk in insensitivity of mind, ignorant, irrational, lacking ability, inhuman, fierce, corrupted by foul morals and unsettled by nature or by reason of their depraved habits of sin. And about such men the Philosopher speaks in a special way in the first book of the *Politics.* So let the ungodly men, and those who have enticed Sepúlveda to defend an evil cause by lies, stop citing the Philosopher in opposition to our position. They do not understand or do not want to understand the distinction the Philosopher and the holy doctors have shown in regard to barbarians. Let them take pity on their own souls and let them pray to Christ so that falsehood may die in them and truth live.

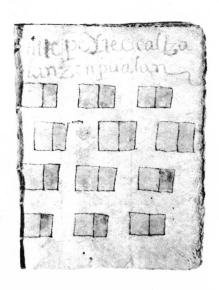

Chapter Six

The second argument by which Sepúlveda justifies war against the Indians is as punishment for the crimes of idolatry and human sacrifice by which these people offend God. Here, as in his other arguments, Sepúlveda is completely wrong because of some mistaken suppositions and expressions.

To make the matter clearer, we have to suppose that we can punish the sins of unbelievers or that they can punish ours, either when we are their subjects or when they are ours or come under our authority. Now this can happen for four reasons. The first is dwelling or habitation; for example, if they should live among Christians. Or [second] it can be by reason of origin or by reason of a person whose case, or that of his parents, is under litigation. Third, a person is considered our subject if he is a vassal and has taken an oath of fealty to us according to proper form, that is, by reason of some feudal right by which he owes us service. The fourth reason is a crime committed in someone's jurisdiction, either against the ruler himself or against the property or persons of his subjects. Similarly, one gains competence by reason of a contract or by reason of property, for example, if an alien acquires ownership of an apple orchard within the jurisdiction of some ruler. By reason of that property, the owner is considered to be within the ruler's competence. None of these persons are subjects properly so called but only under certain aspects: by reason of property or contract they can be summoned by the judge from whose jurisdiction they are exempt by law.

The first kind of subject includes Jews and Moors who live within the kingdoms of Christian rulers, for they are obliged to use and be subject to the same civil laws as the other inhabitants of the kingdom. When they violate the laws, they are punished by means of them, according to the doctors.[1] However, as regards religion and spiritual matters, no matter whether they be Jews, Mohammedans, or idolaters they are in no way subject to the Church nor to her members, that is, Christian rulers. And therefore when they celebrate and observe their rites they cannot be punished by Christian rulers, for [the latter] lack

1. See the Codex, 1, 14 and 3, 13, near the end.

jurisdiction in this area; although those crimes in themselves are most serious and detestable, yet they cannot be punished by men, as is noted by the doctors in canon law. This will be proved later.

Let us now speak about the unbelievers who live in kingdoms ruled by non-Christians, such as the Moors of Africa, the Turks, the Scythians, the Persians, and those with whom the present controversy is concerned, the Indians. Surely, no matter how despicable the crimes they may commit against God, or even against religion among themselves or within their territories, neither the Church nor Christian rulers can take cognizance of them or punish them for these. For there is no jurisdiction, which is the necessary basis for all juridical acts, especially for punishing a person. Therefore, in this case, the emperor, the prince, or the king has no jurisdiction but is the same as a private citizen, and whatever he does has no force.[2]

The case of heretics is different. They are subject to Christian rulers, not only by reason of dwelling, birth, contract, or crime but also by reason of the vow made and the obedience promised to God and the Catholic Church in baptism. And so, when they fail to carry this out it is quite lawful for them to be punished by rulers under the laws of Pope and Emperor, as is quite clear from very many passages in both codes.

If, however, it should happen that a Christian people live under the yoke of unbelievers or in their domains (which God forbid!), certainly they would be obliged by the natural and divine law to observe the civil laws proper to the state, as long as these do not make a man evil or involve a wrong against God.[3]

In this chapter and in those that follow we shall prove that unbelievers who have never embraced the faith of Christ and who are not Christian subjects cannot be punished by Christians, or even by the Church, for any crime at all, no matter how atrocious it may be.

This is proved, first, by the fact that unbelievers who have never accepted the faith of Christ are not actually subject to Christ and therefore not to the Church or its authority. Here is the proof of this. The Eternal Father gave Christ power over all nations, believing and unbe-

---

2. See the Digests, 1, 18, 2 and 3, and the Codex, 3, 13, 3; Innocent on the Decretals, 1, 3, 20. Ancarano treats it at greater length on the rule *Ea Quae* in the rules of law, Liber Sextus, at the word *Iudice.*

3. This is the proof given by Paul in his Epistle to the Romans, chap. 13, and in his first Epistle to Timothy, chap. 6, and in his Epistle to Titus, chap. 3, as well as in other places.

lieving, in heaven and on earth, according to what is said in the last chapter of the Gospel according to Matthew: "All authority in heaven and on earth has been given to me,"[4] and so all peoples of the earth are his [Christ's] subjects by the authority and power over every creature which he has received, not only as God but also as man, from the Eternal Father. Yet, despite this, not all of them are actually or effectively subject to him, not even as regards the exercise of his power. We use the words "actually" and "effectively" in reference to those unbelievers and sinners who, because of their unbelief and the rebellion of their wills, do not specifically subject themselves to him by practicing Christian piety. This is indicated in those words of the Epistle to the Romans: "Not everyone listens to the gospel,"[5] as well as in the following words from Exodus: "How much longer will you refuse to submit to me?"[6] Therefore, since such persons do not acknowledge Christ or obey his commandments, they are not actually subject to him, that is, as regards their actions, but only potentially. However, they will be subject actually and effectively only when they have been regenerated through baptism and bring themselves to the sheepfold of Christ or return to charity through grace.

However, as regards the exercise of this power granted to Christ and on his behalf: as a merciful lord he waits until the day of each person's death or the day of judgment, when he will reward or punish each person according to the person's works, and he will carry out his will concerning all things. Yet in this life he does not use this right of his [for two reasons. The first is that] since, in his mildness and kindness, he gently moves and directs all created things, especially rational creatures, in their acts, he does not want anyone to be forced to give the service that is his due, but he wants it left to each one's free will, so that each one might gladly and willingly knock in order that the door will be opened. [The second reason is that] since man has brought about his destruction by his own will, it is appropriate that he win his salvation by his own will as aided by divine grace.[7]

Therefore, when the unbeliever willingly receives baptism he actually and effectively subjects himself to Christ's jurisdiction and is now a subject by a special reason, that is, by reason of the vow and the solemn promise [he] made in baptism to observe Christ's law, and this

4. [28:18].
5. 10 [16].
6. 10 [3].
7. See Gratian, c. 10, C. 15, q. 1.

also means the rejection of his former master, the devil, whose servant and subject he was previously.[8] Therefore the person who is baptized receives two privileges. The first is that he becomes a member of Christ's flock and his servant in submission to the faith, firmly obliged to observe the law of Christ and even to undergo death for it.[9] Then he is numbered and accepted among the orthodox, that is, the Catholic Church, for he has become a member of the Christian state and a citizen of the City of God, as is proved in Ephesians: "You are no longer aliens or foreign visitors; you are citizens like all the saints."[10] And so, from that time on, he can approach the most holy table of Christ and be strengthened with the sacraments of the Church.[11]

And so, having received these privileges, the baptized person is considered to be somewhat like a feudal subject and vassal of Christ because of the vow and the promise he makes in baptism. Thus baptism is called the sacrament of faith.[12] And this sacrament makes the Christian subject to Christ under a special aspect and in a new way, since he [Christ] acquires a new right of dominion over him, above and beyond the universal right that is his as God and Lord of all creation, as well as beyond the power and authority over every power and principality in heaven and on earth that the Father has conferred on him as man. For example, all men are bound to adore Christ as true God by the adoration of *latria*.[13] If, however, a person should make a special vow by which he promises to adore Christ one hundred times a day, surely he would be subject to Christ on a very special and new basis. From this we infer that if a Christian and a pagan commit the same crime, the Christian sins more seriously because he is actually subject to Christ and has violated a special promise.[14] Therefore pagans who have never received the faith are not voluntary and actual subjects of Christ but potential subjects; not actually, in other words, in fact or on a special basis, or by a new promise, as in the case of Christians.

From all of this it is clear that a twofold power has been granted to Christ insofar as he is man. One of these powers is actual, referring to

8. See Gratian, c. 54, c. 44, c. 61; c. 131 and c. 143, D. 4, *De Consecratione*.
9. Decretals, 1, 1, 1, and the Athanasian Creed.
10. 2 [19].
11. As is proved in Ephesians, chap. 4. See also Saint Thomas [*Summa Theologiae*], III, q. 67, a. 2c.
12. Gratian, c. 76, D. 4, *De Consecratione*.
13. Philippians, chap. 2.
14. This is proved in Hebrews, chap. 10, and in 1 Timothy, chap. 5, as well as in Gratian, c. 5, D. 40.

those who hold his faith and observe his commands through charity; the other is habitual or potential, and refers to those who do not acknowledge that he is true God or do not observe his precepts. This twofold power is laid down in Hebrews: "If he has put him in command of everything, he has left nothing which is not under his command."[15] This is the habitual power conferred on Christ. The Apostle adds: "At present, it is true, we are not able to see that everything has been put under his command."[16] Here he is speaking about the actual subjection that, according to Saint Thomas, will be fulfilled in the world to come, as has already been mentioned. And so Christ's actual power will come to be exercised over those who are now unbelievers and sinners. Again, in 1 Corinthians Paul says: " 'Everything is subjected,' this clearly cannot include the One who subjected everything to him."[17] This is the habitual power. The Apostle adds: "And when everything is subjected to him, then the Son himself will be subject in his turn."[18] This is the future actual power. Similarly, in Philippians he says: "By the same power with which he can subdue the whole universe."[19] But if he "can," then he does not do so in act. Therefore some things are not actually subject to him, for potency, as distinguished from act, is a source of act or operation, according to the Philosopher.[20] Therefore when Paul said "he can subdue the whole universe," he implies potency only, not act. Now what is in potency is not said to be in act under the same aspect. From this we infer that there is a habitual potency in Christ that has not been reduced to act. Therefore some things that are subject to him are not subject in act. But this cannot be said in reference to habitual power, since this would be a denial of any power in Christ and would be contrary to his statement "All authority in heaven and on earth has been given to me." Therefore this statement is interpreted as referring to his future actual power.

In Christ, therefore, is a twofold power: actual and habitual (or potential). And so we say that unbelievers are subject to Christ only potentially, not actually, and thus do not belong to his authority or jurisdiction, insofar as it is potential, until they be converted or die or

15. 2 [8].
16. [Ibid.].
17. 15 [27].
18. [v. 28].
19. 3 [21].
20. *Metaphysics*, Book 5.

until the end of the world, when Christ will exercise his full power over all persons by condemning the evil and rewarding the good. And then all things will be actually subject to him.[21]

Therefore, since unbelievers are not actually subject to Christ, neither are they actually subject to the Church. This conclusion is proved, first, from the fact that persons are subject to the Church only insofar as they are subject to Christ, because Christ is the head of that Christian state which is the Church. But unbelievers are subject to Christ habitually (or potentially). Therefore they are subject to the Church in the same way.

The second proof is that the Church does not have a greater power or jurisdiction in the world, or in any part of it, than that which Christ had or has now. "The disciple is not superior to his teacher, nor the slave to his master. It is enough for the disciple that he should grow to be like his teacher, and the slave like his master."[22] "No messenger is greater than the man who sent him."[23]

Again, Christ did not grant his Church or his Vicar absolutely and without limitation all the power that he has in heaven and on earth. For not even the Supreme Pontiff can institute new sacraments or abrogate those that have been instituted, nor can he forgive sins without the power of the sacraments. Furthermore, he has not been granted other powers that the doctors of the Holy Church attribute to the power of excellence in Christ in keeping with his most holy humanity.[24] And so neither the Church nor the Pope has the same power as Christ with regard to all things, although some persons attribute it to the Pope by way of flattery. I admit that the power of the Supreme Pontiff and the Church is as full as it can be, but only in reference to creatures who are capable of grace and glory, for this power was instituted because of and for the purpose of happiness in heaven and for building the Church. Nor does that power extend to all creatures who are capable of grace and

---

21. Saint Thomas wrote about this kind of twofold power in Christ in his [*Summa Theologiae*], III, q. 59, a. 4, ad 2um, and q. 8, a. 3, as well as in his *Super Epistolam ad Hebraeos Lectura*, lectio 3^a, toward the end, and lectio 6^a.

22. Matthew 10 [24] and Luke 6 [40].

23. John 13 [16].

24. Saint Thomas gives a full explanation of this manner in his [*Summa Theologiae*], III, q. 64, a. 3 and 4c [this explains the power of excellence], and he writes that this authority or power has not been communicated to any creature, ibid., ad 1um et 3um; *In IV Sententiarum*, dist. 2, q. 1, a. 4; q. 4c; dist. 4, q. 1, a. 3, quaest. 1 and 2, as well as in other places.

glory; that is, it extends to men, but not angels; to man the wayfarer, but not all men, because, as Saint Thomas writes, the Pope is the head of wayfarers.[25] But Christ is the head both of angels and of man the wayfarer, according to what is said in Colossians, "who is the head of every Sovereignty and Power, etc."[26] Now those are called wayfarers who strive to attain the kingdom of heaven through faith, whereas unbelievers are not wayfarers at all but are, instead, off the path, that is, blind men and strangers to the way of truth and happiness for which they were created. Thus it is obvious that the power of the Church and the Vicar of Christ extends only to those men who have voluntarily received sacred baptism, that is to all the faithful striving for eternal happiness.

It can be said, however, that the Church has habitual or potential power over unbelievers; that is, that they can be among the believers if they accept the Christian religion and, by entering Christ's sheepfold, want to be subject to his Vicar and to become members of his Church. For just as an unbeliever is potentially one of the faithful, so the Church has only potential power over him, that is, if and when he embraces the faith of Christ. From this it is obvious that just as the unbelievers about whom we are speaking are subject to Christ and are under his jurisdiction habitually and potentially while they live in this life, in the way just explained, so they are subject to the Church and his Vicar and belong to their jurisdiction and care, but habitually and potentially. Now the fact that unbelievers are only habitually and not actually subject to the Church is taught by Saint Thomas in the following words:

Although those who are unbelievers do not actually belong to the Church, yet they belong to it potentially. This potency is based on two things: primarily and principally, the power of Christ, which is sufficient for the salvation of the entire human race; secondarily, the freedom of the will.[27]

From these words it is apparent that Saint Thomas thought that the Church does not have actual but only potential jurisdiction over unbelievers, since he says that this potency is based on the power of Christ,

25. [*Summa Theologiae*], III, q. 8, a. 6 [c].
26. 2 [10].
27. [*Summa Theologiae*], III, q. 8, a. 3, ad 1um.

who does not force anyone, as well as upon the freedom of the will, which cannot be forced either.

The Church, then, does not have contentious jurisdiction over unbelievers, which, according to the jurists, is exercised on an unwilling person (we shall speak about this in chapter 37), nor can the Church exercise it over such persons except in the six cases that I shall cite later. The reason is that, according to the Philosopher, every potency or power is determined toward something it can attain at the time and in the manner in which [the latter] is able to be attained.[28] Again, he says that the acts of agents are proportionate only to a well-disposed recipient.[29] The power of the Supreme Pontiff, then, can be exercised to the extent and in the manner that he has this power, and no more. For if something is good, it must be achieved in the manner and to the extent possible, after all the circumstances have been taken into consideration, in keeping with what Paul says: "All government comes from God."[30] However, as long as unbelievers do not accept the Christian faith or are not cleansed by the waters of baptism, and especially those who have never heard anything about the Church or the Catholic people, they are in no way disposed or proportionate recipients for the exercise of the Pope's power or his contentious jurisdiction. For it is wanting in that case. And even if it is not, what can it accomplish, since it is the power that Christ granted his Vicar for building up the Church? There is also the absence of the "how" and the "when," which are necessary circumstances for the exercise of apostolic power, since the unbelievers are not yet subjects capable of duly and correctly receiving jurisdictional acts.

Consequently, the other circumstances needed for the proper and correct exercise of the above-mentioned acts are lacking, that is, a subject people and the matter over which [these acts] may be exercised. This is habitual possession of jurisdiction, with respect that is, to some persons who are not yet subjects but who, becoming such, are a fit subject and matter upon whom the acts of jurisdiction must be duly exercised. For example, if a teacher is the rector of a college that has not yet been founded, he has habitual jurisdiction. But after the college has been established and completed, he can actually exercise this jurisdic-

28. *Metaphysics,* Book 9.
29. *De Anima,* book 2.
30. Romans 13 [1].

tion. This is the teaching of those who are skilled in the law when they speak about jurisdiction as possessed, as it were, habitually and actually. This is also the case of the pastor of a church that has no parishioners. He is habitually a pastor and rector, but when his parish has parishioners he can actually use and exercise his jurisdiction, because then there is a matter, a subject, a people suited to the exercise of this jurisdiction, and from this potency or habit he can actualize his jurisdiction.

The Pope, then, does not have this subject-material (that is, a people or parishioners) among unbelievers who are completely outside the competence of the Church, because he has nothing to do with judging those outside.[31] Therefore he has no actual jurisdiction over these persons. However, as soon as they enter Christ's sheepfold they belong to the jurisdiction of the Christian Church, they are a part and members of the Christian people, as is evident from what has been said. And then the Pope can judge them by his power and, in the cases contained in law, compel them by his jurisdiction.[32]

Thus unbelievers who are completely outside the Church are not subject to the Church, nor do they belong to its territory or competence.

---

31. 1 Corinthians 5 [12], a text that will be discussed later at greater length.
32. Decretals, 2, 1, 13.

Chapter Seven

The second proof that unbelievers do not belong to the competence of the Church is what Paul says: "It is not my business to pass judgment on those outside. Of those who are inside, you can surely be the judges. But of those who are outside, God is the judge."[1] All doctors, Greek or Latin, sacred or otherwise, interpret these words of Paul to mean that, as a rule, the Church cannot judge unbelievers who have never accepted the Christian faith.

The reason for this is that God, who is the Lord of all things, did not will to grant his Church the power of judgment over these persons but reserved this judgment for himself. Explaining the words "those outside," the interlinear gloss says: "He has committed us to attracting those who are outside the Church." And Jerome says: "Do you not judge only those who are within the Church?" Again, Anselm says: "Concerning unbelievers who are outside," *that is, outside the Church,* "I should judge, as you thought, that they should be avoided by you, since they must be attracted, so that they might be gained for Christ through love and tenderness." And later: "For God did not give those who are outside to you for judgment; rather, he will judge them in the future according to the discretion of his justice and will punish them in a worthy manner." On the same point, Athanasius says: "I am not addressing anyone of those who are outside, since this would go beyond my rights. Therefore it would be useless for me to impose precepts on those who wander outside of Christ's court, since any law concerns those who are under the law." Augustine teaches the same thing in many places. So do Theophylactus and Bede. Again, Nicholas of Gorran interprets the Apostle's words in this way, as if he meant to say: "It is not my business to pass judgment on unbelievers; rather, they must be attracted so that they may be converted. This is what Our Lord wanted when he said, 'My friend, who appointed me your judge or arbitrator of your claims?'[2] [This man] was not one of his disciples." Saint Thomas also explains this passage in this way:

1. 1 Corinthians 5 [12–13].
2. Luke 12 [15].

"For what have I to do," that is, how does it concern me? "with judging," that is, with giving a sentence of condemnation, "on those outside," that is, unbelievers who are completely outside the Church. For the prelates of churches receive spiritual power only over those who have subjected themselves to the faith in keeping with what is said in *2 Corinthians* 10: 6, "Once you have given your complete obedience, we are prepared to punish any disobedience."[3]

Moreover, Saint Thomas gives the same explanation of these words in his treatise *Against Those Who Attack Religion.*[4] In his commentary on Paul's epistles, Saint Bruno offers the same teaching as does Richard of Middletown in his *Commentary on the Fourth Book of the Sentences,* where he teaches that

the Vicar of Christ was not granted any direct power over those who have not received the sacrament of baptism which is the gate by which one enters the Church Militant. Thus in his first epistle to the *Corinthians* (5 [12–13]), the Apostle says, "For it is not my business to pass judgment on those outside, etc." And so the gloss [comments], "That is, how is it my business to pass judgment on those persons but only on those who are within the Church by profession and name? Yes, and God alone will pass judgment on those who are outside. He did not enjoin us to pass judgment on them now."[5]

Similarly, Saint Thomas says: "Now it is not the right of the Church to punish unbelievers who have never accepted the faith, in accordance with the Apostle's words in *1 Corinthians,* 5 [12], 'It is not my business to pass judgment on those outside, etc.' But it can punish by sentence the infidelity of those who have embraced the faith."[6] If it is not the business of the Church to punish the unbelief of unbelievers who have not received the faith, then they do not belong to the competence of the Church. Nicholas of Lyra argues to the same conclusion by explaining the same words in this way: "It is not my business since they are outside the competence of the Church."

Thus, on the basis of the words quoted from Paul, all doctors teach that unbelievers cannot be punished by the Church because they do not belong to the competence of the Church.

---

3. *In Primam Epistolam ad Corinthios Lectura,* lectio 3, #259.
4. *Contra Impugnantes Dei Cultum et Religionem,* chap. 15, answer to the fourth objection.
5. D. 7, a. 2, q. 2.
6. [*Summa Theologiae*], II–II, q. 12, a. 2.

Furthermore, a third proof that the Church cannot punish unbelievers is this argument, which I submit, along with myself and all my other statements, to its correction: It is not the business of the Church to uproot idolatry by force or to punish idolaters, at least if they are not its subjects. Therefore idolaters and unbelievers do not belong to the Church's competence. The conclusion is already evident from the previously cited arguments and authorities. Now the antecedent, as regards its first part (that it is not the business of the Church to uproot the worship of idols by force), is proved from what Augustine says concerning the centurion's servant:

Brothers, it is our business to talk to you. It is our business to speak to Christians. "For what have I to do with judging those outside?" the Apostle asks. We talk to them, *that is, pagans,* differently, as to weak persons. They must be enticed to listen to the truth. Whatever is rotten in you must be cut out. If you want to know how pagans are conquered, how they are enlightened, how they are called to salvation, then give up all their solemnities, give up their triflings. And if they do not agree with our truth, let them be ashamed over their small numbers.[7]

And later:

Do not believe or fear their words. They call us enemies of their idols. May God grant and give all things into your power in the same way as he has given what has been done. For we say to your charity, do not do those things when it is not in your power to do them. It is characteristic of those depraved men, the insane circumcellions, that they rush rashly to vent their rage where they have no power and to die for no purpose. Are you listening to what we are reading to you, you who only recently were in Mapala? "When you shall have been given the land as your possession, before" (he is referring to power) "you shall destroy their altars, cut down their groves and break all their idols" (*Deuteronomy* 7:15; 12:3). Do this when you have received the power. We do not do it when the power has not been given to us. When it is given, we do not neglect doing it. Many pagans have those abominations on their estates. But do we go and destroy them? We first act in such a way as to break the idols in their hearts. When they also have become Christians, they either invite us to such a worthy undertaking or anticipate us. For the present we must pray for them, not become angry with them.[8]

7. *De Verbis Domini, Sermone 6, de Puero Centurionis.*
8. [Ibid.].

And later:

Therefore, since God has so willed it, they think that we seek idols everywhere and that, once we find them, we break them in all localities. Why? Are not the places where they exist here before us? Or are we really ignorant where they are? And yet we do not do it, since God has not given them over to our power. When does God give them over to our power? When the owner becomes a Christian. Then the owner wants it. If he should be unwilling to surrender the place itself to the Church and desires to retain control of his property, I do not think that this property can be considered an idol, since this should be done with consummate devotion so that the absent person may be helped by Christians. The Christian soul which seeks to thank God from the earth does not want anything to be there which would be an insult to God. . . . This is of small concern to them, since we do not expel them from their estates, we do not break idols and some of us want them to be preserved in ours. We preach against idols and remove them from our hearts. We persecute idols, we claim. Are we not their servants? I do not act where I cannot. I do not act where the owner would complain. If, however, he wants it to be done and is grateful, I shall be guilty if I do not act.[9]

From these words, clearly, one can infer that Augustine thought that the Church does not as a rule have jurisdiction over idolaters and that it cannot force those who are subject to it or to its members to abandon the worship of idols or, against their wills, destroy their powerless statues. For when he says "Are not the places where they exist here before us? Or are we really ignorant about where they are?" (as if he were saying "we are not ignorant of this"), "Yet we do not do this since God has not given them over to our power," he is clearly showing that this power denied to the Church is not one of fact but of law, since Christians could forcibly remove idols, as Augustine implies in this quotation. So he wants to teach that the Church, in this regard, has no power at all to uproot idolatry against the will of idolaters, and so it would be unlawful. This opinion of Augustine not only refutes the empty opinion of our adversaries but also proves that this opinion is false.[10]

Now it should be noted that Augustine says that to destroy idols and forbid idolatry before we have power over the idolaters (which means

9. [Ibid.].
10. See Hostiensis on the Decretals, 3, 24, 8, about which I have spoken at greater length elsewhere.

before they belong to the jurisdiction of the Church by baptism) is to act like the insane Circumcellions. According to Isidore, the Circumcellions were certain heretics who killed themselves so that they might be considered martyrs.[11] Augustine writes that those who attempt to destroy idols so that, when they are killed for doing so, they may be considered martyrs are like the Circumcellions. Therefore he says: "They rush to vent their rage where they have no power and to die for no purpose." Unless I am mistaken, then, chapter 60 of the Council of Elvira was directed against them when it said: "If anyone breaks idols and is killed in the act, since this is not recorded in the Gospels and is not found to have ever been done by the Apostles, it has been resolved that such a one is not to be numbered among the martyrs."[12] Note from the words of the Council that neither Christ nor his Apostles ever broke idols or commanded anyone else to break them, although at that time the whole world was given over to the madness of idolatry. If this had been done or commanded, it certainly would be found in the Gospels. Now if it were really advantageous or just, Christ and the Apostles would have done it without any fear of the rulers, whom they would have frightened by miracles or by the word of God. We read that Ananias and Sapphira died when they were rebuked by the words of the Apostle Peter and that, because of this, great fear came over the others. This is how it is recorded in Acts: "When he heard this Ananias fell down dead. This made a profound impression on everyone present."[13] From this we conclude that the Apostles failed to break idols not because they were poor and destitute of all protection but because it was unlawful, since they could destroy a man by word alone, nor were they deterred by the fear of death or disgrace from doing what served to promote the cause of the Gospel. For they were more powerful than all princes, emperors, and tyrants, so that the Holy Spirit calls them lords of the earth: "You will make [them] lords of the whole world."[14]

But if we occasionally read that Apostles or martyrs, as they were being led to make a sacrifice to idols, commanded demons to destroy those images of empty gods, this was with the consent of the pagans. This is what we read in the life of Saint Bartholomew: "If you want all

11. *Etymologiae,* Book 8, chap. 5.
12. Chap. 60.
13. 5 [5].
14. Psalms 44 [17].

these sick persons to be restored to health, tear down and break this idol and I shall consecrate this temple to Christ." When, at the command of the king, they tried to do so but failed, the Apostle said to the demon: "Get out of the statue and break it apart." These things are in his life and legend.

Sometimes they broke up idols by divine power, so that by this display of miracles the truth of the gospel which they proclaimed might be believed. Thus we read that the Apostle Paul went about Athens looking at all the statues of idols and finally noticed an altar dedicated to "the Unknown God," and that, speaking with Dionysius, he led him to the rejection of idols and to the worship of the true God, first by offering arguments and then by performing a miracle, not by seizing or overturning idols.[15] The result was that Dionysius and many other persons broke idols with their own hands. We have frequently seen this happen among the Indians. Indeed, this is the truly Christian reason why God should first give us the land as our possession, that is, in order that the idolaters who own the idols be converted and then, as a result, that they destroy their idols and abolish idolatry—in order that we should teach idolaters the truth of the gospel and lead them to the net of the Church by persuasion. Then, as Augustine says, we shall break [idols] lawfully. In fact, in adoration of the light of the gospel they themselves will break the evil images of the demons and will join us in trampling them underfoot.

As a rule, then, the Church cannot forcibly destroy idols before the pagans hear and freely embrace the truth of the gospel. For it is fatal to the spread of the true religion, unless the pagans possibly had a very strong inclination to embrace our religion or if they voluntarily subjected themselves to our rule, for then the worship of idols could be prohibited by means of adding some slight laws, provided that any kind of scandal be avoided. This will occur but rarely, and only where the actual state of affairs shows that it will be to the advantage of the people. It is fitting that the worship of idols be dislodged not by the violence of men but by the word of God.

What would we do if, after the idols had been destroyed by force, the pagans, still ignorant of Christ, would secretly offer their sacrifices to their gods in the mountain forests and in the deserts, where those

15. Acts 17 [23].

who strenuously preach Christ habitually discover them? The idols may be taken away from the temples but not from their hearts. For this reason Saint Gregory says very appropriately: "We destroy in vain all the ceremonies of unbelievers or [in vain] make rules as to how they should practice religion if thereby we cannot win them."[16] And so, as Augustine says, let us first "break the idols in their hearts." Without the preaching of the gospel and the knowledge of the true God, idolatry will be abolished either late or never, according to Chrysostom and William of Paris.[17] Hence Saint Thomas teaches that the rites of pagans ought to be tolerated by the Church so that, when they hear the preaching of the gospel, they might be converted to the faith.[18] He is speaking about pagan rites that are performed in the territories of the Church, since it would be pointless to say of others that they should be tolerated. The Church is concerned only with persuading men to abandon them by an appropriate preaching of the gospel. Saint Thomas says:

To avoid some evil, namely, scandal or discord (which could result from inter-ference by the Church) or an obstacle to the salvation of those who, by being tolerated in this way, would be gradually converted to the faith, for this reason, whenever there has been a great number of unbelievers, the Church has even tolerated the rites of heretics and pagans.[19]

Indeed, these matters are so clear that I think they will satisfy Sepúl-veda, no matter how stubbornly he holds to his opinion. For why is it that he now commits slander? He even cites Saint Thomas against himself. Surely that saint wants pagans to be tolerated and to be at-tracted to the faith, not to be compelled by violence. To teach is Chris-tian, to compel is tyrannical.

A general argument can be drawn from all the foregoing. Because nature itself teaches that every race of man must worship God and because divine worship is made up of ceremonies, it follows that, just as men cannot live without the true God or a false god believed to be true, they cannot live without the exercise of some ceremonies, espe-

16. c. 3, D. 24.
17. [Chrysostom] *Homilia 7 in Epistolam 1ᵃᵐ ad Corinthios*. [William of Paris] *Liber de Legibus.*
18. [*Summa Theologiae*], II–II, q. 10, a. 11.
19. [Ibid.].

cially since the common opinion among the gentiles has been that the whole status of a country is preserved in happiness by means of ceremonies and sacrifices. Therefore, if against their wills we should completely abolish their ceremonies, they would have, in addition to the great number of other resulting abuses, only an apparent adherence to the Catholic faith and the Christian religion, and we would appear to be openly compelling them to embrace that faith—and this is forbidden.

But when has there been such a multitude of unbelievers throughout the whole world as to constitute a just cause for tolerating their rites if they were subjects of the Church? Or in what other nations could idols be more easily destroyed in hearts, and idolatry thereby totally abolished and the worst scandals avoided, as well as the loss of innumerable souls if they were taught little by little and tolerated, than in our peoples of the Indies? Certainly the holy Church itself knows quite well that it is not its concern to destroy idols and idolatry among the unbelievers about whom we are speaking, but only by the divine word and the mild urging of reason, just as it has known how to use it from its very beginnings and will continue to use it (I hope) until the coming of the just judge and spouse, Jesus Christ.

Therefore they who do the contrary, or claim that the contrary should be done, go against both the custom of the Church and the teaching of the holy fathers and the examples they set and believed. And so, finally, it is evident in this regard that they do not belong to the authority or jurisdiction of the Church. Chapter 48 will deal with this at greater length.

Chapter Eight

In the previous chapter we taught that unbelievers do not belong to the competence of the Church. Now we shall prove that neither the Christian Church nor Christian rulers can punish pagans who worship idols. This, the second part of the antecedent, is proved by ten arguments, the first being from Christ's words in Luke, where he said to a certain man who was not his disciple or a follower of his words: "My friend, who appointed me your judge or the arbitrator of your claims?" as if he were saying "I do not judge those who do not believe what I am saying."[1] Nicholas of Gorran says: "If it is not Christ's concern to judge unbelievers in this life, then it is not the concern of the Church." As a rule, then, the Church cannot punish them, for it does not have a power greater than that which Christ exercised while he was here on earth.

The second proof is from Paul: "It is not my business to pass judgment on those outside," that is, to pass a sentence on them. But the

1. Luke 12 [15].

Church does not have greater power now than it had in Paul's time. If it could not punish pagans at that time, it cannot do so now.

The third proof is from Jerome, who writes that the Church can punish only the faithful. In connection with the citation from 1 Corinthians, Jerome comments: "Do you not judge only those who are inside the Church?" Therefore one must view unbelievers differently.

The fourth proof is that Christ did not give the Church power over the pagans to annoy, persecute, afflict, and arouse them to riot and sedition, and to hatred of the Christian religion, but [only the power] of gentleness, service, kindness, and the words of the gospel to encourage them to put on the gentle yoke of Christ. This is proved by the gloss, by Augustine, Anselm, Bede, and again by Paul in 2 Corinthians, where he speaks of the "authority which the Lord gave me for building up and not for destroying,"[2] as well as in 1 Corinthians, where he says: "Let all things be done for building up."[3] Therefore punishing pagans who worship idols is not the business of the Church since it sets up an obstacle to the gospel.

The fifth proof is that when a superior judge summons some case to himself, an inferior judge cannot make any judgment about this case. Otherwise the judgment is null.[4] Now God wanted to reserve the judgment of pagans to himself, as Paul has said: "But of those outside God is the judge." His judgment is more serious, according to what Paul says in Hebrews: "It is a dreadful thing to fall into the hands of the living God."[5] Now since God has reserved their judgment for himself, surely the Church has no power to judge or punish them, for this would be an injury to God, who has reserved this action for himself. The judgment would be null because of the lack of jurisdiction, which is the basis of judgment, in keeping with Exodus: "Who appointed you to be prince over us and judge?"[6] We can also cite Romans: "It is not for you" (that is, by what authority or power?) "to condemn someone else's servant: whether he stands or falls is his own master's business."[7] In general, the

2. 13 [10] and also 10 [8].
3. 14 [26].
4. Decretals, 2, 18, 56; 1, 5, 3. Gratian, c. 12, C. 2, q. 1, and c. 8, C. 3, q. 6. Codex, 7, 61, 1, #1, and 7, 62, 13.
5. 10 [31].
6. 2 [14].
7. 14 [4].

only lawful judgment is that which has been permitted or granted by divine authority, according to what is said in Deuteronomy: "You must give your brothers a fair hearing and see justice done . . . for the judgment is God's";[8] that is, the judgment is given on divine authority. This is the explanation given for this passage by the gloss and by Saint Thomas.[9]

Now a person who makes a judgment on matters for which he has not been granted the power by divine authority makes a rash judgment, because, lacking the power to pronounce judgment, he usurps the functions of judgment. For example, if a judge who had been delegated for a particular case by the Pope were to pass judgment on some other case, his judgment would be invalid, precisely because it exceeds the form of the mandate and the power granted him.[10]

The theological reason is that no one may overstep the order that divine providence has established in all things. Now this order seems to be especially violated when judges set up by God, and notably ecclesiastical judges, pronounce judgment on matters entrusted to another person or reserved to the immortal God himself. This is the teaching of Saint Dionysius:

Those who are more perfect among the saints (that is, those who are superior or more perfect in holiness), or those who are inferior have no right to act (that is, do anything other than [perform] the proper mysteries of the sacrifice, that is, anything beyond the power granted to them or the sacred ordinances, that is, anything beyond the statutes and commissions established for them by God). Nor may they even subsist in any other way, that is, not only is it unlawful for them to act in any way other than according to what has been granted to them, but they must not even live in any other manner if they are seeking the brightness of God, that is, if they really wanted to be glorified.[11]

It is as if he were stating openly that divine justice will in all fairness remove the rays of splendor and its grace from those who do anything else than what has been granted to them, so that they will go wrong in their acts and fall into more serious crimes. Chrysostom has the same

8. 1 [16–17].
9. *In Epistolam ad Romanos Lectura,* cap. 14, lectio 1, and [*Summa Theologiae*], II–II, q. 60, a. 2, 3, and 6c.
10. Decretals, 1, 3, 22. Digests, 17, 1, 5.
11. Near the beginning of chap. 3 of his *De Coelesti Hierarchia.*

teaching: "Note that it is unlawful to usurp a task which has not been entrusted by God."[12] Now the fact that those who take upon themselves judgment against pagans do injury to God by usurping that judgment is proved from one of Augustine's letters: "Lest I should seem to do injury to the power of divine goodness under whose examination a case is still present if I should seek to anticipate his judgment by my own judgment, just as judges do in dealing with secular cases."[13] The Church, then, confirmed in truth by the light of Christ, its spouse, has never usurped divine judgment but has always been content with the function entrusted to it to judge the Christian people, not others (that is, unbelievers), in keeping with the statement in Ecclesiasticus: "The wise magistrate will be strict with his people,"[14] that is, only with them. Therefore it has never punished or inflicted a penalty upon idolaters.

The sixth proof is clear from the words of Saint Thomas cited above: "it is not the business of the Church to punish the paganism of those who have never been cleansed by Christian baptism." Since he speaks generically and without any distinction, his statement refers also to idolatry.

Our conclusion is proved in three ways. First, because it seems impossible that, at least after the first age of the world, there should exist any nation that is ignorant of the true God and that does not worship idols with varying degrees of unbelief. The reason for this is that since God made man to his image by making him capable of himself, he endowed him with three very noble higher faculties: the rational, the concupiscible, and the irascible. The faculty of reason offers some knowledge of God (although it may be very confused); that is, it teaches that there is a God to whom we should subject ourselves and all we have as to a lord and superior. The concupiscible faculty makes man want to seek and know God as the source for conceiving joy and sweetness for the mind. And the irascible faculty inclines, teaches, and impels man to show subjection and honor to God as befits man's nature, as well as to use some sensible objects as an offering to God, which serves as a sign of due subjection and honor in the same way as those who offer things to their masters indicate a recognition of the latter's

12. *Homelia 7 in Matthaeum*, chap 1, in the unfinished version.
13. Cited in Gratian, c. 12, C. 2, q. 1.
14. 10 [1].

dominion. Now these things constitute the definition of sacrifice, which is a natural aim of the irascible faculty.

However, since it is impossible that the rational faculty should be anything but eager and starved for the knowledge of truth until it reaches the first cause (God), and since, in addition, the concupiscible, which has a more eager craving for what is pleasurable, has to seek some sweet pleasure and goodness until it attains God, it is impossible for the irascible faculty not to subject itself to the service of him whom it deems to be God. Further, it has happened that men, by reason of their crimes and the sin of our first parents, have been deprived of grace and of knowledge of God as long as there was no one to lead their power of reason to the knowledge of the first cause, or to lead their concupiscible faculty to seek him who alone is good and truly gentle, or to lead their irascible faculty to offer true allegiance or divine honors to the true God to whom alone it is due. The totally evil and malicious demons, who have always wanted to usurp the honor due to God, have, in their frenzy, so driven men that they accept false opinions instead of pure and perfect truth and thus fall into various errors. Worshiping the images of empty gods instead of the true God, they lust after evil and miserable things as though they were good and sweet, and offer divine honors to the impious images of demons and animals by means of sacrifice, which is due only to the true God. Therefore, since men are naturally led to the worship of God, or of what they believe to be God, as well as to love true or false goodness, they cannot help offering sacrifices and divine honors to the true God or to an imaginary god. If they give honor to the true God, this is the pious worship called *latria.* If to false gods, it is not called *latria* but *idolatria* idolatry. The reason for this is that it is naturally impossible for men to live without either the true God or a false god. This is indicated in the divine words of Deuteronomy: "If you forget the Lord your God, if you follow other gods,"[15] as if a man who leaves the true God cannot help worshiping false deities. Therefore, no matter how wild and barbarous a nation may be, it cannot live without the worship of the true or a false deity.[16]

Since, then, belief or credulity in false gods is unbelief and the worship offered to them is idolatry, and this worship cannot possibly

15. 8 [19].
16. See Aristotle, *De Coelo et Mundo,* Books 1 and 2; Cicero, *Quaestiones Tusculanae,* Book 1, and the *Liber de Legibus;* Boethius, *De Consolatione Philosophiae,* Book 1, prosa 4.

be removed from those who are deceived by errors of this type unless [the errors are] shown to the one bound by the false belief—just as no nation can possibly live without some deity—it certainly and necessarily follows that there is not and never has been an unbelieving nation that is not or has not been idolatrous. This did not escape Saint Thomas when he wrote that the Church cannot punish pagans for unbelief. Thus he undoubtedly also meant that the Church cannot punish idolaters because unbelief has never existed separately from idolatry anywhere in the world.

In the second place, the conclusion—that the Church cannot punish pagans who worship idols merely because of their idolatry—is proved, first, because the worship of idols presupposes paganism or unbelief and is a superstitious protestation of unbelief and originates from it, just as the virtue of religion is a protestation of and presupposes the Catholic faith. And although idolatry is an immediately subalternate species of superstition inasmuch as it adds [to superstition] external worship and reverence to someone to whom it is not due—according to what is recorded in Acts, Paul, "revolted at the sight of a city given over to idolatry," said to the Athenians: " 'Men of Athens, I see that in every respect you are very religious' "[17] —Yet it is all reduced and referred to unbelief as to its most universal genus. This is true even if unbelief is taken to be a mere negation, as it is in those who have not heard anything about the faith, so that unbelief in them does not have the character of a sin, or if unbelief is taken as a contrary to faith, as when some refuse to hear about the faith or even despise it. In this latter case, the definition of unbelief as a sin is verified. Idolatry, however, always proceeds from ignorance about the true God and divine things or from contempt toward knowing and professing faith in him.

Therefore, whoever for some reason lacks the power to punish unbelief in general for the same reason lacks the power to punish the more specific idolatry. [This is proved] by means of the argument or proof by the removal of a genus: When the genus is removed from something, so is its species.[18]

Nor does it help to object that idolatry, precisely as sin, is a most

17. 17 [16–22].
18. See Aristotle, *Topicorum,* Book 1, and various canonists on the Decretals, 1, 2, 4, and various jurists on the Codex, 2, 4, 32: the gloss on the word *Peremisti* in the Codex, 2, 4, 32, and the Institutes, 3, 5, #4.

serious crime and therefore that the Church, which should be motivated by zeal for the beauty of God's house in order to safeguard and promote the rule of Christ's revered name in the hearts of men, can punish idolaters for committing a most serious crime. But the answer to this argument is that paganism or unbelief that spurns and rejects the truth of the gospel is a more serious sin than the worship of idols. This is proved, first, on the basis that although idolatry is a most serious crime *ex genere suo,* yet, on the part of those committing it (the idolaters)— since they sin through ignorance inasmuch as they think that they are worshiping the true God, according to what the Apostle Paul tells the Athenians: "The God whom I proclaim is in fact the one whom you already worship without knowing it"[19] —[this ignorance] makes the sin less serious as it diminishes the freedom of the act. Nor does the ignorant person cast himself directly into sin. Rather, he sins accidentally, like the person who labors under an erroneous conscience and thinks that he can steal or commit adultery without sinning. For this reason, then, there is less character of sin in idolatry. The true sin of unbelief, as we are speaking of it here, is committed directly, purposefully, voluntarily, and contemptuously by those who resist hearing about the faith. Therefore not only the sin of unbelief but any other sin can be more serious than idolatry.

This is proved, in the second place, by the fact that the sin of unbelief arises from pride.[20] Now sins that arise from pride are the most serious from the point of view of conversion since the proud raise themselves against God, and therefore God himself is their adversary. "God opposes the proud."[21] On the other hand, the sin of idolatry arises from ignorance, as has already been proved. Therefore the sin of unbelief is more serious than the sin of idolatry.[22]

That unbelief is a worse sin than idolatry is proved, in the third place, by the fact that, in keeping with his supreme wisdom and equity, God punishes each sin according to the seriousness of the crime, as we are told in Deuteronomy: "According to the measure of the sin shall the measure also of the stripes be,"[23] although, according to the theologians,

19. Acts 17 [23].
20. See Saint Thomas [*Summa Theologiae*], II–II, q. 10, a. 1, ad 3[um].
21. James 4 [6].
22. Saint Thomas speaks of this in his [*Summa Theologiae*], II–II, q, 162, a. 6c and a. 7, ad 4[um].
23. 25 [1]. Also see Gratian, c. 21, C. 24, q. 1, with its concordances.

he always punishes less than is deserved; that is, the punishment is less than the seriousness of the sin. On this basis, God punishes unbelief more seriously than idolatry or any other sin, due regard being paid to the type of sin.[24] Therefore idolatry is a less serious sin than unbelief. The seriousness of the sin of idolatry, then, does not argue to the conclusion that the Church, which cannot punish unbelievers who are completely outside the Church because of their unbelief, can punish idolaters because of the seriousness of the sin of idolatry. Therefore, whoever teaches that pagans cannot be punished by the Church must surely and reasonably hold the same conclusion in reference to pagan idolaters.

In the third place, also, our main conclusion is proved principally by the fact that it is not the business of the Church to punish worshipers of idols because of their idolatry whenever it is not its business to punish unbelief, because the unbelief of Jews and Saracens is much more serious and damnable than the unbelief of idolaters. In the former, the definition of unbelief and the gravity of the sin are truly verified, whereas in the latter there is the obstacle of ignorance and deprivation in reference to hearing the word of God (as has already been explained). The Jews and the Saracens have heard the words of Christ, and the preaching of apostolic men and the words of gospel truth have daily beat against their hard hearts. But since they do not embrace the teaching of the gospel because of the previously mentioned pertinacity and insolence of their minds, they are guilty of a wicked malice. However, the worshipers of idols, at least in the case of the Indians, about whom this disputation has been undertaken, have never heard the teaching of Christian truth even through hearsay; so they sin less than the Jews or Saracens, for ignorance excuses to some small extent. On this basis we see that the Church does not punish the blindness of the Jews or those who practice the Mohammedan superstition, even if the Jews or Saracens dwell in cities within Christian territories. This is so obvious that it does not need any proof. Rome, the bastion of the Christian religion, has Jews, as also do Germany and Bohemia. And Spain formerly had Saracens, who were commonly called *Mudejars,* whom we saw with our own eyes.

24. See Saint Thomas [*Summa Theologiae,* II–II], q. 10, a. 3, ad 3[um].

Therefore, since the Church does not punish the unbelief of the Jews even if they live within the territories of the Christian religion, much less will it punish idolaters who inhabit an immense portion of the earth, which was unheard of in previous centuries, who have never been subjects of either the Church or her members, and who have not even known what the Church is. For an argument that what is true of the greater [is therefore true of the lesser] is valid, as is evident in the Philosopher and among the doctors.[25]

25. See the Decretals, 1, 6, 7. See also Saint Thomas [*Summa Theologiae*], I–II, q. 76, a. 3 and 4c; q. 102, a. 3, ad 2[um]; II–II, q. 10, a. 1c and ad 3[um]; a. 3c and ad 3[um]. a. 5c and ad 1[um]; *Quaestio Disputata de Malo*, q. 2, a. 10c.

Chapter Nine

The seventh principal proof that the unbelievers about whom we are speaking are not subject to the Church or its competence and, therefore, that idolaters cannot be punished by the Church is that they do not dwell within the borders of the universal Church but live outside her district and territory. Now no ruler, whether king or emperor, nor anyone else, can exercise jurisdiction beyond his borders, since borders or limits are so called because they limit, determine, or restrict the property, power, or jurisdiction of someone.[1] And that these unbelievers do not dwell within the borders of the Church is proved from the fact that the Church is circumscribed by certain "borders." In fact, the Church is nothing other than the whole Christian people, strengthened in faith and united in the society and communion of the sacraments.[2] And these sacraments are the borders or walls by which the Church is surrounded. Or we can say that the borders of the Church are the faith that is promised in baptism to God and the Church by those who are converted, and likewise the unity infused by the Holy Spirit by charity and peace and preserved and perpetuated by the administration and reception of the sacraments. Or surely these limits are the very multitude of the faithful bound in the unity of faith and charity, as Augustine says: "The city is a multitude of men gathered in some bond of association or a multitude of men of one mind."[3]

The gate to this city (that is, the Church) is baptism.[4] Those who are cleansed by baptism according to the word of the Lord are members of the Church and remain steadfast in the Church. But those who have not been regenerated by baptism or who waver in the vows pronounced in baptism and withdraw from the unity of the Church or from the Christian religion by heresy or apostasy are outside the Church, even if they are not expelled. Therefore, even if Catholics live with pagans or heretics in the same house or city, the Church certainly consists of those who are bound by faith and charity and who are called the house or church of God, as Jerome says: "All things considered, I think that I am not afraid to tell you that others are thus in the house of God, which is said to be built upon a firm rock."[5] "The house of God, the temple of God, the kingdom of heaven are just men."[6] Paul, too, indicates this by saying "It is not my business to pass judgment on those outside," and then, in reference to the faith, he says: "Of those who are inside you can surely

1. See the Digests, 18, 6, 7. Codex, 1, 27, 2, #8, and 10 and 11, 60, 1.
2. See Gratian, c. 49, D. 4, *De Consecratione;* c. 18, C. 24, q. 1; c. 22, D. 93; and c. 37, C. 1, q. 1., at the end.
3. *De Civitate Dei,* Book 1, chap. 15, and Book 15 [*sic* for 13], chap. 8.
4. Gratian, c. 112, D. 4, *De Consecratione.*
5. In Gratian, c. 20, C. 24, q. 1.
6. Gratian, c. 11, D. 4, *De Poenitentia.*

be the judges." Gregory teaches the same thing by using the terms "inside" and "outside" in reference to the faithful and unbelievers respectively. "From the Catholic Church alone," he says, "is the truth seen that there is a place in it" (that is, for unbelievers), "the Lord forbids, etc."[7] And again: "The Lord gives a command concerning the sacrifice of the lamb, saying, 'You shall eat in one house but you shall not take any of the flesh outside its walls' "; that is, you shall not share any of it with unbelievers because here they are outside the door of the Church since they lack baptism, which is the door of the Church, as Gregory goes on to explain:

For truly [the lamb] is eaten in one house, since the true sacrifice of the Redeemer is immolated in the one Catholic Church. The divine law forbids taking it outside since it forbids giving that which is holy to dogs. [This is the] only [house] which guards all persons placed within it by the strong bond of charity. The waters of the flood did in fact raise the ark on high but all those whom they found outside the ark, they destroyed.[8]

Again, commenting on Leviticus, Origen says:

When someone departs from the truth, the fear of God, faith, and charity, he departs from the citadel of the Church even if he is not expelled by the word of the bishop, just as, on the contrary, one is not expelled by a correct judgment; but if he has not left before, that is, if he did not do anything to merit expulsion, there is no harm done. For sometimes the person expelled is within and the one who is outside seems to be kept inside.[9]

Moreover, the words "inside" and "outside" are rather frequently repeated in Gratian.[10] Therefore there is a place to which the Church does not extend, specifically, the place where the truth of faith is not known and the true sacrifice is not offered which is not to be shared with dogs (that is, heretics, schismatics, Jews, idolaters, and pagans). Now to be inside or outside the Church is the same as to lack baptism or regeneration by baptism, for those who have been baptized and have that faith that is the door of the Church are in the Church, whereas

---

7. In Gratian, c. 22, C. 24, q. 1.
8. [Ibid.].
9. This comment is quoted in Gratian, c. 7, C. 24, q. 3.
10. c. 32, C. 1, q. 1, as well as in c. 33, C. 1, q. 1, and the canons that follow.

those who lack the faith are outside the Church, where no salvation can be expected for anyone.[11]

And so, even though the Church is spread throughout the whole world, it still has its borders and limits, consisting not of house or city walls or a certain portion of the earth but of baptism and faith, outside of which unbelievers of all types live, if they can be said to live. Indeed, if there are two Christians in the middle of Africa, the Church is there. Even if there are many thousands of pagans in the same locality, the Church consists of those two, in whom its boundaries terminate and over whom it has its only jurisdiction. The others are outside the Church and do not concern it at all. For example, Paul was speaking to a few of the faithful who were living among innumerable pagans when he said "It is not my business to pass judgment on those outside," as if he were openly stating: "You do not judge nor should you judge the others who are outside," that is, unbelievers, since God has reserved their judgment to himself. And this is how the passage should be understood according to the Catholic faith.[12]

In the chapter [of Gratian's Decree] that begins *Cuncta per mundum* it is written that the Roman Church and the Vicar of Christ can pass judgment on the universal Church as well as on particular churches.[13] This should be understood in reference to all Christians, not to all pagans, as is sufficiently proved in the Decretals, 2, 1, 13, where the text reads: "Anyone of sound mind knows that our office is concerned with the correction of any Christian as regards any mortal sin whatsoever." [This concern] does not, therefore, [apply to] any unbeliever; otherwise it would surely have said "any man" in order to include both believer and unbeliever. Thus in the Decretals, 3, 42, it is proved that even if an unbeliever receives baptism unwillingly by reason of coercion (that is, conditionally), he belongs to the jurisdiction of the Church by reason of the sacrament. And, on the contrary, if he does not receive the sacrament, he does not belong to the jurisdiction of the Church. Anthony of Butrio makes the following notation on this passage:

Note here that non-baptized persons are not under the jurisdiction of the Church and that those who have the baptismal character are subject to the

11. Gratian, c. 19, C. 24, q. 1; c. 22, D. 4, *De Consecratione;* c. 45, D. 4, *De Consecratione.*
12. Gratian, c. 16, C. 9, q. 3.
13. Gratian, cc. 17–18, C. 9, q. 3.

jurisdiction of the Church in this respect: that they should be compelled to persevere in the faith which they have accepted.

Furthermore, John Ananias says that neither in spiritual nor in temporal concerns do the Jews belong to the Church, since they are not baptized.[14] Therefore much less do unbelievers belong, since the Jews are servants of the Church whereas the other are not. And thus those who have not received baptism are outside the limits and jurisdiction of the Church. From this we clearly infer that the Church cannot punish idolaters, since they are outside the borders and territory and so also outside the jurisdiction of the Church. For no judge pronounces sentence outside his borders. The king of France does not pronounce sentence in Spain nor does the king of Spain dictate laws for France, nor does the Emperor himself, in his travels, use his imperial authority outside the borders of his empire. [In all these cases] there is a lack of that power and jurisdiction which in his indescribable wisdom the author of nature has prescribed within certain limits for each nation and prince so as to safeguard and preserve the common good of each. For this reason jurisdiction is said to be implanted in a locality or territory, or in the bones of the persons of each community or state, so that it cannot be separated from them any more than food can be separated from the preservation of life.

Further, since the creator of the world has granted this privilege to all kingdoms and communities, the jurisdiction of one kingdom does not extend beyond its borders nor does it extend within the territory of another kingdom or province. Now the law of grace perfects the acts of nature; it does not overturn or abolish them. This is the teaching of all schools, all theologians, and all doctors. And thus it is lawful for pagan rulers to protect their borders as well as to exercise jurisdiction, since, in this respect, their jurisdiction is no less natural than the jurisdiction of Christian rulers. According to what the Philosopher says in the *Politics*, every state should be sufficient to itself and a territory is the totality of lands within the borders of each locality where one has the right to rule.[15] Now "district" is derived from the verb *distringo* [to occupy], "Territory" from *terrendo* [terrifying] or *terrere* [to terrify].[16]

14. *Rubrica de Iudaeis,* col. 3.
15. See the Digests, 50, 16, 239, 8.
16. On the aforesaid law, of which Felinus speaks at very great length on the Decretals, 1, 3, 35.

It is evident, however, that the divine law forbids anyone to violate or transgress another's territory or jurisdiction, for we read: "Do not pass beyond the ancient bounds which your fathers have set."[17] Further, Sacred Scripture holds dire threats for those who transgress another's territory: "A curse on him who displaces his neighbor's boundary mark, and all the people shall say, Amen."[18] And so the decisions of a judge have no validity outside his territory, since jurisdiction is founded in the bones of the men of any territory, as stated by the doctors.[19] And so each person in this visible world is commanded to own things in such a way that he is content only with his own possessions and does not invade another's property, does not seize a poor man's farm, vineyard, conveyance of any kind, servants, fruit, etc. Now the fact that a judge cannot pronounce sentence outside his territory is so true that, even if someone should commit a crime in my territory, I can punish him, although he may be a foreigner and the subject of another ruler.[20] If, however, he escapes beyond the borders of the territory of that judge, the latter cannot then punish him since the jurisdiction arising on the basis of crime is not natural but accidental, like that arising from residence. As a result, as soon as the criminal leaves that territory, the jurisdiction of its judge or ruler ends.[21]

[Therefore when unbelievers, no matter how idolatrous or sinful they may be, who have not embraced the faith, and especially those who have not heard anything about it, but have their own lands, kingdoms, and territories separate from Christian lands, commit crimes and sins outside the boundaries and territory of the entire Church, its jurisdiction does not extend to them. It clearly follows, then, that the Church and its members do not have the right to punish them for idolatry or any criminal or heinous deed, as long as it is committed precisely within the limits of their domination or unbelief, as is the case with our Indians and other similar peoples.]

17. Proverbs 22 [8].
18. Deuteronomy 27 [17]. This conclusion is also proved from the traditions of the law. Codex, 3, 13, final law and the gloss on this section. Digests, 1, 18, 7. Liber Sextus, 1, 2, 2, and the doctors in both laws. Decretals, 2, 2, 12. And the Clementines, 2, 11.
19. Digests, 1, 12, 1, 4; 1, 12, 3; 18, 1, 24; 1, li, 3. Codex, 3, 13, 2. Gratian, c. 6, D. 93, supports this.
20. Digests, 1, 18, 3.
21. As is proved in the Clementines, 2, 11, 2, #*Denique*.

This agrees with what Cajetan writes when he explains the Apostle's words:

"It is not my business to pass judgment on those outside." He punishes Christians as persons who are subject to his judgment but he does not punish non-Christians as persons who are outside his jurisdiction, since it is not his business to judge them. "Of those who are inside you can surely be the judges." He shows that discretion which is commonly employed by judges. The pronoun "you" indicates men exercising the function of judge, because it is common for men to judge those included within the limits of their jurisdiction.[22]

22. On 1 Corinthians 5 [12].

Chapter Ten

The eighth reason why the Church cannot punish idolaters is taken from Augustine's commentary on psalm 145. Explaining the words "the Lord gives justice to those denied it," he adds "to those who are not under its jurisdiction," that is, those on whom the discipline of the Church cannot be exercised (although I cannot find those terms in the commentary). But Gratian quotes Augustine as saying further:

There are some things which should be corrected only by salutary admonition, not punished with bodily chastisements. Their punishment must be left to divine judgment alone when we cannot discipline the culprits, either because they are not under our jurisdiction or because their crimes, though evident to us, cannot be established by clear proofs. Concerning those who are not under our jurisdiction, the Apostle says in *1 Corinthians:* "It is not my business to pass judgment on those outside . . . of those . . . God is the judge."[1]

Therefore, if they are not under our jurisdiction, we have absolutely no right to punish them. Augustine teaches the same thing in homily 50,[2] on the need and value of penance, from which Gratian selected the section that he quotes in c. 18, C. 2, q. 1. Augustine states it more clearly in his book *On Baptism,* where he says:

Were not the men of Sodom heathens, that is, gentiles of the worst sort? Therefore, so were the Jews to whom the Lord says, "It will be more tolerable for the men of Sodom on the day of judgment than for you" and to whom the prophet says, "You justify Sodom," that is, in comparison with you, her deeds are just.[3]

And later:

Holy men have not condemned whatever is discovered to be divine and right in the teachings of the gentiles, even though they ought to have been detested because of their superstitions, idolatry, pride, and other depraved practices and, unless they were corrected, ought to have been punished by divine judgment.

You see, then, that Augustine believes that the punishment of crimes committed by pagans or idolaters is reserved to divine judgment. Therefore such punishment does not belong to the Church.

---

1. 16, C. 23, q. 4, #1.
2. Col. 6.
3. We read this in c. 37, C. 1, q. 1.

The ninth proof of this truth lies in the argument upon which the other, preceding arguments depend. Saint Thomas gives it and it is as follows.[4]

The Pope, (who is the Vicar of Christ), and the other ministers of the Church were established in the Church after it was divinely founded. Hence it is certain that the building or founding of the Church preceded, and is presupposed in, the ministries and the acts of the ministers of the Church, just as the works of creation preceded and are presupposed in the works of nature. Now this establishment of the Church is based upon faith and the sacraments. The sacraments, however, necessarily presuppose the existence of persons capable of receiving them; that is, they have this capacity through faith. But since pagans and unbelievers are totally outside the Church, and are not members of the Church because they are incapable of receiving the sacraments by reason of their lack of faith, the establishment of the Church does not concern them in any way. From this it follows that the functions or acts of the Church's ministers do not extend to them, just as a function of nature does not extend to what has not yet been created or does not yet exist in nature. However, jurisdiction and the judicial functions or acts by which crimes are punished belong to the Church's ministers by reason of faith and the sacraments. These are necessary presuppositions to the acts of the ministers, just as the work of creation must be presupposed for the capacity of nature to function. Therefore the Church's ministers cannot as a rule exercise jurisdiction over pagans or unbelievers because they are not proper subjects for such functions of the Church. From this we infer that if, by some impossibility, the Apostles had not converted a single person to the faith, they could not have exercised the jurisdiction granted them by Christ, since there would have been no Church outside of themselves. There would have been no subject or matter over which they could exercise their jurisdiction. Therefore the punishment of idolatry, or any other sin of pagans or unbelievers, does not belong to the Church.

The tenth proof is that in the case of unbelievers who have never embraced the faith, or to whom the faith has not been preached and who have not resisted hearing about the faith (in this case it will be

---

4. *In IV Sententiarum,* d. 17, q. 3, a. 1, q. 5c.

called the "first preaching"), their conversion must not begin with the punishment of their sins but with an offering of pardon and forgiveness and an exhortation to penance. The proof of this is that if we begin by punishing their crimes, we overturn Christ's express command and teaching and the very form of preaching that he established for preachers. Sending the Apostles to preach the gospel to every creature, he addressed them in these words, given in the last chapter of Luke: "Thus it is written and thus the Christ should suffer and should rise again from the dead on the third day, and that penance and remission of sins should be preached in his name to all the nations, beginning at Jerusalem. And you yourselves are witnesses to these things,"[5] that is, the things that are to be preached, according to the interlinear gloss. With regard to the word "all," the same gloss notes: "not just to one nation," that is, the Jews, "or in some one part of the world." And on the words "beginning at Jerusalem," the ordinary gloss observes:

The ministers who were to preach penance and forgiveness to all nations were obliged to begin at Jerusalem, not only because God's words were entrusted to them [the Jews] because they were adopted sons and had the glory, the covenants, and the giving of the law, but also that the gentiles, with all their various errors and crimes, might be drawn to the hope of pardon implicit in this very great judgment of divine goodness, because pardon is extended to those who crucified the Son of God.

These words prove, in the first place, that Christ commanded the Apostles to preach the gospel by freely offering and promising the forgiveness of sins as well as by exhorting to penance. That this was commanded is proved from the words "thus it is written," that is, thus it has been prophesied, and therefore it was necessary for Christ to suffer. On the supposition of divine foreordination and the necessity of the objective—which was to free and redeem the human race—in the same way and by the same necessity it was necessary to preach penance and the forgiveness of sins to all nations.[6] For just as it was necessary for Christ to suffer and rise from the dead for the redemption of the

5. 24[47–49].
6. See Saint Thomas [*Summa Theologiae*], III, q. 46, a. 1. *In III Sententiarum,* d. 20, a. 1, q. 3.

human race—because it was prophesied and also because the Lord fore-ordained this because of the necessity of the objective—so, also, the preaching of penance and the forgiveness of sins were ordained by God and foretold by the prophets many years before.

Moreover, it was necessary, in order to fulfill the counsel and will of God, "who desires that all men should be saved," especially the predestined, that the truth of the gospel first be announced by exhorting men to penance and promising them the pardon and forgiveness of all sins on behalf of God and Jesus Christ. God so required this that, unless the gospel were announced in this way to men who were ignorant of the truth at that time, surely the predestined would not attain salvation, and so the fruit of Christ's passion would be made null and void, according to the words of the psalmist: "What do you gain by my blood if I go down into the pit?"[7] Now it was impossible that the predestined should fail to attain salvation. It was absolutely necessary, then, that the Apostles preach the gospel according to the form, command, and instruction they received from Christ.

This conclusion is clear, for as God predestined the persons who would attain salvation he also predestined the means by which they would attain this salvation.[8] Yet the first and principal means was the passion of the Son of God, while the second means, next to the first in importance, presupposing divine grace, was the preaching of the gospel according to the command, form, and instruction given by Christ, as the Apostle says: "But they will not ask his help unless they believe in him, and they will not believe in him unless they have heard of him, and they will not hear of him unless they get a preacher."[9] Therefore the preaching of the gospel was a necessary means for the salvation of those whom God predestined, and, consequently, the Apostles were obliged by an absolute necessity to preach the good news of Christ's law in that way.

Now the way to spread the gospel according to Christ's instruction and command is to exhort men to penance and offer them forgiveness of their sins, in keeping with the words of Luke cited above, and as is evident in many passages of the gospel and the prophets. In confirmation of this point, when Christ began to spread his heavenly teaching

7. 29[10].
8. See Saint Thomas [*Summa Theologiae*], I, q. 28, a. 8.
9. Romans 10[14].

he addressed men with these words: "Repent, for the kingdom of heaven is close at hand."[10] Thus Luke's term "should" implies a command and represents a necessity. This is proved also from the words of John: "You must be born from above."[11] The term "must" signifies complete necessity, since it is necessary that men be regenerated by baptismal water to be saved, according to John: "Unless a man is born through water and the Spirit, he cannot enter the kingdom of God."[12] The word "must" signifies necessity also in John, chapter 10: "And there are other sheep I have that are not of this fold and these I must lead as well."[13] These sheep are the pagans who are to be led to Christ's sheepfold by the preaching of the truth of the gospel, in keeping with what is said in Luke: "Thus it is written."[14] The word "should," representing necessity, means that the preachers of the gospel are obliged by necessity to exhort people to penance by offering them forgiveness of their sins. For just as the term "should," as related to Christ's passion and resurrection, implies that these were necessary for the salvation of the predestined, it also implies that the gospel ought to be preached by exhortation to penance and by offering the forgiveness of sins.

No preacher of the gospel, then, can begin by punishing the crimes of pagans, especially in the case of those to whom the faith has not as yet been preached. Since the Apostles thought that they were held by a strict command to preach the gospel in the same way that Christ taught and commanded it to be preached, for that reason, in converting the world, they observed as strictly as possible the above-mentioned form and manner in their words and deeds. Speaking of them, Augustine says:

Filled with the Holy Spirit, they suddenly speak in the languages of all nations, faithfully expose errors, preach a most saving truth, exhort to penance for a sinful past life, and promise the pardon granted by divine grace. Appropriate signs and miracles follow them as they preach the piety of the true religion. Savage unbelief is aroused against them, they tolerate what was foretold to them, they hope for what was promised to them, they teach what was commanded them. Small in number, they spread throughout the world, convert

10. Matthew 4[17].
11. John 3[7].
12. John 3[5].
13. John 10[16].
14. Luke 24[46].

peoples with admirable ease, increase among enemies, grow amid persecutions, and are spread out to the very ends of the earth through their distress and afflictions.[15]

And later:

The temples and images of demons, as well as their sacrilegious rites, are gradually overturned in keeping with what was foretold by the prophets.[16]

These words of Augustine greatly strengthen our position; that is, that the gospel must be announced to pagans by exhorting them to penance and offering them forgiveness of their sins. The canonists teach that Christ's term "should" represents necessity.[17] So do the jurists in other passages.[18]

The reason for all this is given by Augustine:

But a discipline which punishes a person who is leading an evil life is distorted, *that is, inordinate,* unless the severe discipline offers beforehand an instruction about how to live well, that is, unless the culprit is first instructed about the good or unless the one correcting first gives an example of the good life.[19]

That is how the gloss explains it. You see that Augustine teaches that holy doctrine and the example of right living should come before the punishment of the sinner. This must be admitted all the more in the case of sinners who sin from ignorance, such as the pagans who have never heard Christ's words and for whose sake we have undertaken this treatise. Otherwise the punishment or discipline is distorted and inordinate and has been devised by the devil.

Secondly, from the words of our Savior, "thus it is written," it should be noted that the form should be observed by which he commanded that his gospel be announced, no matter which nations of the world are being evangelized, whether they are pagans or peoples sunk in the most atrocious sins. For the words have general application, since Christ says "to all nations" without differentiating among nations.

15. *Ad Volusianum Epistola 3a.*
16. [Ibid].
17. Decretals, 1, 2, 4; 2, 3, 1. Liber Sextus, 1, 3, 1.
18. Digests, 1, 1, 1, on the word *Oportet.*
19. *Contra Petilianum Epistola,* cited in Gratian, c. 33, C. 23, q. 5.

Again we read: "We must turn to the pagans."[20] Now it is a maxim in human law that wherever the law does not distinguish, we should not distinguish. Since, then, Christ's words are general, the proclamation of the truth according to the instruction, example, and command of Christ and the Apostles should be observed wherever the gospel is preached.

20. Acts 13[46].

Chapter Eleven

The foregoing arguments are bolstered by what Paul says: "There is no distinction between Jew and Greek"[1] and "There are no more distinctions between Jew and Greek, slave and free, male and female, but all of you are one in Christ Jesus."[2] Further, he acknowledges that he is obliged to preach the gospel to everyone. "I owe a duty to Greeks just as much as to barbarians, to the educated just as much as to the unedu-

1. Romans 10 [12].
2. Galatians 3 [28].

cated, and it is this that makes me want to bring the Good News to you too in Rome."[3] Saint Peter says the same thing: "Then Peter addressed them, 'The truth I have now come to realize,' he said, 'is that God does not have favorites but that anybody of any nationality who fears God and does what is right is acceptable to him.' "[4] Bede's gloss states on this passage:

God is not a respecter of persons since he sent his only-begotten Son, the creator and lord of all things, to make peace with the human race. According to the testimony of the prophets, not only the Jews but all who believed would receive the forgiveness of sins in his name.

And so the gospel must be preached to all nations without distinction, in a brotherly and friendly manner, along with offering the forgiveness of sins.

This is how Saint Ambrose speaks: "In this command, has any distinction been made among nations or persons? It excludes no one by design, segregates no one by race, sets no one apart by class."[5] So on that point we may summarize Saint Ambrose's teaching thus: God's grace has shone on all men of every nation and the message of the gospel has been sent, and must be sent, to all persons, earlier to some, later to others, since, as Ambrose says: "It must be most firmly admitted that God 'wants all men to be saved and to come to the knowledge of the truth.' " Peace, Christian friendship, and mutual love, then, must be offered to the pagans to whom the gospel is preached for the first time, while at the same time they are offered forgiveness of sins. By "first announcement" I mean the one that is made to nations that have never heard the gospel on any occasion. The "second announcement" is the one that is made to heretics and schismatics, just as the "first Eucharist" is said to be that which Christ instituted.[6]

3. Romans 1 [14–15].
4. Acts 10 [34–35].
5. *De Vocatione Omnium Gentium,* Book 2, chap. 1.
6. This is evident from Gratian, c. 88, C. 1, q. 1: "so that he might give him the first Eucharist, produced by his hands and recommended by his utterance, just as he did for the other apostles."

Thirdly, from Christ's words "thus it is written" we should note that just as the gospel must be announced to Greeks, Latins, Scythians, barbarians, slaves and freemen, men and women, in the same way, no distinction must be established in respect to any nation, no matter how involved it may be in fearful crimes and horrible vices of idolatry or any other kind of evil. For the greater the crimes of the pagans, the more God's immense mercy will shine when the pagans see that the preachers of the gospel offer forgiveness of all crimes, no matter what their number or kind may be. This will very definitely lead them to receive the sweet and light yoke of Christ, as the gloss teaches in this matter. Indeed, if the gospel was preached and the forgiveness of sins was offered to those who crucified Christ—and no more fearful crime can be imagined—who will be so stupid or will think such nonsense as to claim that there are any pagans, no matter how wicked and detestable, who should not hear the gospel announced in the same form and be offered the pardon and forgiveness of sins in a spirit of brotherly love? Thus on this point the gloss observes that Christ's law had to be preached first to the Jews in an attractive and kindly way "so that the gentiles, with all their various errors and crimes, might be drawn to the hope of pardon implicit in this supreme judgment of divine goodness, because those who crucified the Son were pardoned." This is even more obvious in the first sermon Peter addressed to the Jews after he had received the Holy Spirit, for he addressed them in this way:

"For this reason the whole House of Israel can be certain that God has made this Jesus whom you crucified both Lord and Christ." Hearing this, they were cut to the heart and said to Peter and the Apostles, "What must we do, brothers?" "You must repent," Peter answered, " and every one of you must be baptized in the name of Jesus Christ for the forgiveness of your sins, and you will receive the gift of the Holy Spirit."[7]

And it goes on to say that three thousand persons among them received the faith that day and remained faithful to the teaching of the Apostles.

7. Acts 2 [36–38].

So too when Peter doubted whether all nations were capable of belonging to God's kingdom and whether they were to be admitted without distinction to the grace of the gospel or whether some were to be excluded because of the enormity of their crimes, he received from God the sign of the sheet, containing all the unclean and offensive kinds of serpents and birds. When Peter was told "Kill and eat," and he answered "Lord, I have never yet eaten anything unclean," he was told "What God has made clean, you have no right to call profane."[8] Therefore, understanding that no one, however sinful, should be excluded from divine grace, he said:

The truth that I have now come to realize is that God does not have favorites but that anybody of any nationality who fears God and does what is right is acceptable to him. . . . God sent his word to the people of Israel, and it was to them that the good news of peace was brought by Jesus Christ.[9]

Speaking of this vision of Peter, Jerome says:

A voice came to Peter, "Arise, Peter, kill and eat, etc." In this command there is an indication that no man is polluted by nature but that all are equally invited to the gospel of Christ, since the voice said to Peter, "What God has made clean, you have no right to call profane," that is, unclean.[10]

Moreover, the people of Corinth were infamous for their irreligion, their sodomy, and their plunderings. Yet Paul wrote two letters to them in a spirit of fatherly love. Nor did he preach the gospel to them any differently than he did to other peoples. In fact he led them to Christ even more persuasively, and with a greater affability and gentleness. And so he worked with his hands lest he should upset the greedy among them. Thus he says: "Or was I wrong, lowering myself so as to lift you on high, by preaching the gospel of God to you and taking no fee for it? I was robbing other churches, living on them so that I could serve you. When I was with you and ran out of money, I was no burden to anyone."[11] Now the fact that this people was guilty of detestable crimes is proved from the accusing and warning words of the Apostle:

8. From Acts 2 [36–38].
9. Acts 10 [34–36].
10. *Epistola ad Augustinum,* which is no. 170.
11. 2 Corinthians 11 [7–9].

You know perfectly well that people who do wrong will not inherit the kingdom of God; people of immoral lives, idolaters, adulterers, catamites, sodomites, thieves, usurers, drunkards, slanderers, and swindlers will never inherit the kingdom of God. These are the sort of people some of you were once, but now you have been washed clean, and sanctified, and justified through the name of the Lord Jesus Christ and through the Spirit of our God.[12]

Can there be vices that surpass these in number or seriousness? Certainly not! Therefore there is no crime so horrible, whether it be idolatry or sodomy or some other kind, as to demand that the gospel be preached for the first time in any other way than that established by Christ, that is, in a spirit of brotherly love, offering forgiveness of sins and exhorting men to repentance. For to do otherwise would be to upset the way established by Christ. Therefore it is not the Church's business to begin the first preaching of the faith with the punishment of idolatry or any other serious crime. Rather, this preaching should begin with an exhortation to repentance and an offer to forgive all sins on behalf of the divine mercy.

The foregoing agrees with what Almain writes: "The Pope cannot punish a pagan committing any crime, even if the pagan knows that it is a sin, as, for example, if he commits the sin of idolatry or a sin against nature or steals what belongs to another."[13] Almain cites Paul, who, having spoken of idolaters, drunkards, slanderers, and thieves, says: "It is not my business to pass judgment on those outside." On this basis, Almain accuses Panormitanus of teaching that the Pope can punish a pagan who sins against the law of nature, and this in spite of the contrary and common opinion of the doctors.[14] From this Almain infers that no pagan is held to shun an excommunicated Christian since the Pope has no jurisdiction over the pagan. As a matter of fact, however, Panormitanus does not teach that the Pope can punish a pagan, but that he can denounce or warn him and correct him in a brotherly fashion, in keeping with Christ's command. However, Panormitanus is accused of this same thing by Barbatius, who teaches that fraternal correction, as enjoined on us by Christ, does not oblige us in our dealings with pagans, for which opinion he offers sound reasons.[15]

12. 1 Corinthians 6 [9–11].
13. *Liber de Potestate Ecclesiastica*, chap. 21.
14. In reference to [Panormitanus'] interpretation of the Decretals, 2, 1, 13.
15. In his commentary on the Decretals, 2, 1, 13.

Whatever the case may be, Panormitanus is speaking about Jews who sin against their own law, as is indicated in his clause "or if they sin against their own law." Yet a Christian is not obliged to correct other pagans, Saracens, or idolaters who disobey their own foolish and irrational laws in order that they will not transgress them, first, because this would be an approval of their unjust and evil laws, and, second, because among all the holy and pious persons in the Church no Christian has done such a thing or takes the trouble to do it. This is a strong argument that we are not obliged to do things of this sort. In the case of the Jews, however, about whom the Abbot [Panormitanus] is speaking, there is something of a difference since, in sinning against his law in moral matters, the Jew sins against the divine law that we too acknowledge and recognize. And consequently there is an injury to the Christian Church, which can freely coerce and punish the Jews as its subjects.

Whatever the Abbot thinks about other unbelievers, his opinion must be admitted in the case of pagans who in law and fact are subject to Christian rulers. This is the proper interpretation of what Innocent teaches, that is, that the Pope can punish unbelievers who sin against the natural law or Jews who sin against the gospel in moral matters, that is, insofar as they act against the divine law of the Old Testament, which they profess, even though they mingle some heresies with it, provided that they are not punished by their own elders.[16] Furthermore, Innocent reports that Popes Gregory and Innocent burned the books of the Talmud, which contained many heresies, and commanded that those who taught and followed those stupid fables should be punished. His teaching is based on the argument that the Jews are subject to the Church and to Christian rulers. We shall treat this subject at greater length later.

To summarize, no pagan can be punished by the Church—much less by Christian rulers—for a superstition, no matter how abominable, or a crime, no matter how serious, as long as he commits it precisely within the borders of the territory of his own masters and his own unbelief. For there is no judge or ruler in the world who has care of the men of the whole world except the Church and the Vicar of Jesus Christ, (who is the Roman Pontiff) in order to invite and attract pagans to the Catholic faith or protect and strengthen them in the truths of the faith.

16. In his commentary on the Decretals, 3, 24, 8.

Chapter Twelve

Everything said above, including the ten arguments, is bolstered by the praiseworthy government and holy practice of the Church. The practice of the Church must be imitated and emulated in all things, as Thomas teaches: "Whatever holy men have written has its authority only from the Church. Therefore one must praise, follow, and prefer the practice of the Church more than the authority of Augustine, or Jerome, or any other doctor."[1] On this basis, never, from the time of Christ's ascension into heaven, has the Church begun to spread the truth of the gospel by punishing the sins by which pagans offend God; rather, it has attracted them to the faith by gentleness, service, meekness, and charity, by offering them in Christ's name the forgiveness of all sins (later, from chapter 39 on, this will be clearer than light itself).

Under the enlightenment of the Holy Spirit, the Church understands that Christ has reserved the judgment of those crimes to himself and has not entrusted this judgment to it, and that he has wished that his Church lead unbelievers to the truths of faith by gentleness and charity,

1. [*Summa Theologiae*], II–II, q. 10, a. 12c. *Quodlibetale*, II, a. 7c.

not by violence or the use of arms. For this reason we read in the decrees of the Popes:

Whoever seek with a sincere intention to lead those outside the Christian religion to the true faith should seek to do so, not with harshness but with pleasant words and actions, lest adversity drive away those whose spirits can be brought back from death by the return of reason. For those who do otherwise and seek to take them away from their accustomed manner of worship under this pretext show that they are concerned more for their own interests than for God's.

And later:

For what advantage is there when and if they are forbidden to continue what has been long-standing among them and there is no progress toward a change of belief? Furthermore, how can we lay down rules for them if we cannot in that way win them? For we must proceed in such a way that, enticed by reason and meekness, they should want to follow us, not flee from us.[2]

Gregory expresses the same teaching in this way:

For those who are in disagreement with the Christian religion we must gather to the unity of faith by means of meek and kind admonition and persuasion, in order that those who could be invited to believe by gentle preaching and the prospect and fear of future judgment, may not be driven away by threats and fears. Therefore if they are to hear the word of God from you, they should come to you because of your kindness, rather than in fear of an exaggerated austerity.[3]

In these words Gregory clearly indicates what we have already taught at great length, and which will be seen even more fully later. Saint Cyril says:

Now because the creator of all things has wanted man to be responsible for himself and to be guided by his own will in his activities, therefore Christ, the savior of all men, quite properly decreed that men should be freed from their wickedness, not by forcible correction, but by persuasion, so that they would prefer better things, those through which they themselves would most likely become better. But if, in all the splendor of his kingly glory, he who has

---

2. Gratian, c. 3, D. 45.
3. In his book of letters, specifically letters 15 and 34.

unvanquished power had commanded men to believe him, this belief would not go beyond the realm of knowledge but rather would concern only necessary and unavoidable commands. And he would perhaps have been like a person who receives divine honor unworthily on the sole basis of the judgment of men. But because, as one of us, he used a modest and humble appearance and avoided human glory, he leads those who are willing and sure in their knowledge to what is better, partly by very wise teachings and partly by indescribable and divine miracles.[4]

Observe how foreign to the decrees of the Fathers and to Christ's teaching is the desire to lead pagans to the faith by armed terror, warlike force, and empty display. But Gregory has shown, in the citation above, that anyone who does otherwise or teaches that there is any other way of acting, because they are both intent on plunder, is more concerned about his own interests than God's. Finally, the Roman Pontiff Paul III, the Vicar of Christ, in his bull of 1537, has shown that Sepúlveda has gone totally astray in this matter and that, in addition, those who misuse the authority of this otherwise learned man to strengthen their impious cause are instruments of the devil in his envy of man's salvation, the glory of Christ, and the spread of the gospel. This affirms and renews the ancient practice of the Church in the preaching of the gospel and the subjugation of pagans to the true religion. We would like to append the tenor of the bull at this point.

The Sublime God has so loved the human race that he has made man in such a way that not only would he share in goodness like other creatures but also that he should be able to attain that highest and inaccessible good and know it by face-to-face vision.

And later:

Hence that Truth which can neither deceive nor be deceived is known to have said, in sending the preachers of the faith to fulfill the function of this preaching, "Go and make disciples of all nations." He said "all" without any distinction, since all are capable of receiving the discipline of the faith. Seeing and envying this, the enemy of mankind, who always opposes good men so that they might perish, devised a means, unheard of up to this time, by which the preaching of God's word to nations for their salvation would be prevented. And

4. *Adversus Iulianum,* Book 6.

he inspired certain of his satellites who, in their desire to satisfy their greed, presume to assert here and there that the Indians of the south and west and other nations who in these times have come to our knowledge, under the pretext that they are incapable of the Catholic faith, are brute animals who can be enslaved by us. And they actually do enslave them, afflicting them in a way which they would scarcely use on the brute animals which serve them.

Therefore we who, however unworthily, take the place of our said Lord here on earth and seek with all our strength to bring those lambs to his flock who are outside his sheepfold—

Acknowledging that the Indians as true men not only are capable of receiving the Christian faith but, as we have been informed, eagerly hurry to it—

And wishing to provide suitable remedies for dealing with these abuses—

We command that the aforesaid Indians and all other nations which come to the knowledge of Christians in the future must not be deprived of their freedom and the ownership of their property, even though they are outside the faith of Christ. Rather, they can use, increase, and enjoy this freedom and ownership freely and lawfully. They must not be enslaved. Furthermore, whatever else may be done, contrary to this command, shall be invalid and void, without force or weight. And on the basis of our apostolic authority we decree and declare that those Indians as well as other nations must be invited to the aforesaid faith of Christ by the preaching of God's word and the example of a good life. Anything to the contrary notwithstanding.

Given at Rome, etc.

The Archbishop of Toledo was appointed executor and commissary of this bull by the apostolic authority, with complete power, in these words:

To our beloved son, health and apostolic blessing.

Exercising our pastoral office toward those of his sheep who have been entrusted to our vigilant care by heaven, we rejoice in their progress just as we are saddened by their loss. Moreover, not only do we praise their good works but we spread the fruits of apostolic meditation ever more extensively so that they might enjoy what is to their advantage. In fact, we have been informed that our most dear son in Christ, Charles, the ever august Emperor of the Romans and King of Castile and León, has pronounced a public edict on all his subjects with a view to restraining those who, burning with greed, have an inhuman attitude toward the human race. [This edict] forbids anyone whomsoever to dare to enslave the Indians in the south or west or to deprive them of their property. Recognizing then that those Indians, though they are outside the bosom of the Church, must not be deprived of their freedom or their ownership over their property, and since they are men and therefore capable of receiving faith and salvation, they must not be destroyed by reduction to slavery but invited to life by preaching and good example—

Furthermore, seeking to repress the wicked attempts of such evil men, as well as to make provision lest, exasperated by injuries and harm, these nations should be hardened against embracing the faith of Christ—

Desiring to accommodate your foresight, since we have a special confidence in the Lord about your rectitude, foresight, piety and experience in these and other matters—

By this letter, then, we enjoin and command, through you or another or others and as a bulwark for the effective defense of all the aforesaid Indians, that you must very strictly forbid each and every person of whatever dignity, status, condition, degree, or excellence to presume to enslave the aforesaid Indians or despoil them of their property in any way whatsoever under pain of automatic excommunication if they act contrary to this directive, from which they can be absolved only by us or by the Roman Pontiff then reigning, unless they are in extreme danger of death and have made some previous satisfaction. Further, you must proceed to declare that the disobedient have incurred this excommunication and take further steps by making statutes, orders, and dispositions concerning whatever is necessary or opportune in any way in relation to the other matters which we have mentioned, and this as it seems to be in keeping with your prudence, uprightness, and religion. In these matters we give you full power.

All to the contrary notwithstanding.

Given at Rome, etc.

Do you not see, dear reader, that the Roman Pontiff expressly states and teaches that all the claims of the enemies of the spread of the gospel are false?

First, he teaches that the means they have employed were contrived by the devil in order to prevent the salvation of men and the spread of the true religion. And, in truth, this is the word for what they did in treating the Indians as though they were wild and brute animals so that they might exploit them as if they were beasts of burden.

Second, the Roman Pontiff says that because the Indians are men they are capable of receiving beatitude and the means by which they can reach it, that is, Christian teaching. And so he calls them lambs of Christ's flock, entrusted to his pastoral care so that he may lead them to Christ's fold, which they have been outside of up to now.

Third, he teaches that, although they have not embraced the faith of Christ, they must not on that account be deprived of their freedom or their possession and ownership of their property that nature has granted them for their lawful use and enjoyment.

Fourth, he teaches that they must not be exterminated from the face of the earth by violence, tyranny, and the cruelty of arms, lest, as a result of persecution and injuries, they should vomit forth blasphemies against Christ's law.

Fifth, he teaches that those who, contrary to the commands and prohibitions of the kings of Castile, have committed cruel and savage acts against them have been satellites of Satan, the most bitter enemy of the human race.

Sixth, he teaches that the Indians of the south and west who have not heard Christ's gospel must be invited and brought to the faith by gentleness, meekness, pleasant words and actions, and Christian charity. You see that, as regards drawing unbelievers to the faith, the Supreme Pontiff decrees what natural reason dictates, what Christ taught and commanded by word and example, what the Apostles, who always followed his footsteps in everything, eagerly took care to fulfill, what the sacred doctors have taught in their writings, finally what the Church has used in her traditions and practice from the very beginning and what the preachers of the faith should use. Therefore the Indians must not be harassed, despoiled, and persecuted, as Satan's satellites have done and still do in their rage and unbelievable savagery against that pitiable nation. Nor must they be punished for any sins, even the most serious, in which they are involved, as long as these are committed within the limits of their territories or their unbelief, in spite of all that the good Doctor Sepúlveda rashly presumes to affirm.

Seventh, the bull states, and by a new decree provides, that acts to the contrary are invalid and without effect.

By these eleven reasons, our truly spoken opinion—that is, that neither the Church nor any Christian prince has the power and jurisdiction to punish the crimes of unbelievers, about whom we are speaking —is proved to be most true and undoubted, etc.

Chapter Thirteen

It remains for us to answer what Sepúlveda cites from the sacred books, specifically Deuteronomy, chapter 7, and Joshua, where we read that God destroyed the seven nations that dwelt in the Promised Land because of certain crimes. Now he argues that this can be done to the Indians, and he also cites Saint Cyprian, whose meaning he perverts and falsifies, as he has done habitually in many other cases.

And so, in the first place, eminent Doctor Sepúlveda, I should like to learn from you why God did not command the destruction of many other idolaters who flourished at that time? For, with the exception of the Jewish people and the line descending from Adam to Christ, the whole world was given over to the worship of idols, except for some men living among the gentiles who were outstanding for their piety, namely, Job, Melchisedek, and others whom God was pleased to give a knowledge of the truth. This is clear from Genesis, Deuteronomy, and almost all the other books of the Old Testament. Moreover, Paul and Barnabas bear witness to this fact, saying: "In the past he," that is, God, "allowed each nation to go its own way,"[1] that is, with their various rites and idolatrous ceremonies, about which Ambrose has a lengthy treatise[2] and which is sufficiently verified in all the histories of the pagans. Therefore, although the whole world was worshiping idols, God did not command that the Edomites or the Egyptians be destroyed in war, in spite of the fact that they outdid the other nations of the world in their loathsome worship of idols and other crimes. In fact, God said "You are not to regard the Edomite as detestable, for he is your brother; nor the Egyptian, because you were a stranger in his land."[3]

God, then, did not command any idolaters to be killed except those living in the Promised Land, unless there was some fresh cause besides idolatry. This is proved in the twentieth chapter of the same book,[4] where, instructing his people how they should wage war against the pagans living outside the Promised Land in case they should receive any loss or injury from them, God warned them in these words: "If at any time you come to fight against a city, you shall first offer it peace,"[5] and later: "So shall you do to all the cities that are at a great distance from you and are not of these cities which you will receive as your possession. But of those cities that will be given to you, you will permit none at all to live but shall kill them with the edge of the sword."[6]

And so the sufficient cause for war against the Canaanites who lived in the Promised Land was that they were living in that land. Therefore, by divine command, the Jews were obliged to kill them without sparing the oldest, or sometimes the youngest, or even the animals. But even if the other nations were evil and idolatrous, the Jews could not take up arms against them without some other legitimate cause. And even then, they were obliged to offer them peace beforehand. If they did not refuse and thereupon opened their gates, the Jews could not cause them any other burden than the imposition of tribute as a penalty for any loss or injury inflicted on them. Once the tribute was imposed, however, they were left unharmed and free to dwell in their cities. If, nevertheless, the

1. Acts 14 [15].
2. In the two books of his *De Vocatione Omnium Gentium*.
3. Deuteronomy 27 [actually 23:7].
4. As noted by [Nicholas of] Lyra on this passage and by Abulensis, q. 1, and *2 Paralipomenon* [*Chronicles*], chap. 8, q. 5.
5. [v. 10].
6. [vv. 15–17].

other nations obstinately refused peace, the Jews could attack the city and kill the men who were fit for battle, but they had to spare women, children, and animals. In fact, they could spare the men, since they were not obliged by divine precept to kill them, as Cajetan observes. Now although it was generally true that, unless there was some legitimate cause, the Jews could not bring war or any other burden upon the nations living outside the Promised Land, no matter how idolatrous they were, the Lord made an exception for two of these nations, namely, the Midianites and the Amalekites, whom the Jews were obliged by divine precept to attack and destroy, but not because they were idolatrous. For, as has been said, they could not start a war against idolaters, even if they were very wicked, without a just cause; but [these two nations] inflicted certain injuries on the Children of Israel. Indeed, the Midianites were the reason why the Children of Israel committed fornication with the local women and worshiped idols, and therefore why God's anger would come upon them. For this reason the Lord commanded them: "Harry the Midianites and strike them down, for they have harassed you."[7] Now the Amalekites unjustly fought with the Jews in the desert on two occasions.[8] So God commanded the Jews not to forget their injury and to blot out the name of Amalek from the face of the earth when they had first taken possession of the Promised Land.[9] And because Saul sinned gravely by sparing the Amalekite King, the Lord did not let his sons succeed him in the kingship.[10]

The Lord, then, did not want all idolaters to be killed or subjugated indiscriminately, but only if there was some special, just cause. For a case admitted for some special reason does not become a general rule. In fact the common law teaches the opposite in the passage concerning special cases.[11] Therefore they [our opponents] are mistaken and do not know the Scriptures or the power of God.

Nor do they do any better with what they bring forth from [Nicholas of] Lyra,[12] who, when teaching that some just causes for which war was

7. Numbers 25 [17].
8. Exodus 17. Numbers 14.
9. Deuteronomy 25 [17–19].
10. 1 Kings [1 Samuel], 15.
11. The argument for this is in the Digests, 1, 3, 14, and 16, 50, 1, as well as in rule 28 of the rules of law in the Liber Sextus and in similar passages.
12. *Super Numeros,* chap. 31.

undertaken are found in the sacred books, adds that there is a just cause for war if the people of some province blaspheme God by worshiping idols.[13] We hardly deny this as it reads in that passage, but we understand it to be true only when a nation worships idols after embracing the faith. Indeed, if they are warned and told to stop those impure sacrifices and their sacrilegious worship, yet refuse to repent and acknowledge the truth, then it is just to wage war against them. The Lord commanded this procedure through Moses,[14] although the Jews were obliged to destroy the idolaters at that time even without listening to them. See what is said on this subject in the next chapter.

In this era of grace, however, we must think and act quite differently (as I shall teach shortly), whereas the proofs that Sepúlveda cites and foists off on the unwary, in the same way that sleep catches the drowsing man, speak about idolaters living in the Promised Land whose temples and idols the Jews were obliged to destroy completely.[15] Now to argue from the idolaters living in the Promised Land to other idolaters, especially after the coming of Christ, is absurd (as I have taught above). Otherwise, if they oblige us by the authority of those passages, they will also teach that the Spaniards are necessarily obliged to kill the greatest and the least [of the Indians], both guilty and innocent—not excepting even draft animals, dogs, and cats—as commanded in some of those passages. This is completely absurd. If, however, they deny this and hold that the children, women, dogs, and beasts of burden must be spared, I shall ask: By what right do they admit those passages as regards the men but reject them as regards the children, the beasts of burden, and the other things which are commanded to be killed in them? Is that the reason why Sepúlveda is of this opinion? He offers a weak argument for believing him. In short, those passages speak about pagans dwelling in the Promised Land. The Jews could not wage war against the other nations without some other legitimate cause (as has been frequently proved in the foregoing). Nevertheless, I am surprised that a Christian man does not prefer to admit those passages that speak about pagans outside the Promised Land so that we might use their example toward all nations in the world that are found to indulge in idolatry. These

13. Deuteronomy 13.
14. Deuteronomy 13.
15. Deuteronomy, chaps. 9, 12, 18, and Leviticus, chaps. 13, 18, 20.

passages agree more with the teaching of the gospel, with the gentleness, meekness, and charity of Christ, than do those which rest upon that special and rigorous precept.

In order that it may later become more evident to all that the destructive error and ignorance, or certainly the malice, of some of our adversaries have been understood, in support of our argument we want to prove more fully that the rigorous precept against the Canaanite nations was very special, and consequently, the foregoing passages commanding the massacre of idolaters must be admitted only in reference to those who lived in the Promised Land. We prove this by indicating some reasons for this special character that are taken from sacred literature. Saint Thomas gives two of these reasons.[16]

The first is that the malice of those nations had already reached its peak and, since they continued to sin obstinately, the Lord did not want to tolerate them any more. For we read that God said to Abraham: "To your descendants I give this land."[17] And again, as though Abraham were asking the Lord why he did not give it to him immediately, the Lord answers: "For as yet the iniquities of the Amorites are not at their full until the present time." Therefore the iniquity of that nation is believed to have reached its peak when the Children of Israel departed from slavery under the Egyptians and the command to exterminate the Amorites was enjoined upon them. Gratian notes this.[18] The obstinacy of this nation is expressly mentioned in the book of Joshua: "For the Lord had ordained that the hearts of these men should be stubborn . . . so that they might be mercilessly delivered over to the ban."[19] Therefore the Lord had condemned that nation to death because of its crimes and made the Hebrews the executors of his will. Thus he expressly commanded them to kill and exterminate them. If the Hebrews failed to do this, they would sin mortally, but they could not kill any other idolaters.

The second reason why the Lord gave a particular command to the Hebrews to massacre those nations was the danger that threatened the Hebrews, because, as is clear from many passages of Holy Scripture, the Hebrews were especially prone to idolatry. Now in order that the nearness of the Canaanites, the Amorites, and other peoples of that

16. *In IV Sententiarum,* d. 29, a. 1, ad 1[um].
17. Genesis 15 [5–16].
18. c. 49, C. 23, q. 5.
19. Joshua 11 [20].

region should not lead them to the worship of idols, the Lord commanded them to exterminate those peoples: "So that," he says, "they may not teach you to practice all the detestable practices they have in honor of their gods and so cause you to sin against the Lord your God."[20] For the same reason, also, the Lord forbade them to enter into friendship or marriages with any women from those nations.[21] In the work already cited, Saint Thomas notes that the Jews were not forbidden to enter into friendship with the other idolatrous nations, especially if there was no danger that the former would be drawn into the worship of the latter.[22] So we see that the Hebrews were permitted to enter into marriages with the women of those nations. Joseph chose as his wife the daughter of Potiphar, a priest of the Egyptian idols. Moses had an Ethiopian woman as his wife; Esther married King Ahasuerus; Solomon celebrated a marriage with the daughter of the Egyptian King. In fact the Jews were permitted to contract marriage with the idolaters who lived closest to the Promised Land, for we read that Ruth the Moabite, born in the land of Moab, which borders on the land of Canaan, married Boaz.[23] So also the Lord permitted that if and when the Hebrews waged war against other enemies, that is, those who did not live in the Promised Land, and conquered them, and they saw among the captives a beautiful woman who suited their fancy, they could take her for a wife, provided they observed certain ceremonies.[24] In fact, by dispensation, they could take as wives the daughters of the pagans dwelling in the Promised Land. Salmon, the head of the tribe of Judah and son of Naason, married Rahab, a prostitute from the city of Jericho, which is in the midst of the region of Canaan.[25]

Among the fathers, the holy Abbot Serapion,[26] Saint Epiphanius,[27] and Saint Augustine[28] give another reason for this special precept; namely, that the region possessed by the Canaanites fell to the lot of Shem, the oldest son of Noah, when Noah divided the world among his

20. Deuteronomy 20 [18]. See also chapter 7 above.
21. Deuteronomy 7 [2–3].
22. [*Summa Theologiae*], I–II, q. 105, a. 4, ad 6um.
23. Ruth 4 [13].
24. Deuteronomy 21 [10–13].
25. We read this in Numbers 12 and 71 and Matthew 1 [5].
26. *Sermon,* chap. 24.
27. In his book titled *Anchoratus.*
28. *Seasonal sermon #105.*

three sons. Now their father demanded their oath that none of them would invade his brother's portion and that whoever would transgress the precept of this oath would be exterminated together with all his descendants. When, however, the sons of Shem had held possession over that region for a long time, the sons of Ham (who are called Canaanites), whom his father Noah had cursed, went down into that region, violently expelled the sons of Shem, and took possession of their provinces. So the Lord, who is patient, gave ample time for the children of Ham to repent and return the inheritance of the sons of Shem to them, but the Canaanites refused to repent. Then, after many generations, God, who is just, avenged the injury the Semites suffered from the Hamites by wiping out the offspring of Ham in keeping with the oath taken by Noah's sons. And the seed of Shem, that is, the Children of Israel, took possession of their own territory. Thus the measure of the Amorites, that is, the malice of the Canaanites, had to attain its fullness so that the kingdom might be restored to its rightful lords and the crimes of that nation might be punished.

From this it is clear that the Lord's precept about banishing the seven peoples dwelling in the Promised Land had a special cause and that it is not to be inferred from it as a general rule that idolatrous pagans are to be killed. We have established this from passages in the Old Testament. And since this was the case even in the time of the Old Law, which was rigid and severe, much more is it to be held today, since, through Christ's coming, the Lord has distributed the treasures of his mercy throughout the entire earth and every nation. That is why this time is called the time of grace, the time of love, the year of propitiation, the day of salvation, and the freely sent and good messenger of joy. The prophets of the Old and New Testaments are full of such testimonies. Therefore the venerable Doctor Sepúlveda makes a slip here. In this consideration, he has not diligently searched the Scriptures, or surely has not sufficiently understood how to apply them, because in this era of grace and mercy he seeks to apply those rigid precepts of the Old Law that were given for special circumstances and thereby he opens the way for tyrants and plunderers to cruel invasion, oppression, spoliation, and harsh enslavement of harmless nations that have neither heard of the faith nor known whether belief in Christ is in accord with reality or whether the Christian religion can be discovered, and all this under the pretext of religion. Why? Because we admire the examples of things

God commanded to be done in the past; yet we should not imitate them.[29] For in one of those wars Samuel butchered Agag, the King of the Amalekites,[30] whereas in our time consecrated men refrain from shedding blood. Again, Phineas, the priest, killed a Jew who was having intercourse with a Midianite woman, whereas now it would be judged impious for a priest to soil his hands with blood. Further, at that time the Hebrews used deceit in despoiling the Egyptians, and Hosea, seeking to have children by fornication, cohabited with a prostitute. Today, in keeping with the law of the gospel, if anyone did these things he would be guilty of theft and lust and would commit a mortal sin. At that time it was lawful to have many wives, whereas anyone doing that nowadays would be an adulterer. Hence Gregory says:

If anyone, by means of the Old Testament, seeks to defend his lie on the grounds that in that case it would possibly be less harmful to somebody, he should also say that it is necessary to steal others' property, he should say that the revenge of injury, all of which were granted to the weak at that time, cannot harm him. All these matters are evident to everyone in proportion to the attention he gives to the pursuit of that truth which is declared to us as reality once the shadow over its meaning is put aside.[31]

And again, at the end of the second chapter, Gregory says:

For in the New Testament we go forward with higher precepts since the truth has been manifested through the flesh and it is fitting that we give up certain actions which, in that people, were under the shadow of the truth.

Moreover, Augustine says:

The Lord said to Moses, "The man should ask of his neighbor and the woman of her neighbor, vessels of silver and gold and raiment"[32] No person should conclude from this that he should follow this example and despoil his neighbor in this way since this was commanded by the Lord who knew what he had to permit and that the Israelites were not committing theft. But by command of God they were offering a service.[33]

29. Gratian, c. 41, C. 2, q. 7.
30. 1 Kings [1 Samuel] 15 [33].
31. *Moralia,* Book 17, chap. 3, quoted in Gratian, c. 19, C. 22, q. 2.
32. [Exodus 3:22].
33. *De Exodo,* quoted in Gratian, c. 12, C. 14, q. 5.

Those, then, who would try to prove from those passages that in general all unbelievers or idolaters should be destroyed by the arms of war, in which there necessarily occur so many murders, spoliations, plunderings, and scandals, as well as an infinite number of other irreparable evils and losses, on the grounds that God commanded the Children of Israel to do these things to the Egyptians and the Canaanites, should also by necessity admit that it is lawful to steal another's property and avenge personal injuries. They should also acknowledge what I said previously, that is, that this would be nothing else than to practice Judaism. By our Savior's words, however, we are taught that we cannot be saved unless our justice is greater than that of the Jews.[34]

34. Matthew 5 [20].

Chapter Fourteen

Furthermore, in support of his position Sepúlveda distorts the words Saint Cyprian wrote in his book *To Fortunatus: An Exhortation to Martyrdom.*[1] Cyprian relates that the Lord commanded that in general an idolatrous nation should be exterminated.[2] Cyprian argues in this way:

1. *Epistola ad Fortunatum: De Exhortatione Martyrii.*
2. Citing Deuteronomy, chap. 13.

If in the time of the Old Law before the coming of Christ, the state which worshipped false gods was punished in this way, how much more in our own time will the same thing be done and the same precept of the Lord be observed? For the Lord himself, having become man, taught us the truth and the worship of the true God both by word and example.

With his shins exposed (as the saying goes), Sepúlveda uses this authority to urge the Spanish nation to annihilate the Indians and teaches it that when it sheds the blood of that people it consecrates its hands to God, after the example from the past; that is, that a state that had apostatized by idolatry from the belief in the true God, which it had previously accepted, was to be destroyed on the basis of the divine precept given in Deuteronomy, chapter 13. This opinion is worthy of hellfire. For if there has been not only such a great slaughter and loss of life but so much destruction and devastation of vast numbers of people, as well as innumerable evils that can never be undone and that have been perpetrated by tyrants in that world up to now, then nothing has been accomplished by all the many laws, rules, precepts, prohibitions, threats, or penalties issued by the kings of Spain, by the mild entreaties "in season and out" of preachers of God's word, by the very bitter rebukes joined with the threat of the terrible day of eternal judgment and reminders of the pains of hell, by denial of the sacraments by confessors, or, finally, by censures and excommunications by prelates. They have accomplished nothing, I say, to bring an end to all these and many other evils. Rather, the Indians have been subjected to worse and far more harmful evils from day to day. What will be done to these miserable, peaceful, meek, and harmless peoples by their enemies, who seek their blood in order to increase their gold, when the plunderers take notice of the fact that someone is telling them that, in committing those crimes, they consecrate their sacrilegious and bloody hands to the true God, just like those who at Moses' command punished the worshipers of the golden calf?[3] Oh, the deep-rooted blindness of a man catching the popular ear, or trying in a most dangerous way to beguile the ears of royalty!

Although this error has been sufficiently covered by what we said in a previous chapter in reference to a statement by Nicholas of Lyra, we shall now make this refutation even clearer by giving the opinion

3. See Exodus 32 [25–29].

of Saint Cyprian. In stating this, we should note that the whole theory of Saint Cyprian in the above-mentioned work concerns the exhortation that Catholics should persevere in the faith of Christ, which they have embraced, and should undergo torture and therefore martyrdom rather than fall away from the faith.

So, first, in chapter 6 he teaches that, despising death and torture, Christians should profess that Christ is the true God. Invoking a passage of Matthew, "Anyone who prefers father or mother to me is not worthy of me,"[4] he says: "For, redeemed and restored to life by Christ's blood, we should prefer nothing to Christ, for in the Gospel the Lord says, 'Anyone who prefers father or mother to me is not worthy of me.' " In this context he cites chapter 14 of Exodus about the Children of Israel who wanted to return to Egypt. Again in that chapter of his work Cyprian says that one must persist and persevere in faith, virtue, and the completion of heavenly and spiritual grace. And since, in his time, many Christians who had embraced Christian truth were returning to idolatry, he begins by teaching, in the first chapter, that an idol is not God and that man should not worship any idol or element except God. In chapter 2 he proves that all worship of *latria* is due to God alone and that it is worthy of every sacrifice. In chapter 3 he teaches how the Lord threatened those among the Jews who worshiped idols. Further, in chapter 4 he tries to prove that the Lord is very slow to pardon sins committed by idolatry once man knows him by faith. "In Exodus," Cyprian says, "Moses prays for the people but his prayer is not answered. 'Ah, I grieve,' he says, 'this people has committed a grave sin, making themselves a god of gold.' "[5]

Similarly, he relates in chapter 5 that the Lord became so angry with those who had apostatized from the faith by idolatry that he commanded that all of them should be killed, even if it were a son or a brother who persuaded others to return to idolatry. For the Scripture says:

If your brother, the son of your father or of your mother, or your son or daughter or the wife you cherish, or the friend with whom you share your life, if one of these secretly tries to entice you [to serve other gods] . . . gods from

4. 10 [37].
5. Exodus 32 [31–32].

among those of the peoples . . . you must not give way to him nor listen to him, you must show him no pity, you must not spare him, you must not conceal his guilt. No, you must kill him. Your hand is to be the first raised.[6]

Then the Lord says, in that passage, that if all the Jews of any Hebrew city should worship idols, they should all be destroyed. He is speaking not of the cities outside the Promised Land but of those inhabited by the Jews, as is evident from this context, for the Lord says:

If you hear that in one of the towns which the Lord your God has given you for a home, there are men, scoundrels from your own stock, who have led fellow citizens astray, saying "Come, let us serve other gods" whom you have not known, it is your duty to look into the matter, examine it, and inquire most carefully. If it is proved and confirmed that such a hateful thing has taken place among you, then you must kill all the inhabitants of that town without giving any quarter; you must lay it under ban.[7]

He is speaking of Hebrews living in the same city, as is clear from the words "in one of [your] towns" and the words "who have led fellow citizens astray" to serve other gods. Furthermore, he is obviously not speaking of the idolatrous Canaanites since, when the Israelites entered the Promised Land, all the native inhabitants living there had to be killed by reason of the divine command. In citing chapter 13 of Deuteronomy, therefore, Cyprian interprets it as referring to those who, having heard and embraced the truth of the gospel, have returned to idolatry. He teaches that they must be punished and that to punish them is especially pious and holy. And so the ruler is obliged to punish them even if this should introduce a division into his empire. Then, arguing from the lesser point in a holy and learned way, Cyprian says: "If these precepts about adoring God and despising idols were observed before the coming of Christ, how much more must they be observed after the coming of Christ, since in coming he taught us, not only by his words, but also by his deeds."

This is what Cyprian teaches, and we gladly admit and acknowledge it. But what, I ask, does this have to do with the Indians who have never heard the truth of the gospel, not even by hearsay, and have not ac-

6. Deuteronomy 13 [7–11].
7. Deuteronomy 13 [13–18].

cepted it? Moreover, being harmless in warfare and especially inclined
to accept the truth, they must be encouraged by Christian love, rather
than persecuted by arms in a devilish and worse than pagan way.

Now with the expression *si audieris* [if you hear], Gratian begins c.
32, C. 23, q. 5, from which our adversaries take their fragile argument
against the Indians. Gratian, however, uses this chapter, along with the
one before, to prove that, even after the coming of Christ, evil persons
must be punished by death by those who have legitimate power in a
state, and without violation of the commandment "You shall not kill."
And this is Gratian's final intention.

It is clear, then, how the Reverend Doctor Sepúlveda has distorted
the opinion of Saint Cyprian, as well as the testimonies of other saints,
by reducing it to his own opposite meaning.

Chapter Fifteen

Up to now we have taught that neither the Church nor Christian
rulers can punish pagans even if they are guilty of the most atrocious
crimes. Now, for the perfect understanding of this treatise, I shall submit six cases in which the Church can punish pagans, and in the process

I shall refute Sepúlveda's teachings near the end of his second argument.

From the very outset, it must be supposed that the Church can exercise temporal jurisdiction over unbelievers in three ways (the third will be seen later, in chapter 37).

The first is when unbelievers are habitually and actually subject to the Church or to some member of the Church, for example, a Christian ruler. Unbelievers of this type are heretics, about whom we have spoken in chapter 7, and shall speak later. Since they have previously received Catholic truth, they must be compelled to return to Christ's sheepfold. Under this heading we should also include those Jews and Moors who are subject to Christian rulers. Since they are subjects by law and fact, the Church can lay down laws [in their regard].[1] Moreover, we have very many public laws in the Spanish language passed by the Kings of Castile in reference to Jews and Moors, and therefore contentious jurisdiction can be exercised over them, that is, even if they are unwilling.[2] It is lawful for the Church to do this when the unbelievers are actually and habitually subject to Christian rulers, that is, to members of the Church.

Secondly, the Church habitually has contentious jurisdiction over other unbelievers only to the extent that it can reduce this jurisdiction to act when a case occurs or when there is a continuing cause, and not in any other case, because of the above-mentioned ten reasons, especially the reason based on Saint Paul's words: "It is not my business to pass judgment on those outside." Now these unbelievers are persons who have never professed the faith of Christ through baptism, no matter what their religion, worship, rite, or sect may be, as long as they are not Jews and as long as their realms are separate from the realms of Christians, so that they are not subjects of the Church or of any of its members. We have just said "as long as they are not Jews" since, because of the crime they committed in killing our Lord Jesus Christ, they are by law servants of the Church. "Those whom their own guilt has subjected to perpetual slavery, Christian piety should receive and support."[3] But Constantine actually subjected them to slavery.[4] Never-

---

1. This is proved abundantly from the Decretals, 5, 6, as well as from the Liber Sextus, 5, 1, and the Clementines, 5, 3. Also Codex: *De Iudaeis, Paganis et Templis Eorum* and *De Haereticis et Apostatis*.
2. This is taught by the doctors on the Digests, 45, 1, 83, #2.
3. Decretals, 5, 6, 13.
4. According to the gloss on the Decretals, 5, 6, 7.

theless, properly speaking, they are not slaves, nor can tasks be imposed on them if they are unwilling, nor are they to be oppressed in violation of human and divine law.[5] We have also said that these unbelievers are not subject to the Church but have separate realms, since, in this regard, one and the same reason militates against all unbelievers, no matter what the region or rite to which they belong, and this for the reasons given previously. No one can assign any shade of difference.

Therefore the Church can exercise contentious jurisdiction over all unbelievers of any sort in six cases.

The first is if they unjustly possess realms of which they have unjustly despoiled a Christian nation, especially if Christians live in them, such as the Empire of Constantinople, Rhodes, Hungary, Serbia, and Africa (all of which formerly worshiped Christ). Since, in holding these realms, the unbelievers do continuous injury to us, the Church can actualize the jurisdiction it habitually has over them in order to regain what belongs to it through force of war. No other way is open. Among those who speak about unbelievers of this type are Hostiensis,[6] Oldraldus,[7] and Alberic.[8] In these sections, Hostiensis and his followers say that if unbelievers fail to recognize the rule of the Church, they are unworthy of any rule and jurisdiction. And Hostiensis means the jurisdiction and rule that unbelieving rulers have in lands that once belonged to Christians and that they exercise over Christians living in these lands. Or he means the case in which the whole populace or some part of the populace is converted to Christ but the ruler perseveres in his blind unbelief. This is the interpretation of Anthony of Butrio, who harmonizes the opinions of Hostiensis and Innocent:

Hostiensis confirms and moderates Innocent's conclusion that unbelievers could have jurisdiction over Christians when the unbelievers recognize the jurisdiction of the Church, since such persons can have [this jurisdiction] and can have dominion and right with the toleration of the Church.[9]

Thus it is clear and obvious that Hostiensis meant that unbelieving

---

5. See Gratian, c. 3, D. 45. Decretals, 5, 6, 9.
6. On the Decretals, 3, 24, 8, where other doctors also are cited.
7. On the *consilium,* 72.
8. On the rubric, Codex, *De Paganis et Eorum Templis.*
9. On the Decretals, 3, 24, 8, col. 4.

lords who have some Christians under their rule should recognize the dominion and jurisdiction of the Church if they are to be worthy of such a rule or dominion, specifically, rule over the faithful. This agrees with the teaching of the holy Doctor Thomas that, through a sentence or regulation, "the Church could by right take away the right of dominion or rule which unbelieving rulers have over Christians because, by reason of their unbelief, they deserve to lose their power over the faithful who are transformed into children of God. Yet it tolerates them in order to avoid scandal."[10] Therefore the opinion of Hostiensis must not be understood as applying to all unbelievers without distinction but to unbelievers of his time, that is, only when an unbelieving ruler has Christians under his jurisdiction or when he has usurped Christian domains. These seem to be bound to recognize the dominion of the Church. However, in the case of others, such as our Indians, who have not usurped Christian realms or do not rule over Christians or, until our era, have never even heard mention of our world, it is absurd to make them acknowledge the dominion of the Church under penalty of losing their power to rule, since they cannot even guess at this without the teaching of the faith. Any other interpretation of the Cardinal's [Hostiensis] opinion would be heretical, as we have proved at length elsewhere. Moreover, great perils would arise in the world and intolerable absurdities would follow.

Secondly, the Church exercises actual jurisdiction over pagans when they practice idolatry in provinces which were formerly under Christian jurisdiction or when they corrupt a region with evil and hateful vices against nature. In these provinces the true sacrifice of Christ's body and blood has been consecrated, pure honor has been given to the true God, and the holy sacraments have been administered.[11] The purpose of these things is that, by giving honor and glory to the true God, men submit to him both in body and soul.[12] It is utterly irrational that the Church tolerate such conditions, if it can do otherwise, since this redounds to the dishonor and insult of the name Christian. Now no Christian should ignore this insult "since we should not ignore dishonor to him who destroyed our shameful acts for us."[13] And "We decree that

10. See [*Summa Theologiae*], II–II, q. 10, a. 10.
11. See Saint Thomas [*Summa Theologiae*], III, q. 63, a. 2–4, 6c.
12. Ibid., II–II, q. 93, a. 2c. *Contra Gentes*, II, c. 119.
13. Decretals, 5, 6, 15.

what is committed against divine religion is a public crime. It has an injurious effect on all persons."[14] Furthermore, the public law rests on sacred things and priests.[15]

Innocent specifically equates this case with the preceding when, speaking of the Saracens, he says: "The Church should not make war on them if they do not defile Christian lands with their filth or assail them personally."[16] Innocent took the word "filth" from Sacred Scripture, where it especially means idolatry or some other unclean abomination, notably one against nature. Thus we read that King Asa "drove out of the country the men who had been sacred prostitutes and cleared away all the filth of the idols which his ancestors had made."[17] We read further: "Let the sinner go on sinning, and the unclean continue to be unclean."[18] This is also the interpretation of what the same Innocent says in another section, where he is of the opinion that "if a gentile who has only the law of nature acts against the law of nature, he can be lawfully punished by the Pope."[19] And a little later he says: "I say that the same is true if they worship idols for it is natural to worship the one and only God, the creator, not the creatures." This must be supplemented and understood in this way—"if Christian peoples formerly lived in the province where those sins are committed." Otherwise greater absurdities would follow than follow from the teaching of Hostiensis, if Innocent meant to apply his teaching absolutely to all parts of the world where the inhabitants had not embraced the faith and the Church had not been established. First, because this would be contrary to what we have proved above by ten effective arguments, and second, because Innocent does not prove his statement but only offers the fact that the men of Sodom who sinned against the natural law were punished by God.[20] "Now since God's judgments," Innocent says, "are examples for us, I do not see why the Pope, who is the Vicar of Christ, cannot do this as long as he has the power." Surely, if all of God's judgments have to be imitated by us, it would follow that, because of

14. Codex, 1, 5, 4.
15. Digests, 1, 1, 1 [*sic* for 2].
16. On the Decretals, 3, 42, 3, at the end.
17. 1 Kings [1 Samuel] 15 [12].
18. Apocalypse [Revelations] 22 [11].
19. On the Decretals, 3, 24, 8, col. 1.
20. Genesis 14 [10–11].

the sin of idolatry and the sin against nature, the innocent children of such sinners should be slaughtered by reason of the fact that God had done this.

Likewise, because of rebellion against or schism from the Church, not only the rebels and schismatics would have to be killed but also their wives and children, and all their property would have to be destroyed, simply because we read that Korah, Dathan, and Abiram were swallowed by the earth together with their tents and all their possessions because of their disobedience.[21] Likewise, not only would a man who is guilty of a serious theft have to be stoned but his wife, children, cattle, sheep, beasts of burden, and other property would have to be destroyed by fire, since the Lord commanded these things to be done to Achan because he had taken "a fine robe from Shinar and two hundred shekels of silver and an ingot of gold weighing fifty shekels" from the spoils seized from the enemy, which God had commanded to be burned.[22]

Similarly, it would follow that if some boys mocked even the highest prelate, they would have to be thrown to the lions—on the grounds, we read, that forty-two boys were torn to pieces by bears because when Elisha the prophet was going up to the city of Bethel they mocked him, saying "Go up, baldhead! Go up, baldhead!" For this reason they were cursed by Elisha and were torn to pieces by bears coming out of the forest.[23] There are other terrible judgments from God which we omit for the sake of brevity. If we were to imitate them, undoubtedly we would commit a vast number of most unjust and serious sins and thousands of absurdities would follow.

Therefore not all of God's judgments are examples for us, nor can anyone assign any reason other than a frivolous one why we should imitate God's judgments in some matters but not in others. Yet we offer an answer. First, because examples or actions of this type in the Old Testament must be admired rather than imitated, as we have said before and shall say again. Second, because when certain sins were first committed, God would punish them most severely at the very outset, so that by this severe example he would frighten men from committing similar

21. Numbers 16.
22. Joshua 7 [14–15, 21].
23. 2 Kings [2 Samuel] 2 [23–24].

sins. Punishments of this type were the destruction or submersion of
Sodom, the ban on first entering the Promised Land, and the punishment of Achan for his sin against the first ban. In the same way, the
penalty accorded the first case of simony was laid very severely on
Gehazi because he had received money and garments from Naaman in
return for the spiritual power Gehazi had communicated to him. God
struck Gehazi and all his descendants with leprosy.[24] Thus too, in the
first dawn of the gospel Ananias and Sapphira were suddenly deprived
of this light because of only one lie; namely they had concealed a certain
part of their wealth.[25] The ordinary gloss gives the reason for this in the
following words:

Laws in their first stages are always bolstered by penalties. The two sons of
Aaron are consumed as they offer fire. Taking hold of the ark, Aza died. He fell
so that other violators might be frightened by his example. God did not pass
such a severe sentence on the violation arbitrarily but because he foresaw that
there would be weeds which would defile the simplicity of the Church with
depraved morals. He pulled out the harmful sprout from its roots, not to heal
the guilty by penance, but to strike fear in those who were to come.

And the interlinear gloss says: "In the beginning this swift punishment struck great fear." Surely men who came later committed greater
abuses of simony, as well as greater sins and more wicked crimes of the
kind already mentioned, yet God never punished these evils so violently.[26]

---

24. 2 Kings [2 Samuel], 5 [15–27].
25. Acts 5 [1–10].
26. The Master of History deals with this in reference to the Acts of the Apostles in
chapter 22 of his history, as does also Abulensis in his *Commentary on Joshua*, chap. 7, q.
59.

Chapter Sixteen

Therefore when Innocent said that if a pagan sinned against the natural law or worshiped idols he could be punished by the Pope in line with the example of divine judgment, he did not intend to speak absolutely about all pagans or unbelievers but only about those who live in lands or kingdoms in which the name of Christ had been [preached] and when it is known for sure that true divine worship of God had thrived. Otherwise, Innocent would have written something very blameworthy. Now an argument that is chosen to avoid the absurd or any aspect of absurdity, inhumanity, or incongruity is quite valid in law, since it is *rationalis* founded on natural good judgment and is useful even without the support of authority. And it is formulated in this manner: Something must not be asserted or an interpretation chosen from which could follow absurdity, inhumanity, or incongruity. And so each commentary must be interpreted in such a way that no inhumanity or absurdity follows, because absurdity must always be avoided. That is why, to avoid absurdity, a general commentary must be narrowed.[1]

Therefore, since so many and such great inhumanities, absurdities, and incongruities must properly be avoided in the statements of such a great man, [we must necessarily narrow] whatever he said in this article about unbelievers so that it refers only to those who, as we have said, defile places that formerly belonged to the Church by the filth of their idolatry or foul acts. However, even aside from any absurdity that would follow from a general application of his statements, this is proved to be true, first, from the fact that when kingdoms that once belonged to Christians are held by unbelievers and are defiled with their disgusting superstitions, injury is done to Christ, to whom those places were once dedicated and consecrated for divine worship. According to a rule of law, moreover, what has been dedicated to God must not be turned over to human usage; much less, therefore, is it to be turned over to wicked superstitions and heinous and dissolute crimes. For what if Mohammed or empty images are worshiped instead of the true God? The Church should not tolerate or ignore such abuses but, if it can, should compel the unbelievers to restore these places or should lay down prohibitions or even punishments so that filth of this sort will not be enacted, precisely because of its ugliness and seriousness, on the basis of the arguments and authorities given previously. And that this was the mind of Innocent is proved from his words when he was speaking about the indulgences granted to soldiers going to recover the Holy Land. He adds this reason: "What was consecrated by the birth, dwelling, and death of Jesus Christ and in which not Christ but Mohammed is worshiped, can justly be reclaimed by the Pope so that it may be inhabited by Christians."

Secondly, [this narrowing of Innocent's statement] is proved by the fact that—supposing those provinces were once dedicated and consecrated to Christ—they now rightfully belong to the Church, and so all the unbelievers who live there are subject to the Church and its laws by reason of dwelling, for whoever lives in the territory of a foreign

1. See Codex, 3, 41, 2. Digests, 50, 1, 11, #1. As Bartholus says on the Digests, 1, 1, 9. There is abundant writing about and use of this type of argument in the Decretals, 1, 6, 34; 1, 6, 55; 1, 33, 6, and 5, 33, 17. See the doctors of both laws, as well as other innumerable passages of both canon and civil law.

ruler is subject to him.[2] Therefore the Church can both prohibit and punish wicked superstitions and heinous crimes in provinces that were formerly under Christian jurisdiction, because of a special reason not found in other areas.

The third proof is that if Christians live under the yoke of barbarians in these kingdoms, there is a greater insult to Christ's name, and the Christians living with unbelievers are subject to the danger of being contaminated with their impiety, for "wicked communications corrupt good morals" and "frequent association with evil persons corrupts even good persons,"[3] and still more those who are inclined to vice for the same reasons.[4] Speaking about this kind of unbeliever, Innocent rightly teaches that the Pope can issue laws so that they will not harass Christians and that, if they inflict injuries on Christians, the Pope can deprive such unbelievers of their kingdoms which were formerly under Christian jurisdiction. He adds, however, that a serious reason should exist before the Pontiff does this, in view of the dissension and upheaval that would necessarily arise from the Pope's action. Further, Christians should not be endangered. Now the danger in question is that the Christians might fall away from the Catholic faith, or some similar danger. In this situation, everything else must yield so that nothing like that will happen.

Likewise, Innocent teaches that such unbelievers should let the gospel be preached in their kingdoms. Otherwise they can be punished by the Pope, since they would be sinning. However, we shall deal with this later.

In summary, Innocent's words "If a pagan acts against the natural law, etc." must be understood (as we have previously taught) either of unbelievers living in lands that formerly belonged to Christians or of unbelievers who are subject in fact and law to Christian rulers. This has been expressed in the Decretals,[5] where it is said that a certain Sicilian Bishop punished Moors who committed sins against nature. Or again, Innocent's statement must be understood in the way I explained before,

2. Decretals, 2, 2, 17, and 2, 2, 15, and 2, 2, 20. Codex, 5, 32, 1, and what is noted by the doctors on this passage. And Digests, 5, 1, 19, #2.
3. See Gratian, c. 12, C. 28, q. 1.
4. c. 16, C. 24, q. 3.   c. 17, D. 45.
5. 5, 17, 4.

that is, [in reference to unbelievers] who are subject only by law inasmuch as they hold lands usurped from the Church, because of the three special reasons mentioned above.[6]

6. This is also the correct interpretation of what is given by Innocent and the Abbot [Panormitanus] on the Decretals, 5, 17, 4, and 2, 1, 13, as well as by the canonists who follow their opinions.

Chapter Seventeen

Besides his teaching in the chapter cited,[1] Innocent adds that "the Pope has the right to punish the pagan who knows only the natural law if he worships idols," because, as he says, it is natural to worship the one and only God, the Creator and not the creatures. With all due reverence to such a great doctor, we say that if his opinion has to be taken without distinctions it is subject to many contrary arguments. To clarify this matter, we take it for granted that we intend to speak about those unbelievers whom Sacred Scripture calls "nations" or "gentiles,"

1. On the Decretals, 3, 24, 8.

that is, those who were or are without the law and who, as yet, have not heard or believed anything about the Catholic faith. According to Isidore, since these gentiles are such because they were born (that is, they are descended in the flesh) under sin (that is, serving idols and not yet regenerated), they were therefore called gentiles.[2] The world was full of them when Christ came and when the Apostles began to preach, and they are called by our doctors unbelievers in a deprived or negative sense, since they are capable of having the faith and do not have it. All those whom we call southern and western Indians are of this type.

I have said "if [his opinion] has to be taken without distinctions" because, in the case of some unbelievers (those dwelling in the lands of the Church or of her members and in certain situations), the Pope can punish those who worship idols, as you can gather from what has been said, as well as from what will be said later.

On the basis of all these suppositions, we offer the following conclusion as our answer.

Conclusion

It would be unlawful to punish the unbelievers about whom we are speaking, at least by a human judgment, merely on the basis that they worship idols.

Our conclusion is proved in this way. No person can be punished, at least by a human judgment, if he is invincibly or probably ignorant that the act he performs is forbidden or that the act he fails to perform is commanded, even if it concerns the faith. However, the unbelievers about whom we are speaking are invincibly or probably ignorant in their idolatry. Therefore it would be unlawful to punish them, at least by a human judgment, merely on the basis that they worship idols.

The conclusion from the major premise is evident since whoever invincibly or probably commits some act forbidden him or omits what is commanded of him is excused from guilt. According to St. Thomas, the reason for this is that such ignorance is the cause of the act or omission, and therefore makes it involuntary. But there is no guilt or sin unless it is voluntary. Therefore ignorance always excuses, unless the ignorance itself is a sin. Now ignorance is a sin when a person is ignorant of what he should and can know. This is clear in the case of

2. *Etymologiae*, Book 8, chap 10.

a constitution or mandate of the Pope that all persons are obliged to know, each in his own way. If a person fails to know it because of negligence and acts against it, he is not excused from guilt. If, however, a person is sufficiently hindered from knowing it—if, for example, he was in prison or in foreign lands which this constitution has not yet reached, or there is another similar obstacle—his ignorance excuses him from sin, for no one sins in regard to something he could not avoid.[3] Now no innocent person can be lawfully punished by human judgment, at least as regards a penalty involving physical punishment by which he would be killed or mutilated.[4]

The minor premise is proved first in this way. He is invincibly ignorant and so excused from guilt who cannot dispel that ignorance by himself or by asking others. Now unbelievers of this type cannot ferret out matters of faith by their own efforts since these matters are beyond every faculty of nature, nor is there anyone whom they can question or consult or by whom they may be taught in the ordinary course of nature. Therefore they are invincibly ignorant in their worship of idols. The minor premise of this reason is obvious, since the first principle or first truth which must be known about God is that he is one and that he alone is God. But God's existence is not a self-evident truth, and much less so is the fact that he is the only God, since this truth is not implanted in reality in such a way that, in knowing the terms, we would immediately and without any reasoning process assent to the proposition *there is a God and he is the only God* in the same way that, knowing what a whole is and what a part is, we would recognize that every whole is greater than any of its parts. Hence, although the proposition *there is a God and he is the only God* is true and necessary, it is not self-evident. We hold it on faith.

Furthermore, whatever is denied by many persons who have a conception of the terms is not self-evident. But God's existence is a truth of this type, as is clear from psalm 13: "The fool says in his heart, 'There is no God.' " God's existence, then, is not self-evident.

Furthermore, what is proved by someone is not self-evident.

3. See Saint Thomas [*Summa Theologiae*], I–II, q. 90, a. 4, ad 2um et 3um. *Quaestio Disputata de Veritate,* q. 17, a. 3c. And *Quodlibet,* I, a. 19. This is considered by the canonists in reference to the Decretals, 1, 2, 2, with its contents. And the Digests, 22, 6, as noted by the jurists.
4. See Saint Thomas [*Summa Theologiae*], II–II, a. 108, a. 4. Gratian, c. 7, D. 56; c. 38, C. 16, q. 7. Decretals, 2, 13, 7. Digests, 9, 2, 31. Codex, 9, 47, 22; 1, 6, 2. Liber Sextus, De Regulis Iuris, r. 23.

Again, in addition to the efforts of other saints and even philosophers, Blessed Anselm tries to demonstrate God's existence by the definition "God is that greater than which nothing can be conceived." But no demonstrable truth is self-evident. God's existence, then, is not self-evident. Hence if God's existence is not self-evident but is held only on faith, the above-mentioned negative unbelievers cannot suspect God's existence, much less that there is only one God or the other supernatural truths of faith. Therefore they cannot overcome their ignorance by their own efforts.

Likewise, they do not have any person or persons whom they may question or by whom they may be taught (as we are supposing) since they all lack the faith and worship idols. Indeed, they have their own priests, their own theologians, their own prophets and seers who foretell events to them long before they occur, and they hold these persons in very great reverence and esteem. Yet the latter, laboring under the same ignorance, teach what is contrary to the faith. Finally, they have their kings, lords, and magistrates, who by their laws foolishly command the observance of that idolatrous religion and its ceremonies. And so this religion is supported by public authority. The error of the people, bolstered by the authority of their ruler, makes the law and excuses them.[5]

Undoubtedly, too, [these laws] make their errors seem probable to them. Now according to the Philosopher[6] the probable is "what appears to be the case in the judgment of all or very many persons or of the wise and, among these, all or most or especially those who are famous and approved." And what is probable in this sense is said to be morally certain. For they are not obligated to wander all over the world in search of wise men of other nations so that, by their advice or authority, the opinion they happen to follow may become probable. Rather, it is enough that they consult their own wise men or elders or that they follow their examples or teachings.

Since, then, unbelievers who worship idols in a negative way cannot teach themselves and do not have other persons by whom they may be taught the truths of faith, but—rather—all their wise men, kings, provincial governors, magistrates, and all the people and private citizens revere, profess, and follow that religion by reason of custom bolstered

---

5. See the Digests, 1, 13, 3.
6. *Topics,* Book 1. *Rhetoric,* Book 1.

by very ancient usage, so that they are sufficiently hindered [from discovering the truth], it is clear that such an error or ignorance is invincible and probable, and therefore is the cause of their acts and causes them to be involuntary, and as a consequence causes the lack of guilt. For whoever follows public law is not considered to be in error or to make a mistake.[7] It would be unlawful, therefore, to punish negative unbelievers, at least by a human judgment, merely because they worship idols. And so Innocent is undoubtedly mistaken.

7. See the Digests, 50, 17, 116.

Chapter Eighteen

Yet, in opposition to the foregoing conclusions, there is the authority of [Saint John] Damascene, as well as that of some saints and even philosophers who say that the knowledge of God is naturally implanted in the minds of men. But the first knowledge of God must be that God exists. Therefore God's existence is a self-evident truth. Again, the Apostle says: "They knew God and yet refused to honor him as God."[1]

1. Romans 1 [21].

To this we answer that it is true that a common knowledge of God is naturally implanted in the minds of men, but it is very vague and universal and shows only that there is someone who puts order in things that we see functioning according to some order. But who or what he is, or whether he is one or many, is not, as yet, clearly known by this common consideration. And this is not knowledge of God's existence in the full sense of the term. When we see a man moving and doing other things, we perceive that there is in him some cause of these actions which is not in other things, and we call this cause a soul, not knowing, as yet, the definition of soul, or whether, for example, it is a body or how it accomplished the actions referred to. Again, to know that someone is coming is not to know Peter, even though Peter is the one who is coming. And therefore the proposition *God exists* is not self-evident to us but needs to be proved by means of what is better known to us, that is, effects. Now the authority of Damascene is interpreted in the sense that knowledge of God is naturally implanted in us according to his likeness, not according to what he is in himself, just as it is said that all things seek God, not as he is considered in himself but in his likeness, and this because nothing is desired except as it bears his likeness. Nor is anything known [except in this way].[2]

As regards the authority of Saint Paul, we say that he is speaking of the philosophers who, having a knowledge of God, did not use it well but acted foolishly. For they knew that God surpasses all things, and so they owed him the honor and glory which is due that which is superior to all, and so "They knew God and yet refused to honor him as God," either because they did not give him fitting worship or because they placed a limit on his power and knowledge.

Moreover, they knew God as the cause of all good things; so they should have given him thanks for all things. Yet they failed to do this, and ascribed all their goods to their own talent and ability. Thus the Apostle adds "or to thank him; instead, they made nonsense out of logic and their empty minds were darkened." But all this is not commonly true of all persons, and therefore the Apostle is not speaking about them.

The second principal proof of the minor premise in the main argu-

2. See Saint Thomas [*Summa Theologiae*], I, q. 2, a. 1c. *In I Sententiarum*, d. 3, q. 1, a. 2. *Contra Gentes*, III, c. 38.

ment, that is, that negative unbelievers of this type are invincibly ignorant, etc., is taken from the opinion of Saint Augustine and Saint
Thomas, who say that those who have never heard anything about the
faith are excused from sin. "If I had not spoken to them, they would
have been blameless,"[3] that is, of unbelief. This is Augustine's explanation of that passage. Saint Thomas has a similar explanation.[4] And there
is Saint Paul's remark: "They will not believe in him unless they have
heard of him and they will not hear of him unless they get a preacher."[5]
Hence such unbelievers are damned not because they lack the faith that
was never preached to them but because of their other sins, which
cannot be forgiven without faith.

From these considerations it follows that since this proposition *there
is only one God* is undoubtedly a matter of faith, and since those who
worship idols cannot be instructed about their error or about the truth
of the faith by their own efforts or by their elders, they are invincibly
ignorant of the existence of God and even more so of his unique character, just as they are invincibly ignorant that Christ is the Son of God and
the redeemer of the world and other supernatural truths, until the faith
is fully and effectively preached to them. This is proved by the fact that
since the unity of the true God is not implanted in external reality, even
if they finally understand that there is a God, they could still believe
that the true God is the one whom their elders have worshiped and thus
each province could claim that its god is the true god. Nor would they
be obliged to believe that the true God is found among Christians rather
than in other nations. So, just as they could lawfully think that the god
or gods worshiped by other nations is or are not the true god or gods,
they could think the same thing about the God of the Christians, since
he exercises no extra causality in the external world, except by the
working of miracles. Therefore unbelievers who worship idols in the
negative sense labor under invincible ignorance.

But if someone objects that worshiping stones as god is contrary to
natural reason and thus forbidden by the nature of things, and therefore
that they cannot be invincibly ignorant or excused, we answer that the
ordinary and ultimate intention of those who worship idols is not to

3. John 15 [22].
4. [*Summa Theologiae*], II–II, q. 10, a. 1.
5. Romans 10 [14].

worship stones but to worship, through certain manifestations of divine power, the planner of the world, whoever he may be. They naturally recognize that they must be helped and directed by him because of the limitations they detect in themselves. So they try to reconcile him to themselves through a religious, or rather superstitious, worship that consists chiefly of sacrifices.[6]

This is what Jerome says:

So therefore we and all the rest of the human race know God naturally, since there are no peoples who do not naturally understand their creator. Although they venerate stones and trees, yet they understand that there is something greater than themselves and, in their error, they show that they have wisdom, that is, there is no nation which does not naturally know God. Finally, the gentiles worship idols, that is, they venerate stone or wood. And if they have a quarrel and swear an oath among themselves, they do not say, "The stone sees" or "The wood sees," but "God sees" and "God hears."[7]

This is what a certain idolatrous Roman by the name of Maximus seems to have wanted to show in a letter he wrote to Augustine:

Who, indeed, would be so mad or so insane as to deny that there is, most certainly, one god or great and magnificent father without a beginning and without natural offspring? We invoke his powers, spread through his work in the world, under many names, since all of us are ignorant of his proper name. For "God" is a name common to all religions so that, while we honor his [name] with various supplications as though he were divided into parts, we really seem to worship him as a whole.[8]

From the foregoing it is clear that the intention of those who worship idols is principally to strive to honor and adore the true God, whoever he may be.

We said previously "until the faith is sufficiently and fully preached to them, etc." because negative unbelievers of this type are not obliged to believe unless the faith is fully presented and explained to them by suitable ministers, such as any prudent person ought to trust because of the shining example of their lives. Indeed, they could properly say

6. See Saint Thomas [*Summa Theologiae*], II–II, q. 85, a. 1.
7. *Breviarium in Psalmos*, 95.
8. Epistola 43.

what the Jews argued at the very outset of Christ's preaching, and the gentiles later: "What is that teaching? What is this new religion which completely upsets the ancient religion approved by the whole world for so many centuries? How is it possible that God is both three and one and that God himself is crucified?" And because of this newness they can reasonably doubt this teaching and be suspicious of it, and refuse to hear it or to admit its preachers, considering them to be deceivers rather than heralds of the true religion. Otherwise they would be extremely inconstant. "Being too ready to trust shows shallowness of mind."[9]

The reason for this is that truths of this type are beyond every faculty of nature. Therefore a person is obliged to believe them only in the way it becomes possible for him, that is, by having sufficient testimonies for belief: either he witnesses a miracle worked specifically to confirm such teaching or he is moved to believe by effective reasons or by something else that fulfills the function of a miracle. Among these, one thing is sufficiently effective, that is, the blameless and Christian life of the preachers by which the mysteries of the faith are made credible for their listeners; that is, they see that these mysteries must be believed. For no one would believe them unless he sees that they must be believed, either because of the evidence of signs or because of something else of this type.[10]

But as miracles do not occur nowadays, in order to make the truths of faith credible for unbelievers the lives of Christians must shine with virtuous works as an example for them. Hence Chrysostom says:

There would be no need for words if our life shone with the light of holiness. There would be no need for teachers if we performed the upright acts of virtue. Indeed, no one would be a gentile [pagan] if we took the care we should take to be Christians, if we obeyed God's counsels and decrees, if when cursed we blessed, if we returned good for evil. No one would be such a wild beast that he would not immediately hasten to the worship of the true religion if he sees these things done by everyone.

And later:

But, indeed, if they see us also seek the same things as they themselves, covet the same things, and strive for our own private good and honor, how can they

9. Ecclesiasticus 19 [4].
10. See Saint Thomas [*Summa Theologiae*], II–II, q. 1, a. 4, ad 2um. *Quodlibet*, II, a. 6.

admire the Christian religion? On what ground, then, can they believe? By reason of miracles? But these no longer take place. By reason of a holy life? But that is obviously dying out. By reason of charity? But no trace of it is ever discernible. For this reason, we shall surely give an account not only for our sins but also for that injury to another of which we are the cause.

And elsewhere Chrysostom says:

For when many of them, *that is, unbelievers,* see that some of us are called "Christians" by word and name, and that, as Christians, we steal, are greedy for wealth, are envious, scheme, intrigue deceitfully, and do all other evil things, they will not listen to us, no matter how reasonable our admonitions may be. Rather they think that all our actions are lies and that all of us are involved in the same crimes. Think, I beg you, of what torments these persons are worthy when they not only build up unquenchable fire for themselves but also serve as sources whereby others remain in error and deafen their ears lest they should learn virtue. And they are the reason why even those who strive for virtue are accused and rebuked, and (what is more serious than all else) the Lord is blasphemed through them. Do you see how great the calamity of malice is? Do you see how those who pursue evil make themselves worthy of extraordinary punishment? But they shall undergo many very severe punishments for everything, that is, not only by reason of their own destruction but also for being a stumbling block to the straying, insulting the just, blaspheming against God.

Chapter Nineteen

From all this it is clear how a virtuous life in the preachers of the faith takes the place of miracles, so that unbelievers readily hear the words of life and see that it is reasonable to believe them, and thus finally they gain these men for Christ. But it will be just the opposite if their lives are stained by crime, especially by devastating their lands, by looting, invading and unjustly seizing the domains and properties of these same unbelievers. And if for this reason a countless number of them are killed and slaughtered, as we have always done and continue to do in the Indian lands of the west, nothing can be clearer than that we have become an effective obstacle to their conversion.

So we can conclude that a great many unbelievers are excused from accepting the faith for a long time and perhaps for their whole lifetime, no matter how long it lasts, so long as they see the extremely corrupt and detestable conduct of the Christians, even if religious men travel with such as these for the sake of preaching and even if they actually preach. [These natives] have obstacles enough to believing; indeed, even to hearing and dealing with men of this kind. Rather, they have a great many motives to the contrary, as is clear from the words of Chrysostom. For it is written: "If one man builds while another pulls down, what else do they gain but trouble?"[1] And there will be much more trouble if one man preaches and a thousand others do the opposite. Scotus agrees with this when he says that no man is bound to any divine command if it is not made known to him by an authoritative and qualified person or by a public opinion that is based on truth and by the testimony of good men which anyone should reasonably believe.[2] Scotus interprets this in reference to something commanded either by divine or human positive law, which is not known interiorly in the heart.

To return to the point. Such unbelievers do not have "an authoritative and qualified person" whom they should reasonably believe. Nor is there, in their regard, "a public opinion based on truth," since they have not yet seen the preachers of the faith, as we are supposing. Nor

1. Ecclesiasticus 34[23].
2. *In IV Sententiarum*, d. 3, q. 4.

is [the truth] "supported by the testimony of good men," since every unbeliever of this type is held back by ignorance. Therefore those who are unbelievers in a negative sense will not always sin by worshiping idols. As a consequence, it will be unlawful for a human tribunal to punish them just because they worship idols. In my judgment, in view of the evidence already presented, no one should be uncertain about this [conclusion].

Yet, in opposition to what we have said above, one can assert the common opinion of all the holy doctors, that is, that there can be no invincible ignorance about the things that are of faith and the divine law and are necessary for salvation because, if unbelievers do what lies within them, God is ready to enlighten them by his grace. Therefore if they are not enlightened, it is their own fault, since they do not do what lies within them, and so they sin. Hence because of that sin they can be justly punished, even by a human tribunal. The basis for this argument is clear from Saint Thomas.[3] Speaking about a man brought up in the woods, forests, or among animals, he says this:

For it belongs to God's providence to provide for each man the things necessary for salvation, so long as man on his part places no obstacle. For if anyone were reared in such a manner in the forests or among wolves and followed the lead of natural reason with a desire for what is good and an aversion for evil, it is most certainly to be held that God, by an interior inspiration, would reveal the things that are to be believed by necessity, or he would send some preacher of the faith as he sent Peter to Cornelius (*Acts* 10).[4]

To this we answer, first, that God is not always ready to enlighten by his grace the one who does what lies within him, unless it is God's purpose that he should be enlightened and receive grace. And then he is infallibly enlightened and receives grace. Saint Thomas teaches this. He asks whether grace is given necessarily to one who prepares himself for grace or does what lies within him. And he answers that

preparation for grace can be considered in two ways: either inasmuch as it is from free will and under this aspect the attainment of grace does not necessarily follow; or insofar as it is from a movement by God, and then it has a necessity for that to which it is directed by God, not indeed the necessity of violence but

3. Especially in the *Quaestio Disputata de Veritate*, q. 14, a. 11, ad 1um.
4. He teaches the same thing in *In Epistola ad Romanos Lectura*, 10, lectio 3.

of infallibility, because God's purpose cannot fail. . . . Therefore if it is God's purpose in moving that the man whose heart he moves should attain grace, he infallibly attains it.[5]

Therefore, since it is not God's purpose to bestow grace or enlighten those who are foreknown and are to be condemned in the end with the rejected, no matter how much they prepare themselves through free will or do what lies within them, they will not attain grace and consequently they do not sin, since they do not receive grace. The reason is not any fault of their own (since in them it is a punishment of original sin, not a fault, according to Augustine in the citation below); the reason is that God, solely by his own free will, does not will to enlighten them, not because of their sins but because it is not his will, because just as there is no cause for rejection or predestination on our part, there is sometimes no cause for the effect of rejection. The effect of rejection, however, is to deny grace and the means necessary for the attainment of grace. An indispensable means for attaining faith and grace is the external calling by preachers in which predestination itself begins to be put into effect, according to Augustine, and likewise the interior calling by God's inspiration.

Hence Saint Thomas says:

A man is obliged to believe to the extent that God helps him to believe. Now a person is helped by God in three ways: (1) by a call from within; (2) by teaching and preaching from without; and (3) by external miracles.[6]

Therefore if they are not helped by God in one of the ways mentioned —as, for example, the predestined are—they do not sin in not believing or not receiving grace. Augustine implies this in his book *On the Predestination of the Saints*[7] and *On the Gift of Perseverance*,[8] where, among other profound and beautiful statements, he says this in speaking about the people of Tyre and Sidon:

Where, indeed, are the rest left by the just judgment of God, except in the mass of damnation where the men of Tyre and Sidon were left. They also would have

5. [*Summa Theologiae*], I–II, q. 112, a. 3c, and ad 1um.
6. In his second *Quodlibet,* a. 6.
7. Chaps. 9 and 10.
8. Chaps. 13 and 14.

been able to believe if they had seen those wonderful miracles of Christ. But since it was not given to them to believe, therefore the means of believing were also denied them, *that is, preaching.*

And later:

The eyes of the men of Tyre and Sidon were not so blinded nor their hearts so hardened, since they would have believed had they seen such signs as these saw, *that is, the Jews to whom the passage refers,* but it did not profit them that they had the capability to believe because they were not predestined.

Therefore the common teaching of the doctors—that is, that no one is invincibly ignorant about the things necessary for salvation because if a person does what lies within him, etc.—is interpreted of those who, through God's mercy, are foreordained to eternal life. For if such persons would do what lies within them, we must consider it most certain that God would provide them with assistance, but as often as they do not do [what lies within them] they sin, as the holy doctors say. Therefore this is not contrary to what has been determined previously.

Secondly, we answer that whatever may be the situation in regard to sin, that is, if we suppose that they sin, the avenging of that sin is nevertheless reserved to the divine judgment alone and therefore human justice is barred from any concern about these things. Moreover, as is evident from what has been said, it is difficult, indeed impossible, to detect or distinguish those who cannot excuse themselves by reason of invincible ignorance from those who are rendered guiltless by it. Therefore the determination of this matter does not belong to human but to divine justice, because it is God who knows and judges what is hidden.[9] He who sits in judgment on uncertain and doubtful matters usurps divine judgment.[10] Nor can something that God has reserved to his judgment be weighed in the scales of human justice.[11]

Furthermore, as will be asserted at length later, sins that involve only the relation between God and the sinner are reserved to the divine judgment alone (as is clear in many sins, especially sins of thought), even if it became evident to a judge who was in other ways qualified

9. Gratian, c. 11, D. 32; c. 20, C. 2, q. 5.
10. Gratian, c. 12, C. 2, q. 1.
11. Gratian, c. 1, C. 15, q. 6.

that they were sins of the gravest kind. Consequently, no judge has the right to judge hidden sins.[12]

This is likewise evident from the fact that the sin of those Jews and Saracens who are now subject to Christian rulers is not punished by a human tribunal but is reserved to divine judgment. Hence the canonists say that to be a Jew, and by the same reasoning a pagan or Saracen, is an objective fault when considered in reference to God and to eternal punishment, but not with respect to a judge and a law court, and so is not punishable by men.[13] Since, therefore, the sin of idolaters (supposing that they are not otherwise excused from the sin of idolatry) is a matter strictly between God and the sinners themselves, and since it is extremely difficult if not impossible to identify those whom invincible ignorance does not excuse, and since such sins are committed as arise from most deeply concealed thought, it follows that human justice is excluded from the duty of punishing such sins, unless it rashly desires to lay claim to God's judgment.

The logical conclusion, therefore, is that it would be unlawful to punish negative unbelievers merely because they worship idols, at least by a human judgment. And so, at last, it is clear that Innocent makes an enormous mistake in this matter when he says that the Pope has the power to punish an unbeliever who has only the natural law if he worships idols. As to his argument for this, that it is natural to worship the one and only God, the Creator, we grant that it is natural—but only after he has become known as the one true God. For then every rational creature naturally understands that he is to be worshiped and that every act of *latria*, reverence, and sacrifice should be shown to him.

---

12. Gratian, c. 11, D. 32; c. 7, C. 6, q. 1; c. 20, C. 2, q. 5.
13. Decretals, 3, 24, 8. Bartholus and others say this on the law *Apud Iulianum*, #1, and Giasone the same, #*Constat*, col. 5. See the gloss on the Decretals, 5, 19, 12.

Chapter Twenty

It now remains to refer to the position of Augustine of Ancona, a theologian,[1] which he took from the same Innocent who writes that "every creature is subject to the formulator of the canons and the Vicar of the Creator."[2] "Creature" can be interpreted as "baptized Christian," as is evident from what was said above and from the opinion of the holy Archbishop of Florence, who cites the words of this Augustine of Ancona.[3] Sylvester, citing both positions, suggests that Augustine is speaking of unbelievers who hold the lands of Christians.[4] And he says, and we admit, that they are subject to the Church or to its members in law, though not in fact. But if he understands this of all unbelievers without distinction, even of those who do not hold territories that were once under Christian rule, he is obviously very much mistaken. Therefore we must reply to his proofs and arguments: They do not stand in our way.

1. *Liber de Potestate Papae*, q. 23, a. 1 and 4.
2. On the Decretals, 3, 24, 8; 5, 17, 4, and 1, 2, 1.
3. [*Summa Moralis*], p. 3, title 22, chap. 5, #8.
4. *Summa*, under the heading "Pope," #7.

First, we are not hindered by the fact that Christ merited the power of judgment over all creatures by reason of his passion[5] and so, for the same reason, power was given to him in heaven and on earth.[6] From this, Augustine [of Ancona] infers that since the Pope is the universal Vicar of Christ over the whole world, no one is exempt from obedience to him any more than they are from obedience to God. Part of this argument is valid. We admit that the power of judgment and dominion over heaven and earth was given to Christ as man because of his humility and the disgrace of his passion and cross. Moreover, we freely admit that the Pontiff is the Vicar of Christ. Nevertheless, we deny that it follows from this that all unbelievers are subject to the Pope's jurisdiction, for three reasons.

(1) Because the Pope is content to have no greater power over unbelievers than Christ himself has. Christ, however, has habitual, not actual, jurisdiction over them until they receive baptism (as we explained above at some length) and they are subject with regard to the authority and power given him by the Father but not with regard to the effect and execution of that power. For he holds it in abeyance, as was shown in chapter 6. And this is to be subject to Christ habitually and potentially. Hence they are exempt from voluntary obedience to Christ until they receive baptism or until judgment day, as we proved in the same chapter 6. Therefore unbelievers of this kind can quite readily be exempted from obedience to the Vicar of Christ. Therefore the Supreme Pontiff cannot actually exercise jurisdiction over them.

(2) Because in no case can anyone be bound by obedience where obedience was not previously promised and thus submission contracted, according to the words of the Apostle: "Once you have given your complete obedience, we are prepared to punish any disobedience."[7] But unbelievers have not promised obedience to the Church, and thus submission was not contracted. Therefore they can never be said to be disobedient or rebellious against it. For he cannot be said to be disobedient who has never promised obedience.[8] It should be noted that this is contrary to certain stupid, indeed impious jurists who say

5. Saint Thomas speaks of this in his [*Summa Theologiae*], III, q. 59, a. 1c.
6. Matthew, last chapter [28:18].
7. 2 Corinthians 10 [6].
8. As in Digests, 4, 5, 5, #1. Bartholus teaches this when commenting on the Extravagantes, the law *Qui Sint Rebelles,* at the beginning, and on *Tenore,* at the end.

that the Indians who out of fear of the Spaniards flee into the forests and woods are rebellious, since these poor people flee in order that, after they have been despoiled of their goods, they may not be enslaved or massacred by a savage and cruel people. Since, therefore, unbelievers were never subject to the Pope, the Pope cannot judge or punish them, according to the words of Paul quoted above.

(3) We answer the proposition that just as all power in heaven and on earth was entrusted to Christ by the Father, Christ granted all that power to his Vicar. He cannot rule over the angels or over all men because [he cannot rule] over those who have attained their goal, that is, the blessed citizens of the heavenly city. Nor can he work miracles or [control] the things that belong to the power of excellence; he has power over and is the head of only those who are wayfarers, that is, those who strive toward the heavenly kingdom through faith. The unbelievers, however, are not wayfarers but wanderers. Therefore the Pope has no actual power over them, as we have taught above.

In proof of his first argument, Augustine of Ancona quotes the words of Cyril, where he says:

Just as Christ who comes forth from Israel has received from the Father the leadership and authority of the Church of the gentiles over every principality and power and everything else that exists, so that all knees should bend to him, so has he granted the fullness of power to Peter and his successors.[9]

These words have little value because the adverbs "just as" and "so" do not signify equality but similarity, as in the phrase "You shall love your neighbor as yourself,"[10] that is, just as a man naturally loves himself, so also he should love his neighbor. It does not mean, however, that he is bound to love another just as much as himself. Thus the words of Cyril mean that just as Christ has received the leadership and authority of the Church which was to be gathered together from the gentiles, so also (that is, in a similar way) he granted to Peter and his successors such fullness of power as, I say, would be needed for the guidance, government, and preservation of the Church. However, it cannot be inferred from these words that Peter and his successors would have a power

9. *Liber de Thesauris.*
10. Matthew 19 [19].

equal in every way to Christ's power, as we showed above in the exception mentioned.

Again, the similarity of the Pope's power to Christ's power is a similarity of proportion, because just as that power is in Christ in a more excellent way inasmuch as he is both God and man and as such works through it more excellently than any other man whatever, so it is with his Vicar. Although divine power is vested in him by the God-Man, yet he has received it as a mere man and uses it in his own way by imitating Christ to the extent necessary and fitting for the guidance, government, and preservation of the universal Church entrusted to him and for the salvation [of souls]. And so it is clear that those adverbs "just as" and "so" do not signify absolute equality but a likeness of proportion.

Third, in the passage quoted, Cyril does not write that Christ received actual authority in a special way over unbelievers, although by his authority and power he ought to have eminence, dominion, and rule over all creatures. He says that he received authority and government of the Church and in the Church, which was to be collected and gathered together out of all the peoples whom he had asked for and received from the Father as his heritage, according to the prophet: "Ask and I will give you the nations for your heritage, the ends of the earth for your domain."[11] Over and within this Church, Christ has received authority, power, and royal dignity as regards both purpose and accomplishment, according to the verse [6] of the same psalm: "This is my king, installed by me on Zion, my holy mountain. Let me proclaim the Lord's decree." Saint Augustine interprets this mountain as the Church. "On the Church," he says, "which he calls his holy mountain because of its eminence and solidity."[12] Therefore, just as Christ in his own way was appointed by the Father prince over all the princes of the earth insofar as he was man,[13] and is actual king within the Church and potential king outside the Church, as has already been frequently proved, so also his Vicar in his own way has actual power within the Church, in which he obtains sovereignty and royal dignity, spiritual rule, and, by a sort of consequence, temporal power over every kingdom and principality that happens to be within the church, but potential power outside the Church, that is, over unbelievers.

11. Psalms 2 [8].
12. [*Enarrationes in Psalmos*].
13. Apocalypse [Revelations] 1 [5].

Fourth, although Cyril says "over every principality and power and everything else that exists," these words are to be interpreted "over all that is contained within the Church," that is, over all Christian rulers and their kingdoms and dignities and powers, whether spiritual or temporal, that is, in those areas that are necessary for the salvation and the proper government of the flock of Christ. Universal terms are sometimes restricted and limited and at other times are quite properly used in a wide sense, not only in law and in the teaching of the holy doctors but also in that of Holy Scripture. The theologians note this in regard to that verse of Matthew 3 [5]: "Then Jerusalem and all Judea and the whole Jordan district made their way to him." "All Judea" and "the whole district" are not to be understood in a totally universal sense, as saying that everyone without exception went out, but that the majority or a great part of the people went out.[14] This is the interpretation of that verse of Isaiah: "All mankind shall see the salvation of God."[15] For not all men in the world saw Christ in the flesh. For the same reason, "God our savior . . . wants everyone to be saved" [is interpreted in the same way].[16] But God does not will those who die in mortal sin to be saved, but those who observe his commandments until death. But not even these attain salvation without the grace of God, as Saint Thomas notes on this verse: "[He] wants everyone to be saved." And this is a proper use in the wide sense, which includes those who are capable, that is, true Christians to whom it belongs to be saved. And to destroy the conclusion, it is enough to give a single instance. Hence, although Sacred Scripture often uses its universal terms in their full meaning, they are applied universally only to those of whom the predicate is true, as in that verse of John: "The whole world is running after him."[17] It is hyperbole, a figure of speech. This is a grammatical figure, that is, a way of speaking. This is what Jerome teaches in his letter to Pope Damasus in which, applying to the Jewish people the words that are spoken to the prodigal son, "My son, you are with me always and all I have is yours,"[18] he says:

But how does all that is God's belong to the Jews? Are the angels, thrones, dominations, and the other spirits theirs? By "all," therefore, we understand the

14. *In I Sententiarum,* d. 46.
15. 52 [10].
16. 1 Timothy 2 [3–4].
17. 12 [19].
18. Luke 15 [31].

law, prophets, and the divine oracles, according to the usage of the Scriptures, as we have often explained. "All" is not to be referred to the whole but to the greatest part, as in that passage, "All have turned aside, all alike are tainted," and in another place, "All others who have come are thieves."[19]

interpret

From this it is clear that although the texts of Sacred Scripture are expressed in universal terms, they admit of limitation or restriction. The text "Whatever you bind on earth shall be considered bound in heaven" admits this.[20] It is limited [by the condition] "when the key does not err," according to the gloss and the doctors.[21] So also the text "But when the Spirit of truth comes, he will lead you to the complete truth."[22] "Complete," that is, in reference to preaching and the spread of the gospel and the salvation of souls, not truths of philosophy, cosmography, geometry, and similar arts. Therefore the gloss interprets that passage as "truth necessary for salvation." This is also the interpretation of the text of the Decretals, 1, 33, 6, and also Gratian, c. 1, D. 19, that is, all things necessary and useful for the guidance of the Church to the goal of [eternal] happiness. So also in civil law, general words are restricted and interpreted as applying to those who are able and have a right. An example is Codex, 1, 2, 1. And in that place where it is said "Let each one have license to bequeath in his testament to pious places," the doctors comment that it is interpreted according to the gloss as "each one who is able to make a testament." And so Baldus, when he expounds that passage of the Decretals, 1, 2, 1, and cites the words of Innocent, "Every creature is subject to the formulator of the canons and the Vicar of Christ," says that if the constitutions of the Pope can be applied to all, they bind all. If, however, they cannot be applied to all, for example, to unbelievers, then they include only the subjects of the Pope.[23] For general words are always to be restricted so that no absurdity, evil, or scandal follows, as has been sufficiently proved.[24]

Words?

19. [Letter 21. The citations are from Psalms 14:3 and John 10:8.]
20. Matthew 16 [19].
21. On the Decretals, 2, 13, 13.
22. John 16 [13].
23. We see the same thing in Book 1, and there the doctors comment on the Codex, 1, 1, 1, and on the Decretals, 1, 31, 12, and 19; 1, 2, 1, and on the last chapter [13] and the Digests, 29, 1, 40.
24. Anthony [of Butrio] teaches this at length on the Decretals, 1, 2, 1, col. 5, and the other doctors on the same passage.

Cyril's general words, therefore, must be restricted to whatever is contained in the Church (as has been proved), since if we interpret his words in any other sense they are contrary to the words of Paul, and if interpreted in a general sense they produce absurdities, for example, that the Pope can punish those not subject to him or outside his competence for the crimes they commit within the boundaries of a foreign territory. This is as false as it can be, as we have proved with the ten proofs above and the authority of the holy fathers. For who would judge that idolatrous Indians are to be punished when they had never, not even by hearsay, heard of Christ or Christians up to our own time and so are free from all guilt of malice? And Christian meekness favors men of this kind; it does not persecute or afflict them. It teaches; it does not coerce or punish. For unbelievers of this kind are immune, directly or indirectly, to spiritual penalties such as excommunication and the like, and much more so from temporal penalties that the Pope might want to impose on them for their crimes.

The antecedent is obvious: that they cannot be directly excommunicated is clear, for he who is outside the Church cannot be expelled from it.[25] Nor indirectly, as happens when the Church cuts the faithful off from communication with unbelievers in order to punish the unbelievers in certain cases. This is also obvious because we are supposing that unbelievers such as the Indians and the like commit no special crime for which they should deservedly undergo a penalty of that kind, since they are living in their own lands far distant from ours. So much more, therefore, are these unbelievers immune to the temporal or physical penalties of the Church.

The conclusion is proved from the fact that the Church does not judge secular persons except in what concerns their souls, according to the doctors.[26] However, it is not the function of the Church to pass judgment on the souls of unbelievers unless they receive baptism, as is evident from the above. Therefore in no way can the Church impose temporal punishment on them for their crimes, since the jurisdiction that the Church has in temporal matters is dependent on spiritual things. And, as a sort of consequence, [it cannot impose such punishment] outside the lands subject to it in a temporal way, according to the

25. Gratian, c. 32, C. 11, q. 3.
26. On the Decretals, 4, 19, 8; 4, 17, last chapter [15]; 4, 13, 4.

true Catholic opinion of both canonists and theologians, and also the saints. Therefore, when it will be granted that there is no jurisdiction or spiritual power or power in spiritual matters, the result will be to deny that it exists in temporal matters.

The conclusion is evident from the proof, [by which one reasons] from the destruction of the antecedent to the destruction of the conclusion. This kind of argumentation is valid as often as the terms are convertible, as are "rational" and "man." And this is the present case because temporal jurisdiction or jurisdiction over temporal matters either is convertible with spiritual jurisdiction or comes as a consequence of spiritual jurisdiction in ecclesiastical judges or in spiritual things in certain cases that have a relationship to spiritual affairs, that is, inasmuch as it is necessary for the free administration of spiritual affairs.[27]

Therefore in this case (that is, the case of unbelievers, with whom we are dealing here), as the Church does not have spiritual jurisdiction and cannot inflict penalties because of spiritual matters, it follows that as a rule it cannot inflict temporal or physical penalties, etc. And, therefore, the title by which ecclesiastical judges exercise temporal jurisdiction is the spiritual jurisdiction that belongs to the universal Church. There are indeed unbelievers of this kind, subjects directly incapable of penalties which are based on spiritual jurisdiction, that is, excommunication, interdict, and the like. On this account they are considered not to be bound by precepts and canonical penalties.[28] And even indirectly [they are incapable of penalties], because we are supposing that in their relationship to us they are living calmly and peacefully in their kingdoms and are not committing special disturbances against us. Therefore, also, they are not liable to temporal penalties that might be imposed by any ecclesiastical or spiritual judge, as has been proved. The common opinion of canonists proves this conclusion against Innocent.[29] And

27. This is clear from the Decretals, 4, 17, 13, #*Rationibus;* 2, 1, 13. And in both places it is noted at length by the doctors, as well as in many other places.
28. As in the Decretals, 4, 19, 8. Gratian, c. 18, C. 2, q. 1; c. 32, C. 11, q. 3.
29. On the Decretals, 3, 24, 8; 4, 19, 8; 1, 2, 1. And on that point, Anthony of Butrio and the Abbot and Felinus, col. 9, at the words *At Fallit Ergo.* And the doctors on the Decretals, 4, 13, 4; 4, 17. And Peter of Ancarano on the rule *Ea quae* in col. 15 and on the rule *Peccatum,* col. 15, and on *Concilium,* 15, at the beginning, *Spiritualis Iudex.* And Cardinal Zambaralla [Zabarella] on the Clementines, on the second *Notabili,* where he says that "the power of the Pope concerns the Christian people only and thus does not concern the sects of others since it is not our business to pass judgment on those who are outside, etc." And on the Clementines, 5, 5. And John of Anagni on the rubric and on the Decretals, 5, 6, 18.

others in other places write that, in regard to temporal penalties, unbelievers are subject to secular rulers under whose dominion they live, but not, however, to the Church, except in cases in which the Church can exercise jurisdiction over secular persons.[30] However, concerning pagans who live in their own separate kingdoms, apart from the cases noted above and those that will be noted later, it is the concern of neither the Church nor Christian rulers to punish the sins they commit specifically within the limits of their unbelief and territories, as is clearly established by the proofs above.

Now if the punishment of sins of this kind does not belong to the Church, to which God entrusted the care of the whole world (as has been dealt with above and will be seen also below), much less is it lawful for Christian rulers, whose power and jurisdiction is of no weight or authority outside each kingdom, country, or territory (as was proved above), to presume to hold coercive jurisdiction.

30. These are cited in Gratian, c. 18, C. 2, q. 1., by Dominic and others, and this is the interpretation of Gratian, c. 31, C. 17, q. 4., [and] the gloss on Gratian, c. 13, C. 28, q. 1, and it is sufficiently proved in the Decretals, 5, 17, 4, and 5, 19, 12, with the points noted there by the doctors.

Chapter Twenty-One

All of this is in agreement with what Saint Thomas writes: that "the Church does not have the right to pass spiritual judgment on unbelievers who have in no way whatever accepted the Christian faith, that is, pagans and Jews, but may pass a temporal judgment when they commit some crime while living among Christians and are punished by the faithful with a temporal judgment."[1] And in reply to the second objection, he says:

The Church does not have jurisdiction over unbelievers so that it may inflict a spiritual penalty on them. But it does have jurisdiction over some unbelievers on whom it may impose temporal penalties. For example, the Church sometimes forbids the faithful to associate with unbelievers because of certain special crimes which the unbelievers have committed.

Take note of the words "pass a temporal judgment when they commit some crime while living among Christians," and also note the words "it has jurisdiction over some unbelievers." Again, note the words "certain special crimes." From these words there is clear proof that the Church cannot punish unbelievers with temporal penalties, except when they are living among Christians. Nor can it do this except in certain cases; for example, if they do not return usurious profits to Christians, if they hold the bonds of Christians, if they commit blasphemy against Christ the Lord or the saints, and similar cases.[2] And those words of Saint Thomas, "they are punished by the faithful with a temporal judgment," mean that in those cases in which it is lawful to punish unbelievers they are to be punished by their civil rulers and by the ministers of those to whom they are subject, except in those cases in which the Church punishes lay people. Again, by the words "it does have jurisdiction over some unbelievers" Saint Thomas teaches that the Church does not have general jurisdiction over all unbelievers but only over some (I mean contentious jurisdiction), specifically in those cases, as we have taught above in chapter 6, in which the Church can actualize

---

1. [*Summa Theologiae*], II–II, q. 10, a. 9.
2. Concerning these, see Gratian, c. 12, C. 28, q. 1, and the gloss on C. 28, q. 1, and on the Decretals, 5, 6, 2; 5, 6, 13; 5, 6, 16, and on many other passages of both laws.

the habitual jurisdiction it has over unbelievers. Therefore it is quite clear that the Church does not indiscriminately intrude in order to judge the crimes of all unbelievers, nor all their crimes, nor in all cases. [The cases it judges] can be reduced to three, as we can gather from the words of Saint Thomas, Innocent, and the canonists.

The first case is when [unbelievers] who live among Christians commit some atrocious crimes. Then they can be punished as subjects of the Church, or at least of its members.

The second case occurs when they control territories they have wrested from a Christian nation and commit shameful crimes, for example, a crime of idolatry or against nature, by which they defile and contaminate places that had been dedicated to Christ.

Third, when not content with their native kingdoms and territories they invade the lands of Christians and harass the Church with the uproar of war, or when they commit blasphemy against Christ or the saints. All of this is evident from the conclusions drawn above.

Here we must recall the gloss on Gratian, c. 12, D. 1, and some other canonists who, because they speak generally and without distinctions, confuse matters and darken men's understanding. Because they do not distinguish alien from alien and unbelievers from unbelievers, these men say, with the gloss, that "aliens are under Roman rule [or Empire]." I say that it is stupid to take this in such an absolute sense. But since it is incredible that the gloss and those who make similar statements have fallen into this error, we must say that the gloss is to be interpreted as referring to aliens, that is, unbelievers, Jews, Saracens, and those of other religions who live within the provinces of the Church or in the territories of Christian rulers or because they hold lands taken from Christians, since those realms are included within the limits of Roman rule that do not go beyond the limits of the Christian people. For the Roman Empire is and always has been marked by certain boundaries, according to Boethius in the *Consolation* [*of Philosophy*], where he says:

At the time of Marcus Tullius [Cicero], as he himself indicates someplace, the renown of the Roman Republic had not, as yet, gone beyond the Caucasus Mountains. And even at that time, it was mature, *that is, known from antiquity,* and feared by the Parthians and also the other inhabitants of those regions.[3]

3. Liber 2, prosa 7.

Therefore the Roman Emperors were not lords of the whole world, even when Roman power was more widely spread throughout the world. And today the Roman Empire does not extend beyond the boundaries of the Catholic Church, according to the Authenticum: "But caring nothing for the one and being unconcerned about the other, this, *that is, the law,* is extended throughout the world which is bound by Roman Law and the sanction of the Catholic Church and determines what is its own, etc."[4]

Therefore where men are not his subjects and the reason for subjection has ended, the ruler cannot make a law because the justification for his jurisdiction ceases.[5] The kingdoms of aliens, therefore, were exempt from the jurisdiction of the Roman Empire. And the Emperors themselves acknowledged this, and therefore neither in law nor in fact did they win rule over the entire world.

There are those who allege that the Roman Emperor is lord of the world by right though not in fact, but this is a foolish assertion. They cannot prove it with solid arguments. Without doubt it is obviously false. For never in any century until now has anyone been lord of the world, nor did the despotic Roman armies subdue the world. In this sense must we interpret the law: "We command everyone without exception to obey our imperial authority throughout our jurisdiction, on which the sun never sets and which extends to both ends [of the world]."[6] Any ruler can say the same thing. For there is no kingdom that

---

4. Authenticum, *De Non Alienandis vel Permutandis Rebus Ecclesiae,* # *Sicut autem.* And Hostiensis teaches this expressly in his *Summa,* title *Qui Fili Sint Legitimi,* # *Qualiter: a quo filii,* as also by the authority of the saints. Hostiensis says: "For the law of the Emperor can bind only those subject to Roman law and the sanction of the Catholic Church, that is, because outside the Church there is no empire." This is expressly proved in the Codex, 1, 27, 2, at the words "Before the invasion of the Vandals and the Moors, the Roman Republic had boundaries" and "Where the ancient guards were stationed, etc." And in the same place: "And we hope that in our own times it will soon come about that the provinces will be completely preserved within their ancient boundaries in security and peace, etc." And many other paragraphs of that law touch it. Cf. also Bartholus on the law *Hostes,* the gloss on Digests, 49, 15, 7; Angelo of Perugia on the Authenticae, 8, 18; the Digests, *quia vero,* col. 8, second *Notabili,* where he says that "princes make laws against barbarians because those barbarians are subject to him [sic]."

5. This is also proved in the Codex, 11, 60, laws 1, 2, and 3; law 11; and the Codex, 4, 63, 4.

6. Digests, 14, 2, 9. Authenticae, 5, 24, 1.

does not look to east, west, south, and north. Yet it is true that the Roman Emperor is the universal lord of Christians.[7]

However, to say that the Roman Emperor is the lawful master of the whole world is an utterly vain bit of nonsense and a way of deceiving the Emperors by flattery and an occasion for involving the world in strife. Even more ridiculous is what Michael Ulcurrunus (among others) writes in his treatise *On the Rule of the World:* "All the nations of the world are obliged to obey the Roman Emperor elected by the seven distinguished princes of Germany as representatives of the whole world." He cites John Andrea, but John Andrea does not write anything like that; rather, he writes that "those whom these princes have succeeded chose as a college and totality ... consisting of princes and the whole people who were subject to the Roman Empire or the army chose, representing that totality, etc."[8] He does not say "acting in place of the totality of the whole world, etc.," although even if John Andrea had said it he would be no less blameworthy than Michael who attributes it to him, especially because John Andrea does not state it dogmatically but cites a certain doctor by the name of Upoldus who asserts it. But since we hope, with God's help, to show elsewhere, point by point, how full of errors the above-mentioned treatise *On the Rule of the World* is, for the present we shall forgo saying anything more about it.

Therefore the words of Blessed Cyril are not opposed to our Catholic and well-proved teaching, which all the doctors, sacred and profane, follow.

---

7. Baldus teaches this on the introduction to the Digests, col. 2. The doctors on the Codex, 1, 1, 1. Giasone on the same passage, col. 2. Baldus on the same passage, same law, col. 2

8. In his additions to the Speculator [Gulielmus Durandus], on the title *De Rescriptus: Praesentia,* on the final sentence *Item quod obtentum.*

Chapter Twenty-Two

To continue, Augustine of Ancona argues that pagans who sin against nature can be punished by the Pope since each person can be justly punished for a violation of the law he accepts and claims to observe. But pagans and all barbarian nations accept the natural law and can be found guilty by means of it. But the Pope is, or should be, the guardian of the natural law. Therefore the Pope can and must punish all pagans and barbarian nations who violate the natural law.

We answer this argument in three ways.

First, it is true that each person should be punished on the basis of the law he accepts and professes, and so also on the basis of the natural law. Yet a distinction must be made between divine and human judgment according to the characteristics of each of these judgments.

The concern of human judgment is to punish sins that are committed against the natural law by sinners who are subject to human judgment. On the other hand, the concern of divine judgment is to punish the sins of those who, in some way, are not subject to human judgment. And so such a punishment is recognized as reserved to divine judgment. This can be made clear in the following way. Very many heinous crimes can be committed against the natural and divine-positive law, whose primary defender is the Pope and whose [secondary] defender is the competent judge. It is their obligation to punish these [crimes] in their subjects. Yet in many cases neither the Pope nor any other judge has the power to punish such crimes even in his own subjects, because these crimes belong expressly to divine judgment. This can be illustrated by many examples. One is the case in which someone committed some very serious crime against the natural and divine law in the presence of the Pope alone or the king alone, with no other witnesses present, so that only the Pope or the king saw it with his own eyes. Therefore such an offender is left to the divine judgment, since in that case he is not subject to human judgment, whether of the Pope or anyone else. A Pope who punishes such an offender would deserve to hear the words "It is not for you to condemn someone else's servant: whether he stands or falls, it is his own master's business."[1] Pope Evaristus proves this in reference to the above-mentioned case in these words: "We should not judge or condemn anyone prior to a true and just trial, according to the Apostle who says, 'It is not for you to condemn someone else's servant: whether he stands or falls, it is his own master's business, etc.' " Remarking on that passage, the gloss says that the servant of another should be judged by the other, in this case by God. This same Evaristus cites the example of the sin the men of Sodom committed.[2]

An example of this is the unbelief of the Saracens and Jews who live in Christians lands. It is contrary to the divine law that they have received from God, the principal guardian of which is the Pope.[3] The impiety of the Saracens is contrary to the natural law also, for they worship an impious false prophet who is defiled by a whole sewer of vices. Further, they observe certain obscene ceremonies that are contrary to the natural law. Yet they are not punished by the Pope or by any other ruler, since the punishment of their sins is left to divine judgment. Their punishment does not belong to the Pope or any other human judge because in these sins they are subject to no man. Moreover, the doctors teach that to be a Jew is a sin before God, who will punish the crime, but is not a sin before men, for that sin is not punished

1. Romans 14 [4].
2. Gratian, c. 10, C. 30, q. 5; c. 20, C. 2, q. 1.
3. Gratian, c. 6, C. 25, q. 1.

by men but is left to the divine judgment.[4] To be a Jew, they say, is a sin in itself, that is, in relation to God and eternal punishment, but not in relation to a judge and contentious competence and so it cannot be punished by men.[5] The same is true of Saracens, Arabs, and other pagans, since their superstition is not punished by human, Christian judges but is left to God, as is evident from what has been said.

The same judgment must be made about crimes committed by the drunk or insane, since, though they may kill, commit blasphemy, or other notable crimes, they must not be punished while the insanity or drunkenness lasts.[6] An insane person can receive but cannot commit an injury.[7] Offenses of this type are judged as though they were committed by accident. If, however, a man becomes drunk or loses his mind through his own fault and devotes himself to something unlawful, then he is guilty of crime and so will give an account to God.[8] The reason for this is that when someone deliberately gets drunk, the fault committed by him is in some way deliberate, just as if a person should shoot an arrow without first looking to see whether there was someone who could be injured. That is what Lamech did in killing Cain by an accident of this type. For the same reason, the man who desires the wife of another is guilty before God but is not punished by a human judgment.[9] The same is to be said of persons who seek to become wealthy with another's possessions and of those who keep what belongs to others and are bound to restitution, as also of those who hold property in bad faith. Although they are not punished by human judges, yet before God they are guilty of a crime. On these matters Adrian of Florensz, the Roman Pontiff, wrote a quodlibet (that is, *Quodlibetum* I, a. 2) in which he wrote four propositions that fully agree with this treatise. Among these also are the carnal faults of boys who are not capable of malice. They are not

4. Decretals, 3, 24, 8.
5. This is the teaching of Bartholus on the Julian Law, #1, and Giasone, #*Constat*, col. 5; Louis of Rome on the Digests, 45, 1, 34; John of Anagni on the Decretals, 5, 6, 1, at the beginning; Felinus on the Decretals, the chapter *Multorum*, col. 2, under that title [*De Iudaeis*]. And other doctors also hold the same position.
6. See the Clementines, 5, 4, the only chapter.
7. Digests, 47, 10, 3.
8. See Saint Thomas [*Summa Theologiae*], II–II, q. 64, a. 8c. *In IV Sententiarum,* d. 17, q. 2, a. 2; q. 24, ad 2um.
9. A similar example is given in Gratian, c. 12, C. 15, q. 1; c. 9, C. 15, q. 1; c. 7, C. 15, q. 1.

punished by law.[10] Hence a boy under twelve years of age cannot be accused of adultery.[11] Yet before God they commit a mortal sin if they are capable of malice.[12] This last citation also proves that if boys steal, lie, or commit perjury—which are crimes against the natural law—they are guilty of a crime before God, provided they are capable of malice. In some boys this happens at the age of seven. Yet they are not punished by human judgment unless they are very close to puberty.[13]

10. Decretals, 5, 23, 1.
11. Digests, 48, 5, 37.
12. Gratian, c. 3, C. 15, q. 1. Decretals, 5, 23, 1.
13. As is noted in the Institutes, 3, 19, #9, and the gloss on the Institutes, 4, 5.

Chapter Twenty-Three

There are many cases in which men are guilty before God but not before men, so that not even the Pope himself can punish those crimes in Christian subjects, even if these crimes are contrary to the natural and divine law of which he is the guardian and defender. The reason for this is that in some respect the persons who commit those crimes cease to be his subjects in regard to the crimes, as is clear from what has been said. And so the punishment of such offenses is thought to be left to divine judgment, although the Pope does not, on this account, cease to be the guardian and defender of the natural and divine law. Much less, then, can pagans who live apart in their own kingdoms and are not subject to the Pope (as has been established above by many authorities and arguments) be punished by him, although they might commit enormous crimes against the natural law, for they have God as their judge. He alone will judge and punish them according to the same natural law because they are subjects and servants of God alone. This is in agreement with Paul's words "whether he stands or falls, it is his own master's business."[1] Neither does the Pope cease to be the guardian of the natural law just because he does not punish sins of this type, because it is not his concern but God's to punish sins of this type. And so Augustine of Ancona is mistaken and draws a wrong conclusion when he argues that unbelievers who sin against the natural law, which they acknowledge, can be judged according to the natural law. But the Pope is its guardian; therefore he can punish them. As is clear from what was said above, this is not a good syllogism.

Now our second answer to Augustine of Ancona is that God did not appoint the Pope alone as the guardian of the natural law but also kings, princes, and judges, even if they are pagan. "Over each nation he has set a governor." "By me monarchs rule and princes issue just laws; by me rulers govern, and the great impose justice on the world." And "All government comes from God . . . since all government officials are God's officers. They serve God."[2] Here Paul is speaking about pagan rulers, for in that century there was no Christian ruler. Yet I admit that the Supreme Pontiff is more obliged to have the natural law observed than any other ruler, even if he is a Christian.[3] Yet it is the concern of each king or judge, even if he is an unbeliever, to pass laws and decrees by which the natural law, which all men accept, will be observed in every way. In fact, to put this into effect they have been placed by God at the very summit of affairs, as is proved in Wisdom 6 [2–4], where they are called God's ministers for the accomplishment of this task. And so an unbeliever who does not observe the natural law should be punished not by

1. Romans 14 [4].
2. Ecclesiasticus 17 [14]. Proverbs 8 [15–16]. Romans 13 [1–6].
3. This is proved in Gratian, c. 13, C 24, q. 1: "Greater zeal for the Christian religion obliges us more than all others."

a foreign ruler but by his own ruler, so that the natural law may be observed. "Civil authorities were appointed by God."[4] Now if a Christian ruler does not take diligent care about the observance of the natural law, he can and should be corrected by the Pope.[5]

There are two reasons for this. First, because no one violates the natural law, especially in serious matters dictated by nature, without committing mortal sin. Therefore it is the business of the Pope to correct a Christian who violates the natural law.[6] Second, because the Christian religion cannot be practiced or continue to exist without the observance of the natural law. Since, therefore, the task of preserving and strengthening the Christian religion is a special obligation of the Pope, it also follows that it is his concern to cause the natural law to be preserved among Christians. If, however, the person who sins against the natural law is an unbelieving ruler, he has God to punish him, according to the gloss on the words "Against you only have I sinned" [Psalm 50:5]. This is proved by three arguments.

First, it is not the business of the Pope or the Church to pass judgment on those who are outside, that is, pagans.[7]

Second, we are supposing that pagans commit their sins in their own kingdoms outside Christian territories. Also, that their crimes are not in any way subversive or harmful to the Christian religion, for the protection of which the Pope is obliged, more than all kings and rulers to see to the observance of the natural law.

Third, such a ruler has God to punish him, and another's servant is subject to God alone, who, he will discover, is a very severe judge. "Ruthless judgment is reserved for the high and mighty . . . strict scrutiny awaits those in power. . . . Yes, despots, my words are for you, that you may learn what wisdom is and not transgress,"[8] as if he were saying quite openly: "You either stand or fall to me, the Lord, your master." The natural law, then, has its defenders and guardians everywhere, even among the pagans, who, if they violate it by committing crimes, are left to divine judgment and pay their penalties to their rulers. From this it is clear that Augustine of Ancona is drawing an unwarranted general

---

4. Romans 13 [1].
5. See the Decretals, 2, 1, 13; 1, 33, 6. Gratian, c. 3, C. 15, q. 1; c. 10, D. 96; c. 11, D. 96.
6. As in the Decretals, 2, 1, 13.
7. See 1 Corinthians 5 [12].
8. Wisdom 6 [6, 9].

conclusion, since he does not give any special argument or clear authority by which it would be the Church's concern to punish unbelievers
more for acting against the natural law than for other offenses.

Our third answer to Augustine is that the Church does not punish
the crimes of unbelievers who are subject to it or to its members if the
crimes are committed precisely against God, except insofar as their
crimes are harmful to the Christian religion.[9] Here the gloss interprets
Paul's words "It is not my business to pass judgment on those outside"
by adding "inasmuch as they offend God." If, however, men should be
scandalous or prejudicial to the Christian religion, they could be punished.[10] But no matter how abominable and how unnatural the crimes
of pagans, if they are committed within territories held by the pagans
and never possessed by Christians, and if they are not harmful to
Christians or to the advantage of the Christian state, the Church cannot
punish the crimes of such unbelievers or sinners, no matter how serious
they may be.

Besides, in the second place, the Church judges secular persons only
on the basis of matters that concern the soul, as we have established
above. But the Church has the care of the souls of unbelievers only to
the extent of preaching the gospel of Christ to them in a mild and gentle
manner. This, too, is evident from the conclusions we have drawn.
Therefore the Church cannot in any way punish unbelievers because of
crimes against nature, or any others.

Thirdly, we argue with the reason first cited against Augustine's
second argument, that is, that the sin of Jews and Saracens, precisely
because they are Jews or Saracens, and so also their unbelief is a very
great sin. Yet they are not punished by men. The only reason [for
punishment] is if [this sin] is a source of harm or hindrance to the good
of our Christian state, because when it is a matter of the preservation
or general good of any state, crimes must not go unpunished.[11] On the
contrary, not to punish them is to the advantage of the Christian religion, as we see in the case of the Jews whose books bear witness to the
truth of the gospel. Both they and the Saracens praise the meekness,
charity, and gentleness of the Christian state as being long established.

9. This is taught by the gloss on the Decretals, 5, 19, 12.
10. The doctors also teach this when commenting on the Clementines, 2, 8.
11. See the previously cited chap. 35 [Decretals, Book 5, title 39] and the Digests, 9, 2,
51, at the end; 46, 3, 95, #1; 5, 1, 18, #1.

Rather, the Church could possibly remain silent about crimes committed against nature by pagans, even if such pagans might be subject to it, unless there would be enormous harm to the Christian state. This might happen in two ways.

First, if they committed blasphemy against the venerable name of Christ or the names of his saints in the presence of those who worship him. Thus they would not only offend God but they would also injure the Christians themselves. For if they did not avenge such injuries, the faith itself and the Christian religion would be gradually reduced to derision or disgrace even among Catholics.

The same must be said in reference to the unspeakable sin, for if pagans who live together with Christians in the same city were to practice the abominable vice of sodomy and went unpunished, undoubtedly boys, young men, or men who by nature had evil inclinations would sooner or later be corrupted. Therefore they would doubtless have to be punished by the Christian rulers to whom they are [subject], according to what Jerome says: "Decayed flesh must be cut off and the mangy sheep must be driven from the enclosure, lest the whole house, mass, body, and flocks should be in pain, become corrupt, decay, and perish, etc."[12] But no such danger seems to threaten from the other sins of unbelievers who live among believers.

I have said that the Church could possibly remain silent. However, I prefer that heinous sins of this type would always be punished by Christian rulers, even if they are committed by their pagan subjects. Every good ruler, especially if he is a Catholic, should diligently lay down laws and penalties to ban from his kingdom whatever is contrary to nature, unless a prohibition of this type would hinder a greater good or cause a worse evil.

Second, the state would be harmed, inasmuch as plague, famine, and earthquakes usually occur because of the crimes of blasphemy and sodomy, as it says in the Authenticum:

so that men may not be guilty of unnatural lust or swear by their hair or commit blasphemy against God under the penalty of capital punishment, lest, from the toleration of such acts, *that is, of punishing them* [sic] the city and the state should be harmed by these acts.

12. Gratian, c. 16, C. 24, q. 3.

Moreover, it is right that Christian rulers punish [a fault] in their subjects that is so much opposed to the natural law. Therefore if the sins of unbelievers are not harmful to the Christian state, there is no reason why the Church should be involved in punishing their sins, even if (as it seems) the guilty unbelievers are subject to it or its members.

The unbelievers whom we are here trying to accuse do not in any way hurt the Church or its members by any of their crimes, inasmuch as we are supposing that they live in far-distant lands and in their own kingdoms under their own kings and native rulers, and so are not subjects of the Church. Further, if God occasionally punishes them for their sins by plague, famine, earthquakes, and other scourges, these evils are misfortunes and losses to their own kingdoms. They suffer these things among themselves. They do not extend beyond their own regions. Therefore they are not harmful to the Christian state, nor is the Church burdened by them or by their sins.

From all the foregoing it follows logically that it is not the Church's business to pass judgment on this type of sin in unbelievers, no matter how serious it may be, unless (as we shall explain later) it is a matter of working to invite them to the faith of Christ gently and meekly, not with arms or violence, and to have the Christian religion spread and propagated throughout those kingdoms.

Chapter Twenty-Four

In the third place, Augustine of Ancona claims that unbelievers have been judged and condemned by the Church. Of course, if he means that the crimes of unbelievers are punished by the Church by means of contentious jurisdiction, he is obviously wrong, as is clear from what was said above. But if he means that the Church judges and condemns pagans by Catholic judgment, to the extent that it judges by the certitude of its faith that they must be condemned to eternal fire, we do not deny it. For outside the Church there is no salvation.[1] It does not judge or condemn them by a judgment of contentious jurisdiction, in such a way that it would punish them for crimes outside the six cases previously enumerated. We admit that if they have been enlightened with regard to the power of the keys, they can be absolved of their sins by the Church.

Taken absolutely and generally, Augustine's other statement that the Church has power of judgment over unbelievers is false, as has been indicated over and over again in previous rebuttals. One must distinguish whether the unbelievers are subject to Christian rulers and what crimes they commit; whether they are Jews, Saracens, heretics, or schismatics; whether they are unbelievers holding territories that once belonged to the Christian Church; whether they make destructive raids against a Christian people. These cases must be distinguished, as is clear enough from [Saint] Augustine's book *On the True Religion:*

Spread strong and wide throughout the entire world, this Catholic Church uses all who have gone astray for its own advantage and for their own correction whenever they want to come to their senses. It uses pagans as the raw material for its work; heretics as a proof of its teaching; schismatics as a testimony to its stability; Jews as a comparison for its beauty. Some, therefore, it invites. Others it excludes. Yet to all it gives the power to share in God's grace, whether they are still to be formed or reformed, reconciled or admitted.

If individual points are cited, these words embrace all the previously mentioned cases. "As the raw material for its work" refers to the pagans

---

1. Gratian, c. 19, C. 24, q. 1.

to whom the Church must preach the word of God, since this is the proper function of the Church. Again, the term "invites" quite clearly means that the Church does not force but attracts and leads men to the faith by examples of holiness and by reasonable persuasion. In the same way, "are still to be formed" indicates that they have not been formed or instructed in God's word and Catholic teaching. This does not refer to heretics but to those who have not yet received the faith, since, in reference to them (that is, heretics), Augustine uses the term "excludes" and "are . . . to be formed." By these words he means that heretics, and also schismatics, who do not come to their senses must be expelled from the Church by a spiritual penalty, that is, excommunication. If they stubbornly persist in their error, they must be consumed by flames. The expression "are to be . . . reformed" means that Augustine is speaking of those who, once they have been rightly formed, afterward are deformed by errors, and he is also speaking of the judgment by means of which they must be reformed. The words "others it excludes" can be understood of unbelievers who do not come under the Pope's jurisdiction and whose crimes the Pope does not punish (as I have taught previously), since they do not hurt the Christian state in any way. But even if they commit enormous sins, they hurt no one but themselves and thus they have God alone to punish them. The terms "Some . . . it invites" and "are to be . . . admitted" show the kindness of the Church; that is, it is ready to receive the Jews although they committed the horrible crime of killing Christ the Lord. Now if the Church receives into its bosom those who are guilty of such an enormous crime, much more will it receive pagans, whose sin is less serious. The words "to all it gives the power to share in God's grace" refer to the pagan if, that is, he embraces the Christian faith; to the heretic, by compelling him to reconcile himself with the Church; to the schismatic, if he conforms to the orthodox; to the Jews, if they open their eyes to understand Christ's truth and their own ignorance. And in this way the Church offers the certain hope of salvation to all.

All unbelievers, then, no matter what their class or kind, are oriented toward the judgment of the Church but with considerable differences. For those unbelievers belong to the Church who have never heard the faith as far as the preaching and conversion accomplished by its ministers are concerned. For they can, if they want, become its members. Saint Thomas writes that although unbelievers do not belong to the Church actually, yet they belong to the Church potentially. This potentiality is based on two factors: (1) principally on the power of Christ, which is sufficient for the salvation of the whole human race; (2) on the freedom of the will, by which every man who hears the teaching of Christ can by the help of divine grace become one of its members.[2]

And so it is evident that not all unbelievers belong to the judicial power of the Church, contrary to the opinion of Augustine of Ancona. Yet we grant that on occasions all unbelievers would be of genuine advantage to the Church for the above-mentioned reasons drawn from the words of Augustine's *On the True Religion,* as even Ancona admits in his fourth argument. But, as a matter of fact, his teaching in this area is quite as confused as the teaching of Innocent, from whom he takes it almost word for word. Furthermore, his arguments are not worth much attention. And so, having satisfactorily answered (as we believe) the arguments of both Augustine of Ancona and Innocent, we must go on to the other cases in which the Church actually exercises the contentious jurisdiction against unbelievers that it has habitually.

There is, therefore, a third case of this type, that is, if they are maliciously, knowingly, and insultingly blasphemous toward Christ, the saints, or the Christian religion by speaking out of hatred and contempt for Christian truth. The Church should neither ignore nor tolerate these acts, as we have taught in chapters 15 and 16, but should take up arms against them. If, however, pagans speak blasphemously about the Christian religion not out of contempt and hatred of religion but out of anger toward Christians by whom they have been maltreated and injured, that is, with lawful cause, such persons are not blasphemous. Such is the case of the Indians in the province of Jalisco, where, in order to ridicule priests and Christians, the Indians would lift a little cake over their heads with both hands in imitation of the practice of Christian priests, who immediately after consecrating the body of Our Lord Jesus Christ show it to the people. For they do not know what they are doing, nor do they know that what the Christian priests show for adoration is the body of Christ. Nor do they do these things from contempt but from a desire for revenge, when they burlesque the acts of those whom they have found by experience to be totally cruel ene-

2. [*Summa Theologiae*], III, q. 8, a. 3, ad 1um.

mies, for they think that the religion of these very evil men reflects their way of life. It is scarcely believable how much pitiable harm they have received from these men, how much savage tyranny they have endured. Indeed, even if the word of God had been announced and preached to them, they would not be called blasphemous if they spoke about the Christian religion in an impious way. If two or three pious men preach the word of God to them, a thousand men of the same faith, with whom the preachers are on good terms, slander the Christian religion by their evil lives, their monstrosities, their savagery, and their pride. These latter must be called the truly blasphemous, according to what Paul says: "It is your fault that the name of God is blasphemed among the pagans."[3] Again, Peter says: "The way of Truth will be brought into disrepute on their account."[4]

Our adversaries object that idolatry is a blasphemy against God, according to what is said by Saint Thomas,[5] and therefore that idolaters can be warred against according to what Saint Thomas writes.[6] In fact, however, Saint Thomas does not mean that blasphemy is absolutely a just cause for war against idolaters, since it has already been proved that even if idolatry may be blasphemy, yet the punishment of idolaters is not the Church's business. Saint Thomas is speaking only of those who, knowingly and maliciously and by a determined plan, are blasphemous toward Christ and obstruct the preaching of the gospel, so that no one will embrace the faith. I shall add Saint Thomas's words in the above-mentioned eighth article: "If they can, the faithful must compel [unbelievers] not to hinder the faith by blasphemies, evil persuasions, or even open persecutions." In his commentaries, Cajetan explains what sort of blasphemy this is:

Make a diligent investigation about the just cause of war against unbelievers and the ways of compelling them not to hinder the faith in any of the three ways, namely, by blasphemies, saying evil things about Jesus Christ, his saints, or his Church; or by using persuasions or persecutions, leading our people into unbelief.

3. Romans 2 [24].
4. 2 Peter 2 [2].
5. [*Summa Theologiae*], II–II, a. 94, a. 3.
6. [*Summa Theologiae*], II–II, q. 10, a. 8.

It is clear, then, that the blasphemy of which Saint Thomas is speaking in that section, that is, that which deserves punishment by war, is not idolatry but contemptuous words maliciously directed against Christ, our Lord, with the intention that the Catholic faith might not be received. However, war cannot be declared against them for blasphemy against God resulting from sacrilegious rites and ceremonies connected with following a law or a sect of unbelievers, even if they are idolaters (this is, in fact, blasphemy), as Saint Thomas clearly states.[7]

This is proved very clearly. By observing and practicing the ceremonies of the law of Moses in our times, the Jews undoubtedly commit blasphemy against God. The same is true of the Saracens, together with those who observe the law of the most vile Mohammed. Both hate the law of Christ and the whole Catholic religion as though [the latter] were accursed and evil, and this is evident to the Catholic Church. Yet the Church does not declare war on them or punish them, even when they are its subjects. Therefore the Church does not punish every blasphemy of unbelievers against God. Surely, however, the case would be otherwise if, to insult our religion, the Jews or Saracens crucified a man or committed a similar crime, since this would be a blasphemy that would hinder the spread of the faith. Crimes such as these must be punished by war, as the most learned theologian Francisco Vitoria teaches in a most scholarly way.[8]

The error of our adversaries is sufficiently refuted in the foregoing.

7. Ibid., q. 94, a. 3.
8. *Lucubrationes,* II–II, q. 10, a. 8.

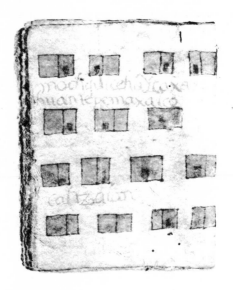

Chapter Twenty-Five

4
war

The fourth case in which the Church can punish pagans by war or some other means occurs when they hinder the spread of the faith deliberately rather than accidentally and when by word or deed they attack those who wish to embrace it or have already embraced it, or, certainly, when they try to do so by entreaties and bribes. For by the natural law the Church can bring force to bear on this type of injury, which obstructs the spread of the faith and which is inflicted upon the members of the Church, as well as suppress them by means of Christian rulers with all the panoply of war. This kind of evil cannot be met with any other remedy,[1] nor is it in accord with right and equity for the Church to allow persons who have been initiated into the Christian mysteries to shrink from their Christian profession because of bribes, flattery, or threats.

The proof of this is that all princes or rulers of a nation are obliged to protect their subjects from every harm and to take up arms against

1. As is clear from many sections of Gratian, c. 23, q. 8

their oppressors.[2] Therefore since the Pope is the ruler and head of the Catholic Church, he is obliged to protect all Christians, no matter where they live, as well as defend them against all harm, no matter under which rulers they may be living, so that they may not fall away under oppression. Pope Leo indicates this when he says: "We never let our subjects be oppressed by anyone but, if there is any need, we personally come to their defense, since in all cases we should be the avengers and foremost helpers of our flock."[3] Again, when the efforts of unbelievers cause Christians to deny the worship of Christ, they take away what has already been planted in the body of Christ and the Christian Church, and by such a denial the sacred name of Christ is blasphemed. The Pope and any Christian ruler whatsoever are obliged to avenge an injury of this kind. Indeed, every private citizen is obliged at least to hinder it, since whatever is done against divine religion does harm to everyone.[4]

Moreover, when pagans prevent those who want to accept the Christian faith from accepting it, they do great harm to the Catholic Church. This is evident, first, because the desire to embrace the Christian faith, like other virtuous deeds, is just and is not prejudicial to anyone, for if pagan rulers accept the word of God they do not lose their kingdoms or jurisdiction. Rather, their hold is made firmer, and is strengthened by a greater legitimacy, and their cities, instructed in knowledge of the truth and good morals, will flourish to the highest degree with the support of the holy sacraments that are administered in them. And so those who punish this desire or prevent it from being carried out hurt both the Christian Church and those who have this desire, in violation of natural justice. Therefore the Church can punish them.

The second proof is that the Pope has been divinely entrusted with the care of the whole world, in which both believers and unbelievers live. This is what Chrysostom teaches: "For when Christ would communicate great things to Peter, he would entrust the care of the world to him."[5] Further, Saint Bernard says:

2. See the Digests, 4, 3, 31; Decretals, 2, 10, 2; 2, 13, 1; 2, 28, 55; Gratian, c. 2, C. 23, q. 2
3. In c. 18, C. 23, q. 8.
4. See the Codex, 1, 5, 4.
5. Homily on John, 87.

Your privilege, then, remains unshaken for you, as regards both the keys which have been given [to you] and the sheep which have been entrusted. Nevertheless, learn something which bolsters one of your prerogatives. The disciples were sailing about [on the Sea of Galilee] and the Lord appeared on the beach. When Peter learned that it was the Lord, he "threw himself into the sea" and so came to him, while the other disciples came in the boat (John 21:1–8). What is that if not a sign of Peter's singular power and pontificate, by which we have received one boat to guide, as have the rest, but he [Peter] received the world for his rule?[6]

Pope Saint Leo also exalts Peter's stature, and says "One Peter is chosen to be in charge of the calling of all nations and of all the Apostles and all parts of the Church."[7] Since, then, the peoples of the whole world have been entrusted to Peter and his successors, and some of them have become actual subjects of the Church but others habitual and potential subjects, and since it is the Roman Pontiff's concern to draw peoples to the knowledge of the truth, it is clear that a war by means of which the Church uses force on unbelievers who hinder the spread of the faith and prevent men from accepting the Christian religion is just. It follows from this that any pagan ruler can be forced by war to let the gospel be preached in his jurisdiction, not because of the sin committed by those who prevent the preaching of the gospel (as the canonists claim, for the Church does not punish their crimes, as has been made clear) but because, without lawful cause, they maliciously and, as we have said, by their own efforts obstruct the spread of the truth of the gospel, which Christ commanded be proclaimed to all nations. They also hinder the good of the souls of those persons who, once they have heard the word of God, will accept it. Therefore the Church, to which belongs the care of peoples throughout the world as regards the preaching of the truth, can justly wage war upon those who prevent the gospel from being preached within their jurisdiction. And this is the interpretation of what the doctors write on this matter, especially Cajetan in his commentary, where he states that the Church can justly wage war on unbelievers who kill preachers because, in forbidding the preaching of the gospel, they resist the spread and propagation of the faith.[8]

6. *De Consideratione Libri Quinque ad Eugenium Tertium,* Book 2.
7. *De Regulationibus Sermo 3.*
8. On the [*Summa Theologiae*], II–II, q. 10, a. 8.

It should be remembered, however, that this is true only when the pagans, knowing what is preached to them, kill the preachers out of the malice and hatred they continually bear toward that faith. Pagans of this sort are the Turks and Moors who are not ignorant of Christian teachings. On the other hand, they may kill them not knowingly, nor maliciously and deliberately as preachers of the gospel, but out of hatred toward a Christian nation from which they have perhaps received great injuries, [inflicted] with inhuman and fierce violence, in the same way that the Indians have killed some innocent preachers, not just because they were preachers but because they had suffered harm to themselves and all their Indian nations from the Spanish people—injuries that have not been heard of for centuries. Not only were their cities devastated but also their kingdoms and very widespread regions, along with the slaughter of an innumerable and undreamt of multitude of human beings. Kings and rulers were despoiled of their high ranks, dominions, and royal honors. Their peoples were enslaved.

When, therefore, such rulers fail to receive preachers, or even kill them cruelly, they prevent the preaching of the gospel accidentally and unintentionally, rather than deliberately. Now an accidental cause is outside the law, and cases must be judged not on the basis of what is accidental but on the basis of what is deliberate.[9] But what is unintentional does not deserve a physical or severe penalty. Therefore when the Indians, afflicted with so many frightful evils, see that the preachers are men of the same nation and speech, white and bearded, and that they mingle and are on familiar terms with their enemies the Spaniards, they will necessarily be ignorant of which ones are the servants of God and, again, which ones are the ministers and instruments of Satan. Moreover, will they not be unaware that the preachers are tonsured, in contrast with the rest of the Spaniards with whom they wage a very just war? What do we want the Indians to do? Whenever they first hear preachers warning them to acknowledge the true God and claiming that they do not belong to the company of those who harm them, should they immediately trust them? They have been summoned a thousand times to Spanish camps under safe conduct and have been killed by treacherous men, and thus have paid the penalty for their gullibility. Has an Indian ever received a benefit from a Spaniard?

9. See Aristotle's *Physics,* Book 2, and *Method,* Book 4.

Therefore it surpasses all stupidity, and smacks of dire ignorance, to say that the Indians can be warred against if they kill two hundred thousand preachers, and even if they were to kill the Apostle Paul and all the other gospel-preaching followers of Christ. For such a war would smack of untamed barbarism and a fierceness greater than that of the Scythians, and it would have to be called the devil's war rather than a Christian war. Furthermore, in warring against the Spaniards the Indians would wage it in such a way that they would deserve to be praised most eloquently by all skillful philosophers.

Indeed, I would dare to say that to wage war against Indian rulers could not be just at the very outset—rather, it would be unjust—if, from fear of losing their property, they refuse to receive preachers who are accompanied by fierce and barbarous men, even in territories or provinces where the unbridled tyranny of Christians had not yet become known. For he [the ruler] would not be rash in fearing for the safety of his kingdom if he were to receive a group of foreigners, whether or not the latter are fearsome in their appearance. For every ruler must look after the security of his kingdom, as I have taught elsewhere at greater length.

So, Christians, stop deluding yourselves with these pretenses. Don't join insatiable greed to the spirit of the devil by shedding the blood of a completely innocent people. Let those keep silent who are swollen with foolish learning and who encourage tyrants to persecute innocent sheep by claiming that the latter kill the preachers of the faith. This is not true (in the proper sense of the term); rather, they kill those who give them reason for killing. For they do not even know what the gospel is or what a preacher is. They kill them not because they are preachers but because they are Spaniards, of the same nation and in the company of those fierce men who are their enemies. Christ will certainly give a crown to those most religious men. But the Spaniards themselves will be accused of having killed them by their crimes, for they have brought the gospel into ill repute and have prevented the spread of the faith. In my judgment, the Indians are not guilty in any way in the sight of the Supreme Judge, since they fall into that crime ignorant and aroused, that is, by so many evils.

It should also be noted that, for the same reason, war against unbelievers can be just when only the rulers or kings maliciously prevent the spread or preaching of the gospel. But if both the rulers and all their peoples, precisely out of love for and devotion to their religion, refuse to hear or admit Christian preachers, then, under no circumstances, can they be forced by war to let them come in. This is contrary to God's words, since Christ said "Go . . . and make disciples of all nations,"[10] that is, those who want to listen. Do not force those who do not want to listen. You will not find any statement, either in the Sacred Scriptures or in the writings of the holy doctors, and you will not produce any argument on the basis of which we could, without blame, compel unbelievers who do not want to hear the teaching of Christ to do so. Consequently, in so doing we would offend Christ. The fruit of his precious death would be made useless. For those unbelievers especially, who have never had the teaching of the truth, would be led by any good reason to the veneration, the love, and, more, the defense of their gods and the rites of their ancient religion.

Moreover, in order to take measures for the peace, freedom, and security of the whole present and future civil status of their republic they would not want to admit foreign and strange peoples into their kingdoms or territories, nor would they want to receive preachers of the faith or listen to their teaching, even in zeal for their own religion, if for this reason alone they would be assailed by war, which is, as it were, an ocean of all evils, by which, after they have been conquered and many of them killed, the rest would be beset with so many irreparable misfortunes, along with sorrows, sighs, tears, and bitterness. Granted that once they have been forced in this way they will hear the gospel, with what disposition, I ask, will they listen to the truth of the gospel? How will they understand it? With what sort of will would they love it? How will they believe the teachings about Christian gentleness and truth?

On the contrary, I shall speak boldly and do not flinch to state openly that if preachers are accompanied by the clatter of arms when they go forth to announce the gospel to any people, by that very fact they are unworthy to have their words believed. For what does the gospel have to do with firearms? What does the herald of the gospel have to do with armed thieves? Instead, those who would believe such preachers would be very inconstant and foolish rather than clever, and those who spurn their words could, to some extent, be excused in God's

10. Matthew 28 [19].

sight. Nor would they be obliged to believe the apostles or even Christ himself, our redeemer, if they preached the gospel in this way. Miracles build up faith in Christ's words, and unless visible or invisible miracles are performed, men would not be guilty of sin if they did not believe. For no one is obligated to what exceeds his powers but only to what is possible for him. Now belief is beyond man's natural power. Therefore it results from a gift of God, in keeping with what the Apostle says: "It is by grace that you have been saved, through faith; not by anything of your own, but by a gift from God." "He has given you the privilege not only of believing in Christ, but of suffering for him as well."[11] So man is obliged to believe insofar as God helps him to believe. God helps someone to believe in three ways, namely, by hidden inspiration, by teaching, or by miracles. We interpret all three as being miracles from God. If they were lacking, the whole world would be excused if it did not believe. This is what the Savior teaches: "If I had not come, if I had not spoken to them, they would have been blameless,"[12] that is, of unbelief, according to Augustine. Again: "If I had not performed such works among them as no one else has ever done, they would be blameless."[13] In the eighth chapter of Deuteronomy we read that the Lord God had commanded the Jews not to believe anyone claiming to be sent by God unless he either produced signs or foretold future events in the name of the Lord.[14]

Since, therefore, an army of soldiers, especially if unexpected, is by its very nature and in its first appearance frightening to all men, even if its members do not put their hands to the warlike acts they are accustomed to perpetrate (such as murder, plunder, theft, and other savage deeds, which are so opposed to natural reason, peace, tranquillity, humility, Christian gentleness, meekness, Christ's teaching and miracles), it follows that if the Apostles had gone forth in the company of an army of soldiers to terrorize the gentiles into listening to the gospel, especially if these men committed acts of war—rather, if Christ himself had been accompanied in such a way as he went out to preach, and unless he had helped his listeners by miracles or internal inspiration

11. Ephesians 2 [8]. Philippians 1 [29].
12. John 15 [22].
13. John 15 [24].
14. Saint Thomas writes on this point in his second *Quodlibetale*, a. 6, and Abulensis, *In Matthaeum Commentarium*, chap. 10, q. 21.

—undoubtedly their words would not have been believed nor would unbelievers be held to believe their teaching. Rather, they would reasonably have started a very just war, as against public enemies.

All these points are evident from Christ's teaching and from natural reason. They are equally evident from many of the truths proved above.

Chapter Twenty-Six

What has been said above is not contradicted in any way by the fact that the Church has the obligation of preaching the gospel to all nations and that, for this reason, we should be able to compel them to listen to the truth of the gospel. I readily grant that the Church is obliged to preach the gospel, as is said in the last chapters of Matthew and Mark "Go out to the whole world; proclaim the Good News [gospel] to all creation"; "Go . . . make disciples of all nations, etc."; "It is a duty which has been laid on me. I should be punished if I did not preach it."[1] These words are commands and indicate necessity.[2] However, it does not

1. [Mark 16:15. Matthew 28:19]. 1 Corinthians 9[16].
2. As in Gratian, c. 3, at the end, C. 14, q. 1.

follow from this that we can force unbelievers to hear the gospel. This is proved in four ways.

The first is that since unbelievers cannot be forced to receive the faith, with much less reason can they be forced to hear the words of the gospel, which are the way to faith. Indeed, if I cannot be forced to a religion, neither can I be forced to hear the dogmas and traditions of a religion. Nor is it valid to say "Faith comes from what is preached, and what is preached comes from the word of Christ."[3] For just as unbelievers are not forced to religion when they cannot be forced to it without warfare, which brings with it all kinds of evil and results in hatred of our religion rather than an argument for the Catholic faith, so also we cannot force unbelievers who live in their own kingdoms to listen to the gospel, except by means of countless killings, arson, and destruction of cities. Thus it would be sacrilegious and stupid to wage war on unbelievers in order that they may hear the gospel, because out of this would arise hatred of our religion instead of the advance of the faith.

The second argument is that since the Church is always vigilant and solicitous about conditions favorable to the Christian flock and never forces unbelievers who are its subjects in law and fact (for example, such subjects of Christian rulers as the Jews and Saracens) to hear the word of God, the conclusion is inescapable that unbelievers who are not subject either in law or in fact must not be forced to hear the word of God.

The third argument is the fact that Christ commanded only that the gospel be preached throughout the world. So wherever the gospel is preached, Christ's command is considered to have been carried out, and those who do not want to listen to the preachers bring guilt on themselves and will give an accounting to God. In this case, one can apply the advice of the wise man: "Where no one listens, do not pour out words."[4]

The fourth argument is that it is quite clear from the instructions with which Christ first sent his disciples to preach the gospel what should be done when unbelievers do not want to hear the gospel. For we read:

3. Romans 10[17].
4. Ecclesiasticus 32[6].

As you enter his house, salute it, and if the house deserves it, let your peace descend upon it; if it does not, let your peace come back to you. And if anyone does not welcome you or listen to what you have to say, as you walk out of the house or town shake the dust from your feet. I tell you solemnly, on the day of judgment, it will not go as hard with the land of Sodom and Gomorrah as with that town.[5]

Note that Christ did not teach that those who refuse to hear the gospel must be forced or punished. Rather, he will reserve their punishment to himself on the day of judgment, just as he also reserves the punishment of those who refuse to believe.

Then he began to reproach the towns in which most of his miracles had been worked, because they refused to repent. "Alas for you, Chorazin! Alas for you, Bethsaida! For if the miracles done in you had been done in Tyre and Sidon, they would have repented long ago in sackcloth and ashes. And still, I tell you that it will not go as hard on judgment day with Tyre and Sidon as with you. And as for you, Capernaum, [did you want to be exalted as high as heaven? You shall be thrown down to hell]. For if the miracles [done in you] had been done in Sodom, [it would be standing yet]. And still, I tell you that it will not go as hard with the land of Sodom on judgment day as with you."[6]

And "He who does not believe will be condemned."[7]

Therefore, just as by punishing unbelievers who refuse to accept the gospel the Church would be usurping a right the Lord reserves for himself, so also would it be called a usurper if it forced unbelievers to listen to the gospel. For the reason is the same in each case, that is, that Christ has reserved the punishment to be inflicted for each offense to himself on the day of judgment. Saint Thomas teaches this expressly. In reference to the passage "shake the dust," he says:

It must be said that the Lord commanded the Apostles to shake the dust from their feet as a testimony against those who do not receive them. For this reason in *Mark* 6:11, it is said, "Shake off the dust from under your feet as a sign against them." And as regards the passage in *Luke* 10:11, that is, "We wipe off the very dust of your town that clings to our feet, and leave it with you," the gloss adds, "as a witness of the earthly labor which they undertook in vain on

5. Matthew 10[12–15], and also Mark 6[10–11] and Luke 9[4–5] and 10[5–12].
6. Matthew 11[20–24]. See also Luke 10[13–15].
7. Mark 16[16].

their behalf." And this testimony is related to divine judgment. So in *Matthew* 10:15, he adds, "I tell you solemnly, on the day of judgment it will not go as hard with the land of Sodom and Gomorrah as with that town." The Lord, then, commands his disciples that if we are not received, we should depart from those whose crimes are reserved for the last judgment. Such are unbelievers of whom it is said (1 *Corinthians* 5:12–13) "of those outside God is the judge," but the judgment of those who are within, that is, the faithful, is entrusted to the Church. As a result, if anyone wishes to be received into the society of the faithful and they unjustly turn him down, he ought not to be reserved for divine judgment but be brought for correction to the judgment of the Church.[8]

Now since Christ's words and actions should be examples for us, I do not know if anything more express or certain can be discovered than the fact that, in instructing his disciples, he taught them that men must not be forced to listen to the gospel. But if this is not enough, note what Christ did and said to strengthen this truth when John and James, when they saw that the inhabitants of a Samaritan town refused to receive Christ, who wanted to enter it, said to him: "Lord, do you want us to call down fire from heaven to burn them up?" But he turned and rebuked them, saying "You do not know what spirit you are made of. The Son of Man came not to destroy men's lives but to save them."[9] It is as if he were saying "It is not a good spirit that tells you this." And it continues: "And they went off to another village." According to the gloss on this passage, the people who at that time did not want to receive Christ were the first to embrace the truth of the gospel by means of the Samaritan woman, as John teaches in beautiful language in his fourth chapter and as Bede and Ambrose note in reference to this passage. Furthermore, we read in the ordinary gloss: "And finally the Samaritans, from whom the fire was held off in this passage, were the quicker to have faith."[10]

Note that Christ taught by word and deed that unbelievers must not be forced to hear the gospel. If they refuse to listen, we must go to other places, until we find friendly listeners. Now by the command of the Eternal Father we are obliged to hear, that is, to imitate Christ: "This is my beloved Son; he enjoys my favor. Listen to him."[11] For he has been

8. *Contra Impugnantes Dei Cultum et Religionem,* cap. 15°, ad 4[um] argumentum.
9. Luke 9[54–56].
10. See also Gratian, c. 26, C. 23, q. 4.
11. Matthew 17[15].

given as "a leader and master of the nations."[12] Nor does it make any difference if someone replies that unbelievers will never become Christians if they cannot be forced to listen to the gospel. To this we say that we must not have more diligent concern for the salvation of men than Christ himself, who shed his precious blood for them: "It is enough for the disciple that he should grow to be like his teacher." "The fully trained disciple will always be like his teacher."[13] Let us imitate the examples and teachings of Christ and the Apostles and let his image shine forth in our conduct. Let us represent our teacher and savior by our deeds, and then those who have been foreordained to go from paganism to eternal life will hasten of their own free will to the sheepfold of Christ, to the city of God, to the place outside of which there is no salvation. If, however, we live like Christians and teach unbelievers in the way mentioned and they neglect to hear us or be converted, it is not our fault. Nor do I think there is any other reason why the Saracens, Turks, and other unbelievers refuse to embrace our faith than that we deny in our practice what we affirm in our speech. It is not impossible, then, for unbelievers to embrace the faith just because it is unlawful to make an armed attack against them in order that they may listen to the gospel. The most effective solution is for them to see the Christian life shine in our conduct. But to advance the gospel by the power of arms is not Christian example but a pretext for stealing the property of others and subjugating their provinces.

The best solution for ending these seditious and diabolical crimes would be to send, from areas that have already been pacified and in which some have embraced our faith, representatives chosen from among the recent converts, in the name of some pious and religious men to whom they are devoted. These representatives would tell the other peoples in that province the purpose for which those pious men, who are vastly different in their conduct from the other, murderous men, come into those provinces, that is, to proclaim to them the way of truth and the worship of the true God. This is how we are destined to bring vast provinces to the faith. Afterward it would be useful to build a fortification in a suitable place where the preachers would have their residence after a garrison of good and honest men had been installed.

12. Isaiah 55[4].
13. Matthew 10[25]. Luke 6[40]. See also John 13[13–16].

Now since these members of the garrison would not seek the death or the wealth of the Indians, the monarch would be obliged to give them an abundant salary.

In this gentle and Christian way, without tumult and the clash of arms, with only the word of Christ and the kindness of our soldiers, and with mildness and good services by which even wild beasts become tame, we have led to the faith some Tecultan provinces that are part of the kingdom of Guatemala. For we sent to them some of the recent converts who both loved and respected us. These men explained to the others that we came to them out of zeal for the house of God and to wake them from the ignorance by which they were bound for so many centuries, not to despoil them of their property and freedom as the other Spaniards were doing. All natural things want to be directed to their end gently. This is how we are moved by the Lord, who "orders all things to good."[14] This great gift was granted to me and my companions by Christ, for we joined so many thousands of souls to their creator and savior by gentleness and kindness, without violence. Thus they were happy that we lived among them, with the result that an area that shortly before was filled with anger and pursued our men with a dangerous hatred because of the tremendous evils they had frequently inflicted upon it, put aside its fierceness; it was made most peaceful. The result is that, under the rule of our most invincible Prince Philip, son of the great Emperor Charles, they are called the provinces of True Peace [*Vera Paz*]. Nor do I doubt that by this work, which he condescended to accomplish through us, the weakest of all, Christ wanted to show the absurdity of the way in which the gospel had previously been preached to those peoples, how far from his teaching were the slaughter and arson committed by most wicked men against those pitiable peoples, and how his gospel was to be preached to them from that time on.

Now whoever, by preaching the gospel in this way, seeks to impose the sweet yoke of Christ on peoples gently, rather than violently, satisfies Christ's command, for he has followed his instruction and example. But whoever preaches the gospel in the other way, that is, with arms, has already strayed from Christ's teaching, nor in his sight can he be excused in any way. For evils must not be committed "as a means to

14. Wisdom 8[1].

good,"[15] nor should impiety be committed under the pretext of piety.[16] Saint Augustine very appropriately says:

Let a man also do what he can for the temporal welfare of men. When, however, it comes to the point that he cannot secure such welfare without sinning, he should then consider that he has no choice, since he has seen that what he may do rightly is beyond his reach.[17]

From the foregoing it is evident that war must not be waged against the Indians under the pretext that they should hear the preaching of Christ's teaching, even if they may have killed preachers, since they do not kill the preachers as preachers or Christians as Christians, but as their most cruel public enemies, in order that they may not be oppressed or murdered by them. Therefore let those who, under the pretext of spreading the faith, invade, steal, and keep the possessions of others by force of arms—let them fear God, who punishes perverse endeavors.

15. Romans 3[8].
16. See Gratian, c. 27, C. 1, q. 1, and the Decretals, 5, 3, 42.
17. *De Mendacio,* cited in Gratian, c. 15, C. 22, q. 2.

Chapter Twenty-Seven

In agreement with what has just been said is a point that we have already established: no one can be forced to give away a good in the lack of a prior promise to do so. In human law, in the same way, a benefit is not conferred on a person against his will.[1]

As for unbelieving rulers who maliciously obstruct the spread of the gospel, the fact that the Church can wage war against them is clearly proved by the following argument. Since Christ is the Lord and King of every creature that lives in every part of the world, to prevent men from acknowledging and worshiping him as the source of every good by accepting the Catholic faith is an injury to Christ that the Church must not tolerate. For this sin is not like one they commit between themselves and God. In fact, it directly deprives God of the honor due him and does direct injury to him. It is true and formal blasphemy, committed with malice against the Christian religion. For this reason, as we have taught, what is done against the divine majesty becomes an injury to all. For it is evident from the arguments used above that the Church can justifiably wage war only against those unbelievers who would maliciously prevent the spread of the faith, either by trying to make those who had already received it abandon it or by placing obstacles in the way of those who, in all probability, would come to believe.

Albertus Pius, the Count of Carpi, speaks about [such unbelievers] when, in writing against Erasmus, he asserts and tries to prove that a war against the Turks is lawful, either to regain the realms stolen from Christian rule or because the Turks prevent or would try to prevent the spread of the faith. This is what Pius says:

Therefore those who oppose Christ the Lord and work against his glory by preventing the spread of the gospel must surely be deprived of all power, since they abuse it against the dignity and grandeur of the Supreme Ruler. For while they are governing, the peoples subject to their tyranny are not allowed to accept the law of the gospel nor is the preaching of it permitted. Therefore, to promulgate this law and increase Christ's glory, it is lawful and advantageous, in keeping with the circumstances of time and place, to invade them and to

1. Digests, 50, 17, 69; 39, 5, 19, #2. Codex, 2, 3, 29.

subject them to the sweet yoke of Christ, even though they do not provoke us in any way or gain control of our territories which we may at any time have possessed. For they belong to the law of Christ, which Christ's servants can justly vindicate. So, provided that the war is undertaken for this purpose, that is, of spreading the gospel and increasing Christ's glory, it will be holy and just.

Anyone who reads the words "even though they do not provoke us in any way" and "for they belong to the law of Christ" will perhaps think that Pius teaches that war against unbelievers, even though they are at peace, is lawful even if there is no cause other than the spread of the gospel and the increase of Christ's glory. But this is not so, because Albertus is speaking of the case in which unbelievers maliciously obstruct the preaching and spread of the gospel, as is evident in the words "therefore those who oppose Christ the Lord and work against his glory by preventing the spread of the gospel." He says the same thing in reference to the Turks and Moors, who are not ignorant of our dogmas and who very effectively block the spread of our religion. The point is also proved by his words when he deals with the fact that waging war is lawful even if there is no other cause than the increase of Christ's glory, so that "in keeping with the circumstances of time and place," "it is lawful and advantageous," that is, to attack unbelievers who resist the spread of the faith and subjection to Christ's sweet yoke. Hence everything he deals with in this section presupposes malicious resistance and hindrances of unbelievers to the spread of the faith—not of unbelievers in the absolute sense of the term but unbelievers like the Saracens and Turks, who obviously bear an age-old hatred for the name of Christ. When he says, then, "it is lawful and advantageous, in keeping with the circumstances of time and place," [he does not mean] that it is always lawful to wage war solely for the purpose of spreading the faith but [only] when unbelievers maliciously prevent the spread of the gospel and when they can be subjected to Christ's sweet yoke without scandal to and hatred of our religion and blasphemies against Christ. Otherwise I do not know how it would contribute to Christ's glory and the growth of religion, or how, if the end is achieved by the sword, the souls of such unbelievers would attain salvation. Rather, it seems to me that by such means the blood of Christ is made useless, and therefore that such a step is not only not advantageous but unlawful.

The fifth case in which the Church can actualize the potential jurisdiction it has over unbelievers is when unbelievers break into our provinces or harass our shores with the accouterments of war, either generally, as in the case of the Turks who daily harass, attack, and afflict Christian lands with their terrible armies, or particularly, [as in the case of rather frequent sorties] by the Saracens. And the justification for the Church is clear. By the law of nature, the arms of all peoples throughout the world are raised against their public enemies. So, to crush the insolence of such enemies, we take them captive, and by inflicting equal destruction we teach them to fear our men and to avoid injuring us, so that they pay for the injuries they have inflicted upon us. Acts of this kind are called "natural defense" and are included under this maxim of the natural law: "It is lawful to repel force with force."[2]

Saint Thomas treats these last three cases (numbers three, four, and five) in these words:

Unbelievers . . . should be compelled by the faithful, if it is possible to do so, so that they do not hinder the faith by their blasphemies or by their evil persuasions or even by their open persecutions. It is for this reason that Christ's faithful often wage war with unbelievers . . . in order to force them not to hinder the faith of Christ.[3]

Cajetan and Carpi interpret these causes together in the passage cited above, although Erasmus never even dreamed of what Carpi cites against him. In fact [Erasmus] very explicitly teaches the Catholic opinion in his commentary on the psalm "Give to the Lord, you sons of God,"[4] as well as in many other passages in his writings. Possibly Carpi was seeking glory by attacking Erasmus, to whom our Sepúlveda, in putting together his little book, did not devote much attention, contrary to rumor.

The reason for Saint Thomas's teaching is that in those three cases the pagans are brought within our competence by reason of their crime and we can punish them, although they may not otherwise be subject

2. Digests, 1, 1, 3. Decretals, 2, 13, 12. Liber Sextus, 5, 11, 6, and other passages of both laws.
3. [*Summa Theologiae*], II–II, q. 10, a. 8c.
4. [Psalm 28].

to us.[5] And concerning unbelievers of this type who offend us, Baldus says that all unbelievers can be punished by temporal judges according to the territory of the person pronouncing the judgment.[6] Nor are they distinguished according to domicile, according to book 3 [of the Digests], where it is said that the head of a province sometimes has power even against foreigners if they commit some evil, etc.[7]

5. See the Decretals, 2, 2, last chapter [chap. 20]; 5, 17, 1. And the Novellae, 69, c. 1. And in many other laws where it is said that by reason of crime someone may be brought under the jurisdiction of another who ordinarily would not be his judge. The reason is that there is no other way of remedying the situation, and besides, natural reason demands it, that is, when there is no superior to whom recourse can be had.
6. *Proemium in Libros Decretalium.*
7. Digests, 1, 18.

Chapter Twenty-Eight

There is another case, let it be the sixth, in addition to the five cases already cited and known to everyone. And this is indeed a new case, not heard of until our times, although I shall not say that it was unthought of, in which the Church can exercise actual coercive jurisdiction over any unbelievers; that is, if they are found to oppress and injure any innocent persons or to kill them in order to sacrifice them to their gods or in order to commit cannibalism. According to reports, some tribes in the Indian world do this. This is the third argument or cause that Sepúlveda introduces in order to justify those expeditions of his. His error in this, too, will be eliminated by the following explanations.

The first consideration in this explanation is not that human sacrifice is against the natural law (about which I shall speak at greater length later). Nor is it that every person is obliged by the natural law to free those who are oppressed and are put to death unjustly, according to Proverbs: "Rescue those being led away to death,"[1] and that the Church is not exempt from this obligation. [Rather, the reason is] that those innocent persons belong to the Church potentially and therefore are under its protection. For this reason it is the concern of the Church and of the Pope, who is the head of the Church, to take care that they attain eternal salvation. But innocent persons would not attain this if they were killed. Therefore it is the concern of the Church and the Pope, to whom the pastoral care of the whole world has been entrusted by Christ, to prevent the slaughter of such innocent persons lest their souls, whose salvation should be of special concern, should perish forever. It is the business, then, of the Church and the Vicar of Christ, as the universal pastor and curate of the whole world, to exercise jurisdiction authoritatively and in Christ's name in this case, not in order to punish or subjugate unbelievers by reason of their crime, since it is not the business of the Church "to pass judgment on those outside . . . but of those who are outside, God is the judge,"[2] as has been proved at great length, but in order to take the steps necessary to prevent the slaughter of such innocent persons.

Now all the rulers in the world are the equivalent of private persons in regard to this sin and others like it, and they cannot pronounce judgment outside the boundaries of each individual kingdom. For although each private person is obliged by the natural law to set such innocent persons free, this is true only when there is no one else to free them. For this reason, if the Church should entrust the liberation of these persons to some Christian ruler or some other private person, no

1. [24:11].
2. See 1 Corinthians 5 [12–13].

one else could take up arms or do anything to free them. This is proved by three arguments.

The first is that the obligation of liberating innocent persons, like the obligation of other works of piety or charity, has force only in the special case in which there is no other suitable person to free them, just as the obligation of giving alms to a poor person ceases if there is some other person to supply this need. The gloss uses a similar argument in reference to the words of Ecclesiasticus, "Save the oppressed from the hand of the oppressor,"[3] by saying "just as he says that giving to the poor is almsgiving, so he shows that freeing the unjustly oppressed person is mercy."

The second reason is that when the superior who has charge of some state provides or designates someone to effect that [liberation], it would be blameworthy rashness if someone else involved himself in this matter, and especially if the superior had forbidden it. And acts done contrary to the prohibition of a superior have no value in law.[4] It is the duty, then, of the Church or its head, who is superior over the whole world, to provide a suitable remedy for those who suffer such things innocently. If [the Pope] has entrusted or should entrust such a rescue of innocent persons to some Christian ruler, others would be presumptuous in putting their hands to doing anything of this sort.

The third reason is that the obligation to free innocent persons, which nature teaches to all men and Christian charity teaches to the faithful, ends as soon as there is effective opposition to the evils. Hence, since in this case all other rulers are [equivalent to] private persons, there is nothing for them to do. The Church, however, must go further, since it should not only oppose all evils but also, after removing all obstacles, should care unceasingly for the salvation of souls, so that all peoples in the world may attain salvation. Although we admit that it is the business of the Church to prevent such an evil (the unjust death of innocent persons), it nevertheless must do this with such discretion as not to give rise to some greater evil to the other peoples that would be a hindrance to their salvation and would thereby frustrate the fruit and purpose of Christ's passion. For since the salvation of men is the end intended by

3. [4:9].
4. See the Decretals, 2, 14, 8. Gratian, c. 6, D. 32, at the paragraph beginning *Verum*. Also to the point is what we read and note in the Decretals, 1, 6, 44, in the final gloss.

Christ, every remedy that would hinder the accomplishment of such an end would be vain, as the Philosopher says. And for this reason, also, he says that whoever destroys the end destroys every good, as we have explained previously at great length. Moreover, Gregory makes this observation: "Of what use is it when and if their practices of long standing are forbidden to them? It contributes not at all to their conversion to the faith." He is speaking of unbelievers.[5]

Furthermore, since the rescue of this kind of oppressed persons, who are killed as sacrifice or for purposes of cannibalism, cannot be accomplished (if it is a question of areas belonging to the oppressors) unless we take up arms, we should most carefully consider the tumult, sedition, killings, arson, devastation, and furor of the goddess of war that necessarily attend the prevention of this evil. Making its decision with prudence, the Church will at times take up arms, at other times it will overlook [such provocation]. For circumstances sometimes make what is just in itself be unjust.[6] This is sufficiently established by what we read in Genesis in the Septuagint translation: "If you offer rightly, but do not rightly distinguish, have you not sinned? Do not fret."[7] Commenting on these words, Augustine says:

A sacrifice is "rightly offered" when it is offered to the true God to whom we must sacrifice in only one way. And it is "not rightly distinguished" when we do not rightly distinguish the places or seasons or materials of the offering, or the person offering, or the person to whom it is offered or those to whom the offering is distributed as food. "Distinguishing" here is used for discerning either when an offering is made when it ought not . . . or when that is offered which in no place or at any time [ought to be offered] or when a man keeps for himself choicer specimens than those that he offers to God or keeps those that are equally good.[8]

Augustine concludes his explanation with John's words:

"Not to be like Cain, who belonged to the Evil One and killed his brother. And why did he kill him? Because his own works were evil and his brother's good"[9] He thus gives us to understand that God did not respect his offering. . . . For

5. Gratian, c. 3, D. 45.
6. See the Decretals, 5, 12, 6; 2, 20, 37. Digests, 48, 19, 16.
7. [4:7].
8. *De Civitate Dei,* Book 15, chap. 7.
9. 1 John [3:12].

this all do who follow not God's will but their own, that is, who live not with an upright but a crooked heart, and yet offer to God such gifts as they suppose will procure from him that he aid them not by healing but by gratifying their evil passions.

This is in agreement with the remark of a certain wise man, to the effect that "God rewards not nouns but adverbs"; that is, God does not reward the good that is done but the good that is done well. For this reason God did not reward the Jews, who crucified Christ, although Christ's death was a good. "Giving alms to a needy person is a pious work. If, however, I give an alms so that the recipient might betray someone to me in order that I might kill him, the work is evil."[10] And so Dionysius says: "What is good comes from the entire cause, while what is evil comes from particular defects"; that is, if a work is to be perfect, it is required that no circumstance be lacking.[11] Otherwise the good work will become evil. Moreover, after describing virtue in the second book of the *Ethics* the Philosopher says: "A good act occurs in only one way, while evil occurs in many ways"; that is, if a work is to be good, it must be in keeping with right reason, which is unique. But to be evil, it must lack reason, and this can happen in many ways.[12]

10. Gratian, c. 1, C, 15, q. 6.
11. *De Divinis Nominibus,* Book 4.
12. Saint Thomas writes about the cause of this in his [*Summa Theologiae*], I–II, throughout q. 19 and 20.

Chapter Twenty-Eight [*bis*]

[handwritten marginal note: economy : which = less loss of souls? lesser evil]

Therefore when unbelievers are discovered to be committing a crime of this kind (that is, killing infants for sacrifice or cannibalism), they are not always to be attacked by war, although it may be the business of the Church to try to prevent it. But there must be lengthy consideration beforehand, so that in trying to prevent the death of a few innocent persons we should not move against an immense multitude of persons, including the innocent, and destroy whole kingdoms, and implant a hatred for the Christian religion in their souls, so that they will never want to hear the name or teaching of Christ for all eternity. All this is surely contrary to the purpose intended by God and our mother the Church. Instead, war must be avoided and that evil tolerated at least for a while—indeed, in some cases permanently—as will be explained. One must, rather, think out some prudent and Christian argument by which they will cleanse everything by the word of God, or they will refrain from that inhumanity because of warnings, entreaties, or exhortations. For that practice is not that common among all the Indian peoples. And if it is, no great number of persons are killed. Otherwise all would have been totally destroyed before this. And yet we find that all the regions are densely populated.

Now the fact that one must refrain from war, and even tolerate the death of a few innocent persons, is proved by arguments and many authorities.

The first argument is this: According to the rule of right reason when we are confronted by two choices that are evil both as to moral guilt and punishment and we cannot avoid both of them, we ought to choose the lesser evil. For in comparison with the greater evil, the choice of the lesser evil has the quality of a good. This is what the Philosopher teaches.[1] Now the death of a small number of innocent persons is a lesser evil than the eternal damnation of countless numbers of persons killed in the fury of war.

Again, the death of the innocent is better or less evil than the complete destruction of entire kingdoms, cities, and strongholds. For not all of them eat the flesh of the innocent but only the rulers or priests, who do the sacrificing, whereas war brings the destruction of countless innocent persons who do not deserve any such thing. Therefore if those evils cannot be removed in any other way than by waging war, one must refrain from it and evils of this kind must be tolerated.

Furthermore, it is incomparably less disastrous that a few innocent persons die than that Christ's holy name be blasphemed by unbelievers and that the Christian religion be brought into ill repute and be hated by those peoples and by others to whom word of this flies, when they hear how many women, children, and aged people of their nation have been killed by the Christians without cause, as will unavoidably happen, and indeed has happened, in the fury of war. What, I ask, will be the result, if not a perpetual barrier to their salvation, so that there will be no further hope for their conversion? Therefore when there is a question of war over a cause of this kind it is better to let a few innocent persons be oppressed or suffer an unjust death. In fact it would be a very great sin, and against the natural law, to wage war on these unbelievers for this reason. This is proved in the following way.

According to right reason, and therefore the natural law, it is evident that in every case and in every matter that concerns two evils, especially those involving moral guilt, one must choose that which is less harmful or is thought to be less harmful. Therefore to seek to free innocent

---

1. 2 *Ethics,* chap. 9. 3 *Ethics,* chap. 5. 5 *Ethics* [sic], chap. 6. And 2 *Topics.* The same point is proved from the text of cc. 1–2, D. 13. The canonists note this on Gratian, c. 1, D. 14, and c. 7, C. 22, q. 4. And the lawyers on the Digests, 18, 6, 1, next to the last paragraph, and Digests, 50, 17, 20.

persons in the case proposed, within their territories, as has been proposed, would be against the natural law and a sin, which, although not mortal, is very serious indeed. This is evident because the greater the damage sin inflicts, the more serious it is, according to Saint Thomas.[2] And this is true even if that damage is not intended or foreseen, since everything that necessarily follows upon a sin belongs in some way to the very species of the sin. From such a war a countless number of innocent persons of both sexes and all ages will unavoidably perish, and the other evils that have been mentioned will necessarily follow upon that war. Therefore anyone who would try to free those who suffer evils of this type by means of war would commit a very serious mortal sin.

This argument is strengthened by the rules the doctor-jurists give concerning the well-known permission, which happens when evils and even serious sins are permitted so that more serious evils in the state may be avoided or so that the good by which the condition of the state is strengthened should not be obstructed. This is evident in the permission for prostitutes in the cities and for Jewish rites. For this reason, in the case proposed, the ruler or governor of each state ought by right to tolerate an evil from which it is hoped there will arise some advantage to the state or some impending evil will be prevented. If he should fail to do this, he would surely commit a mortal sin.[3]

The second outstanding proof of the conclusion mentioned above is this: We have a negative commandment, that is, "You shall not kill," which must be observed in every case, nor is it lawful to violate it in any place or circumstance. This is found in the twentieth chapter of Exodus.[4] Again, in the twenty-third chapter of this book is another, stricter commandment. God says "See that the man who is innocent and just is not done to death and do not acquit the guilty."[5] The same thing is also in the thirteenth chapter of Daniel.[6] And so Saint Thomas says

---

2. [*Summa Theologiae*], I–II, q. 20, a. 5; q. 73, a. 8c.

3. These things are proved especially in Gratian, c. 25, D. 50; c. 28, D. 50. Decretals, 2, 1, 4, #*De Adulteriis*, 3, 46, 2. Gratian, c. 6, D. 4, and other passages. John Andrea has a very lengthy commentary on permission in his commentary on the rule *Peccatum* in the rules of law, q. 3. And the learned Master Vitoria approves our position here when he speaks about not waging war on the Indians in his second *Relectio de Indis*.

4. [V. 13].

5. [V. 7].

6. [V. 53].

"To hand an innocent man over to suffering and death against his will is wicked and cruel."[7] For God added threats against the transgressors of laws he wished to have observed inviolably and strictly. This is a strong sign that the Lord wants them to be scrupulously observed, according to the words of Exodus in the passage cited above: "You must not be harsh with the widow or with the orphan; if you are harsh with them, they will surely cry out to me, and be sure I shall hear their cry; my anger will flare and I shall kill you with the sword, your own wives will be widows, your own children orphans, etc."[8] Another negative commandment, which we have in God's name, is in the twenty-fourth chapter of Deuteronomy: "Fathers may not be put to death for their sons, nor sons for fathers. Each is to be put to death for his own sin."[9] Now if, for this reason, wars are waged against the Indians, an enormous multitude of blameless and innocent persons who are completely free of those crimes will perish; and the son will bear the iniquity of his father, the father the iniquity of the son. Therefore such a war is wicked, and God will pursue with a mortal hatred those who wage the war, along with those who command it and those who give advice or help to them.

To make clearer what we said (a short while back) about another, stricter commandment, that is, "See that the man who is innocent and just is not done to death,"[10] we must note that there are four kinds of human acts.[11] Some are good in the absolute sense, so that they cannot be evil in any way, for example, to adore, worship, and love God and one's neighbor for the sake of God. Some are evil and foul in the absolute and full sense, so that they cannot be good in any way but are inseparable from their depravity and wickedness, according to the Philosopher throughout the second book of *Ethics*. For this reason they can never be lawful. Adultery, ingratitude, theft, and even lying (which, being evil in itself, must be avoided, as he says in the fourth book of the same work) are of this class. Others, when considered in themselves, connote some depravity and seem to be foul, but once some quality or

7. *In III Sententiarum,* d. 47, a. 3, ad 1um.
8. [22:21–23].
9. [V. 16].
10. Exodus 23 [7].
11. According to Saint Thomas, *Quodlibetale,* 9, a. 15, and Henry of Ghent, *Quodlibetale,* 2, a. 17.

circumstance is added, they are lawful. Of this type is killing or striking a man, both of which, considered in themselves, display disorder and depravity. However, if you add [the circumstance] that a judge hangs a thief, he acts well and brings the grace of Christ to himself. To be sure, certain human acts are indifferent; that is, they are neither evil nor good, for example, going to the marketplace.

The killing of innocent persons, then, belongs to the second type. This can never be lawful by reason of any accidental circumstance, according to Saint Thomas,[12] who concludes that it is not lawful to kill an innocent person under any circumstance, and he says that human law cannot permit that a good man be killed without cause.[13] Moreover, Abulensis, in his commentary on Genesis, says that killing an innocent person is always evil and in no way can it become good.[14] From this it is clear that this commandment is most strict and that by no argument or circumstance can it ever be lawful by human law or by the command of a ruler to kill innocent and harmless persons in order that other innocent persons might be freed from death, especially when the latter, who are killed unjustly, are few, as is true in our case, and those to be killed in order to free these few are many.

12.. [*Summa Theologiae*], II–II, q. 64, at the end of the body of a. 6.
13. [I–II], q. 100, a. 8, ad 3um.
14. Chap. 22, col. 6, at the beginning and the end.

Chapter Twenty-Nine

There is no opposition between the foregoing and the fact that God killed both the guilty and the innocent, fathers and sons, of Sodom and Gomorrah, and likewise that because of the sin of Achor [*sic*], women and small children were consumed by fire,[1] and that the tribe of Benjamin, because of the violence committed by one of its members against the wife of a certain Levite, was entirely destroyed by the other eleven tribes without distinction of age or sex. Nor is there any opposition in the fact that when we wage war it is customary, because of the sin of the ruler or of the nobles of the state, to pillage and kill the innocent and inoffensive, who have neither given cause for war nor taken part in it, either by active participation or by advice. For, according to some teachers, when a city is justly condemned to be destroyed or given over to plunder, we are not obliged to investigate whether there are persons in it who are innocent and undeserving of such treatment, since all citizens are presumed to be enemies of the state or ruler who is waging a just war. And so soldiers do not sin when they plunder a city or kill, nor are they bound to restitution, since the killing of the innocent happens (as they say) accidentally, not by a deliberate plan. But the city is not to be seized just so that they may be killed.

However—to return to the first argument—it is not valid for four reasons, the first being that, as stated above in chapter 15, the examples of the Old Testament are to be admired but not always imitated.

The second reason is that God's judgments are inscrutable. Therefore just because God commanded something to be done, it does not follow that we too can do it. For men throughout the whole world belong to God. Therefore he can freely dispose of them inasmuch as men are his possession and, far more certainly, are their creator's very own. Man, on the contrary, does not have a political right to his property, according to the Philosopher,[2] especially since men, no matter how just they may be, will die and death is their due. "Men only die once."[3]

1. Joshua 7[16–26].
2. *Ethics,* Book 5.

Among men, nevertheless, political justice (that is, the equality of justice) must be observed. Judges, then, do not have men subject to them in such a way that they can punish or kill them contrary to right and law, for a human judge does not have the authority to pass judgment except as the law commands, especially the natural and divine law.

My third answer is that no matter how innocent and guiltless a man may be in the judgment of men, in God's judgment he is guilty by reason of original sin. "No man of himself is innocent before you";[4] that is, there is no one who is not bound to you by his own or another's sin. Therefore God in justice kills or orders killed whom and when he wills, just as he commanded Abraham to sacrifice his son Isaac.[5] Moreover, he visits the sins of parents on their children up to the third and fourth generations and, on the other hand, punishes the sins of children upon their parents, as we read in the thirty-fourth chapter of Exodus. It can never be true to say, then, that God kills or punishes an innocent person either in this life or the life to come. But the case of a ruler, who punishes crimes committed against the state, is quite different, for an innocent person is not guilty of offense either against the state or the ruler. Therefore rulers cannot punish either the father for his son or the son for his father. A man ought not be punished for a crime he did not commit.

My fourth answer is that since God knows the most hidden secrets of the heart[6] and truly understands what is best for each person, he sometimes takes a person because it is better for him to die at that time lest he should fall into sin, according to what we read in Wisdom: "He has been carried off so that evil may not warp his understanding or treachery seduce his soul . . . his soul being pleasing to the Lord, he has taken him quickly from the wickedness around him."[7] Possibly this was also the case of the children in Sodom, as well as the sons of Dathan, Abiron, and the Canaanites. God commanded them to be killed because, if they were to reach adult age, they would perhaps imitate the wickedness of their parents. For sons usually repeat the vices of their parents: "You knew very well they were inherently evil, innately wicked and

3. Hebrews 9[27].
4. According to the words of Exodus 34[7].
5. Genesis 22[1–19].
6. 1 Kings [1 Samuel] 10[17–24].
7. Chap. 8 [sic for 4:11–13].

fixed in their cast of mind; for they were a race accursed from the beginning."[8]

Sometimes, too, the Lord does this so that those who are killed before attaining a mature age might suffer milder penalties, as in the case of the sons of the Sodomites and the Canaanites who had already reached the use of reason. For we ought to consider that the Lord is merciful even toward the unbelievers from whom he takes life in their very first years, since, by escaping this life, they can avoid being more wicked than their parents and so, after death, would have to suffer more bitter punishments. Thus whatever the Lord does concerning the human condition, even by untimely death, must be judged to be right, since he directs and disposes it to a better good or at least to a lesser evil. Because we do not really know the causes of these events, we think that, in the case of some persons, events should have turned out other than they did. Boethius deals with this ignorance in us when he says: "But although you are ignorant of the reasons why things are so arranged, yet because a good governor directs the world, do not doubt that all things are well done."[9]

Since no judge in the world has the power to lead persons to a better state by killing and punishing them, but rather [leads them] to a worse condition, that is, from existence to non-existence, and further, if death catches them in mortal sin, they fall into the worst state of all, and this for all eternity; therefore it is unlawful for any mere man to punish someone physically, that is, by death or some penalty afflicting the body, for the crime of another without committing a most serious mortal sin. The man who kills an innocent person or punishes him physically because of another's offense acts wickedly and commits a great sin, since we cannot think that a judge kills an innocent person in order to improve his state. For what is better than life, since by tears and prayers we can appease the Lord who has been provoked by our crimes? For this reason a law that must not be violated in any way has been imposed on human judges: "The innocent and the just you shall not put to death" and "Fathers may not be put to death for their son, etc." Thus Augustine says "Man is commanded, 'A son is not to be put to death

---

8. Wisdom 12[10–11].
9. *De Consolatione Philosophiae*, Book 4, prose 5.

for his father' (*Deuteronomy* 24 [16]). But God, who can free or destroy even after death (something which it is impossible for man to do), judges by a far more mysterious justice."[10] Saint Thomas says:

> But human judgment cannot imitate God's hidden judgments by which he punishes certain persons in this life without any fault of theirs, since man is unable to grasp the reasons for these judgments, so as to know what is for the good of each individual. And therefore a man should never be condemned without fault of his own to a physical punishment by a human judgment, such as death, mutilation, or flogging.[11]

Innocent teaches the same thing.[12] Furthermore, this is the proper interpretation of the passages Gratian cites[13] where the question is discussed "whether God punishes one man for the sin of another man." These agree with Saint Thomas. From these it is clear how much weight is in what the jurists teach[14] in arguing against Innocent,[15] that everything can be destroyed along with the guilty, on the basis that, as we read in the Old Testament, God sometimes commanded that cities be completely destroyed and that all children and women be slaughtered without distinction. They bring up the destruction of Troy, as if a military feat accomplished by pagans ought to affect Christians. We answer these arguments by saying that God's judgments are always right and holy, whereas the judgments of men are not always just or good, unless it is clear that they agree with natural reason as well as with divine law and equity. Therefore it does not follow that there is necessarily no sin just because rulers or emperors issue or have issued certain laws ordering that innocent persons be punished physically and by flogging for the guilt of other persons. Many laws are unjust and the will of a ruler is sometimes taken to be law.[16] Such a will, however, is quite changeable, and according to the Philosopher[17] the human will is a very

---

10. *On Joshua*, q. 8.
11. [*Summa Theologiae*], II–II, q. 8, throughout the entire last article and especially in his answer to the third [*sic* for second] objection.
12. In his commentary on the Decretals 5, 39, 53.
13. Gratian, c. 11, C. 1, q. 4; c. 12, C. 1, q. 4; and q. 3., D. 24, in general, as well as what is said generally in the gloss on this point and generally in q. 4, D. 1.
14. [*Summa Theologiae*], II–II, q. 64, a. 6, ad 1um; and I–II, q. 108, a. 8, ad 3um. Digests, 48, 19, 16. Decretals, 5, 3, 330.
15. On the Decretals, 1, 31, 19.
16. Institutes, 1, 2, #6.
17. *Politics*, Book 3.

poor criterion, especially since the error of a ruler makes the law according to human laws.[18] Furthermore, we must not imitate what we read in those sections of the Codex where it says:

> But his sons, *that is, the sons of the person committing the crime of lèse majesté,* whose life we spare, particularly by reason of the Emperor's leniency (for they ought to die in the punishment of the father), in whom, that is, the examples of the hereditary crime are feared.[19]

This law is truly unjust in [saying] "they ought to die in the punishment of the father." The words of the jurists, then, must be carefully weighed, distinguished, and interpreted in this sense: if innocent persons must be punished for the crimes of others, this ought to be done by a penalty of deprivation, not a physical penalty, so that the son would become infamous on account of his father's crime by reason of divine or human *lèse majesté* and would suffer deprivation through a loss of goods and by an exclusion from dignities. Other than this, an innocent person ought never be punished by human judgment for another's crimes, and whoever acts to the contrary is guilty of a most serious crime before God.

18. Digests, 33, 10, 5, toward the end.
19. Codex, 9, 8, 5.

Chapter Thirty

This argument—that once a city has been condemned in a just war, all its inhabitants are presumed to be enemies—is false, because a presumption of law should not have effect in impossible situations. For who would presume that children, who are weak in physical strength and deliberation and devoid of all malice, are guilty? Who will surmise that frightened women have given grounds for war, unless it is obvious that they have aided the war by collecting materials?—a very rare case indeed. That these persons are innocent is obvious from the nature of the case. Therefore, in this case, a different presumption has no effect.[1]

Again, the fact that women and children are innocent and thus do not deserve this penalty is proved by the divine law, specifically in the twentieth chapter of Deuteronomy, where the Lord commanded the Hebrews that when they would attack some city for some just cause (such as an injury inflicted on them) they would spare the women and the children but use the force of war against the men. Now God would not have commanded this unless it was obvious, at least in the majority of cases, that persons of that type are not enemies but are innocent. Therefore they are innocent by divine testimony.

The second proof of this point is from Innocent[2] and from doctors in both canon and civil law, who presuppose as obvious fact that there are many innocent persons in every nation. Again, if a war is waged between Christians, in each city there are priests, monks, nuns, and many other persons dedicated to divine worship. There are farmers, workmen, foreigners, merchants, and pilgrims, all of whom the law considers to be innocent, so that they are exempt from all force of war by reason of the decree of the Church.[3] If they are despoiled by soldiers, then the soldiers commit mortal sin and are bound to restitution. Therefore, since in every city there are many innocent persons, it is false to claim that once a city has been condemned, all those within it are presumed to be enemies. Consequently, soldiers must refrain from doing violence to persons who show themselves to be innocent. The high-

1. Gratian, c. 4, D. 8.
2. On the Decretals, 5, 3, 330, and 1, 31, 19.
3. Decretals, 1, 33, 2.

ranking army officers should warn them about this, exactly and seriously, unless they want to share in the same sin and loss.

At the same time, we must recall that confused opinion of the doctors that once a city has been condemned to destruction in a war (a just war, that is), the soldiers are not obliged to investigate who are guilty and who are innocent, because, as they say, killing innocent persons in this case is accidental, that is, unintentional. This opinion is true when, were some circumstance omitted, a victory for that just war could not be won or the enemies would not be subjugated, and it happens that innocent persons are involved in that act or circumstance. Now if such an act or circumstance is not necessary [for victory] but can be omitted, they are undoubtedly guilty of the slaughter of such innocent persons and their other injuries. As an example of the circumstance, imagine an army waging a just war against a city condemned to destruction by a decree of a ruler. The soldiers run through the squares and quarters of the city and kill all those they encounter. If, in this case, they kill a merchant or a pilgrim, they certainly do not commit sin, since, at that time, they are not obliged to investigate whether the person they encounter is a citizen of that city or a foreigner, lest, while they do this, their victory should be endangered and by a switch of events the conquerors should become the conquered. So, in this case, innocent persons are killed accidentally, not directly.

Nevertheless, this interpretation is valid only if those [who are so] encountered are not clearly among those who ought to be spared as innocent, such as a child, a woman, an old person, a defenseless person, or a person who should be respected for his priestly or monastic state. If the soldiers kill these persons, they commit a mortal sin, for here they do violence to them not accidentally but directly and by special intent. Furthermore, it is obvious that they are obliged to presume, by probable signs, that such persons would be innocent, and therefore they should refrain from inflicting evils upon them, for the injuries inflicted in war are not of such slight importance that they can be inflicted in doubt, or easily and indiscriminately, without the fear of offending God and the neighbor. Christian warriors, then, are held to presume, even in the course of conflict, that the persons whom they see bearing such signs are innocent rather than hostile.

Let us take another example. Women, children, the elderly, and other innocent persons have retreated to a fortress. If it is not absolutely necessary to attack that fortress for the favorable outcome of the whole war, surely it would be a most serious sin to destroy that fortress by setting fire to it or by mining it, with the result, necessarily, of great disaster to the innocent persons inside. This would be killing innocent persons directly. However, if such an attack should be necessary, the innocent would be killed accidentally and unintentionally. This is proved by the fact that war is lawful only when it is necessary, and thus in no other way can it be excused, inasmuch as war is a pestilence and an atrocious calamity for the human race.[4] For war in itself is an evil deed, belonging to the third genus of acts mentioned previously in chapter 29; that is, unless it becomes just by reason of circumstance and need. Augustine says: "War should be a matter of necessity, so that God may free from need and preserve in peace."[5] Again, Pope Nicholas says: "If no necessity is present, fighting must be abstained from, not only during Lent but also at all times. If, however, unavoidable provocation arises, the waging of war for the defense of one's self, as well as one's country or the laws of one's forefathers, undoubtedly must not be put off during Lent, etc."[6]

This is in agreement with God's words: "Do all you can to live at peace with everyone."[7] Similarly, Cicero never approves war unless unavoidable necessity is so compelling that it cannot be avoided in any way.[8] Therefore if a fortress filled with harmless persons can be left undestroyed without jeopardizing the victory for the entire war, certainly the ruler who destroys it by means of a bloody attack is guilty before the Supreme Judge, since he kills innocent persons directly and the circumstance that would make the war just is missing, that is, necessity. Therefore both he and his soldiers will give an account to God for all the evils that are done there and will be bound to restitution.

This truth is confirmed by the words of Saint Thomas, who, explaining the words of the Apostle, "We have no power to resist the truth,"[9] says that if the Apostle were to punish the innocent, he would be acting against truth and justice. Now to act against justice is a mortal sin,

4. Gratian, c. 47, C. 23, q. 4. Liber Sextus, 2, 13, 2.
5. Cited in Gratian, c. 3, C. 23, q. 1
6. Gratian, c. 15, C. 23, q. 8.
7. Romans 12 [18].
8. *Officiorum*, Book 1.
9. 2 Corinthians 13[8].

according to Saint Thomas,[10] and those who steal in the course of acts of this type also commit a mortal sin, and are bound to restitution. In order to punish a few guilty persons, then, one must not kill a few— much less many—innocent persons, since evils must not be committed so that good may come from them.[11] Nor does God want these evils to be rewarded by such a gain, according to Augustine.[12] And in another place he says: "For God does not want such a loss to be compensated by such a gain; without doubt this compensation is admitted with the greatest of dangers."[13] The gloss on this passage is notable and agrees with Saint Thomas, when he says that no one may sin venially so that another may not sin mortally.[14] Augustine also asserts this in these words: "Let a man also do what he can for the temporal welfare of men. When, however, he reaches the point where he cannot take care of it without sinning, he should then consider that he does not have anything more to do in this regard."[15] Indeed, Saint Thomas says that a man should prefer death and cruel torture to committing even venial sin.[16]

From this arises the rule that when evil and good are so conjoined that, from the good I wish to do, evil would necessarily or almost always result, if the evil is greater than the good I seek to accomplish, the good [action] must always be omitted lest the evil should result. The reason for this is that if a person who is endowed with the greatest virtues is guilty of even the least mortal sin, he will be damned for all eternity. Saints Thomas and Augustine also understand this rule in reference to the case in which venial sin results. In the same way, this rule must be interpreted not only in reference to ourselves but also when we want to do good for someone else. We should be careful that no evil happen to him, for we must be watchful whether a greater evil may result from the good we seek to do for him than from that [evil] which we seek to avoid. And so, in his *Third Quodlibetale* (a. 11, ad 5um), Saint Thomas says: "So some good must be forgone only because of a consequent evil,

10. [*Summa Theologiae*], II–II, q. 59, a. 4
11. See Romans 3[8].
12. Commentary on psalm 146, cited in Gratian, c. 1, C. 33, q. 5.
13. Gratian, c. 1, D. 14.
14. [*Summa Theologiae*], II–II, q. 26, a. 4c, and ad 2um; q. 43 [a. 7, ad 5um].
15. Quoted in Gratian, c. 15, C. 22, q. 2. See also cc. 1, 14, 16. Also the Decretals, 3, 50, 3 and 5, 19, 4.
16. [*Summa Theologiae*], II–II, q. 110, a. 3, ad 3um, and in other places.

since the consequent evil would be much greater than the good, as would happen rather frequently."[17]

17. Abulensis, *Super Matthaeum,* c. 23, q. 19.

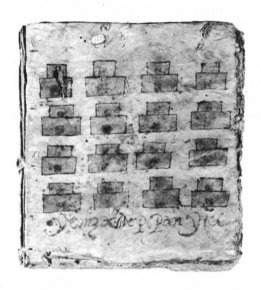

Chapter Thirty-One

Now, in order that rulers and governors of states may weigh cases of this type more accurately, I shall prove by other arguments that it is not lawful to kill or inflict harm on a large or on even a small number of innocent persons in order that a few innocent persons may be rescued from death, and that the ruler or governor who does or permits [such things] commits a mortal sin and is bound to restitution.

In the first place, this is proved to be a sin because it is the direct killing of an innocent person. Therefore it is a mortal sin. In this case, moreover, many persons who do not deserve such treatment are killed or are afflicted with harm, as is evident from what has been said. Therefore such a ruler commits a mortal sin.

The second argument is that this deed is wicked and displeasing in God's eyes, and no different at all, in this respect, from the sacrifice of Cain or the vow of Jephthah, who sacrificed his daughter.[1] Augustine affirms that [Jephthan] acted violently and cruelly. A similar act was committed by Agamemnon, who, because of a vow, sacrificed his daughter Iphigenia to Diana. Tullius [Cicero] relates and censures this deed in Book 3 of his *Offices*.

The third argument is that a particular deed is wicked and imprudent when it is offered to God without the due circumstances in a place and time and by acts that are not pleasing to God. For God does not delight in the suffering of the innocent and harmless. To kill them is a greater sin than that which pagans commit in sacrificing innocent persons. These men sacrifice thirty or a hundred or a thousand persons every year out of probable ignorance (as I shall explain later), whereas the soldiers waging war for this reason in one day kill ten thousand innocent persons, with great loss to their own souls. Inasmuch as the soldiers have been instructed in Christ's teaching, they ought to be aware that innocent persons must be spared. Hence they do not rightly distinguish, as Augustine said in reference to Cain. Therefore they are guilty before God of a most serious crime, and worthy of eternal damnation.

As regards restitution, the common teaching of the doctor [*sic*] is that booty seized from innocent persons who are in no way to blame for the war must of necessity be restored. Saint Thomas gives the reason for this, that a lawful war results from the guilt of those against whom it is waged.[2] But innocent and guiltless persons have deserved nothing like this, and so war against them has not been lawful. However, what is seized in an unjust war must of necessity be restored. Saint Thomas comments on this in the same section.[3] Furthermore, speaking specifically about innocent persons who suffer harm in an accidental way, as in the example given previously, Raymond [of Péñafort] teaches the following: "I believe that subjects who refuse to contribute advice and help or encouragement to their lord in an unlawful war must not be

---

1. Judges 11 [30–39].
2. [*Summa Theologiae*], II–II, q. 40, a. 1.
3. [*Summa Theologiae*], q. 66, a. 8c and ad 1ᵘᵐ. In addition, this point is proved in the Decretals, 2, 24, 13, as well as by the doctors on this section.

despoiled or punished in any way whatsoever. Rather, punishment ought to bind the authors [of the war] themselves, and ought not be prolonged further than the extent of the sin."[4] Ulrich, a disciple of Albert the Great, also teaches this in his *Summa,*[5] and in chapter 9 he adds: "The third condition is that the subjects must not be harmed even if, in an unjust war, their master uses the property which he has taken from them by violence for the support of his war." Hostiensis teaches the same thing.[6] It is also found in the *Summa Confessorum.*[7] Astensano proves the same point in his *Summa.*[8] The *Summa* of Sylvester also proves this, in the following words:

If a person waging a just war or finding himself involved in one despoils clerics, religious, monks or pilgrims, even though they are with the enemy, he commits a mortal sin and is obliged to make restitution. Such persons commit theft if they despoil country folk or travelers or farmers or the animals with which they plow and the seed which they carry. Indeed, subjects who do not contribute either directly or indirectly advice, help, or encouragement to their masters engaged in waging war unjustly, must not be despoiled or punished in any way. Yet they are bound to make restitution lest the punishment reach beyond those who start the war. With greater reason, however, one who injures innocent persons who are not subjects of the enemy is bound to restitution, unless he does this unintentionally, for example, if he is unable to capture the city and sacks or burns it, since he cannot otherwise punish the many guilty persons there.[9]

These words of Sylvester prove that innocent persons must not be molested or injured unless there is no alternative, in line with what was said in the previous chapter: a large number of innocent persons must not be harmed in order that a few guilty persons may be punished, and those who do otherwise commit a mortal sin and are bound to restitution, and are considered murderers of those innocent persons. Brother John of Tabia teaches the same thing in his *Summa* (which is called the "Tabian") on the word "war" #8, as also does the most learned Father Francisco Vitoria in his *Second Lecture on the Indies.*

4. *Summa,* under the title "On War," #17 and #19. See also the Decretals, 3, 11, 2.
5. *Summa,* Book 6, tract 3, chap. 7.
6. *Summa,* under the title *"De Poenitentia et Remissione."*
7. Book 2, title 5, q. 44.
8. 1a, Book 1, title 32, a. 6, and Book 2, title 64, a. 7.
9. "War," 1, #10, particle 3.

In those provinces where unbelievers eat human flesh and sacrifice innocent persons, only a few persons commit these crimes, whereas innumerable persons are not guilty of them, and moreover do not participate in these acts in any way. And since we ought not endanger a large number of innocent persons in order to free a few persons who also are innocent, it follows that neither the Church nor any ruler or other member of the Church ought to wage such a war, since they would not be doing this under the pretext of defending their kingdoms, which are far removed from the realms of the unbelievers, but merely under the pretext of freeing innocent persons, when, in fact, a countless multitude of innocent persons would be annihilated under this pretext. Moreover, this does not militate against what has been determined previously by our argument, since, according to judicial authority, that whole state is not, and should not be presumed to be hostile or inimical, but rather innocent and friendly.

Chapter Thirty-Two

There is a third reason why this crime of sacrificing innocent persons must be overlooked when it can be corrected only by war and when no innocent persons can be rescued without harm to other innocent persons, that is to say, when the guilty cannot be distinguished from the innocent. This is something that clearly happens in wars because of the confusion and disorders with which they abound. This is proved by the words of the Lord forbidding the uprooting of the weeds lest perhaps the wheat too should be uprooted. "Do you want us to go," say the Apostles, "and weed it out?" And he says "No, because when you weed it out you might pull up the wheat with it. Let them both grow until the harvest,"[1] lest perhaps in seeking to uproot the weeds you should at the same time uproot the wheat also. The wheat is symbolic of the innocent and good, or those who can return to a state of mind worthy of God. However, in order that these innocent persons may not be harmed, the Lord forbids the uprooting of evil men and puts off their punishment until the day of judgment. The only reason for this is that the good or innocent may not perish with the wicked and guilty. And so Our Lord gives this explanation:

The sower of the good seed is the Son of Man. The field is the world, the good seed is the subjects of the kingdom; the weeds, the subjects of the evil one; the enemy who sowed them, the devil; the harvest is the end of the world; the reapers are the angels. . . . The Son of Man will send his angels and they will gather out of his kingdom all things that provoke offenses and all who do evil and throw them into the blazing furnace.[2]

Christ, then, does not seek but forbids that the guilty be judged, punished, or uprooted by men as long as they cannot be distinguished from the innocent without endangering them. And this is another case in which the Lord reserves the judgment of sinners to himself. This is taught by the gloss in the explanation of the words "Lord, do you want us to go?" It says:

1. Matthew 13[28–30].
2. Matthew 13[37–42].

He looks to the justice of God to see whether he ought to act and whether God wants this task to be the concern of men. But truth answers: In this life man does not know what he is going to be like who at the present time has gone astray and what effect his error will have on the good, and therefore they are not to be uprooted, lest by chance they may be killed who by chance are going to be [good], or lest it be prejudicial to the good, to whom they [the wicked] are of advantage.

And later:

Indeed it may be done advantageously at that time, since the time for bartering life and profiting from others has not yet arrived and then, he says, it will be done not by men but by angels.

In these statements is a clear implication that they who, in the case proposed, kill the guilty with loss and harm to the innocent, who are unavoidably involved by the onslaught of war, act wickedly by usurping a task that the Lord has reserved to himself and the angels. Chrysostom teaches the same thing. "See," he says, "how unlawful it is to usurp a task which has not been commissioned by God, etc."[3] And so does Saint Thomas: "But if someone wreaks vengeance contrary to the rule of divine instruction, he usurps to himself what belongs to God and he sins against God."[4] Saint Thomas asserts the same thing in various places when he discusses the same parable, that is:

The Lord commanded that the weeds should not be uprooted in order that he might spare the wheat, that is, the good. The reason for this is that the evil cannot be killed without at the same time killing the good, either because they are hidden among the good or because they have many followers, so that they cannot be killed without danger to the good, as Augustine says in his *Contra Parmenianum*. And so the Lord teaches that it is preferable for the wicked to be allowed to live and punishment to be delayed until the last judgment than that the good should be killed at the same time. But when there is no real danger to the good from the killing of the wicked, then the wicked can be lawfully killed.[5]

---

3. *Super Matthaeum*, c. 1, homily 1, not in the unfinished work.
4. [*Summa Theologiae*], II–II, q. 108, a. 1, ad 1um.
5. [*Summa Theologiae*], II–II, q. 10, a. 8, ad 1um. And q. 11, a. 3, ad 3um, and q. 64, a. 2, ad 1um, and q. 108, a. 1, ad 5um, and a. 3, ad 1um. And *In IV Sententiarum*, d. 13, q. 2, a. 3, ad 3um, and *Contra Gentes*, Book 3, c. 146, at the end, and *Quodlibetale*, 10, a. 5, ad 2um.

Explaining the Lord's parable, he gives four reasons for his command that the wicked should not be uprooted lest the good be endangered. First, to exercise the patience of the good. Second, that those who are evil may perhaps be changed from weeds to wheat and, hating their evil life, be converted to the Lord and from wolves be made lambs, as we have seen in the case of Saint Paul. The gloss also gives these two reasons. Third, many people seem evil but lack evil intentions. Fourth, if some evil person is very powerful, he cannot be punished without a disturbance in all divine and human affairs.

Saint Ambrose gave an example of this holy teaching when he sharply rebuked the Emperor Theodosius—in other respects a good man —because in a fit of anger he ordered the Thessalonians, under some pretext, to gather in their forum. There, because they had murdered a judge sent by him, he ordered the guilty and innocent massacred indiscriminately. We read this in the *Ecclesiastical History*, which says:

In Tripartite Thessaly there is a large and populous city where, when there was an uprising, some judges were stoned and killed. Aroused by this, Theodosius did not curb his fit of temper but ordered swords to be unjustly drawn against all of them and the innocent massacred with the guilty. Some seven thousand people, as it is said, were killed.[6]

But in our case it is necessary to kill not seven thousand but seventy thousand, or even seven hundred thousand. Perhaps almost all of them are completely innocent before God, at least of those crimes for which we consider war to be just, that is, the sacrifice of infants and cannibalism. Again, this truth is proved from the writings of the jurists. For we read that "it is better" (and some say more pious) "for the crime of the wicked to remain unpunished than for the innocent to be harmed."[7] Commenting on this, Bartholus says that if it is clear to a judge that someone did not commit a crime (that is, either he did not commit the crime or he is not at fault), the judge may not comdemn him even on his genuine confession.[8] And this is what is meant by *the judge ought to seek the defense of the guilty*.[9] The same interpretation is given when there is doubt about the guilt.

6. Book 11, chap. 13. See also Book 9, chap. 30.
7. Digests, 48, 19, 5.
8. Digests, 9, 2, 23, at the end, and also the following law.
9. Digests, 48, 18, 9, at the end, and 48, 19, 19.

Chrysostom also speaks in this way. He says:

In an uncertain case it is better that a convicted prostitute go free than that an innocent person die. It is more just for the unjust to go free justly than for the just to perish unjustly. For even if the guilty person go free once, he can perish at another time, but once an innocent party has perished, he cannot be recalled.[10]

From these words of Chrysostom you see that our teaching is absolutely true and that it is a sin worthy of eternal death to punish and kill the innocent in order to punish the guilty, because it is against justice. Likewise, extreme care is to be exercised lest the innocent be punished under the pretext that they are guilty.[11] Concerning this latter point, Baldus says that innocent people ought not be taken captive nor burdened with costs or anything else. He also says that whoever causes another to be taken captive, who afterward is seen to be innocent, should be punished with a like penalty. And so he says: "For this reason were certain Perugians beheaded."[12] He also writes that an unfair condition ought not be imposed by one on another[13] and that punishment ought to bind only the instigators [of the war].[14]

He proves the same thing from the canonical decrees, in which Ambrose notes: "Finally, if one person cannot be helped unless another is injured, it is better that neither. be helped than that the other be troubled."[15] On this, and on Gratian, c. 24, C. 23, q. 4, the Archdeacon says that no one should give help to another from which injury to another would follow directly and necessarily. And rightly, for no one is to be provided for to the detriment or injury of another.[16]

---

10. *Super Matthaeum*, c. 1, homily 1, in the unfinished work.
11. Codex, 9, 39, 2, at the end.
12. In the previously cited law 1, same title, paragraph beginning *Tribuni*.
13. Digests, 50, 17, 74.
14. Codex, 8, 47, 22. Digests, 48, 19, 20. Codex, 4, 12, 2. Gratian, c. 87, C. 11, q. 3. Liber Sextus, 5, 17, 5. Gratian, c. 3, C. 1, q. 4; c. 6, C. 1, q. 4; c. 1, C. 1, q. 4; c. 7, C. 1, q. 4; Decretals, 3, 11 [inaccurate citation].
15. Gratian, c. 10, C. 14, q. 5.
16. Gratian, c. 8, C. 22, q. 2; c. 13, C. 11, q. 3. And on the rule of law that "no one is to be enriched, etc.," Digests, 50, 17, 206.

Chapter Thirty-Three

In the din of wars the innocent (although it is well known that they are innumerable) cannot be distinguished from their oppressors because of (1) the large number of persons, (2) the fury and turbulent uproar in which son does not respect father nor father have mercy on son (although, for the time being, we omit the greed for booty and the shameless and cruel license of invaders to inflict evil), and (3) the confusion and the fear of the invaders. Also, there are many who seem evil and are not evil, and in such a doubtful matter, as Chrysostom says, it is more just that the unjust go free justly than that the just or the innocent, as such, perish unjustly. Hence, according to him, the first is in accord with justice, the second is unjust. Likewise, it is more virtuous to leave the crime of the wicked unpunished than to condemn the innocent. Further, we should not help one person to the injury or harm of another, etc.

For these reasons, human laws, both canonical and civil, seem to be in agreement with the prohibition of Christ. It follows that [war] will be forbidden by the natural and divine law, and even by human laws.

In case such hardships of the innocent cannot be avoided by any remedy other than war, we are bound by the natural, human, and divine law to tolerate and overlook them, lest a countless number perish cruelly for eternity, who, after being drawn to the yoke of Christ (gently and by moderate arguments), might perhaps achieve salvation, changing from the corruption of weeds to healthy wheat. All of this is in Chrysostom's [commentary] *On Matthew,* homily 47, where he says that even heretics are not to be killed, in these words:

The Lord forbids that they uproot the blades of wheat together with the weeds. This he said to forbid wars and bloodshed. For, if the wicked were put to death without entreaty or inducement to peace, it [war] would be brought to the world. He has forbidden it, therefore, for two reasons: (1) because they do little injury to the wheat; (2) because unless they are healed, they cannot avoid the worst punishments. For these reasons, even if you wish them to be punished and not to harm the wheat in any way, you must wait for the right moment. But why is it that you will tear up the grain along with them? Certainly because if you take up arms *(he says),* when you slaughter the heretics, it is necessary at the same time to kill many of the saints or those who by a drastic change may alter their condition from that of weeds to that of wheat. Thus, if by anticipation, you uproot them, the wheat which might come out of the change in the weeds will perish.[1]

You see, then, that divine and human decrees, and natural reason itself, uphold this opinion, full of Christian moderation and justice. Therefore let us admit that for the Indians to be assailed with war for such reasons is unjust and evil.

A fourth reason can be added to this argument by a comparison with the punishment of crimes, for the punishment of crimes is not an act of justice except insofar as the criminal returns to a better state of mind by reason of the punishment or except insofar as peace and quiet are restored to the state. For if the punishment of crime or a remedy that is applied to prevent offenses gives rise to crimes greater in number or kind, or if the whole state is destroyed, to punish crime is a vice, not a virtue or an act of justice. This is proved by Augustine when he says "Punishing or pardoning is done well only if men's lives are corrected."[2] For a punishment is not imposed in this life for its own sake, nor is this

1. *Super Matthaeum,* homily 47.
2. *Epistola Secunda ad Macedonium,* cited in Gratian, c. 4, C. 23, 1. 5.

the place for full retribution. Therefore punishment in this life is imposed as a medicine, not a penalty.

Again, it can be shown that the punishment or the prevention of crimes is accepted as a kind of medication or a medicine for a disease. If, however, a medication increases the sickness of the body, it is poison rather than medication. For what if you injure the eyes to cure the foot? Would he be a very good doctor who cuts off the hand to heal the finger? Medicine sometimes hurts the lesser parts in order that it might bring health to the principal parts, but not vice versa. So, if the punishment or prevention of crimes increases crime, either directly or as an occasion, it could be a crime to seek to punish or prevent crimes, and it would be contrary to all virtue. Saint Augustine asserts this, saying:

Indeed when the contagion of committing sin invades the multitude, the severe mercy of the divine discipline is necessary. The counsels for separation, *that is, through death or excommunication,* are empty and destructive and sacrilegious because these are impious and proud and they disturb the weak good more than they correct the bold wicked.[3]

In this passage Saint Augustine sufficiently disparages inopportune punishment or a remedy that is adopted for healing the wicked but gives birth to greater evils than it is intended to avoid. He calls it sacrilegious, destructive, impious, and proud.

Again, this same Augustine says:

Truly in cases of this sort where, because of the serious divisions resulting from disagreements, there lurks, not danger to this or that man, but the massacre of peoples, one must withdraw somewhat from severity, so that true charity may aid in healing very great evils, etc.[4]

His words should be noted because he is speaking of the Church's subjects whom it may punish. Therefore punishment should not be administered, nor should one strive to apply a remedy, when many would have to be killed in order to punish or prevent a crime. Now "many," according to the law, means more than forty.[5] On this point

---

3. *Adversus Epistolam Parmeniani,* cited in Gratian, c. 32, C. 23, q. 4.
4. *Epistola ad Macedonium,* cited and read in the same place in Gratian.
5. Decretals, 5, 27, 3; 2, 20, 26 and 27.

the gloss and the doctors note that we must look to the matter under consideration and determine who are many and who are few. What if not a mere forty or fifty but uncounted thousands of persons are endangered, and almost all of them innocent and free of the crimes mentioned above? In such a case, would not such a warlike prevention be wicked?

The same thing is proved, in a third instance, by the fact that even in civil law the punishment or severe prevention of crime ceases when a large group is involved.[6] In these passages it is said that when a sin is committed by the populace or by a crowd, it usually goes unpunished because it is impossible to proceed against everyone on account of the large number.[7] Out of this has arisen the saying "Because of the large number the crime has gone unpunished."

But if a guilty crowd is spared, much more will the same thing occur in this case. Many thousands of persons have never committed a crime or deserved punishment; yet these innocent ones will have to perish and be included in the extermination of the few who are guilty. All this is in keeping with what Chrysostom writes: "A sin committed by many people generally remains unpunishable."[8] For the same reason, one ought not punish or attempt to prevent the crime of a very powerful person, who has many people to protect him, so that it is impossible for his crime to be punished or prevented without the death of many persons who are forced, as a body, to protect him, for example, a prince. Saint Augustine teaches the same thing:

Profitable correction by many is impossible except when the person corrected does not have a large number of allies. When the same disorder seizes many people, the good have no recourse but sorrow and sighs.[9]

Likewise, in the same book he says:

When a person's crime is known and is recognized as evil by everyone, so that the criminal has absolutely no one to defend him so as to cause a division, severe discipline must not be delayed.

6. Decretals, 5, 27, 3; 1, 11, 2. Gratian, c. 14, C. 1. q. 7.
7. Gratian, c. 113, C. 1, q. 1; c. 25, D. 50; c. 1, D. 44; c. 6, D. 4.
8. *Super Matthaeum,* chap. 1, homily 1.
9. *Contra Epistolam Parmeniani,* Book 2, cited in c. 32, C. 23, q. 4.

Therefore severe discipline must lie idle if there are those to defend him. And a little later he says: "This should be done when there is no danger of a division, etc."[10] From this it happens that the sin of a ruler is punished by punishing his kingdom or his people, who have never sinned—by punishing them, I say with the penalty of harm—something we touched on previously.[11]

On the whole, it is the general teaching of theologians and canonists that a penalty should not be imposed or a correction made nor, for that matter, should a work that is good in itself be done if an uprising or some great scandal will follow. Without attempting a scholarly definition, we may call it scandal if there should arise a sudden, violent commotion, an uprising, or a war between individuals. So says Dominic,[12] and, according to the Cardinal,[13] what hinders a pious work is also called scandal after the manner of Matthew, chapter 16, where Christ says to Peter, who wanted to prevent his death: "You are a scandal to me" [22, 23]. It is not a sin, then, to omit pious works, except those necessary for salvation, such as baptism, if scandal is anticipated from them. Rather, not to omit them at some places and times could be sinful. Indeed it is true that all the penalties imposed by the Pope, including excommunication and any other major spiritual penalty, can be disregarded, and we would be obliged by divine law to do so if the observance of a papal precept that binds under excommunication would lead to uprising, violent commotion, war, or any other great evil. This is the teaching of Innocent,[14] and according to Philip Probus it is lawful to violate all laws in order to avoid scandal.[15] The doctors agree that a penalty that is to be imposed in general should be omitted if it would lead to scandal.[16] Similarly Hostiensis: "Scandal is to be avoided by avoiding penalties, unless the person who avoids them commits a mortal sin"—by the very act of avoiding them, as is proved later.[17] We shall also offer the short verse the gloss cites in Decretals, 5, 41, 3. Later in

---

10. Same cause and question, canon 19.
11. As is evident in the Decretals, 4, 1, 11.
12. Gratian, c. 4, D. 45. Liber Sextus, 1, 15, 1.
13. After Paul on the Clementines, 1, col. 2, *De Officio* [*ludicis*] *Ordinarii.*
14. Decretals, 5, 39, 43. And the authorities on the Decretals, 1, 3, 5. Felinus deals with this section more than the others.
15. In his additions to the gloss of John the Monk on the canon *Licet,* col. 3, Book 6.
16. Decretals, 1, 9, 10, #*Pro gravi scandalo,* and on the Decretals, 5, 41, 3.
17. Decretals, 5, 32, 2, #*Super eo.*

the same work [Hostiensis says]: "It is true of life, doctrine and justice: hold fast to the first; let the other two go to avoid scandal. And then the saying is true, 'It is better to omit discipline than to let scandal arise.' "

Saint Thomas agrees with this view when he says:

The imposition of penalties is not to be sought for its own sake. Penalties are imposed as a medicine to stop sin and they partake of justice to the extent that sin is stopped by them. But if the imposition of penalties leads to many greater sins, it will cease to be a function of justice.[18]

So while it is true that the assassination of a tyrant who is a plague to the state is a good and meritorious deed, this is not the case if his death will lead to rebellion or a serious war that doubles the evils within the state. In such a case it is unjust to kill a tyrant, and those who suffer will be consoled by their own tears. Saint Thomas also teaches this.[19] Further, even though an unjust law does not have the force of law[20] and does not oblige in conscience, yet, to avoid scandal or rebellion, those who are subject to it are obliged to observe it, at least externally.[21] It has now been sufficiently proved that greater, rather, the greatest evils would arise if war is waged to prevent the sacrifice and cannibalism of innocent people. In truth, such a war would be totally evil, a fact that we shall attempt to show with greater clarity.

Let us put the case that the Spaniards discover that the Indians or other pagans sacrifice human victims or eat them. Let us say, further, that the Spaniards are so upright and good-living that nothing motivates them except the rescue of the innocent and the correction of the guilty. Will it be just for them to invade and punish them without any warning? You will say "No, rather, they shall send messengers to warn them to stop these crimes." Now I ask you, dear reader, what language will the messengers speak so as to be understood by the Indians? Latin, Greek, Spanish, Arabic? The Indians know none of these languages. Perhaps we imagine that the soldiers are so holy that Christ will grant

---

18. [*Summa Theologiae*], II–II, 1. 43, a. 7, ad 1um. See also q. 66, a. 6, ad 2um; q. 68, a. 1, in corpore, and in other places.
19. [*Summa Theologiae*], q. 42, a. 2, ad 3um. See *De Regimine Principum*, Book 1, chap. 4.
20. See Saint Augustine, *De Libero Arbitrio*, Book 1.
21. See [*Summa Theologiae*], q. 96, a. 4.

them the gift of tongues so that they will be understood by the Indians? Then what deadline will they be given to come to their senses and give up their crimes? They will need a long time to understand what is said to them, and also the authority and the reasons why they should stop sacrificing human beings, so that it will be clear that evils of this type are contrary to the natural law.

Further, within the deadline set for them, no matter what its length, they will certainly not be bound by the warning given them, nor should they be punished for stubbornness, since a warning does not bind until the deadline has run out. Likewise, no law, constitution, or precept is binding on anyone unless the words of the language in which it is proposed are clearly understood, as the learned jurists say. It is enough to cite Felinus, who makes a number of points on this subject,[22] and Gómez, who considers the subject at great length in his commentary on rules for the chancery.[23]

Now, I ask, what will the soldiers do during the time allowed the Indians to come to their senses? Perhaps, like the forty monks Saint Gregory sent to convert the English, they will spend their time in fasting and prayer, so that the Lord will be pleased to open the eyes of the Indians to receive the truth and give up such crimes. Or, rather, will not the soldiers hope with all their hearts that the Indians will become so blind that they will neither see nor hear? And then the soldiers will have the excuse they want for robbing them and taking them captive. Anyone who would foolishly and very unrealistically expect soldiers to follow the first course knows nothing about the military mind. They would hope with all their hearts that the Indians would either misunderstand or reject the warning out of hand. Then the army might realize its wishes and proceed against them with fire and sword and all the misfortunes of total war, so that, after shedding the blood of innumerable persons, the soldiers will seize their goods and make slaves of the survivors in violation of the Lord's command and the rule of charity, by which they were bound to give up property and life for the salvation of their neighbor. Even the presence of the Emperor would not restrain them from thievery and bloodshed for more than two days, especially if the enterprise was of a type to encourage greed. I know for sure of

22. On the rubric *De Constitutionibus,* col. 4.
23. *Regulae de Idiomate,* p. 231 and the following.

occasions when many of our soldiers inflicted sword wounds on Indians who were approaching the Spanish camps weighed down with chickens, fruit, and all sorts of food to offer the Spaniards in deference. Returning to camp, they said that the approaching Indians were armed. To have their story accepted, they told of the Indians' treacherously shooting arrows at them. Thus, under this pretext, the soldiers attacked and either killed or made slaves of people who were quite innocent and had not thought of such a thing.

Further, let us suppose that such a thing does not happen to the Indians and, after more or less time, they may come to understand the warnings of the Spaniards. What if they say that they do not kill the innocent for sacrifice or cannibalism but only those condemned to death for their crimes, or those captured in a just war, or those who have died a natural death? Therefore they do no harm to innocent people but only to themselves in eating the flesh of humans like wild beasts. In this case, will not the reason for freeing innocent people from an unjust death cease to be valid? Therefore there is nothing with which the Christians can reproach them, for there can be cases in which it is lawful to eat human flesh, for example, necessity and extreme hunger. Without committing a sin, one may eat someone who starved to death or who was condemned to death. The eating of human flesh, which is called a wild and bestial act by Aristotle[24] is against the natural law for two reasons: (1) if innocent people are killed so that their flesh may be eaten and (2) because eating human flesh is so savage that even beasts that eat the carcasses of their own kind are rare indeed. When, however, human flesh is eaten out of necessity and innocent people are not killed, but the corpses are of people already dead or of criminals, then surely it is not against the natural law, and no sin is committed. Saint Augustine cites a case of this sort: "Both ancient history and current unhappy experience provide instances of people, famished and overcome by hunger, using human flesh as food."[25] Here he cites the story from 4 Book of Kings [2 Kings] of the two women of a Samaritan city who ate the son of one of the women when the city was besieged by the Assyrian army. They sinned because they killed an innocent person. If their own children had died naturally and the women were suffering extreme

24. *Ethics,* Book 7.
25. *De Civitate Dei,* Book 22, chap. 20.

hunger, they would not have committed sin in eating the flesh of the dead boy.

There is a story of some Spaniards who once ate the liver of a dead companion. Returning to the island of Cuba from the recently discovered Yucatán, they left their ships and, without any food, went toward the mountains. One of them, named Biver, whom I knew very well, died of hunger, and his companions, hoping to avoid the same fate, ate his liver. The same thing happened in the famous Spanish city of Numancia. Its citizens, oppressed by extreme hunger during a siege by Scipio, ate human corpses. This event was reported by the Bishop of Gerona in these words: "Besieged and driven in the end by hunger to eat human flesh, the people of Numancia offered to surrender to Scipio if he would give them humane treatment."[26]

Suppose, then, the unbelievers were to maintain that they eat only people of this kind, that is, those who have died or who have been legally condemned to death, but do not kill the innocent, when the matter can be fully known, especially if the ruler, whose word is in law presumed to be true, [should say so]. Would it not be unjust to wage war on them before the matter is certainly and fully understood?

Let us suppose, further, that it is true and that it is known that, of their own free will and out of a bestial inclination, they eat the bodies of those who have died naturally or who have been executed for their crimes, or even those who were prisoners of war (and undoubtedly this is a crime and a bestial vice), I ask can war be waged against them—justly—simply for this reason? Certainly we cannot wage war against them for any crime they may commit, including idolatry, as we have proved already by ten reasons. Other than their own rulers, judges, or kings, there is no ruler or judge in the world who can punish crimes of this sort.

26. *Parallipomenon Hispaniae,* Book 7.

Chapter Thirty-Four

We have to come to the same conclusion about the crime of human
sacrifice, which is said to be one of their practices. It would not be right
to make war on them for this reason because, as has been said, it is
difficult for them to absorb in a short time the truth proclaimed to them
through messengers and also because the Indians are under no obligation to believe the Spaniards, even if they force the truth on them a
thousand times. Why will they believe such a proud, greedy, cruel, and
rapacious nation? Why will they give up the religion of their ancestors,
unanimously approved for so many centuries and supported by the
authority of their teachers, on the basis of a warning from a people at
whose words there are no miracles to confirm the faith or to lessen vice?

Even though the Indians cannot be excused in the sight of God for
worshiping idols, they can be completely excused in the sight of men,
for two reasons. First they are following a "probable" error, for, as the
Philosopher notes, that is said to be probable which is approved by all
men, either by the majority of wise men or by those whose wisdom has

the greatest following.[1] Further, he says: "That must necessarily be judged to be good or better which is so judged by all, or the majority of persons of good judgment, or by those who are thought to be the more prudent, even if only one person is forming the judgment."[2] Judgments of this type, approved by the opinions of such men, are called "morally certain," according to the same Philosopher, whom all philosophers and theologians follow.[3]

Convictions about the gods, the duty of offering sacrifice to them, and the manner and things to be sacrificed are fully agreed on by all the known Indian nations, and these gods are worshiped by those who are reputed to be sacred and holy men (that is, their priests) and their idolatry is established by the decrees of their laws, the sanction of their rulers, and the penalties leveled against transgressors. Finally, since their idols are not worshiped secretly but publicly and religiously in their temples—and this from the earliest centuries—it is clear that the error of these people is probable. Nor should we be surprised if they do not immediately respond to our first preaching.

Also, they are surely in probable error about their practice of human sacrifice, since the ancient history of pagans and Catholics alike testifies that almost all peoples used to do the same thing. This is what Eusebius says:

It was common for all men, on the day customarily set for human sacrifice, to sprinkle the altar with human blood. This was the practice in ancient times when calamity or danger threatened. The ruler of the city or nation would offer to the avenging demon his favorite child as a ransom for the redemption of the whole people and the one chosen would be slain in a mystic rite.[4]

He goes on:

Human sacrifice is demanded by the demons who from time to time afflict many cities and nations with plagues and sudden calamities and ceaselessly harass the people in frightful ways until appeased by the blood of the victims offered them.

1. *Topics*, Book 1.
2. *Rhetoric*, Book 1, chap. 20.
3. See *Ethics*, Book 1, chap. 2.
4. *De Praeparatione Evangelica*, Book 4, chap. 7.

Again, Clement says that some of the peoples of western India, who may have been very much like those we are dealing with, used to sacrifice foreigners to their gods and then eat them.[5] Eusebius writes the same thing in the work we have already cited.

In addition, Lactantius says:

Among the people of Taurus, an inhuman and savage nation, there was a law that a stranger should be sacrificed to Diana and sacrifice was offered for a long time. The Gauls placated Hesus and Teutates with human blood. Even the Latins were not free of such barbarism. Indeed, even now the Latin Jupiter is worshiped with human blood. However, we should not be astonished at the barbarians whose religion matches their morals. Are not our own people who boast of their meekness and gentleness often more inhuman than those who practice such sacrilegious rites?[6]

Further on he notes: "It is now evident that this practice of human sacrifice is very ancient, for in honor of Saturn people used to be thrown into the Tiber from the Milvian Bridge."

And in regard to innocent children, he says:

I find no words to tell of the children who were sacrificed to the same Saturn because of a hatred for Jupiter. Men were so barbarous and so inhuman that they labeled as sacrifice that foul and detestable crime against the human race which is parricide, when, without any sign of family love, they blotted out tender and innocent lives at an age which is especially dear to parents, etc.

And again:

The Carthaginians had the custom of offering human victims to Saturn and when they had been conquered by Aglothocles, the King of Sicily, they thought their god was angry with them and so that they might more diligently blot out their crime, they sacrificed two hundred noble children.

Plutarch writes that the Romans failed to punish some barbarians who were sacrificing men to the gods, because they knew that it was done from custom and law.[7] Plutarch also says that the Romans themselves did the same thing at times. Here are his words:

5. *Recognitiones ad Iacobum, Fratrem Domini,* Book 9.
6. *Divinarum Institutionum,* Book 1, chap. 21.
7. *Problemata,* p. 465.

When the Romans discovered that certain barbarians had sacrificed a man to their immortal gods, the magistrates thought that they should be summoned and punished. Later they released them when they learned that the barbarians did this because of a certain law and custom and so they forbade them to do it again. This was because a few years before they themselves had struck down two men and two women in the cattle-market at Rome. It does not seem right that they should do this and yet find fault with the savages who did the same. Were they persuaded that to offer a man to the immortal gods was evil, but to offer him to the demons was a necessity? Did they think that those who did this sort of thing from custom and law committed sin, while they believed that by following the command of the Sibylline Books, they were not guilty of the same crime?

The Greek historian Herodotus tells us that the Scythians had a custom of sacrificing to their gods one out of every hundred prisoners of war.[8] He also says that the Scytho-Tauran peoples in Germany sacrifice everyone who is shipwrecked on their shores, as well as strangers, to Iphigenia, daughter of Agamemnon. The same thing is recorded by Solinus[9] and Pomponius Mela.[10] Diodorus Siculus writes that the Galatians sacrificed to their gods captives or those condemned for their crimes. Strabo reminds us that our own Spanish people, who reproach the poor Indian peoples for human sacrifice, used to sacrifice captives and their horses.[11] He says that they forced some to live next to the Duero River in a Spartan manner. He continues:

Those who are given to sacrifice also practice divination with entrails, especially those of their captives. They cut off the right hands of their victims and offer them to the gods. They eat a goat which they sacrifice to Mars, as they do with prisoners and horses.

Moreover, similar practices of other peoples are narrated in other works of Strabo.[12] Polydor Vergil also has recorded many similar and significant details.[13] Because, then, human sacrifice to the gods has been customary among so many different peoples, surely the Indians, in sacrificing men for many centuries, are in probable error.

8. Book 4, p. 299.
9. *Polyhistoria*, chap. 20.
10. Book 2, chap. 1.
11. *Polyhistoria*, Book 6, fol. 190.
12. *De Situ Orbis*, Book 3.
13. See *De Rerum Inventoribus*, Book 5, chap. 8.

We know that famous philosophers have lived in many parts of the world. According to Augustine, even though they knew the stories about the gods to be mere fables and judged them to be undeserving of divine honors (this group included Cicero and Seneca), they did not wish to turn the people from an ancient custom that had been accepted for so many centuries.[14] Why, then, should it be thought that at the words of Christian soldiers, [who exceed the barbarous peoples in their wicked deeds, and are a nation not yet known and frightful in appearance, that does not eat human flesh but surpasses them in all wicked deeds], the Indians ought to turn from a religion that has been accepted for many centuries, sanctioned by the laws of many rulers, and strengthened by the example of so many of their prudent men? As Chrysostom says, in matters that are sacred and of great importance and very difficult to give up they would be fickle and worthy of reproach and punishment if they put aside the many and great testimonies of such great authority and believe these soldiers in this matter, without being convinced by more probable reasons (which cannot be done in a short time) that the Christian religion is more worthy of belief.[15]

They should be ashamed who think to spread the gospel by the mailed fist. Men want to be taught, not forced. There is no way, however, for our religion to be taught in a short time to those who are as ignorant of our language as we are of their language and their religion, until those who prudently hold fast [to these beliefs] are convinced by reason. For, as we have said, there is no greater or more difficult step than for a man to abandon the religion he has once embraced.

.

14. *De Civitate Dei,* Book 6, chap. 10.
15. *In 1ᵃᵐ Epistolam ad Corinthios,* homily 7.

Chapter Thirty-Five

The second major proof why the Indians should not immediately believe that human sacrifice to their gods is evil is that evidence cannot be presented to them in a few, or even many, words [to show] that human sacrifice to the true God or the presumed god (if he is worshiped as the true God) is forbidden by natural reason. Rather, by the same natural reason they can show not only that men should be sacrificed to God but that it would not be enough to sacrifice angels (if it were possible to sacrifice angels).

We argue this point by first offering four principles.

The first principle is that no nation is so barbarous that it does not have at least some confused knowledge about God. Now all persons understand God as that than which there is nothing better or greater. This is the teaching of [John] Damascene.[1] He says: "God does not leave us totally engulfed in ignorance of himself. Rather, the knowledge that God exists has been naturally engrafted and implanted by him in all

---

1. At the beginning of his book *De Fide Orthodoxa*.

persons."² Again, Cicero says: "No man is so inhuman that an opinion about the divinity has not filled his mind."³ And, "No nation is so wild or fierce that it does not know that a god must be had," even if it does not know what sort.⁴ Aristotle says that all men are agreed that this glorious first body, that is, heaven, is the dwelling place of the supreme being, that is, God, [the expression "all men" referring] to the Greeks and others of the early nations who knew God exists and is divine.⁵ Boethius teaches both points in these words: "The common reasoning of human minds proves that the true God, the ruler or source of all things, is good. For since nothing can be imagined better than God, who doubts the goodness of him who has no better?"⁶

The second principle is that, by a natural inclination, men are led to worship God according to their capacities and in their own ways. The reason for this is that they naturally conclude and believe that they belong to him and that their lives and whatever they have come from him. And so Saint Thomas writes: "Now since men believe that all things are given by and proceed from him, the intellect judges that everything is owed to God."⁷ Moreover, the Philosopher writes: "Even natural reason itself dictates that the very highest and best things must be offered to God because of his excellence."⁸ Again, he says: "Man's friendship for the gods is the same as toward those who excel others in goodness. And in friendships, the greater the excellence of the friend, the more he deserves."⁹ Again, he says: "No one can ever give to the gods in accordance to their dignity, but each must do the most he can."¹⁰ Saint Thomas has the same teaching:

Man is in debt to God for two reasons. (1) Because of the benefits received from him; (2) because of the sins committed against him. . . . Man can never completely satisfy these two obligations to God, since, even according to the

2. Chap. 3. See also Gregory of Nazianzen, *Theology,* col. 11; Lactantius, *Divinarum Institutionum,* Book 3, chap. 11.
3. In his book *Tusculan Questions*.
4. *De Legibus*.
5. In the first and second books of *On Heaven and Earth* and in the third book of the *Physics*.
6. *De Consolatione Philosophiae,* Book 3, prose 10.
7. *Contra Gentes,* Book 3, chap. 119.
8. *Politics,* Book 7, chap. 9.
9. *Ethics,* Book 8, chap. 10.
10. *Ethics,* Book 8, chap. 10.

Philosopher, in honors due to parents and to God, it is impossible for man to repay in any adequate way. However, it is enough that man repay proportionately what he can.[11]

From these statements it is obvious that, by natural law, men are obliged to honor God by the best means available and to offer the best things in sacrifice. The conclusion that follows from this is that neither a particular man nor a whole community, taken as a unit, nor a whole kingdom can repay God for the benefits it received, even if they were to give their property and endure labors, vigils, and finally life and death itself for God's glory, no matter how unwilling God may be to reward such deeds in the other life, because God, who by his indescribable generosity has given us so many and so admirable benefits, owes us nothing. For this reason the Psalmist says: "What return can I make to the Lord for all his goodness to me?"[12] As if he were saying: "I have nothing and can do nothing to repay God for these things for which I recognize that I am indebted to him." The reason for this is that a man in no way injures his property even if he makes use of it without rewarding it because there is no political or civil right between a man and his property, according to the Philosopher.[13] But all creatures, including us, are the property of God. Therefore it is absolutely impossible that God would do us harm if he were not to reward the services we might perform for his honor, because there cannot be a political right —or right in the strict sense—between God and us. For although God gives eternal happiness to those who have charity, he is not obliged to do so from justice, insofar as this implies a strict right that denotes complete equality between the two parties. As the Apostle says, "What we suffer in this life can never be compared to the glory as yet unrevealed, which is waiting for us."[14]

Yet there is said to be between God and man a certain right of condescension; that is, the Lord, drawing on the riches of his mercy, is pleased to set up a certain kind of proportional equality between himself and men. In other words, he wills to be obligated to men, and men to him. Thus he is bound to give eternal life to those who persevere in faith

11. *In IV Sententiarum*, d. 10, q. 1, a. 2c.
12. Psalms 115[12].
13. *Ethics*, Book 4.
14. Romans 8[18].

and charity until death, not because our merits demand it but from the disposition established by him by which he wishes a kind of justice of condescension and, as it were, a kind of agreement between him and us, so that, in the works of charity, God may be bound to give us eternal life. And this is called justice, not in the strict sense but after a manner of speaking. Moreover, in this sense God would be said to do an injustice if he did not give eternal life to those who die in charity. And this is the meaning of the Apostle's words "All there is to come now is the crown of righteousness reserved for me,"[15] that is, of justice by reason of this agreement or pact. God, then, owes us nothing except by right of condescension. But we must offer him whatever we have and are: our wealth, energies, life, and our very soul for his service. We are bound to this by a greater bond since he has given his life for us.

The third principle is that there is no better way to worship God than by sacrifice, which is the principal act of *latria*, which is owed to God alone. Nor is there any better way for men to show in their external acts that they are grateful and subject to God. For sacrifice is the sign that he to whom it is offered is God, and it is most certain that there has never been a nation so barbarous, brutal, and foolish as to offer sacrifice to anyone other than the one who was thought to be God. As Saint Augustine says:

For who has ever thought that sacrifice should be offered, except to the one whom he knew or thought or imagined to be God? . . . That the worship of God by means of sacrifice is ancient is sufficiently indicated by those two famous brothers, Cain and Abel. God found fault with the sacrifice of the older and looked favorably on that of the younger.[16]

Saint Thomas teaches the same thing: "Now no one has ever thought that sacrifice should be offered to anyone for any other reason than that he believed or thought he believed that he was God."[17]

The fourth principle is that offering sacrifice to the true God or to the one who is thought to be God comes from the natural law, whereas the things to be offered to God are a matter of human law and positive

15. Timothy 4[8].
16. *De Civitate Dei*, Book 10, chap. 4.
17. *Contra Gentes*, Book 3, chap. 120.

legislation. For this reason this matter is either left to the whole community or to those who represent it, such as the ruler, or, lacking this, it is entrusted to each private individual to decide what he will use for his sacrifice.

The first statement is evident from the three preceding principles. By nature, all nations know that God surpasses anything that can be imagined and that they have life and every possession from him. And by nature they understand that they owe God the greatest reverence and worship because of his incomparable excellence and majesty, and all agree that the principal act of *latria*, which is owed to God alone, is sacrifice. It follows, then, that they are obliged by the natural law to offer sacrifice, by which men show, more than by any other external act, that they are grateful and subject to God. And so there has never been a nation so barbarous as not to judge by a natural impulse that sacrifice is owed to the true God or to him whom they mistakenly thought is the true God.

The second proof of the first statement is what Saint Thomas says:

At all times and among all nations there has always been some offering of sacrifices.

And the reason for this is that

natural reason tells man that he is subject to a higher being, on account of the defects which he perceives in himself, and in which he needs help and direction from someone above him, and whatever this superior being may be, it is known to all under the name of God, and consequently the offering of sacrifice is a matter of the natural law.[18]

The same statement is proved, in the third place, from the lawyers who teach that religion belongs to the law of nations.[19] They call the natural law the law of nations only because men use it.[20] Men put the law of nations into practice as soon as they began to grow in numbers, since the peoples who lived during the first centuries taught many things by natural instinct. From this, then, arose the practice of sacrifice

18. [*Summa Theologiae,*] II–II, q. 85, a. 1.
19. Digests, 1, 1, 2.
20. Digests, 1, 1, 1. Institutes, 2, 1, 11.

as produced by natural instinct. Offering sacrifices, therefore, is a very old practice, introduced by the natural law.

The second statement—that offering this or that thing as a sacrifice is a matter of human law, whereas the law of nature does not prescribe anything definite—is also proved by the fact that even if something may generally be of the natural law, the disposition and arrangement of when and how it should be done is positive; that is, a certain determination of the natural law is laid down by the ruler or the state. For example, men are obliged to give some time to divine matters and to worship God by some external acts, which the theologians call acts of *latria*. This is dictated by natural reason. But the fact that the seventh day should be dedicated to divine worship is a human statute that is laid down by the Church, to which Christ gave the right to establish laws concerning divine worship, even though the seventh day (Sunday) has taken the place of the Sabbath, which God commanded by positive law to be dedicated to divine things. So, too, the law of nature teaches that the guilty must be punished, but human law teaches what the penalty should be. In the same way, although nature itself teaches and leads man to offer sacrifice to God, it is not the law of nature but men themselves who, by means of human laws, teach what should be offered as sacrifice, that is, cattle or sheep or the like. This is clear in the sacrifices of the various nations cited above. Likewise, some sacrificed swine to Ceres, horses to Phoebus, geese to Diana, asses to Priapus, and other such things.[21]

The second statement is also proved by what the Philosopher says in the Fifth Book of the *Ethics*, where, speaking about the natural law and positive law, he writes that all men have the same opinion about natural truths but differ in laws and practices. For when he speaks about sacrifices, he says:

One law is natural, the other legitimate, that is, the legal or positive law. Now the natural is that which has the same force everywhere, for example, fire burns both here and in Persia, not because it seems so or does not seem so. But the legitimate, that is, the legal, is that which does not differ one way or another

21. As Ovid mentions in *Pastores*, chap. 1; Lucan in his *De Bello Civili*, Book 6, and Juvenal in the next to the last satire. I have taken the above-written argument from Saint Thomas [*Summa Theologiae*,] II–II, q. 85, a. 1, ad 1um; *in IV Sententiarum*, d. 26, q. 2, a. 1, ad 1um; and *Quodlibetale* II, a. 8c.

at its source but differs when it is established, as, for example, that the ransoming of captives be done at a certain price or that a goat be offered in sacrifice instead of two sheep, and whatever is provided for by individual laws, such as performing sacred rites to Brasis, etc.

Notice that he teaches that the law of nature does not change because one person wishes to fulfill it while another does not. For what is good cannot be made evil by the will of men. For example, the law of nature teaches us to redeem a captive who is suffering injury and to offer sacrifice to God. And, willingly or unwillingly, all men are obliged to do so, but how large the amount to be paid for captives and what should be sacrificed are taught by human laws. Once these are passed, they should be observed, and it is unlawful to violate them. For example, we read that the Athenians and the Spartans, during a war with each other, made an agreement that the freedom of prisoners could be bought for a certain price. Likewise, if it were established that not one but two sheep should be offered as a sacrifice or that sacrifices should be made and feasts celebrated by some well-deserving person in the state—as the Amphipolitans decreed that sacrifices should be offered by Brasis (who some think was a Spartan king, others a Spartan queen) because of the favors granted to his nation—it is in no way lawful to violate these sacrifices and the form as sanctioned by law. If, however, the law provides no sanction, each private individual could sacrifice whatever he wishes and could redeem a prisoner at any price he wishes. For the natural law does not teach these matters, and in morally indifferent matters each person can follow his own judgment and lay down rules for his wife and children as he wishes, according to the Philosopher.[22] Speaking about families in his city, he says: "Every household is ruled by its oldest member, and so are the descendants who branch out from it, because of the blood relationship. And this is what Homer means, 'And each one must give laws to sons and to wives,' for people used to live scattered about in this way in ancient times."[23]

Now Genesis (chapter 4) proves that unless a certain form or definite victim for sacrifice were defined by law, each person could lawfully sacrifice what he willed. In this chapter, Cain is said to have offered ears

22. In the first book of *Politics,* chap. 1.
23. Saint Thomas speaks of this in the [*Summa Theologiae,*] II–II, q. 57, a. 2, ad 2um; q. 60, a. 5, ad 1um et 2um; q. 66, a. 7c.

of wheat and the fruits of the earth, while Abel, who was a shepherd, sacrificed the firstborn of his flock to the Lord. However, after he made a covenant with Abraham and his descendants, the Lord, through Moses, regulated the sacrifices that were to be offered to him, that is, cattle and sheep from among the four-footed animals and turtledoves and pigeons from among the birds.[24]

24. This is clear in Genesis 17 regarding the covenant and in Leviticus 1 regarding the offerings. Abulensis treats these matters in a learned way in his *Commentary on Leviticus,* q. 11 and 12; *Commentary on Exodus,* q. 9, col. 7, c. 25; and his partial *Commentary on Genesis,* chap. 15.

Chapter Thirty-Six

On the basis of these principles one can arrive at what we taught previously: within the limits of the natural light of reason (in other words, at the point at which divine or human positive law ceases and, one may add, where grace and doctrine are lacking), men should sacrifice human victims to the true God or the reputed god, if the latter is taken for the true God. We draw this conclusion: Just as men naturally know that God exists and think that there is nothing better or greater than he, since whatever we own, are, or are capable of is given to us by his boundless goodness, we do not adequately repay him even if we offer him all that is ours, even our life.

The greatest way to worship God is to offer him sacrifice. This is the unique act by which we show him to whom we offer the sacrifice that we are subject to him and grateful to him. Furthermore, nature teaches that it is just to offer God, whose debtors we admit we are for so many reasons, those things that are precious and excellent because of the surpassing excellence of his majesty. But, according to human judgment and truth, nothing in nature is greater or more valuable than the life of man or man himself. Therefore nature itself dictates and teaches those who do not have faith, grace, or doctrine, who live within the limitations of the light of nature, that, in spite of every contrary positive law, they ought to sacrifice human victims to the true God or to the false god who is thought to be true, so that by offering a supremely precious thing they might be more grateful for the many favors they have received. For the natural law teaches gratitude in such a way that we not only do good to our benefactor but also try to repay him in an abundant manner for the benefits we have received, giving due consideration to the benefits, the benefactor, and the motive for which he confers the benefits on us.[1]

The kindness by which the Lord created us, endowed us with so many gifts, and enriched us with so many good things comes from his immense charity and boundless goodness and gives birth in us to innumerable good things, and even life itself, and, finally, whatever we are. However, since we cannot give adequate thanks for so many favors, we are obliged to present what seems to us to be the greatest and most valuable good, that is, human life, and especially when the offering is made for the welfare of the state. For the pagans thought that through sacrifices of this type they could divert evils from their state and gain good will and prosperity for their kingdoms. Therefore whoever sacrifices men to God can be drawn to this action by natural reason, especially if he lacks Christian faith and instruction. All of this is corroborated by what Dionysius of Halicarnassus writes:

1. See Seneca [no specific reference given] and Saint Thomas [*Summa Theologiae*], II–II, q. 107, a. 5 and 6.

When the peoples of Italy tried to appease the gods by offering various first-fruits after they had been afflicted with many evils, a certain old man told them that they were deceiving themselves if they thought that there was no reason why they were being tried by the gods. For, as he said, they rightly and justly gave the first-fruits of other things but, in the judgment of the gods, they still owed the first-fruits of what was most valuable to the gods, that is, their offspring. If, then, the gods would accept one of these or the part still due, their petition would be complete. When they had heard this advice, some thought that he spoke correctly, while others thought that his reasoning was deceptive. When someone suggested that they seek the opinion of the god as to whether he would be willing to receive men as tithes, they sent soothsayers and the god answered that they should do so.[2]

Possibly the idea of human sacrifice spread from here through the whole world. Yet someone will loudly protest that this idea must not be admitted, since innocent persons are sacrificed against their will. But I shall answer this objection as I have previously: Every man, no matter how innocent he may be, owes God more than his life; and so, although these persons do not will it by an explicit act, yet they perform an act that is owed, since all men are obliged to give their blood and their life whenever God's honor demands it. We Christians, like all those who knew God during the early centuries, are obliged by divine law to do this. Now apparently there was a case in which God's honor was involved when those upon whom the lot fell were offered as sacrifice by reason of a law in force in some kingdom. Therefore, even if they were otherwise innocent, no harm was done to them, at least in the judgment of those who did not have grace and doctrine. And this is bolstered by the fact that, according to the Philosopher, any outstanding citizen is obliged to give his life for the welfare of the state (this welfare, according to the erroneous opinion of the pagans, was thought to consist of the worship of the gods).[3] Those who do not have the faith, then, have probable error concerning human sacrifice.

Nor is there any validity to the objection that whatever a man can conveniently do without his own destruction is considered to be within his capabilities, according to Saint Thomas.[4] He teaches that

2. Book 1.
3. This is proved in Gratian, c. 5, C. 23, q. 3; c. 9, C. 23, q. 8. Saint Thomas [*Summa Theologiae*], I, q. 60, a. 5, and I–II, q. 109, a. 3c, as well as *In III Sententiarum*, d. 29, a. 3.
4. *In IV Sententiarum*, d. 15, q. 2, a. 2, ad 3um.

although man owes his every capability to God, yet it is impossible according to the condition of our present life that a man devote all his ability to some one thing, since he must be concerned about many things. Yet there is a certain measure imposed upon man and demanded of him, that is, the fulfillment of God's commandments, and in regard to these he can do something extra to satisfy them.

Again, he says:

By his command the legislator does not demand of a man everything that he is capable of, since the former does not intend to regulate a man's condition with regard to a single day or a short time, but rather for a whole lifetime, so that a man would fail to carry it out if, at any single time, he would do everything he could, etc.[5]

So my answer to the first objection is that even if it is true that God, in his immense mercy, does not demand of men as much as they are capable of, yet not all men grasp this. Nor does nature teach this in such a way that it is perceived so clearly by the light of the intellect alone that no man can deny it, as is the case of things that are self-evident. These latter are things which all persons admit through the light of the agent intellect solely, through knowing the terms and without any reasoning process, such as the principle of affirmation and negation of the same thing and the principle that both affirmation and negation cannot be predicated of the same thing. Nor is it grasped even by an imperceptible act of reasoning, as in the principle that "if equals are subtracted from equals, what remain are equal," and in other principles that are not proved but presupposed. This is sufficiently evident from what the Philosopher says in his book the *Posterior Analytics.*

The same is true of what Saint Thomas teaches, that when men do not perceive something by natural light alone, they need grace and doctrine, which unbelievers do not have. However, the barbarians who have only the natural light of reason understand that we owe God whatever we have in this life, and this is the common way of thinking among them, even without God's special grace or teaching, with the supposition, however, that there is always the universal influence or divine providence. So it is not surprising that when unbelievers who

5. q. 3, a. 2, q. 4c.

have neither grace nor instruction consider how much men owe to God, they devise the most difficult type of repayment, that is, human sacrifice in God's honor. And, absolutely speaking, this is within their capabilities.

An answer can also be given to Saint Thomas's teaching that when God's honor is endangered, man is obliged by divine precept to do all he can absolutely, and thus to expose his life so that God's honor and glory may not be diminished, since God wants every man to die in defense of his glory. Even if we did not have God's positive precept, yet we would know it from the very law of nature, for all living creatures, both rational and irrational, naturally love more than themselves him from whom they proceed and by whom they exist. This is evident in the following example. If the body is endangered, the hand, which is part of the body, stretches out so that the body may not be injured, because the hand is a part and member of the body. Now this natural instinct is based on the fact that the welfare of the part depends on the welfare of the whole, and the welfare of the whole is more useful to the part or member than its own welfare, since it would not be good for the part if it were bad for the whole from which the part has whatever it is. For what would be the condition of the hand if the body were corrupted? Therefore, since all creatures are from God, and since God is the good of the whole universe, it follows that, with a love implanted by nature, every creature loves God more than itself, and consequently that it should expose its life to death for the defense of the glory of God, from whom it has whatever welfare it has.[6]

So it happens that all we Christians are obliged to expose our lives to death whenever God's honor is endangered, or whenever it is probable that our neighbor will run into some deadly stumbling block, according to Saint Thomas.[7] We have an example of this in the external profession of faith, to which we are obliged by its necessity for salvation, even by exposing our lives to the danger of death, that is, when, by the omission of this profession, the honor due to God and the help that should be given to our neighbor would be withdrawn. For this reason, Saint Thomas's statement is irrelevant to our case.

6. Saint Thomas speaks of this in his [*Summa Theologiae*], I, q. 60, a. 5, and I–II, q. 109, a. 3c.
7. [*Summa Theologiae*], II–II, q. 3, a. 2; *In III Sententiarum*, d. 29, a. 8, q. 2, ad 3[um].

In regard to Saint Thomas's other declaration that the legislator does not obligate a man to do everything he can, etc., we say that there is a difference in regard to God, who is the absolute lord of all things, and to laws he has made and in regard to men and the laws they make. For, since each legislator has the authority to make laws not from himself but from the people or the community, he can oblige subjects to do or undergo something by law only as it is conducive to the welfare and happiness of the whole state or community, in proportion to the needs of the state. He must keep in mind the truth that the condition of each citizen should be regulated and preserved for as long a time as possible. But if the need of the state demands that a man do or undergo all that he is capable of, that is, that he expose his life to the danger of death for the welfare of the state, undoubtedly the legislator, by his command, can lawfully obligate each suitable citizen to do so. And the citizen is obliged by the natural law to obey the mandate. This is proved from what was established just a short while ago concerning the whole and the part. For, since the citizen is a part of the whole state and his happiness or welfare depends on the welfare and good of the state, he is obliged to love the common welfare and good more than his private welfare, and therefore, in order to preserve that common welfare, he is obliged by the natural law to do and suffer all he can, even by sacrificing his life.

Since, then, the pagans believe that the universal good and welfare of the whole state consists in sacrifices and immolations, that is, human victims, as we have proved elsewhere from Augustine, Chrysostom, and Valerius, it is not surprising that, when afflicted by needs, they sacrifice what in the judgment of all is most precious and pleasing to God, that is, men. This is evident from the previously cited examples. This is evident also from what Titus Livy writes: "When their city was in very great danger, the Romans placated Mars by sacrificing a man and woman of Gaul and a Greek man and woman."[8] Moreover, on the supposition that the error of the pagans is probable, a legislator can and should bind some of the people by his command when there is a great need involving the whole state, so that a sacrifice should be offered by killing them. And they can be obliged to will this by an explicit act, as is clear from what has been concluded.

You see, then, dear reader, that there is some probable natural reason

8. 2 *Decadis,* 3.

by which men can be led to sacrifice human beings to God and, as a result, that it is not easy to persuade the Indians, within a short period or by a few words, to refrain from their traditional practice of human sacrifice.

Chapter Thirty-Seven

All of the preceding conclusions seem to be established, and therefore it can be persuasively argued, from the fact that God commanded Abraham to sacrifice to him his only son Isaac, that it is not altogether detestable to sacrifice human beings to God. Although it is clear from the words of Sacred Scripture[1] and the interpretation of the holy doctors that God gave that command to show men the faith and obedience of his servant Abraham and to foreshadow that sacred mystery by which God the Father offered his only son Jesus as a sacrifice to death for the salvation of men, nevertheless we can say that God also wished to indicate that he would do no injustice to anyone in any way if he had commanded him to be offered in sacrifice. For God is the maker of every creature and all creatures are his possession, as has been said: "To the

1. Genesis 22[1–19].

Lord belongs the earth and all that it holds"[2] and "You, O Lord of all things,"[3] and consequently [he is the Lord] of life and death. Although the Lord asked only once that a human victim be offered to him as a sacrifice, (that is, Isaac, as Abraham understood it) and did not will it to be carried out, this was not because everything, even human life, should not be offered up to him but rather because of his limitless love for the human race. And so, taking pity on Isaac, he refused to have him sacrificed to himself because of the covenant he had made with Abraham and his descendants. And from this the justice that made him worthy had its origin, as we said in the beginning of the second chapter.

Again, the truth that all things, even men, are owed to God and [can be] offered in sacrifice seems to be proved by another passage in Scripture, for he commanded his people to sacrifice every firstborn to himself, in these words: "Consecrate all the firstborn to me, the first issue of every womb, among the sons of Israel. Whether man or beast, this is mine."[4] However, he later exempted them from this mandate so long as they offered him two turtledoves or a yearling lamb. For when God commanded every firstborn to be sacrificed to himself and when he added "All the firstborn are mine,"[5] he gave sufficient evidence that all things are owed to him in justice and that he can command, without injustice to anyone, that they be sacrificed to him or serve him perpetually in the tabernacle of the covenant in the ministry of divine worship. Similarly, we see today how God now and then takes the firstborn in death, as it pleases him, but in doing this he does no injustice to anyone, as we have said. In this way, too, God willed that certain persons be dedicated to his service, that is, the tribe of Levi.[6] Finally, without doing an injustice to anyone he can freely kill or save all men, or use them in any way whatever. When, however, he wants the precept "Consecrate all the firstborn to me" to be ransomed by the offering of a pair of turtledoves or certain other animals, he clearly makes known to us his boundless mercy, condescension, favor, and the justice that makes a person worthy.

In harmony with this is what we read in Judges, chapter 11, that

2. Psalms 23[1].
3. 2 Maccabees 14[25].
4. Exodus 13[2]. Numbers 8[16–17].
5. As is clear from Leviticus 12 [8] and Luke 2 [24].
6. As is clear from Numbers 3 and 8 [throughout].

Jephthah sacrificed his only daughter to God. He was led to do this, perhaps, because God had demanded a similar sacrifice from Abraham and therefore thought that it would be pleasing to God, as Abulensis notes on that passage.[7] For the Israelites were the best known and celebrated among all the nations of the world because of the astonishing works and miracles God wrought among them, according to Eusebius when he asserts that Plato and the Greeks learned many things about religion and government from the Hebrews. "The Greek philosophers" he said, "borrowed from Jewish teaching," and a little later: "When they admit very properly that they stole everything from the Jews and barbarians, no one will be surprised who knows that they were both talkers and thieves."[8] Therefore one might reasonably surmise that the practice of human sacrifice spread to all nations because they heard that the all-powerful God of the Jews ordered his dearest servant Abraham to sacrifice his own son to him, and again that a most renowned leader of that nation offered his only daughter to God in sacrifice after he had won a victory, something he surely would not have done unless he thought it would be acceptable to God. It is no wonder, therefore, that nations and states that are deprived of Christian faith and teaching, when they recognize God's supreme majesty and most abundant kindness toward all and their own obligation to offer him sacrifice from their precious possessions (the number and kind being left to their free choice), should be persuaded to prescribe that on certain days and for various needs some persons of the population, regardless of how innocent, should be sacrificed to the gods for the welfare of the entire state.

Thus it is clear that it is not possible, quickly and in a few words, to make clear to unbelievers, especially ours, that sacrificing men to God is unnatural. On that account, we are left with the evident conclusion that knowledge that the natives sacrifice men to their gods, or even eat human flesh, is not a just cause for waging war on any kingdom. And again, this long-standing practice of theirs cannot be suddenly uprooted. And so these entirely guiltless Indians are not to be blamed because they do not come to their senses at the first words of a preacher of the gospel. For they do not understand the preacher. Nor are they bound to abandon at once their ancestral religion, for they do not understand that it is better to do so. Nor is human sacrifice—even of the

7. Books 43 and 52.
8. *De Praeparatione Evangelica,* Books 11 and 12.

innocent, when it is done for the welfare of the entire state—so contrary to natural reason that it must be immediately detested as contrary to the dictates of nature. For this error can owe its origin to a plausible proof developed by human reasoning.

The preceding arguments prove that those who willingly allow themselves to be sacrificed, and all the common people in general, and the ministers who sacrifice them to the gods by command of their rulers and priests labor under an excusable, invincible ignorance and that their error should be judged leniently, even if we were to suppose that there is some judge with authority to punish these sins. If they offend God by these sacrifices, he alone will punish this sin of human sacrifice.

However, insofar as they sacrifice to idols, it does not seem that they can be excused because of invincible ignorance, according to the common teaching of the doctors, who say that in those things that are necessary for attaining eternal salvation, no one has invincible ignorance. For if men do what lies within them, the Lord will give them light or the inspiration of the Holy Spirit, either by imparting to each a knowledge of himself or by opening the eyes of unbelievers through men or through angels. In a parallel case Saint Thomas, speaking of a man who is brought up in the woods and forests and among wild animals, says:

For it belongs to Divine Providence to provide for each person whatever is necessary for salvation, so long as no obstacle is placed on man's part. For if someone were thus reared in the forests or among wolves and were to follow the lead of natural reason to seek good and avoid evil, it is most certainly to be held that God would reveal to him by an interior inspiration whatever must be believed by necessity, or he would direct to him some preacher of the faith, as he sent Peter to Cornelius.[9]

9. *De Veritate,* q. 14, a. 11, ad 1um. He teaches the same thing in his *In Epistolam ad Romanos,* c. 10, lectura 3. However, the fact that they are excused as far as men are concerned is shown in Digests, 22, 6, 9, where probable error excuses from penalty. This is proved also in the Decretals, 4, 15, 6, and on that passage the Abbot teaches the same thing, col. 2, #*Praepositi.* Also the Cardinal on the Clementines, 5, 7. It is proved still further by the principle that the error of the populace which is confirmed by the authority of the ruler establishes a law and is an excuse, according to the jurists on Digests, 1, 13, 3, and on the Codex, 7, 45, 2, and on the Digests, 33, 10, 3, at the end, and on the Codex, 23, 3, and by the canonists on the Decretals, 1, 6, 44, and as the Abbot treats extensively in cols. 9 et seq.

Since, then, in some regions of the New World, either by law or a very ancient custom that is confirmed by order of the rulers and scholars and priests and so by public authority, it is thought to be reverent and holy to sacrifice men to the gods who are taken for the true God, it follows that this custom and common error establishes a law among them and, consequently, will excuse those who sacrifice, since he is not considered to err or be mistaken who obeys a public law.[10]

10. According to the Digests, 50, 17, 116.

Chapter Thirty-Eight

To sum up this fourth argument, we shall recapitulate everything that has thus far been established by the reasons and citations given earlier, but especially after chapter 30, which has tried to show that unless a war can prevent the evils of which the innocent are victims, the war should be brought to an end and one should pay no attention to those who commit these wrongs. This is our position, for it is well known that evidence, or even probability, that human sacrifice is at least contrary to reason cannot be easily imparted to unbelievers of this type,

[who] believe that they and all their possessions are owed to God and that the idols they worship are the true God, a belief that is supported by a great many witnesses of the highest authority and superior to all others, such as kings, princes, high priests, theologians, prophets, or soothsayers. These latter are held in greatest reverence because the people think these men have frequent communication with the gods, from whom they receive secrets and the knowledge by which they predict future events. For these things they have approved custom, positive law, precept, and common error, and so they have a basis for a plausible argument in favor of human sacrifice.

Again, by reason of their corrupt morals they can eat human flesh so long as they do not kill anyone for this purpose. Although this is a bestial vice, except under pressure of necessity, it is in no way punishable by a foreign nation, nor can war be waged against them on this account, especially as they can offer some pretext in excuse for eating human flesh, as we have said. Nor can those who are so concerned to free the innocent easily convince them of the contrary.

Also, since they rejoice in holding that blasphemous notion that in worshiping their idols they worship the true God, or that these are God, and despite the supposition that they have an erroneous conscience, even if the true God is being preached to them by better and more credible as well as more convincing arguments, together with the good example of Christians, they are bound, without doubt, to defend the worship of their gods and their religion by going forth with their armies against all who attempt to take those things from them or injure them or prevent their sacrifices—to fight, kill, capture, and exercise all the rights consequent on a just war according to the law of nations. Furthermore, it is certain that among those who have been defiled by these detestable rites are kings and great lords, whom a large number of persons must follow: subject peoples, relatives by blood and marriage, allies (friendly or otherwise), and also persons imbued with the greatest zeal for their gods and religion. For this is a common cause for all of them who, in what appears to be a just cause that they hold to be in their favor, rouse their communal spirit to fight courageously, and who prefer death rather than failure in avenging their own injuries and those of their gods and in driving such aggressors from their country.

Equally clear is the kind and number of evils that will follow from this: many massacres, many burnings, many murders, the butchery of infants, children, women, the old, the doddering, the weak, the sick, and other harmless persons as well as the devastation of provinces, the destruction of cities, towns and peoples, many kings and lords stripped and pillaged of their dignities, dominions and honors, the loss of freedom and property, and the many foul and disgraceful crimes that will be committed by the licentiousness of the soldiers—what debauchery, rape, incest, and adultery!

With what hatred, surely, will those who suffer such evils pursue the Christian people and the God of the Christians, the true God who should be adored? How many thousand souls will meanwhile plunge into the deep pit and perish forever? And all this, indeed, that we might rescue a few innocent persons. Will these, our sacrifices, be pleasing in the sight of the divine goodness? In truth they will be as acceptable as the offering of a person "slaughtering a son before his father's very eyes."[1] Who but a man that is wicked or foolish admits a cure that is worse than the disease? Who, to prevent a few from being sacrificed to idols, would want the eternal death of countless souls who do not deserve such a fate? These things are foreign to the teaching of Christ and the example of the Apostles, nor are they pleasing to anyone but cruel and inhuman plunderers or certain ignorant enemies of Christ's glory, who in their own way make Sodom look just. So ends the fourth argument, which we began to treat in chapter 30.

Let us add a fifth argument to prove that even if the infamous deeds the Indians commit by human sacrifice and cannibalism can be stopped only by war, these practices should be passed over in silence and not corrected (or rather, worsened) by war. And this is by reason of the common good and public interest, for public interest takes precedence over private interest and the interest of the many comes before the interest of the few.[2]

1. Ecclesiasticus 34[24].
2. As in the Decretals, 1, 5, 2, in the section that says "Rightly preferring the general interest to the special and the greater interest to the lesser." And in the Decretals, 3, 31, 18: "Just as the greater good is put above the lesser good, so is the common interest preferred to the private interest." And Gratian, c. 35, C. 7, q. 1, where Pope Pelagius says "For the interest of the many is to be preferred to the interest or will of one person." The same is said in Gratian, c. 9, C. 8, q. 1, and the Digests, 17, 2, 84, and the Codex, 6, 51, 1, in the next to the last paragraph, and also in other laws. Now although these passages of the glosses teach that the public good is to be preferred to the private when the interest of the individual is included in the public good, at other times wellordered charity begins with one's self (Gratian, c. 9, C. 23, q. 5; c. 19, D. 3, *De Poenitentia*, and c. 2, C. 19, q. 2.); nevertheless, a judge or ruler ought to prefer the public to the private interest even if the public interest is not beneficial to each private citizen, as stated in the laws quoted.

This is also proved by reason, because the public good is something godlike, according to the Philosopher:

And that end . . . can only be the good for man. For even if the good of the community coincides with that of the individual, the good of the community is clearly a greater and more perfect good both to get and to keep. This is not to deny that the good of the individual is worthwhile. But what is good for a nation or a city has a higher, more divine quality.[3]

However, since the office of ruler has been established especially that its holder might be diligently concerned with the good of the state, so that the state may enjoy true happiness,[4] it follows that the ruler must set the public interest before the private interest, and also that of each citizen, and even more so if what is in the interest of the state is harmful to the judge or the ruler. Indeed, whoever undertakes the duty of governing is by that very fact obliged to set the public interest before his own, just as a soldier who is hired to defend a city is obliged to expose his life to all dangers, even the most certain, so much so that if anything else is endangered while he, in seeking his own safety, abandons control of the ship [of state], he will be liable for all the losses.[5]

This is proved also by the example and teaching of our Savior. "The good shepherd," he says, "is one who lays down his life for his sheep."[6] However, the interest of the Christian religion and the universal Church must take precedence over every public interest of any kind whatever, for Hostiensis, commenting on Decretals, 3, 33, 7, says that the interest of the state, and especially of the Church of God and the salvation of souls, must be preferred to private interest in all things. He argues[7] that if the civil state and the Christian religion are endangered at the same time and it is impossible to provide for both, certainly the interest of religion is to be preferred, since there is no greater interest than that

---

3. In *Ethics,* Book 1 [chap. 2].
4. According to the Philosopher, *Politics,* Book 1, and *Ethics,* Book 8, and Saint Thomas, *De Regimine Principum,* Book 1.
5. As the doctors say on Digests, 19, 2, 40; 19, 2, 13, #7; 19, 2, 29, and the Decretals, 1, 9, 10.
6. John 10[11]. Bartholus and the doctors treat this matter in connection with the Digests, 24, 3, 1. See Felinus on the Decretals, 1, 3, col. 21.
7. Decretals, 3, 31, 18, #*Illa;* 1, 5, 3, #*Hinc fit.*

which works for the good of religion.[8] However, between two things of special importance, that is considered greater which will do more good for the state.[9] For nothing helps the state more than that which leads to the exaltation and preservation of the faith for the salvation of souls. Moreover, the master's cause is worthier than the servant's and the soul is to be preferred to anything bodily, "For what does it profit a man if he gain the whole world but suffer the loss of his own soul?"[10]

Once we accept the principle that every good king or ruler is obliged to prefer the common good to the private good, the interest of the many to that of the few, the greater good to the lesser, and, above all else, the spread of the Catholic faith, the prosperity of the Church, and the salvation of souls, and therefore to avoid everything contrary to these and whatever could hinder them, it is absolutely clear that for no reason should he allow, for the sake of any greater, or even the greatest, public interest, the slaying of a countless number of persons so that a few may not be sacrificed to idols. For this concerns the spread of the Christian religion, since the Indians will never accept the truth of Christianity if they are hardened [against it].

Again, it is in the public interest that so many souls do not perish and that the goods of our brothers who do not know God not be plundered, according to Deuteronomy:

If you see your brother's ox or one of his sheep straying there must be no evasion; you must take them back to your brother. And if he is not close at hand or you do not know who he is [you must . . . return them to him]. You are to do the same with his donkey, the same with his cloak, the same with anything your brother loses and you find. There must be no evasion.[11]

And "If you come on your enemy's ox or donkey going astray, you must lead it back to him, etc."[12]

---

8. According to the Digests, 11, 7, 43, at the end. Bartholus supports this teaching in commenting on the Authenticae, col. 9, t. 14, 6, where it is said that a privileged person uses his privilege against another privileged person since his privilege is stronger. And on the Digests, 4, 4, 11, #7.

9. According to Philip Probus on the Liber Sextus, 5, 2, 11.

10. According to Matthew 16[26] and the Decretals, 5, 38, 13; Gratian, c. 9, C. 12, q. 1; c. 1, C. 24, q. 3; Codex, 1, 2, 21 [probably].

11. 22[1–3].

12. Exodus 23[4]. See Saint Thomas on this in *De Virtutibus*, q. 3, a. 1c.

If, then, we are obliged to prevent the loss of a brother's ox or the injury or death of a person, much more are we bound to avoid the plundering, killing, destruction, and enslaving of so large a number of our brothers. But if we cannot save and free all of them from death, certainly the interest of a great many is to be set ahead of the interest of the few, who can be saved only by the loss of a great many. Therefore we may turn our backs on the killing of the few so that countless numbers of men may avoid death. For Seneca does not admit remedies that are worse than the disease. But if this evil is to be cured by war, countless human souls and bodies will perish forever, not just for these crimes of which only a minority are guilty but for other sins that cannot be forgiven without faith.[13] They are thus deprived of the time or period for conversion and repentance. This is the worst evil that can be inflicted on our neighbors, as has often been said above. Likewise, those who survive will pursue the Christian religion with an eternal hatred when they see those who profess it committing so many heinous crimes, setting so many horrible fires, and destroying so many towns under the pretext of preventing sacrifice to idols.

To sum up, rulers and governors, who have the duty of protecting the public welfare, cannot in any way permit war to be waged against the Indians without being responsible for all its evil consequences, even if crimes of this sort can be prevented in no other way. The public interest must be preferred to the private. In conclusion, anything should be tolerated to avoid waging war, the sea of all evil, against this unfortunate people, naked, unarmed, and led astray through ignorance. For this is not helpful to the spread of the gospel and in no way is it in harmony with Christian teaching.

---

13. Saint Thomas treats this in his [*Summa Theologiae*], II–II, q. 10, a. 1.

Chapter Thirty-Nine

There still remains the sixth and last reason in support of the truth established previously: the great hope and strong presumption that such unbelievers will be converted and will be set right against these errors, for they do not commit them out of obstinacy but out of ignorance about divine things (as has already been proved on many grounds). Sins of this type, especially the impurity of idolatry, can in no way be uprooted or corrected, since it [*sic*] has a very strong hold on the hearts of the idolaters by its root, its trunk, its branches, or even its residue.[1]

On the contrary, idolatry has been uprooted at all times, in every age, and in every nation solely by the preaching of the gospel with divine help, as we are taught by the examples of the Apostles and the traditions of the doctors. For when the truth of the gospel is most effective, it softens hearts of stone and steel by its splendor, in keeping with the words of Jeremiah: "Does not my word burn like fire—it is the Lord who speaks—is it not like a hammer shattering a rock?"[2] and Paul:

1. As William of Paris has beautifully explained in his *De Legibus,* fol. 34.
2. 23[29].

"The word of God is something alive and active; it cuts like any double-edged sword but more finely; it can slip through the place where the soul is divided from the spirit, or joints from the marrow; it can judge the secret emotions and thoughts."[3]

Saint Peter also testifies to this truth when he speaks about the effectiveness of preaching, which is the means of receiving that faith by which the hearts of unbelievers are purified of all error:

My brothers . . . you know perfectly well that in the early days God made his choice among you: the pagans were to learn the Good News from me and so become believers. In fact God, who can read everyone's heart, showed his approval of them by giving them the Holy Spirit just as he had to us. God made no distinction between them and us, since he purified their hearts by faith.[4]

Saint Thomas says that this is the proper and special effect of faith, insofar as it is "the first principle for the purification of the heart" (in other words, to blot out the impurity of error). "If this faith is perfected by means of living charity, it causes a perfect purification."[5] In fact, Saint Peter's words show that the gentiles believe that after being taught through the act of belief under the guidance of the Holy Spirit they are cleansed of the errors of unbelief as well as from the impurities of other sins with which the unbelievers have been contaminated.

Eusebius treats this matter in a very learned way. He frequently repeats that idolatry and other infamous vices were removed not by war or conflagrations but by the preaching of God's word. Speaking about the effectiveness of God's word, by which the world was converted to Christ, he says, among other things:

Now when the very good and peace-making teaching of our Savior appeared, the worship of many gods was widespread, wars came to an end, the whole human race was resting from great evils and dangers. I do not hesitate to say that this was the greatest sign of his divine and indescribable power. Now if you use your eyes to notice how much men have advanced and how many benefits even of this life they have obtained, you will admit that never in the memory of man has there been accomplished by any illustrious man or people what is

3. Hebrews 4[12].
4. Acts 15[7–9].
5. [*Summa Theologiae*], II–II, q. 7, a. 2.

presently being so extensively accomplished merely by their words and their teaching, which is spread throughout the world, so that the laws of all nations are just and humane in the very areas in which laws extant before their coming were offensive, foul, and inhuman. For now the Persians who have followed him do not have heinous intercourse with their mothers. The Scythians do not eat human flesh because the preaching of Christ has reached them, nor are they impelled by a false religion to slaughter their very dear children. Certainly these and an almost infinite number of similar practices formerly plagued the life of man. The Massagetes are said to have considered the neighboring Derbices and related peoples who had attained old age to be most unhappy and so, sacrificing their bodies, they feasted on those whom very many had sacrificed. The Tibarani were said to throw their aged over cliffs, the Hyrcanians had the custom of casting their aged to a kind of ravenous bird, the Cassians used to throw theirs to the dogs. They used to do all these things as acts of religion. Now, however, this most savage plague has been dispelled everywhere solely by the power of the gospel, because the malevolent demons dwelling in the empty and insensible idols, or the elements of this world which are looked on either as the ghosts of the dead or the harmful spirits of animals, are not now considered gods. But in place of all these, solely by the teaching of the Savior, Greeks and barbarians who sincerely listened to the word of Christ have attained the wisdom of worshiping and striving for the true God, king and lord of heaven and earth, creator of the sun, the stars, and the whole universe, etc.[6]

Again, Saint Jerome says:

The Indian, the Persian, the Goth, and the Egyptian philosophize. The fierceness of the Bessians and the crowds of peoples clad in skins, who formerly practiced human sacrifices on the days of festival in honor of their deceased parents, dashed their shouts against the sweet song of the cross and Christ is the one voice of the whole world.[7]

Saint Augustine agrees with him:

In my opinion those evils are moved not by harshness, not by hardness nor by force, but by teaching rather than commanding, by admonishing rather than by threatening, for this is the way in which one must proceed with a large number of sinners.

6. Book 1, chap. 3. He teaches the same thing in other passages of the same work. Before him, Clement taught this in his *Recognitiones ad Iacobum, Fratrem Domini,* Book 9, fols. 43 and 47.
7. *Epitaphium Nepotiani ad Heliodorum.*

And later:

The admonition *to believe or give up such evils* should first be presented to spiritual persons or those who are closest to being such, *in other words, those who in comparison with others are more capable of reasoning and of spiritual matters, such as the nobles and chief lords, so that they may acquiesce and agree and by this means others will be attracted more easily.*[8]

These words [in italics] are from the gloss of Cardinal Torquemada.[9]

After this, Augustine adds: "The remainder of the multitude may be made docile by the authority of these nobles, as well as by very gentle, yet earnest admonitions." It must be noted, however, that Augustine is speaking here about the crimes of Christians. For if he wants their evils to be removed not by violence but by Christian teaching, how much more shall we use the same moderation toward those who sin through ignorance and have not yet entered God's Church?

This opinion is in harmony with what we cited from Gregory previously, as well as with what the same Saint Gregory writes below:

What advantage is there when, although unbelievers are forbidden to commit evils contrary to long usage, this is of no help toward their conversion to the faith? Do we lay down rules as to how the unbelievers should develop their ceremonies, or do we take them all away from them, if we cannot gain them through such action? We must act in such a way, then, that, attracted rather by reason and meekness, they should want to follow rather than flee from us.[10]

Furthermore, Pope Leo says the same thing in these words:

Toward those who must be corrected, let benevolence play a greater role than severity, encouragement than threats, charity than power. But those who seek what is their own rather than what is Jesus Christ's easily depart from this law, and while they find greater pleasure in dominating than in taking care of their subjects, honor is inflated into pride and what has been established for harmony tends toward injury.[11]

Gregory is speaking about the sins of priests and says that if they want to be treated with so much moderation, surely they must use the

---

8. Letter 164, to Bishop Aurelius.
9. On Gratian, c. 1, D. 44, which contains a fragment of Augustine's letter.
10. Gratian, c. 3, D. 45. We have made a few insertions. He makes the same assertion in the following canon 6.
11. Quoted in Gratian, c. 6, D. 45.

same moderation in healing the vices of unbelievers who have never heard the truth of the gospel.

This sixth argument is given by Saint Thomas, Ulrich,[12] the *Summa Confessorum*,[13] and Cardinal Torquemada.[14] These doctors cite Ulrich, who (as we have said) was a man of very great authority among the Dominicans, as the author of the *Summa Confessorum* asserts in his first preface. I add Ulrich's words to the effect that sinners must be spared if they offend by reason of ignorance: "The third case is when there is a credible presumption that they will be corrected and that they sin from weakness or ignorance and not from stubborn malice."

This agrees with what Saint Gregory says in answer to Archbishop Augustine of England:

Now there are many persons in England who, while they were unbelievers, are said to have been involved in this heinous [incestuous] wedlock. When they come into the faith, they must be warned to give it up. And they should recognize that this is a serious sin and should fear God's terrible judgment lest, because of sexual delight, they should incur the torments of eternal punishment. But they are not for this reason to be deprived of communion with the sacred Body and Blood of the Lord, lest we should seem to punish these acts in those who became involved in them through ignorance before they were cleansed by baptism. For at this time Holy Church corrects some things through fervor, tolerates some things through meekness, glosses over others through consideration, so that it frequently curbs an evil that faces it by bearing and glossing over it. However, all those who come into the faith must be warned against taking the opportunity of doing such an evil. If, nevertheless, some do it, they must be deprived of communion with the Body and Blood of the Lord, for, just as a fault must be tolerated to some degree in those who have acted out of ignorance, so it must be strongly censured in those who unhesitatingly and knowingly commit sin.[15]

Note that Gregory wants vices that are committed through ignorance to be restrained by holy admonitions, the word of God, and the fear of hell, not by lances or bombardments—something as far from Christ's teaching as heaven from earth. Moreover, Saint Gregory suggests three points: (1) it is not the Church's concern to punish the sins

---

12. *Summa,* Book 6, tract 3, chap. 8, #*Ad quod respondemus.*
13. Book 3, tract 30, q. 8.
14. On #*Hinc Etiam,* 2ae, q. 4, on conclusion 3.
15. Book 13, answer 7.

of unbelievers that are committed within the limits of their unbelief and territory; (2) the sins committed through ignorance ought to be corrected with meekness; (3) those who are new to the faith must be deterred from doing evil by the threat of eternal pain rather than by inflicting present sufferings.

Chapter Forty

Now God's word uproots idolatry and every other vice and softens the hearts of any nation, no matter how wild it may be, by its admirable power. For this reason his word will have a much greater effect upon the Indians than upon any other people, since the former have a docile character and are far more gentle, meek, and receptive than most peoples of the world in their well-known disposition to receive the faith. Experience has taught this, and for Christ's glory I candidly give to posterity what I have seen with my own eyes over a period of fifty years.

The Spaniards made an extremely bold entry into this New World, which was unheard of in past centuries. There, contrary to the intention of their ruler, they committed enormous and extraordinary crimes: they massacred uncounted thousands of persons, burned villages, drove away flocks, destroyed cities, and without cause or pretext of plausible cause did abominable and shameful things to a miserable people [. . .] fierce, rapacious, cruel, could they have a knowledge of the true God, to whose worship the religious were exhorting the Indians? Nevertheless, take note of the power of God's word and the docility of the Indians. Listen to the mercy of Christ, whose blessed name these very wicked men slandered by their crimes. The Indians embraced Christian truth very willingly, which true religious consider a great miracle. Yet some of the Indians persecuted the consecrated men and the religious monks who proclaimed the truth of the gospel to them. Alas, what if those gentle lambs should have the great Paul as their teacher, or someone who would seek to imitate Paul's virtues? How much and what [devout] service they would offer their Lord! How abundant would be the spiritual harvest, the fruit of divine exultation! If they do not spurn the gospel, which, unhappily, the preachers themselves sometimes disgrace by their way of life, what would happen if men who emulated the virtue of the Apostles were to go alone into those provinces whose inhabitants have embraced the faith of Christ, despite very bad examples and the crimes of enormous ferocity the Spaniards have committed against them?

Now whatever I say about the faith of the Indians I have seen with my own eyes, not only in one place or one nation but in very many. They honor the holy sacraments of the Catholic Church and receive them with a great indication of piety. If they cannot be helped by the sacraments because of a lack of priests, these sincere people grow pale, lament, grieve, and weep. Again, at the time of death you may see in them a wonderful concern about their salvation and their soul—a clear sign of eternal predestination that is characteristic of Christians. Would there be more among us who would be troubled with concerns of this type? Finally, with great solicitude they request the sacraments for themselves and their children. I shall speak at greater length about this in the second part of this apology.

From the foregoing we can gather that in the case of those who are idolaters only because of their ignorance of divine truths, there can be a plausible hope that once they listen to Christ's message they will be roused from this and similar vices, and we undoubtedly have to consider this hope more probable in the conversion of the nations in that world. The reason is that experience has taught us so many [favorable] things about the goodness and docility of their character. Therefore, in recovering these brothers of ours from error let us follow the example of the Apostles and apostolic men. Let us uproot idolatry and the worship of demons, as well as other sins, by the word of God and the teaching of the gospel, in the way that Christ commanded it should be made known —with the example of a good life, not by war, since malice does not remove but spreads malice.

Therefore the sixth case is clear. We began to treat it above, in the twenty-fourth chapter, in which we said that the Church can actualize its potency of coercive jurisdiction over all unbelievers, that is, in order to free innocent men from unjust oppression. The truth and determination of this matter is in these terms: Although, because of the very full power granted it by God, it is the Church's concern to prevent the previously mentioned troubles, which are inflicted upon innocent persons by reason of jurisdiction, and even to punish them when those committing these crimes are unyielding in their resistance, yet, if some human, lawful, and morally good means are first tested and these troubles of innocent persons can be avoided only by war, one must forsake this means entirely and overlook those who commit and those who suffer such things. [The reasons are:]

(1) If one cannot avoid both of two evils, he must choose the lesser evil, according to the dictates of right reason;

(2) It is clear that more innocent persons would perish than would be rescued, and we are forbidden by a very strict negative precept to kill an innocent person;

(3) In war, the innocent cannot be distinguished from the guilty;

(4) Such a remedy has already lost the character of justice or virtue;

(5) The common benefit involved in avoiding the temporal overthrow of a whole nation, and, especially [the danger of] spiritual harm;

(6) The probable hope and the strong presumption of their conver-

sion by the preaching of the faith, as long experience has taught and as has been made clear before.

To these we add this universal reason: God and his holy Church, by means of which he wants men to be saved and to come to the knowledge of the truth, would be frustrated.

And so we conclude that there are six possible cases in which the Church and its head, the supreme Vicar of Christ, can by the right of its apostolate put into practice, that is, exercise, the contentious jurisdiction it has potentially over all unbelievers, as was stated previously. And this is the second application of that distinction by which, as we said in the fifteenth chapter, the Church can exercise temporal jurisdiction over unbelievers.

There is a third mode of that distinction by which the Church can exercise temporal jurisdiction on or over unbelievers. This, however, is not just any temporal jurisdiction but that which lawyers call "voluntary." Now lawyers say that voluntary jurisdiction is that which cannot be exercised on an unwilling person but only on one who is willing. This is why it is called voluntary. Now the law enumerates the acts of voluntary jurisdiction, that is, emancipation, adoption, etc.[1] And this jurisdiction extends even to outsiders who are not subjects.[2] As the universal Vicar of Jesus Christ, the Pope has this type of jurisdiction over all unbelievers throughout the world. It is his concern to spread the gospel to all the nations of the world through his ministers and apostolic legates. This jurisdiction, however, is said to be voluntary or quasi voluntary, since unbelievers who have never professed the faith must not be compelled by the Roman Pontiff but exhorted and invited peacefully and graciously. But if they refuse to receive the gospel, they have only God as their judge. Those who do not believe are reserved for divine judgment, according to the last chapter of Mark: "He who does not believe will be condemned."[3] But if they enter Christ's sheepfold by baptism and faith, the Roman Pontiff has contentious jurisdiction

1. Codex, 3, 12, 7.
2. This is treated in the Digests, 1, 16, 2, and in the last chapter, *"De Feriis."*
3. 16[16].

over them, but only potentially, as we have previously explained at great length.[4]

Now I call this jurisdiction voluntary or quasi-voluntary for two reasons. The first is that although the duty of preaching the gospel belongs to the Pope, the unbelievers to whom it is preached are not forced to accept it, but [acceptance] is left to their free will since belief is an act of the will, as explained previously. Therefore, since the Church's power of preaching the gospel should be adapted and suited to voluntary acceptance of the faith as a means to an end, inasmuch as the same law and disposition are in one of two connected situations as much as in the other,[5] and what is accessory follows the nature of its principal,[6] it follows that such a power can be said to be a voluntary or quasi-voluntary power or jurisdiction after the manner of the jurists who call it voluntary in reference to those upon whom it is to be exercised, since they must be not unwilling but willing.

The second reason is legal and quite adaptable to our purposes. For one of the well-known acts of voluntary jurisdiction is adopting someone as a son who is not a son, just as art imitates nature.[7] This is a voluntary acceptance of an outsider who is not as yet under the power of the person who is adopting him as a son. This acceptance is the step by which the adopted person is admitted to a share in the inheritance of the adopting parent. Now this acceptance should be voluntary on the part of the adopted person.[8]

Unbelievers, who also are outsiders and strangers, are completely outside the Church's competence and so do not belong to its authority as regards coercive jurisdiction, as has been established previously at great length. It follows that if the Church wishes to adopt them as children of God, this should be with their voluntary consent: "He gave

---

4. According to [the Decretals], 2, 1, 13.
5. Gratian, c. 7, C. 1, q. 3; c. 10, C. 3, q. 6.
6. According to the rules on what is accessory, Liber Sextus, 5, rule 43.
7. See the Institutes, 1, 11, #10, in the gloss. Saint Thomas, *In IV Sententiarum*, d. 42, q. 2, a. 1c; *In III Sententiarum*, d. 10, q. 2, a. 1; q. 1, a. 1. [*Summa Theologiae*], III, q. 3, a. 5, ad 2[um].
8. Digests, 1, 7, 24.

power to become children of God"[9] to them; that is, he left this in the power of their free will so that, if they so willed, they would become sons of God. Thus Ambrose says: "Christ has chosen the voluntary soldier."[10] Hence by voluntarily receiving the sacrament of baptism they become adoptive sons of God: "The spirit you received . . . is the spirit of sons, and it makes us cry out, 'Abba, Father!' "[11] Now this power of the Church in preaching the gospel throughout the world—which is nothing else than to persuade and invite the peoples outside (unbelievers) through the teaching of the faith to become adopted sons of God willingly—is known to be established, after Christ's power and grace, only by voluntary acceptance on the part of the unbelievers, according to Saint Thomas.[12]

Beyond this and the six cases cited previously, the Church has nothing to do with judging those outside, as has been fully established in the foregoing sections of this work. It follows that such power, or jurisdiction, or the right to preach can be called voluntary because of its similarity to what the jurists call voluntary, although it is obligatory and necessary for the Church and the supreme Vicar of Christ, as was made clear in one of the previous chapters. Furthermore, as regards this necessity imposed on the Supreme Pontiff by Christ, since the Pope has been commanded to ensure the preaching of the gospel throughout the whole world, the whole world has been assigned to him as his parish, according to Chrysostom: "For when Christ communicated great things to Peter, he entrusted to him the care of the world."[13] And so the Supreme Pontiff has the care of the whole world. Hence Bernard says: "A sign, namely of Peter's singular power and pontificate is that, unlike the others, he received for his rule, not one ship but the world itself."[14]

Concerning this voluntary jurisdiction, which is based on the preaching of the faith and the voluntary conversion of the pagans, Pope

---

9. According to John 1[12].
10. Gratian, c. 10, C. 15, q. 1.
11. According to Romans 8[15].
12. [*Summa Theologiae*], III, q. 8, a. 3, ad 1um.
13. *Super Ioannem*, homily 87.
14. *De Consideratione ad Eugenium*, Book 2.

Leo speaks more expressly when, citing many points of excellence in Peter, he says: "Of all persons in the world, one Peter is chosen to be placed over the calling of all nations, all the apostles, and all parts of the Church, etc."[15]

And thus the Roman Pontiff is the first among all heralds of the truth of the gospel in the calling of all unbelieving nations, as well as the head of the universal Christian Church and of all who are considered members of the Church.

This is in harmony with what Bernard says:

Go out into the field of your Lord, go out into the world, for the field is the world and it has been entrusted to you. Go out into it not as a lord but as a steward to see and inspect those things for which you will have to give an account. Go out, I say, by some steps of your attentive care and careful attention, etc.[16]

And thus the Supreme Pontiff is not the lord of the world but the steward of the Supreme Prince and Universal Lord of the whole world, inasmuch as in his field, that is, the whole world, among all nations, by the cultivation of his apostolic teaching and in keeping with the prophecy of Jeremiah he should plant and build up virtue and uproot vice.[17] In this context, calling the Roman Pontiff the teacher of nations, Bernard says: "Furthermore you must be the form of justice, the mirror of holiness, the example of piety, the defender of truth, the defender of the faith, the teacher of nations, the leader of Christians, etc."[18] The Vicar of Christ, then, is the primary and antonomastic teacher of all men, so that one must accept his definition in matters that concern both faith and morals, according to the words of Jerome to Pope Damasus.[19]

Thus, from this obligation of the Supreme Pontiff to go into the field of his Lord (that is, into the world) to teach all nations through his ministers, the capable preachers of the faith, he is known to be the head, administrator, and shepherd of all persons throughout the world, both

15. *Third Sermon on His Ordination.*
16. In the above-mentioned Book 2, *De Consideratione ad Eugenium.*
17. 1[10].
18. Book 4 of the same work.
19. Quoted in Gratian, c. 10, C. 15, q. 1.

believers and unbelievers. And in this regard all persons are subject to him: believers absolutely in regard to spiritual matters; but unbelievers, about whom we are speaking now, according to nature or the hope of voluntary jurisdiction, but not beyond the mode we have explained. This is because he is the form of justice, confirmed in truth, as is evident from what has just been said and from what we have shown elsewhere at greater length. Moreover, these conclusions are gathered from the mind of Saint John Chrysostom when he explains the passage in Matthew 16 [19]: "I will give you the keys of the kingdom of heaven, etc." "Now Christ placed him, that is, Peter, over the whole world so that he might be able to spread everywhere the seed of the revelation of both the Father and his Son."[20]

In agreement with these statements are the words the Church sings on the feast of Saint Peter: "You are the shepherd of the sheep, the Prince of the Apostles. To you God has given all the kingdoms of the world." From this it is clear that the Supreme Pontiff is the prelate, king, and shepherd not only of those sheep who have already entered Christ's sheepfold through sacred baptism (that is, Christians), as well as their kingdoms in regard to spiritual matters, but also of all those who are outside and have not yet reached the gates of the Church (that is, unbelievers). And yet the latter must be enticed and led by the proclamation of Christ to enter the sheepfold of the Church: "And there are other sheep I have that are not of this fold, and these I have to lead as well."[21] Now these sheep are all unbelievers, especially those who have never heard anything about the faith of Christ and have not out of hatred maliciously set up obstacles to the preaching of the faith, as has been explained in chapters 3 and 6.

Furthermore, the Supreme Pontiff has been accustomed to exercise over these sheep, and should exercise, only and precisely a completely voluntary jurisdiction or authority, not contentious or coercive, as has been said. But he has been accustomed to, and should, exercise both, that is, voluntary and contentious jurisdiction, even to the extent of

20. Homily 51, in the unfinished work.
21. John 10[16].

passing judgment on temporal affairs in cases in which it is advantageous for the promotion, direction, and preservation of spiritual affairs. This is the common opinion of theologians and jurists and is in harmony with the truth.

It is evident, then, that all the kingdoms of the world and all persons throughout the world, bearing in mind the distinction mentioned, are the concern of the pastoral office, princely power, prelacy, rule, and kingship of the Vicar of Jesus Christ—of Christ who is God and Man, the Good Shepherd, King of Kings, and Lord of Lords—as we have proved at length in our treatise testifying to the right of our Spanish kings to rule over the Indian world and at greater length in other works we have written.

Chapter Forty-One

It is clear from the foregoing that there is a difference between heretics and other unbelievers, especially those who have neither heard nor embraced the faith. Furthermore, it is clear what right or jurisdiction the Church has over certain unbelievers, either potentially and actually or only potentially, as well as how and when it can actualize its habitual jurisdiction, whether it be coercive or voluntary. Now ignorance of this truth has given rise to very great evils in the Indian world and has provided turbulent men the opportunity to afflict their brothers with uncommon brutality, at great expense to the divine honor and, among those who did not know God, with great harm and hindrance to the faith and horror toward the Christian religion.

This point—that is, when can war be waged against unbelievers—has been treated by Oldraldus,[1] Alberic,[2] and Corsetus.[3] Others try to harmonize Hostiensis and Innocent, for example, Peter Ancarano,[4] Peter Bertrand,[5] Corsetus (in the previously cited passage), and others.[6] All of them are in error, however, except Bartholus.[7] He helps one understand the truth of this matter by a distinction he makes with regard to nations subject to the Roman (that is, Christian) people. Yet all of them have spoken very confusedly, possibly because they did not think or know of such unbelievers. The Lord Cardinal Cajetan, however, is far ahead of all theologians and jurists in this regard, inasmuch as he casts considerable light on this subject,[8] [and] those who slander the Indians have not understood the distinctions drawn by this very learned man. Moreover, even as they scratch their heads [about what he says], they have no qualms about disagreeing with the teaching of this scholar, and yet do not give any legitimate reason why they are led to have a different opinion. For they say that the words of Cajetan, when he teaches that it is not lawful to wage war on unbelievers solely on the basis of unbelief, must be interpreted as referring only to unbelievers, not to idolaters. In this case they proudly reject Cajetan's teaching. Moreover,

---

1. On *Consilium*, 72.
2. On the rubric *De Paganis et Sacrificiis Eorum*.
3. In his treatise *De Potestate et Excellentia Regia*, q. 82, col. 5, #*Primum ponam*.
4. On the rule *Peccatum*, q. 3, cols. 13 and 14, *De Regulis Iuris*.
5. In the treatise *De Origine Iuris*, q. 4.
6. On the Digests, 3, 24, 8.
7. On the Codex, 1, 11, 6, and on the Digests, 49, 15, 24, toward the end.
8. In his commentary on the [*Summa Theologiae*], II–II, q. 66, a. 8, ad 2um.

they have a false supposition when they say that one of the bases offered by Cajetan is that the inhabitants of the Promised Land were not destroyed because of unbelief joined with idolatry. Now these pompous men add that this is false because of what is said in Deuteronomy, chapters 9, 12, and 18, and Leviticus, chapters 13 and 20. In fact, those who make these assertions have not understood, or have refused to understand, Cajetan. For Cajetan does not deny that the inhabitants of the Promised Land were destroyed because of idolatry and other sins, since Scripture says the contrary in many passages of Deuteronomy and Joshua. Rather, [he says] that he does not read in the Old Testament that war was waged against unbelievers, taking the term "unbeliever" as meaning all those who did not live in the Promised Land. For the command which God gave the Jews to wage war involved only those dwelling in the Promised Land, not others living outside that region. And yet all these persons were idolaters and, like all the other peoples, they sacrificed their children to demons.

This was the mind of Cajetan, who, being very well versed in Sacred Scripture, must not be thought to have been ignorant of the fact that the unbelievers living in the Promised Land were conquered because of idolatry and other sins. Here are Cajetan's own words:

Not even in the Old Testament, where the possession of the land of the unbelievers had to be seized by force of arms, do I read that war was declared against any nation on the basis that they did not believe, but because they refused to give passage or because, like the Midianites, they offended them, or to gain what was granted to them by God's bounty.

This opinion is also proved by the most learned Brother Francisco Vitoria.[9]

Falsely, then, do the slanderers of the Indians attribute to Cajetan errors he neither dreamed nor thought of. He says only that no sins of the unbelievers, no idolatry, no sins against nature were the direct basis for waging war against the unbelievers, other than in the three cited cases.

9. *Relectio de Indis,* title 5.

Again, in opposition to the argument Cajetan uses in citing the example of Christ and the Apostles to establish his position, they claim that his was the argument used by the heretics against whom Augustine wrote. However, we have already refuted this deadly opinion of theirs at very great length by citing Sacred Scripture and the traditions of the holy fathers. Furthermore, other theologians, unworthy of this title, whose names will not be mentioned now for fear of publicly shaming them, devise some ridiculous and absurd fancies against Cajetan's teaching, which throws much light on this subject.

We must not fail to mention that a certain would-be jurist, possibly (as human affairs go) hunting for some greater opportunity to attack Cajetan's teaching in order to please the King by flattery, has presented the following argument. The Indians in the New World are descendants of Hagar, the handmaid of Abraham. Therefore it follows that they must be despoiled of all their possessions and kingdoms. First, although she was not his principal wife, Hagar was a wife of Abraham, not an accursed handmaid, as he claims. So who can fittingly declare how stupid, dense, and shameless the argument of this vain man is? Immortal God, how sad it is that our Spain, the most blessed mother of geniuses in other respects, should take such thick heads to be great men! And so men who should be the light and rule of virtue offer, with the destruction of their own souls, a vain, dangerous, and wicked opinion that is worthy of the flames, so that, in opposition to the example and teaching of Christ and the Apostles, innumerable human beings, redeemed by the blood of Christ, will perish forever and be most cruelly slaughtered by a plundering Spanish nation. But I shall depict very briefly, though vividly, the emptiness of this opinion which he and others use to attack the truth of the gospel under the pretext of these arguments and to lead so many thousands of persons to hell, so that all those involved may come to their senses, do penance, and, when they recognize the truth, administer an antidote to their poisons which they have given the world to drink.

Again, this absurd jurist cites Bartholus against Cajetan,[10] and intro-

10. Digests, 49, 15, 24.

duces a new distinction; that is, that there are some unbelievers who recognize the dominion of the Church, while others do not. But Bartholus, if one reads him, will make this man's stupidity and ignorance clear, for he has skillfully treated this matter.[11] We have taught the same thing at greater length in some of our short treatises. [The jurist] proceeds like a shyster rather than as a jurist, and totally exposes his ultimate senselessness before the world when he asserts something intolerable to Christian ears, that is, that without any previous warning the Spaniards can draw their swords against the Indians and seize their property, since, he says, the warning of the Apostles, "Their voice has gone out through all the earth,"[12] is enough for them. And, furthermore, the Spaniards have warned them to embrace the faith of Christ. Whenever they do not obey this warning but instead prepare their arms, they can quite rightfully be despoiled of their kingdoms without previous warning. The shameless sycophant piles up laws and paragraphs. He cites numberless names of doctors, but irrelevantly, and no less unlearnedly than stupidly. I pray that he may have a saner mind, although he considers himself very learned.

Moreover, by means of all the matters discussed and concluded from chapter 24 up to now we believe that we have sufficiently answered the third cause by which Sepúlveda seeks to justify those satanic expeditions or *conquistas* (as they are called), waged by our people against the nations of the south and west. Now if you add to this what has been previously proved by our twelve replies at the most solemn meeting of great theologians and canonists—gathered by command of the Emperor —to the Council of the Indies at Valladolid in 1551, by such light you will see more clearly what thick darkness most dangerously binds the famous doctor and those who cling to his error.

---

11. On the Digests, 49, 15, 24, and the Codex, 1, 11, 6.
12. [Romans 10:18].

Chapter Forty-Two

At this point we shall refute Sepúlveda's fourth argument or cause [for war], in which he says that war can be waged against the Indians so that, once the path has been totally cleared for the preachers of the gospel, the Christian religion may be spread. Indeed, I cannot cease being astonished by Sepúlveda. For what spirit leads a theologian, mature and well versed in humane letters, to set these poisons before the world so that the far-flung Indian empires, contrary to the law of Christ, would be prey for most savage thieves? In the same way, and to this very moment, the greed of the Spanish people has led to such crimes among those peoples as—according to history—have never been committed by any other nation, no matter how fierce it may have been. In fact, Sepúlveda tries with all his might to increase these crimes, until the last nation in that world will finally be wiped out, when the just and upright God, provoked by these actions, will perhaps pour forth the fury of his anger and lay hold of all of Spain sooner than he had decreed.

And so Sepúlveda first cites what Augustine writes in his letter to the heretic Donatus. Sepúlveda claims that Augustine teaches that peoples during the first period of the nascent Church were to be led to the faith of Christ courteously and gently, whereas later, when the powers of the Church had increased, they could be forced to enter Christ's sheepfold, as in the parable of the wedding feast. Surely Sepúlveda speaks wickedly and commits many errors to the destruction of his soul, especially on three points.

The first is that he says the decrees of the Church against heretics, published by the Pope and the Emperors, should be observed even against unbelievers [in general]. He fails to distinguish the four kinds of unbelievers. Some are unbelieving Moors and Jews who live under the rule of Christians. Others are apostates and heretics. Others are Turks and Moors who persecute us by war. Others are idolatrous unbelievers who live in very remote provinces.

The second error is that Sepúlveda gives a distorted interpretation of the parable of the wedding feast.[1]

The third error is that by not distinguishing unbelievers who are subject to the Church or to rulers who are its members from other, nonsubject unbelievers he grants the Church jurisdiction in cases where it does not have it. In chapter 6 and the following chapters I have proved by clear arguments that this stand is false.

However, as regards the principal question, certainly that gospel parable does not in any way prove what Sepúlveda would have it prove. He tries to prove that Christ wanted the Church, once it had been strengthened by resources and rulers, to force men to embrace the truth of the gospel, not by forcibly baptizing them but by uprooting the worship of idols and crushing their power, so that they could not obstruct the preaching of the gospel. Above all, I would gladly learn from Sepúlveda why God should want force to be used on unbelievers by the Church and Christian rulers rather than by angels, by whose ministry God frequently leads unbelievers to knowledge of himself.[2]

Again, I ask whether the compulsion recorded in the parable should be bodily or material and whether it should be brought to bear by the angels or by God himself. Indeed, if Sepúlveda and his associates have nothing else to offer but their own comments, I shall cite in opposition the words of Saint Jerome to Paulinus:

1. Luke 14[15–24] and Matthew 22[1–14].
2. According to what the great Dionysius says in his *De Coelesti Hierarchia*, chap. 9.

If perhaps some should come to the sacred writings after studying worldly literature and delight the ears of the people by their sermons, they think that whatever they say is God's law. They do not bother to learn the interpretations of the prophets and apostles, but shape conflicting testimonies to their own meaning, as though perverting opinions and dragging contrary scripture texts to their own will were a great rather than a most vicious way of teaching.[3]

In fact, Venerable Doctor Sepúlveda, you would do well to ponder the truth that a parable is an obscure teaching or figure of speech, according to Saint Thomas.[4] Now parables may be explained in very many ways and receive very many interpretations, and the same parable can be applied to different things according to the various points of similarity.[5] Moreover, the literal sense, upon which other meanings are based and which cannot be false, is not that which anyone may want it to be but what the author of Sacred Scripture, that is, the Holy Spirit, intends it to be. The determination of what or what sort that meaning may be, however, is not the function of just anybody but only of the sacred doctors, who have surpassed other men by their way of life and their teaching. Now among all these doctors there has not been one who has explained that gospel parable as Sepúlveda explains it; that is, that unbelievers, and especially the gentiles who have never heard the truths of faith, must be compelled by rulers and the help of force to abandon the worship of idols and enter Christ's sheepfold (that is, the Church). And the same is true of external and bodily compulsion. There is tremendous rashness, then, in presuming to prove by means of that parable that Christ commanded his Church that, once it had grown, it should use physical compulsion on unbelievers before the faith is preached to them. Furthermore, all theologians teach that nothing that concerns the faith or the salvation of men is proposed in sacred literature in a parable or a spiritual sense and is not clearly presented by other passages of scripture in a literal sense. This is the teaching of Augustine[6] and Saint Thomas.[7]

3. Letter 53 to Paulinus [Pl 22:544].
4. [*Summa Theologiae*], I, q. 1, a. 10, ad 3[um], and *Super Isaiam.*
5. Saint Thomas [*Summa Theologiae*], I–II, q. 33, a. 1, ad 1[um]; *In I Sententiarum,* d. 17, a. 1, q. 1, quaestiuncula 3c.
6. *De Doctrina Christiana.*
7. [*Summa Theologiae*], I, q. 1, a. 9, ad 2[um]; a. 10, ad 1[um]; *Quodlibetale,* 7, a. 14. ad 3[um].

At this point I would like Sepúlveda and his associates to produce some passage from sacred literature where the gospel parable is explained as he explains it; that is, that the gospel (which is the good and joyful news) and the forgiveness of sins should be proclaimed with arms and bombardments, by subjecting a nation with armed militia and pursuing it with the force of war. What do joyful tidings have to do with wounds, captivities, massacres, conflagrations, the destruction of cities, and the common evils of war? They will go to hell rather than learn the advantages of the gospel. And what will be told by the fugitives who seek out the provinces of other peoples out of fear of the Spaniards, with their heads split, their hands amputated, their intestines torn open? What will they think about the God of the Christians? They will certainly think that [the Spaniards] are sons of the devil, not the children of God and the messengers of peace. Would those who interpret that parable in this way, if they were pagans, want the truth to be announced to them after their homes had been destroyed, their children imprisoned, their wives raped, their cities devastated, their maidens deflowered, and their provinces laid waste? Would they want to come to Christ's sheepfold with so many evils, so many tears, so many horrible massacres, such savage fear and heartbreaking calamity? Does not Paul say, "Treat each other in the same friendly way as Christ treated you"? And a little earlier: "And indeed everything that was written long ago in the Scriptures was meant to teach us something."[8] Therefore, just as they would not want to be led to Christ's sheepfold in this way, so too they should refrain from all violence toward their brothers—just as this moderation of the gospel was used by Saint James and his disciples toward their [the Spaniards'] ancestors, who were contaminated with possibly worse crimes, and were more given over to the filth of idolatry, and abounded in more barbaric customs than the other nations, as can be seen in the great difficulty in converting Spain to Christ.

Let the Spaniards refrain, I say, from exercising this kind of excess toward other nations and let them use that gentleness with which they were called, whether these peoples are barbarians, idolaters, or infected with any other vices whatsoever. The reason for this is clear, for there is no longer [distinction between] man and woman, "Greek and Jew, between the circumcised or the uncircumcised, or between barbarian

8. [Romans 15:7 and 4].

and Scythian, slave and free man. There is only Christ: he is everything
and he is in everything."[9] "There is no distinction between Jew and
Greek: all belong to the same Lord who is rich enough, however many
ask his help."[10]

Chrysostom says the same thing:

Just as there is no natural difference in the creation of men, so there is no
difference in the call to salvation of all of them, whether they are barbarous or
wise, since God's grace can correct the minds of barbarians so that they have
a reasonable understanding. He changed the heart of Nebuchadnezzar to an
animal mind and then brought his animal mind to a human understanding. He
can change all persons, I say, whether they are good or bad: the good lest they
perish, the bad so that they will be without excuse.[11]

Therefore, since the nature of men is the same and all are called by
Christ in the same way and they would not want to be called in any
other way, it should not be argued that Indians should be led to the
Church in any way other than that by which other men are led.

Again, there is the following argument against the famous doctor
and his obstinacy. The literal sense of any scriptural passage, which
according to Augustine and Saint Thomas is the only basis for an argument, is that which its author, the Holy Spirit, intends and wants us to
grasp. Now by the words of the parable "Force them to come in" Christ
means that, immediately by himself or through angels or men, he usually moves and attracts to himself in an intellectual fashion and, as it
were, compels by a visible or invisible miracle those who do not know
his truth, yet without exercising any force on their will. That is the
literal sense. By that parable, then, Christ wished to signify not external
but persuasive violence. This is sufficiently clear from the words of
Chrysostom cited above, as well as from what Saint Thomas says when
speaking about this parable: "That compulsion which Saint Luke mentions in chapter 14 is not one of force but one of effective persuasion,
as, for example, through harsh or gentle words."[12] This means moving
the hearts of men by infusing within the powers of the soul either fear
or sadness, or by externally afflicting the body with diseases or suffer-

9. Colossians 3[11].
10. Romans 10[12].
11. *Super Matthaeum,* chap. 22, homily 41, in the unfinished work.
12. *De Veritate,* q. 22, a. 9, ad 7um.

ings, or by illuminating the soul itself with the light of the Holy Spirit. Now God either does this himself or through angels or men, by depicting the sufferings of hell, the eternal damnation of the soul, and other troubles of the present life and the life to come. The command "Force them to come in" is carried out in these ways, that is: "Persuade them unceasingly and motivate them to be converted through threats of this type," in keeping with the commands of the Apostle: "Proclaim the message and, welcome or unwelcome, insist on it; refute falsehood, correct error, call to obedience."[13] "Exhort . . . with all authority."[14] "So you will have to be severe in correcting them, and make them sound in the faith."[15] This is how this parable is interpreted by Cardinal Hugo and Dionysius the Carthusian. For God uses the ministry of angels to impart light and salvation to men and commands them to compel men in these ways, according to Dionysius, who says that by the ministry of angels God drew many pagans to know him. "Performing the function of the priesthood, the angels pursued persons in each nation and led them to the one source of all things, etc."[16]

By the same words the Lord instructs men by means of prelates and preachers whom he selects for a similar ministry, just as he instructed Peter, whom he was sending to Cornelius,[17] and Paul when he sent him to Macedonia,[18] and Philip whom he sent to meet the eunuch of Queen Candace.[19] By reason of the duty enjoined on these men, it [was] their obligation to exhort and not to omit rebukes and threats, both in season and out of season. And in this way it can be said that many unbelievers come to the knowledge of the true God as if they were compelled. And so unbelievers are compelled to know the truth by poverty, hunger, disease, suffering, and fear. They are compelled also by the word of God, which is most effective, according to what we read in Jeremiah: "Does not my word burn like fire . . . is it not like a hammer shattering a rock?"[20] Or they are moved to believe because they are convinced by miracles or arguments, just as we also say that the demons have a kind

13. 2 Timothy 4[2].
14. Titus 2[15].
15. Titus 1[13].
16. *De Coelestia Hierarchia,* chap. 9.
17. Acts 10.
18. Acts 16[9–10].
19. Acts 8[26, 39].
20. 23[29].

of forced faith. For although they are unwilling, their intellect is convinced by effective arguments in the things they see and understand, for they see manifest signs by which they perceive that the teaching of the Church is from God, who can neither deceive nor be deceived, although they do not see the realities the Church teaches, for example, that God is one and triune, and other truths of this type. Therefore they are forced to believe on the basis of their intellectual acuteness.[21] Thus in his *Posterior Analytics* and in the fourth book of his *Metaphysics* Aristotle writes about ancient philosophers who, even if they denied first principles in their speech, were forced to admit them once they were convinced by evident and necessary arguments, which he presents in the eleventh book of his *Metaphysics,* chapter 4. Augustine says of this type of interior and persuasive compulsion: "O happy necessity which compels one to what is better." And Seneca says: "I give thanks for my weakness which forces me to be unable to do what I ought not want to do." And this is the compulsion that Christ means to teach by means of the parable in its literal sense.

21. See Saint Thomas [*Summa Theologiae*], II–II, q. 5, a. 2c, and ad 2[um].

Chapter Forty-Three

With regard to persuasive compulsion of this type, please observe what Saint Thomas said:

Now it was not right that man should be justified unless he was willing, for this would be both contrary to the nature of justification, which implies right disposition of the will, and contrary to the very nature of man, which must be led to good freely, not forcibly. Christ, then, justified men inwardly by his divine power but not against their will.[1]

And after many other observations, Saint Thomas continues:

Nevertheless, Christ has worked some miracles on the souls of men, especially by changing their lower powers. Hence, commenting on *Matthew* 9 [9], "He (*that is, Matthew*) got up and followed him," Jerome says, "Such was the splendor and majesty of his hidden divinity which shone forth even in his human countenance that it could draw those who gazed on it to him at first sight."

His purpose was to invite and attract those people gently, by inspiration and illumination, as well as by infusing them with wisdom and divine love. Saint Thomas, in the passage cited, adds:

When commenting on *Matthew* 21 [12], "Jesus drove out all those who were selling and buying there," the same Jerome says, "Of all the signs worked by Our Lord, this seems to me more wondrous—that one man, at that time the object of contempt, could, with the blows of one whip, expel so many persons, for a blazing and heavenly light flashed from his eyes and the majesty of his divinity shone in his countenance." Again, on *John* 18 [6], "They moved back and fell to the ground," Augustine says, "One word, without any weapon, struck, drove back, lay prostrate that crowd wild with hate and frightening with arms; for God lay hidden in that flesh."

And later Saint Thomas draws his conclusion:

From all of this it is clear that, when he willed, Christ changed the minds of men by his divine power, not only by granting them justice and infusing wisdom,

1. [*Summa Theologiae*], III, q. 44, a. 3, ad 1um

which is the purpose of miracles, but also by outwardly drawing men to himself or by terrifying or amazing them, which is part of the miracles themselves.

From this it is also clear that the very way in which Christ was drawing believers [*sic*] to knowledge of himself was miraculous. Furthermore, there is no doubt that he also uses such methods daily to enlighten men by means of men or angels. This is evident in the conversion of Saint Paul. We learn that Paul was changed from a wolf into a lamb by a certain divine miracle by which he was thrown from his horse when a light from heaven shone about him.[2] Since we do not read of a similar calling in any other passage, the Church celebrates it as unique and extraordinary, according to Saint Thomas.[3] A calling of this kind, then, must not be offered as an example, since it was special, and particular privileges do not make a common law, etc. Now Saint Thomas explains the ordinary way in which the Lord draws men to himself without compulsion. Saint Thomas says:

God can change the will by necessity but he cannot force it, for no matter how much the will may be moved to something, it is not said to be forced to it. The reason for this is that to will something means to be inclined to it, whereas force or violence is contrary to the inclination of the thing which is forced. Therefore when God changes the will, he makes another inclination follow the preceding one. And so the first is removed and the second remains. Hence that to which he moves the will is not contrary to the presently existing inclination but to the inclination which was there before. There is not, then, any force or violence here. For example, by reason of its weight, a rock has the inclination to fall. Now as long as this inclination remains, if the rock is thrown upward, there is violence. If, however, God were to remove the inclination of weight from the rock and give it an inclination to weightlessness, then being borne upward would not be violent for it. And therefore an opposed movement can be without violence. And this is how we must understand that God changes the will without forcing the will, etc.[4]

Therefore the Lord gently moves each thing to its end: "She [divine wisdom] deploys her strength from one end of the earth to the other,

2. Acts 9[4–5].
3. [*Summa Theologiae*], I–II, q. 113, a. 10c, at the end.
4. *De Veritate*, q. 22, a. 8. [*Summa Theologiae*], I, q. 105, a. 3–4, throughout, and in various passages of the *Contra Gentes*.

ordering all things gently."[5] Certainly that movement by which divine wisdom draws to itself created things, especially rational creatures, is absolutely contrary to that movement which our adversaries dream up with drawn swords, destructive means, and bombardments. For the truly human means is the desire to be taught, led, and attracted gently, not to be compelled by force of arms. For, according to the Philosopher, each thing is acted on or drawn in the way that it is naturally inclined to be acted on or drawn.[6] And, as is evident from experience, men naturally want to be attracted by gentleness and kindness.

Furthermore, it is said that "a kindly turn of speech multiplies a man's friends, and a courteous way of speaking invites many a friendly reply. . . . A mild answer turns away wrath, sharp words stir up anger."[7] And according to Valerius Maximus: "The gentleness of humane conduct penetrates the temperaments of barbarians."[8] The cause of this is nobility of character, which, according to Seneca, is led rather than drawn, for the mind has something sublime, passionate, and impatient for what is higher. But it is brought into subjection by the delight of some reverence or mildness, through which it suspects that what is higher can come down to an equal status with it and that it does not have to rise above its level. Thus in the eighth book of the *Ethics*, the Philosopher says that good will is the beginning of friendship.

God, then, uses his unutterable wisdom as he draws men to himself in these ways. For no one but God can do those things to the human will, that is, that it should wish and love today what it shrank from and avoided yesterday, by interiorly disposing and inclining men's minds gently to the contrary, all of which is a miracle. For the tongue of the preacher would labor in vain unless the grace of the Savior were present within, as Augustine says. Now this is obvious because many persons heard Christ's preaching yet not all of them were converted, since Christ did not produce the above-mentioned effects in the minds of all those who heard him. Whoever, then, comes to the faith and changes his outlook receives this change from God, for no human terrors can change the human will unless Christ is working interiorly.

Again, among all of God's miracles the conversion of the sinner is

5. Wisdom 8[1].
6. *Physics*, Book 2.
7. Proverbs 6 [*sic* for Ecclesiasticus 6:5 and Proverbs 15:1].
8. Book 6.

considered the greatest, both because of the magnitude of the work itself in view of the obstacles arising from sin, which separates man from God by an infinite distance, and because the end of this conversion is the eternal good. And in regard to this, and in explaining the phrase "He shall perform even greater works,"[9] Augustine says: "To make a just man of a sinner is a greater work than to create the heavens."[10]

Therefore, in order that Christ might show us the greatness of his truth and the surpassing strength of his divine word, by which he cures and heals those who, because of their sins, especially idolatry and unbelief, cannot be healed naturally (that is, without his help), thus making them children of God and heirs of the kingdom of heaven, he has used the expression "Force them to come in" in order to indicate a change that is beyond human power. We might even say that idolaters who [formally] refuse to reject the worship of idols and other sins have nevertheless rejected [them], under the interior working of divine grace and by reason of Christ's word and truth. This is helped by the example of the good Christians who preach the gospel.

Now in order to know that this literal explanation of the truth is correct, let us see what Theophylactus says about the same parable:

Those "in the highways and hedges" must be interpreted as the gentiles since the Israelites were within the city as those who had embraced the law and attained a more civil way of life. But the gentiles were alien to the covenants and law of God and had not become "citizens with the saints" and were involved, not in one, but in many kinds of evil and great coarseness. [They were] "in hedges" which I interpret to mean "sins." For sin is a large hedge and gap separating us from God. By "highways" then, he means the special [bestial] life of the gentiles, divided into many opinions. By "hedges" [he means] their life in sin. He does not simply command that they be called but "forced", he says, although belief is a voluntary act on the part of all. Moreover in order that we may know that peoples involved in such dismal ignorance are subject to God's great power, he said "force." For, unless it were preached that the power and the truth of the Word are great, how would men who have gone mad in the worship of idols and done vile things be persuaded to have a sudden recognition of the true God and a love for the spiritual life? Therefore, seeking to indicate a remarkable turnabout, he stated a necessity, as though someone were saying, "Even the gentiles who refused to give up idols and pleasures have been forced

9. John 14[12].
10. In his commentary on John. Saint Thomas deals with this in his [*Summa Theologiae*], I, q. 105, a. 7–8, throughout.

to abandon them by the preaching of the truth." Or, in another way, the power of his signs, too, necessitated their changeover to the faith of Christ.

And later:

Therefore, to those sinners astray along the broad and spacious highways of sins, the Father sends his Son to invite them to the feast. He was a servant according to the flesh who came to call not the just, but sinners. These he invites after having freely taught beforehand both the wealthy and the self-indulgent. By sending them many diseases and dangers, even if they are unwilling he makes them renounce this life by those judgments by which he usually brings them to his feast, by imposing a necessity and a trial upon them. There are many examples of this. Now this parable teaches us that it is to be given to the simple, the poor, and the weak, rather than to the wealthy, just as he had advised a little before. We learn something else too, that is, that we should be quick and free to receive the poor and that, even when they are unwilling, we should force them to become sharers in our goods. Teachers, too, are warned that it is worthwhile to teach students, even when they are unwilling.[11]

At the end he said"teach," not "inflict war or bodily" (that is, exter-nal) "violence." For, as we have frequently said, the weapons of war are by their very nature directed to the subjugation not of souls but of bodies, property, and places. Surely Theophylactus' explanation of the parable previously cited, "Force them to enter," is vastly different from that which our adversaries devise. I ask them: In explaining Scripture, shall we give greater credence to holy men, who probably had God's spirit as they interpreted the sacred writings, or to Sepúlveda and his accomplices, who in violation of Christ's law try to destroy that im-mense world by ruinous war? These men do not hesitate to claim, rashly and unjustly, that Christ, through the parable cited above, commanded us to disturb unbelievers, who are living peacefully and quietly, with the inhumanity and turbulence of war, to inflame the gentlest peoples, to despoil the poorest, to teach the humblest and simplest persons pride, cunning, and malice, to lead free peoples with tyrannical ferocity into bitter slavery in violation of natural law and the law of nations, and finally to make it forever impossible for nations that are most ready for the faith to enter Christ's sheepfold.

Away with those who offer us not solid doctrine but the emptiest dreams! What do they offer against the truth of the gospel and the

11. This is a summary of Theophylactus' teaching.

examples of the Apostles, except calumnies, lies, and adulterated passages of the Scriptures? Knowing neither the Scriptures nor God's power, those wretched men go astray.

Chapter Forty-Four

These men claim that Constantine the Great waged wars on unbelievers in order that, once they had been subjected to his rule, he might remove idolatry and the faith might be introduced more freely. But where is the evidence that war was waged against them just because they were pagans? Is it what we read in the *Church History?*—

Meanwhile, relying on his piety, Constantine overcame on their own soil the Sarmatians, the Goths, and other barbarian nations, except those who offered peace either by friendship or by surrender. And the more religiously he subjected himself to God, so much the more did God subdue all things for him.[1]

From these words there is absolutely no evidence that Constantine waged war on them simply because they were pagans, that is, in order

1. Book 10, chap. 9.

to uproot the worship of idols. Indeed, if he had taken up arms against them only for this reason, surely the *Church History,* which we have just quoted, would not have been silent about it, since it would closely concern God's glory and the exaltation of the Catholic faith.

We shall be able to argue the contrary by plausible reasons.

The first is that since the Goths against whom Constantine fought had violently troubled the Roman people with war and were provoking them by daily attacks, it is probable that Constantine waged war against them because he was seriously moved by old and new injuries, but not for the express purpose of uprooting idolatry. For the Gothic race was terrifying in its wild and inhuman cruelty, very hostile to the Roman nation, and troublesome to all nations. For this reason Constantine had every right to wage war against them, since they had afflicted the peoples under Roman rule, whom Constantine was obliged to protect from harm, with very many misfortunes. Hence the Tripartite History says: "Since that nation was prone to war and was stronger than other barbarians in the number and size of its constantly ready troops, they had only the Romans fighting against them."[2] And a little before this the same history states that at that time those who were called Goths had very recently made solemn treaties with Constantine to win his favor. Therefore it cannot be gathered from these statements that Constantine waged war against that people to uproot idolatry and draw them to the faith.

The second reason is that the Goths, Sarmatians, and Gelonians were Scythian nations, who lived in Europe differing only inasmuch as some dwelt in rugged mountain regions and others lived on the plains.[3] Yet all of them were Scythians, just as the Cantabrians, the Gallicians who live in the mountains and ridges of Spain, and the Beticans are Spaniards. Now in the second part of his history the Archbishop of Florence writes that these Scythians, a wild and inhuman people, made devastating raids within the confines of Roman jurisdiction at the time of Constantine or shortly before. Constantine, then, warded off injury or inflicted similar devastation as revenge for theirs, but he did not seek to lead them to the knowledge of Christ by means of war.

The third reason is that very frequently the Goths greatly weakened the Roman Empire by warring against it, and even triumphed over the

2. Book 1, chap. 9.
3. According to Pomponius Mela, Book 2; Pliny, Book 4, chap. 12; and Strabo, Book 11.

city of Rome, the conqueror of all nations.[4] Therefore Constantine had
many different reasons for waging war against the Goths, so ruinous to
the Roman people both in his century and in the following centuries.
They plagued the Roman provinces and brought them under their rule.
Therefore it is not certain that Constantine waged war against foreign
peoples in order to draw them to the faith.

The fourth reason is that, besides being idolaters, the Goths were
infected with the Arian heresy and favored this deadly error.[5] Perhaps
they waged war on Catholics in order to defend their sect. Thus in
defending the Catholic people Constantine very justly brought all his
power to bear against the Goths. Therefore, on the supposition that
these reasons are likely and probable, it will be impossible for our
adversaries to boast that they are producing evidence to the contrary.
That Constantine is said to have invaded their provinces and subjugated
them by war [implies] the action of a skillful Emperor. For since he knew
that those people were dangerous and hostile to him and that they
always sought an occasion to harm him and his subjects as much as
possible, he cleverly invaded their provinces with his army. That war
was just in the eyes of the law. For in this case, that is, when one's
enemies are arming and looking for a chance [to strike], it is lawful to
wage war against them, since I should not wait for the enemy to wound
me before I defend myself and ward off his violence. Natural reason
dictates this and civil law makes provision for it.

The fifth reason is that the Irish, a barbarian people who lived in the
forests and were totally given over to the worship of idols,[6] received the
faith of Christ at the time of Constantine the Great not because they
were compelled by any fear of war from Constantine but because of the
faith and activity of a certain Christian female slave, and finally because
of the working of a divine miracle. The *Church History* says that Constantine was happier about the conversion of this nation than he would
have been had the great Roman Empire been enlarged by the addition
of new kingdoms and empires.[7] Again, in the same *History*, it is said
that, at the time of Constantine, remote India received God's word

4. See Orosius, Book 7, chaps. 37, 38, 39; Paul the Deacon, *Roman History*, Book 12.
Jerome weeps over this (*Epistola ad Heliodorum*), as does Augustine (*De Civitate Dei*, Book
9, chap. 23).
5. This is proved in the *Tripartite History*, Book 8, chap. 13.
6. According to Caesar, Book 5, and Strabo, Book 4.
7. Book 10, chap. 11.

because of the persuasion of two servants of a certain merchant or curious philosopher who went about with avid desire of seeing and learning about new territories and kingdoms.[8]

The sixth reason is that it is unlikely, and so improbable, that Saint Sylvester, with a view to promoting the faith, would induce Constantine to do the very thing by which the faith would be made most hateful to unbelievers. For if Constantine should attack the nations of unbelieving idolaters who had never received the faith in order to subject them to his rule and to destroy idolatry after he had overcome them, and in order that the preaching of the faith might follow immediately, the faith itself would become hateful to them, as we have amply demonstrated. Therefore it is unlikely, and so improbable, either that the holy Bishop would advise Constantine to undertake such a war or that Constantine himself would start a war of this type. Neither Pope Saint Sylvester nor the Emperor Constantine, therefore, waged war on pagans so that they would refrain from the worship of idols out of fear of war.

From this it is evident that the passage in the *Church History* in no way supports the anti-Christian cause that Sepúlveda has undertaken to defend. Nor would Pope Sylvester, who is numbered among the saints, have persuaded Constantine about a matter that is not only useless for the spread of the Christian religion but is quite harmful to it. For if pagans are afflicted with the misfortunes of war (which are worse than any plague or calamity) by Christians, by whom they should have been taught rather than forced, they will consider the Christian religion duplicitous, seeing that there is so much fierce cruelty in those who worship Christ, as the massacres, violence, burnings, and plunder mount against them. Nor will they ever believe that the gospel (that is, the Good News) is being announced to them but that a hellish calamity is being unleashed on them by demons, especially since we may suppose that they are in probable error and will consider as just a war against anyone in their own defense and that of their gods. Still more would a war be just that is aimed at avenging evils they have already received. Will they hear the words of shepherds and fathers who want to lead them to Christ's sheepfold by Christian charity? Or will they see plunderers and robbers, greedy not for the salvation of souls but for plunder?

8. Book 5, chap. 10.

And so there is a reason why these peoples will hate the faith, since they think it is not what it is, that is, not the truth but a lie.

These conclusions are supported by the fact that Blessed Sylvester led idolaters to the faith by service and inducements, as we read in his history and as is recorded by the canonists.[9] So too did Gregory offer a remission of the rents the Jews owed from the possessions of the Church that were rented to them, so that they might be converted.[10] How far removed are these from the approaches of war? Far indeed! For pagans should be attracted by way of inducement and charity, in keeping with the command of Christ: "Your light must shine in the sight of men, so that, seeing your good works, they may give the praise to your Father in heaven."[11] But war is an occasion for blaspheming Christ's sacred name, according to Chrysostom.[12] Explaining these words of Christ, he says:

God is glorified through those who teach and act, but blasphemed through those who teach but do not act. For example, if they teach well and live even better, the gentiles, on seeing this, say, "Blessed be the God who has such servants, for truly their God is the true God, since, unless he was just, he would never have a people so devoted to justice. The discipline of the master is shown in the behavior of his family. They are not like our philosophers who talk of great things but do not perform even the least."

If, however, they teach well but live badly, the gentiles, on seeing this, say, "What sort of god is the god of those who act like that? Would he let them do such things if he did not consent to their deeds? Like them, our parents think that those who worship idols have preserved the whole of justice, whereas they speak glorious sermons and perform ignominious deeds."

You see how God is blasphemed through bad Christians, nor can one have a good opinion about the master who has a bad family. Hence it was said to God's people, "For the name of God is blasphemed through you among the gentiles."[13]

Then, explaining the same words in the fifteenth homily of his complete commentary, he says:

---

9. In c. 2, C. 1, q. 2. Liber Sextus, 3, 4, 25 [a faulty citation].
10. This is clear in his sixth letter, Book 4.
11. Matthew 5[16].
12. Homily 10, in the incomplete commentary.
13. Ezeckiel 36[20]. Isaiah 52[5]. Romans 2[24].

Nothing but the lack of love holds back the gentiles, nothing converts them so much as the virtue of the soul. Nothing is so scandalous as malice. For when they see a person who enjoins the opposite profiting by avarice and theft and that from those who are of the same clan, as if he exercised jurisdiction over them, the observers will say that what this person said is madness. Whoever sees a Christian love the highest rank and enslaved to his other passions will remain firm in his own beliefs and will not imagine anything great. For we are the reason why they remain in error. In fact, they would have despised in former times the teachings which they now hold and would admire our teachings in the same way, but they are held back by our lives. Now since we almost destroy the properties of our neighbors, they call us a detriment to the world.

And again he says: "Christians gain the benevolence of the gentiles if they are ready, not to commit but to endure evil."[14]

14. In the same fifteenth homily on Matthew.

Chapter Forty-Five

All of these things are in agreement with what Augustine writes:[1]

God wanted his people to be holy and he wanted them to be so free from every contagion of injustice and evil, so just, so pure, so unspotted, so simple, that the gentiles would find in them nothing to reproach, but only what they would admire, so that they would say, "Happy the nation whose God is the Lord, the people he has chosen for his heritage."[2] Such should be the worshipers and servants of God: serious, prudent, pious, blameless, and unspotted, so that whoever sees them may be astonished and may marvel and say, "These persons who live in such a way belong to God." The man of God should present himself and act in such a way that there may be no one who would not want to hear him and see him, that anyone seeing him would think that he is a child of God, so that truly that prophecy may be fulfilled in him, "His conversation is sweetness itself, he is altogether lovable."[3] For if the Christian, the servant of God, presents himself in such a way that, by his way of life, he is no better than those who serve demons and idols, God will begin to be blasphemed through him and they will say, "O Christian! O servant of God! Your way of life is so wicked. Your acts are evil, your deeds loathsome, your life ungodly, criminal, luxurious, and foul." And he will be guilty of that prophecy, "For the name of God is blasphemed through you among the gentiles."[4] But woe to those through whom it has been blasphemed. Moreover God desires and demands of us nothing more than that, by our actions, his name might be glorified by all persons, as it has been written, "Whoever makes praise his sacrifice honors me."[5] This is the sacrifice which God seeks and loves more than all victims so that, through the works of our justice, his name may be praised everywhere and that he is the true God may be proved by the actions and works of his servants. Those persons truly love God who accomplish nothing else than the glory of God's name.

From these words of Chrysostom and Augustine it is quite clear how great an opportunity is given pagans to blaspheme Christ if war is waged against them and how great a hatred for the Christian religion is implanted in the hearts of pagans by war. Thinking they have a strict

1. In his book *De Vita Christiana.*
2. [Psalms 33:12].
3. [Song of Songs, 5:16].
4. [Romans 2:24].
5. [Psalms 50:23].

opinion about the gods, they will think that those who profess Christian truth wage war against them unjustly. And far more reasonably, they will become incensed against the Christian religion and those who profess it when they have learned that they suffer these evils because of their worship of their gods. For when, in such a war, which they think they are suffering unjustly, parents see that they are being deprived of their children, husbands of their wives, masters of their servants or subjects, and vice versa, and that they are led into slavery and cruelly slaughtered by a Christian people to whom they have done no wrong —from such deeds of Christians, what, I ask, will be their judgment about these men and their teaching? For, according to Chrysostom: "The gentiles were accustomed to form their judgment about teachings, not from what was said, but from deeds and the way of life."[6] And a little earlier: "Whoever causes great harm even for unbelievers is blameworthy in his speech and teaching."

Now if the religion of each person is evaluated from his actions and his way of life, what kind of religion will pagans think Christians have? What opinion will they form about Christ, the Son of God, the true God of the Christians? It will be the opinion the Indians have already formed, especially in provinces where no religious are living, that is, that Christ is the most detestable of all the gods.

Why is it that Christ's sacred name is brought low by these blasphemies? The reason lies in the lives of Christians and their atrocious wars, which surpass all barbaric ferocity. All Christians, then, are obliged to avoid wars of this type and the hellish expeditions by which Christ's sacred name is blasphemed, since as Paul says:

Whatever you eat, whatever you drink, whatever you do at all, do it for the glory of God. Never do anything offensive to anyone—to Jews, or Greeks or to the Church of God; just as I try to be helpful to everyone at all times, not anxious for my own advantage but for the advantage of everybody else, so that they may be saved. Take me for a model, as I take Christ.[7]

This holy teaching of Saint Paul is to be observed at all times and in all centuries, as is clear from the words "Take me for your model, as I take Christ."

6. *Commentary on the Epistle to Titus,* chap. 2, homily 4.
7. 1 Corinthians 10[31–33].

And:

You know how you are supposed to imitate us: now we were not idle when we were with you, nor did we ever have our meals at anyone's table without paying for them; no, we worked night and day, slaving and straining, so as not to be a burden on any of you. This was not because we had no right to be, but in order to make ourselves an example for you to follow.[8]

In this passage Paul is speaking about the preaching of the gospel, and his words are relevant not only for the Apostles of that time but for all preachers and all times, and they should be observed in every age. Now, as is clear from his words, the Apostle in no way denied that this form should be followed in dealing with idolaters or other pagans involved in horrible sins, for the Apostles made no exceptions. For, indeed, if we are not bound to imitate his manner of preaching the faith now that the Church has grown, what reason will our opponents give for not imitating him in humility and the other virtues? If, in fact, the Church is now strong, with even the widest powers, nevertheless it is obliged to show moderation and meekness toward everyone. "I have given you an example so that you may copy what I have done to you." "Learn from me, for I am gentle and humble in heart." "This is my commandment: love one another, as I have loved you." And again, Paul said to the Romans: "Love does no evil." And "While we have the chance, we must do good to all, and especially to our brothers in the faith."[9]

Pagans, therefore, must be treated most gently and with all charity. Nor should any trace of evil be visible in our actions. "And then you will be innocent and genuine, perfect children of God among a deceitful and underhand brood." "Let your moderation be known to all men." "And in everything you do make yourself an example to them of working for good: when you are teaching, be an example."[10] Moreover Peter, the first Pontiff, says: "Always behave honorably among pagans so that they can see your good works for themselves and, when the day of reckoning comes, give thanks to God for the things which now make them denounce you as criminals."[11]

8. 2 Thessalonians 3[7–9].
9. John 13[15]. Matthew 11[29]. John 15[12]. Romans 13[10]. Galatians 6[10].
10. Philippians 2[15]: 4[5]. Titus 2[7].
11. 1 Peter 2[12].

Now if Christians unsettle everything by wars, burnings, fury, rashness, fierceness, sedition, plunder, and insurrection, where is meekness? Where is moderation? Where are the holy deeds that should move the hearts of pagans to glorify God? Where is the blameless and inoffensive way of life? Where is the humanity? Finally, where is the meek and gentle spirit of Christ? Where is the imitation of Christ and Paul? Indeed, thinking about this pitiful calamity of our brothers so torments me that I cannot overcome my amazement that a learned man, a priest, an older person, and a theologian should offer deadly poisons of this type to the world from his unsettled mind Moreover, I do not think that anyone who fails to see that these matters are clearer than the noonday sun is truly Christian and free from the vice of greed.

Furthermore, with what swords and cannons did Christ arm his disciples when he sent them to preach the gospel? Let us listen as Our Lord commands the Apostles and says: "And as you go, proclaim that the kingdom of heaven is close at hand. Cure the sick, raise the dead, cleanse the lepers, cast out devils. You received without charge, give without charge."[12] As for our preachers, however, surrounded by a troop of soldiers, or rather thieves, in what tone of speech will they tell the Indians "The kingdom of heaven is at hand"? They should say instead: "The kingdom of hell is at hand, both for us, who will kill you and plunder your homes, and for you, too, who will breathe forth your lives without faith and the grace of the sacraments." Will they heal the sick, those who massacre and inhumanly destroy the defenseless multitude of a nation by the bloodiest battles? Do they raise the dead, those who commit terrible massacres and pollute the pure air with rotting corpses? Do they cast out devils, or do they give souls to the devils instead? Is this the way we fulfill Christ's command, "You have received without charge, give without charge"? Devastating provinces and exterminating natives or putting them to flight, is this freely sharing the faith? How blind are men's minds! What a truly deplorable calamity! When Christ sent his disciples to preach the gospel, he recommended meekness to them. "Remember," he says, "I am sending you out like sheep among wolves."[13] Explaining these words, Chrysostom says: "He

12. Luke 9[2–6]. Matthew 10[7–8].
13. Matthew 10[16].

commands them to have complete meekness, yet not only that, but also the simplicity of the dove."[14]

And later:

It is surely greater and more wonderful to change the mind and outlook of our adversaries than to overcome them by the sword, especially since twelve in number would be sent out to all other men who ordinarily were more ferocious than wolves. Let those blush, then, who, doing the opposite, pursue their adversaries like wolves, for we see that innumerable wolves are overcome by a very few sheep. And surely to the extent that we are sheep, we easily conquer our enemies, but when we pass over into the nature of wolves, then we are defeated since, according to Luke, we have no support from the shepherd who feeds, not wolves, but sheep.

Shame, shame on those who in violation of Christ's law greedily lay waste to Indian realms, which are filled with innocent persons, like most rapacious wolves and ferocious thieves under the pretext of preaching the gospel! But the Lord lives, and they shall not escape his hand.

It is not likely or probable, then, that the Blessed Bishop Sylvester suggested war to Constantine, nor did that Emperor wage war on unbelievers, who did not embrace the faith or attack it, simply because they worshipped idols or with a view to spreading the religion of Christ and removing the barriers to its spread.

14. *Super Matthaeum,* in the completed work, chap. 10, homily 34.

Chapter Forty-Six

Now we must see what other commands Christ gave his disciples when he sent them to preach. Luke says: "Take nothing for the journey: neither staff, nor haversack, nor bread, nor money.[1] Commenting on this section of chapter 9, Ambrose says:

The qualities of the person preaching the good news of the kingdom of God are designated by the precepts of the gospel, for example, being without a wallet, without sandals, without money, that is, not needing the assistance of worldly support and safe in faith, he will consider that he can do more without seeking those things.[2]

And concerning chapter 10 the same Ambrose says: "And therefore the good shepherd sends his lambs among wolves, because they are guided not to plunder but to grace."[3] Therefore Christ does not want his faith to be preceded by servants who are intent upon nothing but looting the property of others.

1. [Luke 9:1].
2. [PL 15:1771].
3. [PL 15:1798].

Moreover, explaining the expression "Provide yourselves with no gold,"[4] the same Ambrose notes: "If we are forbidden to possess gold, why do we try to snatch, to steal? If you are commanded to give what you have, how do you accumulate what you are forbidden to keep?" All persons who are truly Christian should weigh these words. For if Christ allowed us to receive gold from those to whom we preach the gospel, the pagans would think that the preachers announce the faith for the sake of profit. Now if preachers are forbidden to accept the gold that is offered them, how much less right have they to steal or damage the property of others? Ambrose continues in that section:

You who preach that one must not steal, do you yourself steal? You who say that one must not commit adultery, do you commit adultery? Do you who curse idols commit sacrilege? Do you who glory in the law dishonor God by violating your duty? "For the name of God is blasphemed through you among the gentiles." This was not the case of Peter, the first to carry out the Lord's teaching, who, when asked by a poor man to give him some money, says, "I have neither silver nor gold, etc.," in order to show that the Lord's commands were not given in vain.[5]

Now in waging war on the Indians under the pretext of spreading religion will the Spaniards give their own money, or will they instead steal and rob others by violence? Then will not the Indians, when they see the Christians greedily hunting for gold and diligently collecting small bits of it from the broken idols, saving it, and falling just short of adoring it, will they not surely think that gold is the god of the Christians, which we know they have often believed? Moreover, will the belligerents meanwhile be so chaste, so continent, and temperate that they will not violate other men's wives? Will they not rape their daughters? But after those peoples learn, from the teaching of the religious, that such deeds are sins, forbidden by the law of the Christians, and that so few observe it (for example, the religious) and that many act against it (that is, all others without exception), will they not reasonably judge that whatever the preachers of the faith proclaim to them about the faith, about religion, and about Christ himself is nonsense or contrived lies? Can this wickedness in those who have given cause for so much scandal and for infamy to Christ be expiated by some sacrifice?

4. [Matthew 10:9].
5. [Acts 3:6].

How, then, do those servants of Satan object to us that they are increasing Christ's glory while, by their works, these impious persons profane Christ's sacred name among idolaters and make it hateful? Is not Paul's statement—which Ambrose lamented in the passage just quoted—truly applicable to them: "The name of God is blasphemed through you among the gentiles"?

Listen, dear reader, to Saint Ambrose himself as he comments on Luke:[6]

What is a rod except an insignia of power to be made known and an instrument for revenging sorrow? Therefore the command of a humble Lord—for "in humility his judgment was taken away"[7] —the command of a humble Lord, I repeat, his disciples carried out by their humble services. He sent those out to sow the faith who would teach, not force. Nor would they exercise the strength of power. Rather, they would raise on high his teaching on humility. In this passage he judged, too, that patience must be coupled with humility since, according to Peter's testimony, "He was insulted and did not retaliate with insults; when he was tortured he made no threats,"[8] that is to say, "Be imitators of me. Put aside the desire to revenge. Bear the insolence of those who scourge, not by returning injury, but by the magnanimity of patience." No one should imitate in himself what he blames in another.

And a little later:

And from another passage you know that when the apostles wanted to bid fire from heaven to destroy the Samaritans, who refused to receive the Lord Jesus into their city, he turned to them and rebuked them, saying, "You do not know what spirit you are made of. The Son of Man came not to destroy souls but to save them."[9]

A little later on he says of Paul: "He cast the rod aside and took on the disposition of charity." What can be more expressly offered against those mouthpieces of Satan who do not know Christ—blind, miserable men who fight against the teaching of Christ and the traditions and examples of apostolic men and who throw into confusion the New World and even our own provinces with pestilential teachings and fatal

6. Book 7, chap. 44. [PL 15:1802 ff].
7. [Isaiah 53:8].
8. 1 Peter 2[23].
9. [Luke 9:56].

dissention? From Christ we learn "What I say to you I say to all."[10] But if Christ instructed his disciples in such a way as to command them to teach, not force, to exemplify and extol humility, not surround themselves with military pride and a troop of thieves, why does Sepúlveda dare say that the Indians must be subdued by war before the gospel is preached to them? Is it that they may begin to hate the gospel before they understand it, that they may be subjected to a savage troop of soldiers before they grasp the truth of the gospel? What do they have to say against the words of Christ and the holy Fathers? Did Christ teach us to deal with the Indians differently than with other idolaters? Has that precept, given to the Apostles, been revoked, namely: "As you enter his house, salute it, saying, 'Peace to this house' " and "Let your first words be 'Peace to this house.' "[11]

How does it agree with the example of Christ to spear unknowing Indians before the gospel is preached to them and to terrify in the extreme a totally innocent people by a display of arrogance and the fury of war, or to drive them to death or flight? See what Gregory says about this type of preaching: "However, that preaching which demands faith by the threat of scourges is novel and unheard of.[12] The words that Christ commanded his disciples to speak, "Peace to this house," mean every type of happiness, according to Augustine,[13] for they mean that peace by which men enjoy their possessions in peace, not harming anyone or suffering harm from anyone. For this reason peace is loved by all creatures, even irrational ones, as Augustine records in this passage and as Dionysius teaches.[14] The words "Peace to this house" as spoken by the Apostles have the same meaning as if they were saying "We did not come to seize your possessions or to disturb your peace." These holy words led the pagans to listen to the messengers of the gospel. We, before we announce the gospel, put innocent persons to death, and by waging war we overthrow kingdoms and banish all peace. Let Sepúlveda cite one passage where Christ or the holy Fathers taught that pagans must be subdued by war before the gospel is preached to them. Now Pope Sylvester was a holy man, and so it is unlikely that

10. Mark 13[37].
11. [Matthew 10:12]. Luke [10:5].
12. Book 2, letter 25.
13. *De Civitate Dei*, Book 9, chap. 13.
14. *De Divinis Nominibus*, Book 11.

he did not know how Christ instructed those disciples whom he sent to proclaim the gospel. Did Sylvester want to disagree with Ambrose or Chrysostom, who in interpreting the Scriptures probably had the help of the Holy Spirit? Truth does not fight with truth, nor does the Holy Spirit contradict himself. Sepúlveda, therefore, is dreaming. For Constantine did not wage war on pagans, with Sylvester's encouragement, just because they were pagans. Nor is there any passage in which the opposite opinion can be found. Nor, despite his boast, has Sepúlveda diligently read all the sacred doctors. Indeed, were he versed in them he would not give out these impious teachings.

Chapter Forty-Seven

Again, the seventh proof that Sylvester, a holy man, did not persuade Constantine to lead pagans to Christ by warfare is the fact that preparing kingdoms for war is characteristic of tyrants and thieves, not Christians, or even prudent men. For nothing violent is lasting, and establishing a tyrannical rule by force is odious and abominable, according to the Philosopher.[1] On the other hand, rule that is acquired by

1. *Politics*, Book 3. *Ethics*, Book 8.

service, gentleness, and virtue, peacefully rather than violently, deserves to be cherished, is most pleasing to all peoples, and can last for many centuries, according to what Cicero says: "There is no better garrison of troops than the love and good will of citizens, with which the ruler must be fortified, rather than with arms."[2] Caius Sallust was of the same opinion.

Now such is the rule of Christ: "See now, your king comes to you ... humble."[3] Moreover, according to Isaiah:

He does not cry out or shout aloud, or make his voice heard in the streets. He does not break the crushed reed *(which Jerome interprets to mean the Jews)* nor quench the wavering flame *(that is, the pagans).*[4]

Furthermore, according to Isaiah:

In the days to come, the mountain *(that is, Christ)* of the Temple of the Lord *(that is, the Catholic Church)* shall tower above the mountains and be lifted higher than the hills. All nations shall stream to it, peoples without number will come to it; and they will say: "Come, let us go up to the mountain of the Lord, to the Temple of the God of Jacob, that he may teach us his ways so that we may walk in his paths."[5]

This is the mountain that grew from the stone that was hewn from a mountain and that destroyed the statue (that is, all empires) and grew until, having become a huge mountain, it filled the world.[6] Note the words of Isaiah: "All nations shall stream to it, peoples without number will come to it; and they will say, etc." These words rule out all violence, all terror, and mean the spontaneous will to come to Christ's sheepfold, so that a little later Isaiah condemns those wars that we excuse under the pretext of uprooting idolatry in the following words: "They will hammer their swords into ploughshares, their spears into sickles. Nation will not lift sword against nation, there will be no more training for

2. *Philippics*
3. Zechariah 9[9]. See also Matthew 21:[5].
4. Isaiah 42[2–3].
5. Isaiah 2[2–3].
6. Daniel 2[31–35].

war."[7] According to the gloss on this passage, these words mean that a Christian nation shall not lead anyone to the faith by sword, spear, or warfare. "Now once Christ was born, who is our peace, who made both one, at whose birth the angels `sang 'Glory to God in the highest heaven, and peace to men who enjoy his favor,'[8] all wars ceased."

Moreover, the gloss on 1 Maccabees, chapter 8, interprets the treaty which Judas Maccabaeus made with the Romans in this meaning, by saying:

By sending envoys to the Romans to establish friendship and an alliance with them, Judas signifies our Redeemer as offering nations the gospel of peace and calling them to his faith through his preachers. . . . And why did Judas send two envoys to the Romans in order to make peace if not because, in order to call nations to the faith and the alliance of peace, our Redeemer sent two testaments into the world?

Again, explaining the twelfth chapter, where it is related that after his brother Judas Maccabaeus had died, Jonathan renewed the alliance he had made with the Romans, the gloss says:

The fact that Jonathan sends envoys to the Romans, to the Spartans, and to other places, in order to renew that peace with them which his brother Judas had previously and willingly made with them, shows that it should be the concern of holy preachers to strive to renew and preserve everywhere, with Christ's own full zeal, that peace which Christ offered in the world, since the Son of God himself, who came to earth in order to establish in his flesh peace between heaven and earth, wished, at the very moment of his birth, that the angels sing Glory to God in the highest heaven, and peace to men who enjoy his favor." Surely the mediator of God and men, after his incarnation, recommended this peace to his disciples by saying, "Be at peace with one another." "Peace I bequeath to you, my own peace I give you."[9] Moreover, the entire body of Christ is joined, ruled, and stabilized by peace and harmony.

Now the verb "is joined" means that different things are united into one and that the remotest nations, infected with various rites and errors, are engrafted to Christ's body (that is, the Church) by peace.

7. [Isaiah 2:4].
8. [Luke 2:14].
9. [Mark 9:50. John 14:27].

This is also proved by reason. Christ's kingdom is spiritual, since Christ rules in the souls of the faithful who are endowed with charity, faith, and hope, according to Jerome.[10] Now these three virtues are virtues of the soul in which God rules. "The kingdom of God is within you."[11] The human spirit, however, cannot be coerced, as has been shown. Therefore, in order that Christ may truly reign in the souls of pagans, they must not be forced to the faith by war but attracted and led to Christ's sheepfold by service, attraction, and Christian charity. Leading to faith by massacre and terror is Mohammedan, since Mohammed said that he was sent in the terror of the sword and the violence of weapons, according to Vincent.[12] Further, Vincent says: "Take note whether God's prophet should be involved in expeditions of this type, in which nothing was accomplished but deceit, violence, bloodshed, and, in short, whatever is done by thieves and highwaymen."[13] And he says: "Nothing was done or thought of except to kill people, seize the property of others, commit incest and adultery."[14]

Why, then, Sepúlveda, can you want Christ's law to be propagated not by Christian but by Mohammedan means? Do you want Christ's name, which should be adored by angels, to be blasphemed by pagans? Do you want the ocean of all evils (that is, war) to [surge] against the pagans instead of Christ's meekness, which we ought to teach them? What do the heralds of the gospel have to do with armed robbers, who throw everything into confusion by fire and sword? What is there in common between Christ's instruction and these contrivances of frenzied men?

As a matter of fact, I think that Sepúlveda wrote that little book hastily and without sufficiently weighing the materials and circumstances. And if there are (I know not) more impious or stupid persons following his authority, let them fear God, who punishes perverse undertakings. Let them listen to Christ and the sacred doctors of the Church, not to Sepúlveda, who will cheerfully yield to Christ, Ambrose, Augustine, and Chrysostom. Sepúlveda says that he does not want the Indians to be baptized unwillingly or to be forced to the faith. But what

10. *Super Matthaeum,* chap. 28.
11. Luke 17[21].
12. *Speculum Historiae,* Book 23, chap. 49. See also Saint Thomas, *Contra Gentes,* I, 6.
13. Chap. 42.
14. Chap. 45.

greater compulsion can there be than that which is carried out by an armed phalanx, shooting rifles and cannon, so that, even if no other effect should follow, at least their flashes of light and terrible thunder could dishearten any strong person, especially one not accustomed to them and ignorant of how they work? If pottery shakes because of the cannon, the earth trembles, the sky is hidden in heavy darkness, the old, the young, and women are killed, homes are destroyed, and everything resounds with warlike fury, shall we still say that these persons are not really driven to the faith? Is this not a just fear? Once they have been affected by these measures, what will the Indians refuse? Or what freedom of mind is left for embracing Christ's faith sincerely, so that they may persevere in it?

I should like the reader to answer this question: What will the Indians think about our religion, which those wicked tyrants claim they are teaching by subjugating the Indians through massacres and the force of war before the gospel is preached to them? When I speak of the force of war, I am speaking about the greatest of all evils. Furthermore, what advantage is there in destroying idols if the Indians, after being treated this way, keep them and adore them secretly in their hearts? Listen to what Saint Augustine says about the violent destruction of idols. "Many pagans have those abominations on their estates. But do we go and destroy them? We first act in such a way as to break the idols in their hearts."[15] And a little further on, speaking about those who destroy idols violently, he adds that the indiscriminate destruction of idols is characteristic of depraved men who act like the insane Circumcellions. We have explained this passage from Saint Augustine at greater length in chapter 7.

All of this is supported by the prohibition against direct or indirect violence when a man is embracing the faith.[16]

---

15. Sermon 6 on the words of the Lord concerning the centurion's servant.
16. Decretals, 3, 42, 3. Gratian, c. 3, D. 45; c. 5, D. 45; c. 33, C. 23, q. 5. This is what the doctors teach on these sections and elsewhere in Gratian.

Chapter Forty-Eight

This truth is further corroborated by the fact that not only did the Church have temporal power at the time of Sylvester, it gained greater power at the time of Pope Gregory, when the pious Maurice and Phocas and other great Emperors ruled the Roman Empire. Yet Gregory never had them wage war against pagans who did not inflict injury on the Church, although Maurice was a spiritual father together with Pope Gregory. For this reason it is probable that there was an uncommon friendship between them.

This is clear, in the first place, because if Saint Gregory had encouraged them to wage war of this kind, it would have been worth recording and would be related by the writers of that era. Secondly, to lead the English nation to the faith, Gregory sent them not armed forces but a certain monk, Augustine, and forty pious monks noted for their Christian integrity, who, before entering a city in England, habitually appealed to the Lord with these words: "O Lord, you have created and redeemed these souls. Be pleased to take away your anger from them

so that mercy and pardon may go forward with us to them."[1] Those
holy monks advanced and performed many miracles that astonished
Gregory himself, as he writes in his letter to Eulogius, the Bishop of
Alexandria, as well as in his letter to Augustine.[2]

Do you not see that at the time when the Church enjoyed the
greatest power it used not material but spiritual weapons in preaching
the gospel, and did not depart in any way from the example and instruction of its teacher? Again, in the days of this Blessed Gregory, even
before he was raised to the supreme pontificate, the Popes and Emperors
were most Christian men, such as Pope John III, Benedict I, and Pelagius
II. Yet the Roman Pontiffs did not induce Justin I or Maurice, who were
Roman Emperors of their century, to uproot idolatry by war. Furthermore, Gregory, that very holy man, explains Christ's words "Force them
to come in" (written in the parable of the wedding feast) in reference
to the compulsion that is accomplished by holy warnings, examples, the
Christian way of life and behavior, and the effective power of God's
word.[3]

Moreover, lest their [our opponents] error be refuted only by the
teaching of the sacred doctors, let it be compared with the previously
cited explanation of the saints, which has been interpreted by the doctors of canon law, especially Innocent, who says the following[4]:

And so no one can be forced to become a Christian. Nor is this opposed to the
fact that the servant is told to force those invited to the wedding feast to come
in,[5] since this refers to compulsion accomplished through the urgings of reason,
not through the severity of the material sword or temporal violence,[6] because
the Lord forbids that servant, that is, the Order of Preachers or the Apostles in
the person of Peter, to use such a sword.[7]

Therefore the servant who bears the invitation to the wedding feast
(that is, the preacher of the gospel) should proclaim the gospel not

---

1. This is given in the life of Saint Gregory, written by Paul the Deacon, as well as in his
History of the Lombards, 3, 12. The Venerable Bede also writes at length about this prayer
and the preaching of those holy monks in the history he wrote about the peoples of that
island.
2. Book 7. Book 9, letter 58.
3. Homily 28 on the Gospels.
4. On the Decretals 3, 42, 3.
5. Luke 14[23]. Gratian, c. 38, C. 23, q. 4.
6. Gratian, D. 45, c. 5.
7. C. 23, q. 1, introduction.

armed with cannon, like the wolf seeking to kill and rob the sheep, but equipped with a holy way of life and the word of God, risking his life for the spread of the gospel and Christ's glory. For the preaching of the gospel will be effective only when its preachers suffer death, not when they kill others and put them to death, according to Chrysostom:

In heralding the gospel, the prophets and the apostles were despoiled of their lives. Christ also died for us. Nor did the fruit of their preaching appear before the deaths of Christ and his apostles for, just as no one eats the flesh of a living animal, so no one embraced the words of prophets and apostles while they were alive but only after they were dead. Accordingly, just as in the case of the flesh of a lamb, men consumed Christ's sermons only after he was killed because, after his death, the gospels were preached and believed and men are daily nourished in them. And the same is true as regards the flesh of his prophets and apostles.[8]

This is what Christ, the Eternal Truth, sought to indicate to us when he said "Unless a wheat grain falls on the ground and dies, it remains only a single grain; but if it dies, it yields a rich harvest."[9] Now in this passage he is speaking about preaching and the conversion of the gentiles, according to Saint Thomas.[10] Moreover, explaining these words of Christ, Saint Augustine says: "He called himself the grain which would be put to death in the unbelief of the Jews and multiplied in the faith of all peoples, for that death explained the teaching of the holy apostles and added credibility to their words."[11] Innocent concludes: "From these points, then, it is evident that war must not be declared against the Saracens so that they may become Christians."[12]

Therefore war must not be chosen as a means of preparing the minds of unbelievers or removing idolatry. As Innocent has said, therefore, the gospel is spread not by lances but by the word of God and the Christian way of life and by the urgings of reason. Saint Gregory also teaches this. "We must act in such a way, then, that, challenged rather by reason and meekness, they should want to follow us, not flee from us."[13] Here

---

8. *Super Matthaeum,* chap. 22, homily 41, in the unfinished work.
9. John 12 [24].
10. [*Summa Theologiae*], III, q. 42, a. 1c.
11. *Treatise on John.*
12. C. 23, q. 1, introduction.
13. To Pascasius, Bishop of Naples, Book 11, letter 15.

Gregory is speaking about the Jews. But if the Jews who are servants of the Church and are ready to serve[14] must be drawn to the faith by meekness and teaching, how much more so must this be taught in reference to pagans who have not yet been instructed with any of God's words and who are not obliged to desert their religion or their rulers until they see what is better?

Therefore, to proclaim the gospel with armed forces is completely foreign to Christ's teaching. His whole life and teaching breathe forth meekness and charity. The Lord sent his disciples to preach the gospel after they had been trained with pious words. "As you enter the house, salute it, saying 'Peace to this house.'" "Remember, I am sending you out like sheep." "I have come so that they may have life and have it to the full." "Learn from me, for I am gentle and humble in heart."[15] Armed troops, however, are suitable for the pseudo-prophet Mohammed, who said that he came in the terror of the sword, as we have already mentioned.

Since the Indians have a persuasive reason for following the practices of their ancestors, which have been established for so many centuries and upheld on the authority of so many rulers, priests, and learned men among them, they are not obliged to desert them because of the exhortation of thieves who surpass all Turks and plunderers in cruelty and ferocity. For who would believe that such tyrants are messengers of the true God? By their depraved morals, these men dishonor the gospel and weaken the cause of Christ. Those things which are taught by good and trustworthy men please human souls and are planted in their hearts as things that are in accord with reason. If these latter persons perform visible works which are in conformity with reason, for example, if they manifest charity, meekness, and modesty, they will please everyone and their words will be believed.

Scotus wisely confirmed this point by saying that "no one is held to any positive precept, even a divine precept, unless it is promulgated to him by some suitable and authentic person or by the truthful report and testimony of good persons, which anyone should reasonably believe, etc."[16]

---

14. c. 11, C. 23, q. 8. Decretals, 5, 6, 13.
15. [Matthew 10:12. Matthew 10:16. John 10:10. Matthew 11:29].
16. *In IV Sententiarum,* d. 3, q. 4. Cajetan also speaks learnedly on this matter in his commentary on the [*Summa Theologiae*], II–II, q. 1, a. 4, ad 2[um].

Now what belief will be placed in the Spaniards—greedy, violent, and cruel men who put unarmed and harmless Indians to the sword and rob them with extraordinary avarice? From this we conclude that the Indians, seeing their wicked deeds, commit no sin and do not deserve punishment if they do not accept the gospel. Nor would any nation have been guilty for not accepting the faith of Christ if, supposing the impossible, the Apostles had behaved like the Spaniards. In this regard we have the Lord's statement: "If I had not performed such works among them as no one else has ever done, they would be blameless."[17]

From what has been deduced so extensively, it is evident what literal meaning was intended by Christ in the phrase from the parable cited above, "Force them to come in"; that is, the compulsion signified here is that which concerns unbelievers who have never heard the truths of faith, and the compulsion is accomplished through the urgings of reason and human persuasion or through the spiritual and interior persuasion attained by the ministry of angels. Consequently, it is false and impious to say that Christ bound us by precept through the phrase quoted above and that, when the Church has great power, war against peaceful unbelievers must come before the preaching of the gospel, as the illustrious Doctor Sepúlveda has not been ashamed to advance in his new teaching.

17. John 15[24].

Chapter Forty-Nine

The fact that in his letters and other works Saint Augustine explains that gospel parable as meaning physical and violent compulsion does not run counter to what we have concluded above, since his explanation is true in reference to heretics, whose status and case are vastly different from those of pagans who have never accepted the faith, as we have shown at length in chapter 6 and subsequent chapters. For so great is the richness of divine Scripture that each word has many literal and pious meanings, according to Saint Thomas.[1]

Now the thesis that heretics may be compelled to return to Christ's sheepfold by the application of force is proved by the fact that he who has promised nothing, as in the case of the pagan, is forced to give nothing. But because the heretic has vowed himself to Christ in baptism, he can be compelled to return to his sheepfold. For the natural law dictates that each person must give what he has promised, according to the words of the Apostle: "Pay to every man whatever he has a right to ask. . . . Avoid getting into debt."[2] Furthermore, according to the natural law an unconditional promise obliges in such a way that whoever does not keep it commits a mortal sin.[3] The heretic, however, is obliged not only to Christ but also to the Church. Therefore he must be forced to keep his promise, just as the person who has taken a vow is forced to keep the vow. "Fulfill the promises you make to the Lord our God."[4] For although a vow is voluntary, once it has been taken it must be fulfilled by necessity.[5] Thus a free man and free cities can subject themselves to a king or ruler, and once they have subjected themselves they cannot in any way change their minds. For a free man can subject himself to someone else.[6] Therefore heretics who do not live

---

1. He gives the reason for this in his [*Summa Theologiae*], I, q. 1, a. 10c, at the end.
2. Romans 13[7–8].
3. Gratian, c. 12, C. 22, q. 5. Decretals, 1, 35, 1, as well as the glosses and the doctors on this section. Saint Thomas [*Summa Theologiae*] II–II, q. 10, a. 3, ad 5um, and *In IV Sententiarum*, d. 27, q. 2, a. 1, ad 2um.
4. Psalms 76[12].
5. Decretals, 3, 23, 7; 3, 33, 6.
6. This is noted in the Liber Sextus, 1, 8, 2. Codex, 11, 48, 22. L. 1, #1. And Digests, 2, 14, 7, #7.

up to the vow taken in baptism can be lawfully compelled to fulfill it, for whoever is a heretic offends Christ and commits the crime of *lèse majesté*. This offense is punished by the Church, of which the heretic is a subject, as he is also a subject of its head, the Roman Pontiff.

The root and basis of this subjection are threefold.

The first is the solemnly pronounced vow, the spontaneous confession of faith, and the promise made in the reception of baptism.[7]

The second basis is that, by agreement, the baptized person is obliged by the words "Do you believe in God, etc."[8]

The third basis is the obedience the baptized person tacitly and implicitly promises in baptism to Christ and to the Church. Moreover, each person through baptism gives himself over to the Lord and to the authority of Christ, and becomes [Christ's] subject and debtor by fleeing and divesting himself, through renunciation, from the slavery and possession of the devil, his former master and owner. And so he professes that in the future he will live according to the divine law of the gospel. Moreover, he is numbered with others in the assembly of the faithful and the Christian state.[9] For this reason it is lawful for the heretic to be forced by the Church to keep the faith, offer obedience, and live according to Christ's law, which he vowed and freely promised to observe, since every subject of any ruler or every member of a state is bound to obey its laws, live according to them, and act like other good citizens.[10] And this is the opinion of Augustine in explaining the phrase of the parable "Force them to come in," as it is also that of Saint Thomas.[11]

Further, the Council of Toledo expresses this difference between heretics and pagans in canon 56, which rules that those who have never accepted the faith must not be forced to accept it, but it rules otherwise in the case of those who have accepted it and, through heresy, depart from the unity of the Church, that is, the body of Christ, for they must be compelled to return to the faith.[12]

Now the reason [for this] is that the Church's compulsion, which is carried out by holy warnings and the word of God, was insufficient to

---

7. Gratian, *De Consecratione,* D. 4, cc. 61 and 73.
8. See the gloss on the previously cited canon 61.
9. See Gratian, *De Consecratione,* D. 4, cc. 44, 54, and 61.
10. Gratian, D. 8, c. 2. Decretals, 1, 2. Codex, 1, 1, 1.
11. [*Summa Theologiae*], II–II, q. 10, a. 3c, and ad 3um.
12. This is contained in D. 45, c. 5.

compel heretics precisely because, in its early years of existence, the Church lacked the means and power since it had no Christian rulers to help and defend it. Writing to the heretic Donatus, who complained that, contrary to the example of Christ and the Apostles, the Church was forcing people to the faith by the use of weapons and the physical resources of secular rulers, Augustine gives a fuller explanation of the difference mentioned above and answers that two periods must be distinguished in the development of the Church.

The first is that in which it blossomed forth as a new sprout, for at that time it only invited persons to the faith. As yet the prophecy "All kings will do him homage, all nations become his servants"[13] had not been fulfilled. The second period is that in which the prediction has been fulfilled. Indeed, the more it is fulfilled, the more the Church uses its power so that it not only invites but also moves to what is good. Our Lord wished to indicate that he who had great power decided first to commend humility. He makes this point sufficiently clear, also, in the parable of the wedding feast, etc.[14]

This prophecy, then, was fulfilled during the second period. Therefore at the time when the Church had kings and rulers whose arms it could use it restrained those who refused to persevere in the faith they had accepted. But the case of pagans, and especially the Indians, is different. Not only have they not accepted the faith of Christ, they have not even heard of it, and so, since they have not promised anything and are not subject to the Church, there is no reason for forcing them as in the case of heretics. Saint Augustine is speaking only about the latter. It is clear that all such unbelievers that have not received the faith belong to the first period of the Church, that is, when in order to convert unbelievers the Church was using (and has always used) reasoning and persuasion, not weapons or violence, even if it had rulers among the faithful, because there is no longer reason for using these means. But heretics, on the other hand, must be forced to keep what they have promised—to discharge the allegiance owed to God and the obedience owed to the Church.

Nevertheless, although there were heretics during the first period, the Church patiently tolerated their wicked assaults because it did not

13. [Psalms 72:11].
14. This teaching of Augustine is given in Gratian, c. 38, C. 23, q. 4, and c. 41, C. 23, q. 4.

have the protection of rulers from among the faithful. However, after the kings of the world, by the divine goodness, were converted to Christ and thus the Church began to have believing rulers as sons and subjects, it began to use their services for punishing and forcing heretics by laws and arms. And this is the second status or period of the Church, the period to which heretics, apostates, and schismatics are said to belong. And thus Augustine's intention in explaining the frequently cited phrase of the parable "Force them to come in" as meaning external and physical violence is clear.

Again, explaining these same words, "Force them to come in," in his fiftieth letter, to Count Boniface, Augustine teaches that heretics must be judged differently from pagans, who must be attracted and invited to the faith with kindness and mildness, but not forced. And so Augustine says:

Is it no part of the shepherd's care when he has found those sheep, also, which have strayed from the flock, not because of violence but because they have been coaxed away with kindness and gentleness and have begun to be claimed by others, to call them back to the master's sheepfold by the fear or even the pain of blows if they seek to resist? And especially if their numbers are increased by their fertility while in the possession of runaway slaves and bandits, has he not even more right over them because he recognizes on them the brand of the master ... ? So also the wandering of .the sheep is to be corrected without destroying in it the brand of the Redeemer.

And later:

Therefore the Church imitates its master in forcing them, although in its early days it did not expect to have to force anyone in order to fulfill the prophetic utterance concerning the faith of kings and nations. Indeed, this is not an unreasonable interpretation of the well-known statement of the Apostle, when Blessed Paul says, "Once you have given your complete obedience, we are prepared to punish any disobedience."[15] So it is that the Lord himself commands the guests first to be brought in to his great supper but afterward to be forced. For when the servant answered the King, "Sir, your orders have been carried out and there is still room," he said, "Go to the open roads and the hedgerows and force people to come in." In this way obedience was complete in those who were first brought in gently, but disobedience is curbed in those who are forced. But what is the sense of the phrase "Force them to come in," after he had first said, "Bring them in," and had been answered, "Your orders

15. [2 Corinthians 10:6].

have been carried out and there is still room"? If he meant us to understand that they are to be compelled by the fear which arises from miracles, many more divine miracles were wrought for those who were invited first, especially for those of whom it is said "The Jews demand miracles."[16] Among the gentiles, too, in the time of the apostles, such miracles supported the gospel so that, if the command was given to force them by such means, it is more reasonable to believe, as I have said, that the first guests were forced to come. Consequently, if by the power which the Church has received through religion and faith in the era of kings by the divine goodness in fitting measure, these who are found in the open roads and hedgerows, that is, in heresy and schism, are forced to enter, let them not blame the fact that they are forced but let them look to how they are forced.

And a little further on:

Indeed, before those laws were sent to Africa by which they were forced to enter, it seemed to some of the brothers—and to me among them—that although the madness of the Donatists raged everywhere, it would be better not to petition the emperors to outlaw that heresy altogether by setting a penalty for those who would persist in it, but they should rather decree that those who either preached Catholic truth by word of mouth or gathered others to it by laying a foundation should not have to suffer the mad violence of these men. We thought this could be accomplished to some extent in this way: by means of the law which Theodosius, of pious memory, promulgated against all heretics in general.

All of this is quoted from Augustine.

You see, dear reader, that Saint Augustine felt one way about heretics and another about those who have not yet received the faith, so that the former should be forced by the arms of kings, the latter should be drawn by arguments, so that the preaching of the gospel might be carried out by the faith of kings and gentiles, etc. "Sheep . . . which have strayed from the flock . . . with kindness," that is, the Church or the assembly of the faithful, "and have begun to be claimed by others," that is, heretics, "without destroying in them the brand," that is, the character "of the Redeemer" that the soul receives indelibly in baptism, "when he has found those sheep . . . to call them back to the master's sheepfold by the fear or even the pain of blows." In imitating its Lord, what does the Church do but investigate whether an unbeliever freely embraces

16. [1 Corinthians 1:22].

the faith—before it asks whether, after having abandoned it, he must be forced to return to it? Augustine bolsters all his statements with the authority of the Apostle: "Once you have given your complete obedience, we are prepared to punish any disobedience."[17]

17. 2 Corinthians 10[6].

Chapter Fifty

The words of Saint Augustine that we have quoted show clearly that the Church does not use force on pagans, in accord with the passage "It is not my business to pass judgment on those outside," but forces only those who have already become guests through baptism to come into the feast. This is indicated by his statement: "So it is, the Lord himself commands the guests first to be brought in to his great supper but, afterward, to be forced." Therefore the first obedience is made complete in those who were first brought in by kindness. And later he teaches that the hedgerows are heresies and schisms. He teaches this also in *Against the Letter of Gaudentius,* Book 2, where he says that various errors and heresies are the open roads while hedgerows symbolize depraved opinions and schisms. Likewise, this same Blessed Father Augustine gives his teaching on those two stages and the difference between pagans and heretics who have already accepted the faith (that is, the former must be attracted, the latter forced) in his forty-eighth letter, to Vincent, the Donatist heretic. In it he explains the words of the parable "Force them to come in" as applying to heretics.

As we have already said, Innocent does the same thing, in these words:[1]

Say that he first commanded his servant, that is, the Order of Preachers, which is great in God's Church[2] to go into the streets and alleys of the city and bring in the poor and the crippled, the blind, and the lame, not to force them to come in. Later he told him to go also into the open roads and the hedgerows and force those who were found there to come in.[3] By this he intimates that Jews and others like them, who do not have the faith, must not be forced to the faith by the material sword but introduced through effective reasoning and the law, so that they may be convinced from their own books.[4] But those who turn away from the bosom of the Church, such as heretics and schismatics, must be forced to return to it, even by means of civil power, since they belong to the Church's competence.

Just as, speaking later about the former [Jews and unbelievers], he says:

Indeed, he wants them to be called to the wedding feast, yet without compulsion since it is not our business to judge those who are outside.[5] However, by telling him to go out into the open roads and hedgerows, he means heretics and schismatics who tear with their thorns the Lord's seamless robe, that is, the unity of the Church. Moreover, since they belong to the Church's competence, they must be forced to enter and keep the faith which they received in baptism.

Augustine's explanation, then, must refer to heretics.[6]

And note that it is a general truth that men must be forced to carry

1. On the Decretals, 3, 42, 3.
2. Decretals, 5, 7, 12.
3. As in the previously cited c. 38, C. 23, q. 4.
4. As in the previously cited D. 45, c. 5.
5. Decretals, 4, 19, 8.
6. In addition to the previously cited passages, this is also proved in Gratian, C. 23, q. 4, cc. 24, 25, 37, 38, 39. And this is the explanation and teaching of the glosses and doctors on these passages.

out anything good which they have promised and that no one is forced to carry out anything good if it has not been promised.[7] This is the correct interpretation of that commonly cited statement of Augustine that "many goods are lavished on unwilling persons,"[8] since provision is made not for what they want but for what they need. And in that statement he is speaking specifically of subjects who do wrong. And so Augustine says:

He who corrects a person over whom he has received power by punishment or forces him by some discipline . . . not only in forgiving and praying for him but also in correcting him and punishing him by some corrective penalty, gives alms. The reason is that he shows mercy. For many goods are lavished on unwilling persons, etc.

Note that Augustine is speaking about persons who are subject to us. But pagans are not subject to the Church, a point we have frequently touched and previously determined.[9]

Therefore no one is forced to accept the faith unless he has already embraced it.[10] Now by using the services of Christian rulers the Church not only compels heretics to return to its fold but also lawfully punishes them with terrible penalties, both because the crime of heresy is most serious, for it is committed directly against the honor of God and results in lessening the dignity of Christ,[11] and because an offense against the eternal majesty is far more serious than one against the civil majesty,[12] and is most dangerous and contagious. And so heretics are the worst of men and most harmful to the whole universal Church, since they destroy harmony, nourish strife, and disturb peace.[13] Saint Thomas says: "They try to corrupt the simple faithful."[14] For this reason the Apostle

---

7. See the gloss and the doctors on Gratian, D. 45, c. 1 and c. 11, and on c. 37, C. 23, q. 4, where it is proved that, from the beginning, one should be forced to do good but a person also is forced to persevere in what he has started, as in c. 33, C. 23, q. 5. This is proved from the previously cited glosses.
8. *Enchiridion,* chap. 71.
9. This point is treated in Gratian, c. 11, D. 45; c. 2, C. 23, q. 1, at the word *agenda;* c. 38, C. 23, q. 4; c. 42, C. 23, q. 5; c. 3, C. 23, q. 6.
10. As in Gratian, D. 45, c. 5.
11. Liber Sextus, 5, 2, 19. Saint Thomas, *In IV Sententiarum,* d. 13, q. 2, a. 2.
12. Authenticae: *De Haereticis, Manichaeis, et Samaritanis,* L. *Gazaros* [Codex with Authenticae, 1, 8, 19].
13. See Saint Thomas [*Summa Theologiae*], II–II, q. 39, a. 1, ad 3[um].
14. *In IV Sententiarum,* d. 13, q. 2, a. 2.

says of heretics that "they only lead further and further away from true religion. Talk of this kind corrodes like gangrene."[15] And for this reason they must be cut off from fellowship with the faithful by harsh penalties.

And so Jerome says:

Decayed flesh must be cut off and the mangy sheep must be driven away from the sheepfolds, lest the whole house, the dough, and the flocks should burn, corrupt, decay, and die. Arius was a spark in Alexandria but because he was not checked, his flame ravaged the entire world.[16]

The third reason is that, because heretics are disloyal to Christ and the Church (that is, the Christian state) by that disloyalty which comes under the definition of treason, they are rebellious traitors, disobedient enemies, and active workers against the state. We have spoken about them at great length in the first book of *The Only Way of Drawing Unbelievers to the True Religion.* Therefore, since heretics have come under the jurisdiction of the Church (as has been proved), it can lawfully punish them by the hands of Christian rulers for the reasons we have frequently cited.

However, since other unbelievers do not belong to the Church as members, nor do they corrupt the Christian people by their superstitions (because, according to our supposition, they live in their kingdoms which are far removed from our lands and, as a result, they are not under the jurisdiction of the Church), surely their status should be quite different from that of heretics. For that reason Saint Augustine applies the parable to heretics. He does not speak of unbelievers.

So the confusion of the illustrious doctor [Sepúlveda] is quite clear inasmuch as he has tried with all his might, and with his customary inept and prejudiced pleading, to turn what the holy fathers and Christian emperors have said or legislated regarding heretics against simple unbelievers who do not know God's law and Catholic teaching.

15. 2 Timothy 2[17–18].
16. [Quoted in Gratian, c. 16, C. 23, q. 3].

Chapter Fifty-One

In almost the same way Doctor Sepúlveda twists the true and correct interpretation of the original teachings of Blessed Gregory the Great and other saints. Sepúlveda claims, in the first place, that Gregory approved wars Christians waged against unbelievers on the sole grounds that the faith would be more easily preached to persons who are subject to the jurisdiction of Christians, and further that Gregory praises and thanks a certain Exarch, Genandius, for waging war against certain unbelievers.[1]

The truth is that Gregory, a very holy man, did not even dream of such a thing. Because of his outstanding piety, when he sought to lead the English to the faith he sent them not armed forces but Augustine and forty other monks, who brought that nation to Christ by miracles and the word of God, as we have related in chapter 45. From the words of his letter, quoted by Sepúlveda, we gather that Gregory praised Genandius not for waging war against pagans so that they might become Christians (as Sepúlveda falsely attributes to him) but for re-

1. In his seventy-third letter, quoted by Gratian, c. 49, C. 23, q. 4.

claiming from the power of pagans or heretics territories that had once belonged to Christians.

Here are his words:

For we have learned that Your Excellency has provided many useful measures for pasturing the sheep of Blessed Peter, the Prince of the Apostles, with the result that you have returned to the proper owners those things which have been despoiled, (*that is, the settlement or resettlement of Daticii,*) and have restored important parts of the patrimony to the inhabitants of the Dacians, (*that is, certain peoples, according to the archdeacon*).

You see, dear reader, that Gregory is not speaking about a war waged against pagans with a view to subjecting them so that they might become Christians, as Sepúlveda would like to have it, but about recovering provinces that had once been under Christian jurisdiction. For it is clear from much of what has been introduced and fully proved that in territories of unbelievers who live peacefully and do not harm the Church Blessed Peter does not actually have any sheep or a patrimony that must be restored, since by our supposition they have not received the faith. This is obvious, too, from the word "restore," which presupposes a plundering. For it is clear that at the time of Blessed Augustine the Vandals, who were first pagans and then Arians, occupied Africa and held it for more than ninety years, until the time of the Emperor Justinian.[2]

Now Gregory flourished fifty years after Justinian. In his time the Vandals were laying waste to Africa, as is clear from various histories, especially that of Eutropius, Books 16 and 17. Therefore the pagans held Africa during Gregory's era. Nor is this contradicted by Sepúlveda's argument that the Vandals had already been conquered by Belisarius, since, as is evident from Eutropius' *History,* book 16, in the seventh year of Justinian's rule he went to Africa to fight the Vandals on three occasions.[3] It is possible, then, that they were not completely conquered by Belisarius (although some claim they were), and consequently that they endured until the time of Gregory the Great and made a new attack against the Roman (that is, Christian) populace.

2. See the Codex, 1, 27, 1; the introduction to the Institutes and the Authenticae, 1, 1. Vincent writes about this in his *Speculum Historiae,* Book 21, chaps. 28 and 31.
3. Volateranus has something on this, as does Rubertus in his *Dictionary.*

Now whatever the case of the Vandals may have been, there were other pagans and other peoples in Africa, as Eutropius says in the history we cited above. Among these were the Moors, who were descendants of the peoples whom Joshua and the Children of Israel drove from the Promised Land, or rather who fled from their sword, and these were Canaanites or one of those seven peoples. Coming to Egypt and not being received by the Egyptians, they went to Libya, which they called Hoen, and placed two inscriptions on white concave stone slabs at the top of a large fountain. These had Phoenician letters, which read "We are the people who fled from the presence of Jesus [Joshua] the thief, the son of Nava." This is what Eutropius relates in the work cited.

These Moors made war against the Africans in the time of Justinian. Solomon, who was made substitute governor of Africa by Belisarius, went out against them and killed fifty thousand. This shows that at the time of Gregory there could have been unbelievers in Africa who troubled the faithful and usurped properties belonging to the entire Church. And so Saint Gregory thanked Genandius, the Exarch of Africa, for reclaiming that region for the Church. This is quite clear from the title of the letter, "Gregory gives thanks to Genandius, the Patrician and Exarch of Africa, for benefits gained for Saint Peter." And since the subjugation of those pagans meant the spread of the Church, Gregory says: "Your reputation is that you frequently seek wars, not out of a desire to shed blood, but only for the sake of spreading the state in which we see God worshiped, seeing that Christ's name is spread everywhere among the subjugated peoples by the preaching of the faith." Gregory closes his letter with these words: "We ask Our Lord and Savior to grant holy and merciful protection to Your Eminence for the consolation of the state and to strengthen it by the power of his arm so that his name may be ever more widely spread among neighboring nations." In the same way, we pray vigorously that the Lord may give us daily help against the Turks and Moors who plague the Christian Church, not only that they may become Christians but also because they inflict injuries on the Church and have a tyrannical hold over its lands.

Therefore Gregory praises Genandius not because he took up arms against the pagans in order to make them become Christians but because he reconquered provinces or places from them that had once belonged to the Christian Church, and because, once those fierce foes were thoroughly subdued, the light of the gospel could be spread through the neighboring regions that had been occupied by them. These were Gregory's pious desires.

Again, at that time the churches of Africa were held by Donatists, very fierce heretics, who boasted that they alone were the Church and added many other heretical teachings, which Augustine cites.[4] Now the fact that there were still Donatists in Gregory's time is proved from his seventy-second letter, in which he exhorts Genandius to see to it that a council of the Catholic Bishops be held against the heretics, and in his seventy-fifth letter he orders the orthodox Bishops not to consecrate as Bishop any Donatist who has been reconciled to the Catholic Church. Gregory, therefore, praises Genandius for having subjugated the Donatist heretics and taken the churches away from them, just as before, after he had driven out the pagans, he had recovered Christian provinces. Gregory says this in his seventy-second letter, referred to above:

Just as the Lord has made Your Excellency shine forth in this life with the brilliance of victory in wars with the enemy, so you must proceed against the enemies of the Church with all the vigor of your mind and body, seeing that your renown will shine out more and more as a result of your twofold triumph when, in lawful wars, (*those waged against pagans*), you take a firm stand against the enemies of the Catholic Church in behalf of the Christian people and fight the battles of the Church, (*those waged against heretics*), as the Lord's own warrior. For it is known that men of heretical religion make a vigorous attack against the Catholic faith if they have at hand freedom to harm it (which God forbid!), inasmuch as, if they can, they pour out the poisons of their heresy to destroy the members of the Christian body. For we know that, although the Lord is against them, they raise their necks against the Catholic Church and seek to bring down the faith of the Christian state. Yet Your Eminence should restrain their efforts and press their proud necks firmly under the yoke of uprightness. . . . Surely the glory of Your Excellency advances with great progress before our Creator, if through you the fellowship of separated churches is restored.

From these words, dear reader, note that Genandius subjugated the Donatist heretics by war, restored to Catholic bishops the scattered churches held by the heretics, and fought against pagans in order to

4. In his book *De Haeresibus,* as well as in the book he composed especially against them. See also Isidore, *Etymologiae,* Book 7, chap. 5.

claim provinces for the Church that had once been under Christian jurisdiction and in which Christians were perhaps still living. Because of these things, which Genandius achieved with all piety, Gregory thanks him in the next letter (that is, number seventy-three), which Sepúlveda cites pointlessly. For in it Genandius is not praised for having used armed forces to subjugate Vandals, Moors, or other unbelievers in order that afterward the pagans might be converted through the preaching of the gospel, as we have already proved. And the fact that Gratian inserts these letters into the Church's [Gratian's] *Decree* (C. 23, q. 4) is beside the point, for he uses these passages only to prove that it is not contrary to Christ's law to kill the wicked. This is indicated in the summation of each chapter. For example, the meaning of canon 48 is put down in these words: "Enemies of the religion of the Church must be restrained even by war." And for canon 49 we read this entry: "Victory in war is achieved by the merit of faith." Now who will deny that the foes of the Christian religion must be restrained by war whenever they cannot be checked by any other means? Who will deny that victory is achieved by faith?

But what does this have to do with Sepúlveda's opinion, which is completely foreign to all reason and Christian teaching? Sepúlveda goes on, and to strengthen his error he cites the same Saint Gregory in his sixtieth letter,[5] where he exhorts Ethelbert, the King of England, to uproot the worship of idols and to destroy pagan temples after the example of Constantine the Great, who did the same thing throughout the Roman Empire. Now since King Ethelbert was already a member of the Church through the faith he had accepted, Pope Gregory had every right to exhort him to uproot idolatry, and that exhortation had the force of a command. For that King was obliged by divine law to take all possible measures by which his subjects would be led to the faith, although in an appropriate manner, according to Augustine.[6]

It must be noted also that the subjects of that King were already in some way subjects of the Church, even if they were pagans, because once a king has become subject through baptism, his whole kingdom is

---

5. Book 9.
6. *De Civitate Dei,* Book 5, chaps. 24 and 26; Book 19, chap. 16. See also Gratian, c. 35, C. 23, q. 4, at the words *Regi regentem gentem suam.*

considered to be subject to that to which the king has subjected himself.[7] Now the King was obliged to do what was urged by Saint Gregory since the pagans in question were his subjects in some way (as has been said) and the King, without resorting to arms, could uproot the worship of idols in his own kingdom by edict, especially since it is probable that the nobles received the Christian religion at the same time he did. As Saint Thomas writes, subjects always imitate their ruler.[8] This was the mind of Gregory the Great in citing Ethelbert the example of Constantine with these words:

For Constantine, the very pious emperor in times past, when he was calling the Roman state away from the perverse worship of idols, subjected it, along with himself, to our all-powerful Lord and God Jesus Christ and he was converted to him with his whole heart together with his subject peoples.

A ruler can and should forbid idolatry in his kingdom, as he can other public sins, provided that this is done without any great turmoil or scandal and without greater drawbacks than those that come from the idolatry, as has been treated at length above. Yet in place of the worship of demons, which he seeks to uproot, he should offer what is better: knowledge of the true God. If, however, a king were to prohibit idolatry by issuing laws but would not instruct his subjects in another religion, he certainly would be wrong. For it is impossible for men not to worship the true God or what they think is the true God. Therefore rulers, upon whom lies the task of providing for the good of their kingdoms, can uproot impious religion and introduce the worship of the true religion, since he [*sic*] has power over them by a natural right.

And so, precisely because they were subjects, Constantine forbade the worship of idols under the penalties of death and confiscation of property, possibly on the advice of Blessed Sylvester, who was motivated by this reason.[9] And since, according to Hugh of Fleury, Julian the Apostate restored the worship of idols after the death of Constantine,

7. See the doctors on the Authenticae, 9, 14. Baldus on the Digests, 1, 7, 15, reading 1. Giasone on the Authenticae, 1, 5, 5, col. 8; Codex, *De Sacrosanctis Ecclesiis;* Anthony of Butrio in the recapitulation of the end of the chapter *"De Causa Possessionis et Proprietatis"* [Digests, 2, 12].
8. [*Summa Theologiae*], II–II, q. 10, a. 10c.
9. Codex, 1, 11, 1, and the following.

the pious Emperor Theodosius completely uprooted idolatry throughout the empire and destroyed the temples of the pagans. According to
Vincent, the example of Theodosius was followed by his sons Arcadius
and Honorius, who reigned after him.[10] Likewise, in cases where unbelievers are subject to the Church or its members, we see that laws were
enacted for them by Theodosius, Arcadius, and Valentinian, all of
whom passed laws preventing Jews from celebrating marriages according to the Mosaic law, and in the Christian rite within the second, third,
or fourth degree [of consanguinity].[11] But if unbelievers were not subject to the Church, the Church could not in any way enact laws for
them, as has been proved.[12] No pious person disapproves of laws of this
type. And if a similar case should occur where idolatry could be checked
in subjects by the authority of their rulers without [inducing] a greater
evil, who would not see to it that a similar law would be enacted, if he
really loved Christ from his heart?

But what does this have to do with our case, in which pagans who
have never been subject to the Church or to its members and whose
ruler is a pagan are killed not by their ruler but by Spanish soldiers, and
are cruelly subjugated by war, so that, after innumerable persons have
been massacred, the worship of idols may be uprooted at last? But
someone will object that if it is pious to kill a person who persists in
the worship of idols after the law has forbidden it, it is also pious to
uproot idolatry by war. This argument surely has no force, first, because
power and jurisdiction, and so the authority by which a just war is
waged, are lacking in persons who are not subjects, and, second, because
an idolatrous subject is killed who can still be converted to Christ
through the ministry of preachers, since he sins through ignorance.
Moreover, a guilty person should be executed without harm to the
innocent. But in war, thousands of innocent persons are killed along
with a small minority of the guilty, as has been proved. Therefore to

10. *Speculum Historiae,* Book 19, chap. 5.
11. Codex, 1, 9, 7.
12. Laws enacted by Theodosius in this area are recorded in the *Church History,* Book 11,
chap. 19, and Book 9; in the *Tripartite History,* Book 9, chaps. 27 and 28; and Augustine's
De Civitate Dei, Book 51, chap. 26; by the Archbishop of Florence in the second part of
his history, vol. 8, chap. 7, #2; and Augustine in his forty-eighth letter, against Vincent
the Donatist heretic, quoted in Gratian, c. 41, C. 23, q. 4. And in his thirtieth and
thirty-first letters, Ambrose exhorted Theodosius to do the same thing.

subjugate unbelievers by war in order that they may accept the faith is evil. And so the examples of Constantine, Theodosius, and the other rulers who, by enacting laws, commanded that the temples be closed and forbade the worship of idols in their kingdoms, have nothing to do with our case for the reasons we have given above, and especially since, as rulers, they could impose on their subjects whatever laws they wished. The Indians, however, are subject neither to us nor to the Church, since they are pagans who have lawful and free sovereigns in their own kingdoms. Therefore we cannot impose any kind of law on them. That a person cannot pass a law except for his own subjects is a most certain tenet of law.[13]

The Church [in the time of Constantine] also had a special reason because the converted rulers or kings of the unbelievers, as well as a considerable part of their kingdoms, already belonged to and were members of the Church. However, the other people, who were not yet converted, belonged to the Church in a certain way because, as we have said, they were in closer potency than previously. So if, in a kingdom that was in the first stages of conversion, the ruler allowed temples to remain open and the worship of idols to be practiced publicly, not only the ordinary and common people but also the ruler would have been in imminent danger of apostatizing from the faith. For this reason it was most proper—rather, very necessary—that the Church and its prelates exhorted Christian rulers to destroy idolatry and to strive with all their power to destroy temples. And this is what Gregory [urged] vigorously in his letter to Ethelbert, the King of England. However, in regard to other nations or unbelievers that, along with their rulers, had never heard anything about the faith, nor inflicted any offense on the Church by means of any of the cases previously mentioned and never had the smallest suspicion of what the Church is or whether it really exists, and therefore were completely outside the Church, it is perfectly clear that none of the conditions mentioned before are verified in them. In fact, all the conditions are exactly the opposite. Therefore, the status of all unbelievers is completely different, no matter how given over to idolatry they may be, provided they are not guilty according to any of the six cases already mentioned. It is quite different, I say, from the situation that motivated Gregory, Ambrose, and Augustine to exhort

13. Codex, 1, 1, 1; 5, 5, 9. Digests, 1, 18, 3. Decretals, 5, 29, 21.

Christian rulers to destroy idolatry and to commend their Christian laws concerning this matter.

From the foregoing, then, the true interpretation of the original opinions of the holy doctors of the Church is obvious, as well as their interpretation of human laws, whose arguments the Venerable Doctor Sepúlveda ineptly introduces in support of his position, although they clearly militate against his position.

Chapter Fifty-Two

Furthermore, Sepúlveda cites Augustine and Thomas as teaching that the Romans had a just cause for subjugating the world because God wanted the world to be ruled by them since they were superior to other peoples in skill and justice.

Now, in the first place, the Roman Empire did not arise through justice but was acquired by tyranny and violence, as we have proved elsewhere from historians, lawyers, and theologians. I shall submit what Augustine and Thomas taught in good faith: that those Romans who were the first inhabitants of the city of Rome were endowed with some moral virtues, specifically, love of country and zeal for the public welfare, which they put ahead of their own convenience. Likewise, they established just laws and dealt kindly and gently with the peoples who were subject to their rule by reason of war or some other reason.

However, according to Augustine[1] these were not true virtues, and the Decree states: "Where faith does not flourish, there can be no justice."[2] Therefore Augustine teaches that, in his unutterable prudence and goodness, God granted them rule over the world since he would not give them eternal life.[3] In the *City of God,* Book 4, chapter 33, Augustine says: "Therefore God, the author and giver of happiness because he alone is the true God, gives earthly kingdoms to both the good and the bad." And in the fifth book, chapter 28, he says:

Since this is so, we should attribute the power of granting rule and sovereignty only to the true God who grants happiness in the kingdom of heaven only to the good, but earthly sovereignty to both the good and the wicked, as is pleasing to him who is pleased only by what is just. . . . Therefore, when and as much as he wished, the one true God, who does not abandon the human race as regards either judgment or help, granted a kingdom to the Romans, just as he did to the Assyrians or even to the Persians.

Again, in chapter 15, he says:

Therefore, with regard to those to whom God was not going to give eternal life with his holy angels . . . if he had not also granted them this earthly glory of a very excellent empire, a reward would not have been granted to their good arts, that is, their virtues.

And he concludes the chapter by stating: "There is no reason why they should complain against the justice of the supreme and true God. 'They have received their reward.' " As Augustine says in various passages, the reason for this fact is that it is in keeping with God's marvelous goodness to attach a reward to virtue, even the least. This is proved from Ezekiel where God says of Nebuchadnezzar, who did a deed pleasing to him by waging war against the people of Tyre:

1. *De Civitate Dei,* Book 5, chap. 12.
2. Gratian, c. 29, C. 24, q. 1.
3. *De Civitate Dei,* loc. cit. Jerome, quoted in Gratian, c. 14, C. 28, q. 1, #*Ex his.* Saint Thomas, *De Regimine Principum,* Book 3, chaps. 4–6.

Son of man, Nebuchadnezzar, king of Babylon, mobilized his army for a great expedition against Tyre. Their heads have all gone bald, their shoulders are all chafed, but even so he has derived no profit from the expedition mounted against Tyre either for himself or for his army.[4]

And since such tyrants do not merit an eternal reward for their merits or the services rendered to God, the Lord adds:

I am going to give Egypt over to Nebuchadnezzar, king of Babylon. He will levy his share of riches there instead, will loot it and carry off the booty to pay his army. In reward for his efforts against Tyre I am handing the land of Egypt over to him, since he has been working for me—it is the Lord who speaks.[5]

Similarly, the Lord addresses Cyrus, the King of the Persians, in these words:

Thus says the Lord to his anointed, to Cyrus, whom he has taken by his right hand to subdue nations before him and strip the loins of kings . . . I will go before you leveling the heights . . . I will give you the hidden treasure, the secret hoards.[6]

For although this man's rule was unjustly possessed, it gave rise to very many things that were pleasing to God. First, it granted freedom to the Jews who were held in captivity and gave them the freedom to rebuild the city of Jerusalem and its temple, so that God might be worshiped there.[7] Then Cyrus showed himself the instrument of divine justice by killing Belshazzar, who, wishing to worship his idols, had the vessels Nebuchadnezzar had brought from the temple in Jerusalem brought to him, and he, his wives, and his concubines drank from them.[8]

Therefore divine providence rewards the tyrants whom he uses as instruments for the execution of his justice. This is why the Romans received their reward. In the same vein, Gratian says:

4. 29[18–19].
5. [18–21].
6. Isaiah 45[1–3].
7. Ezra, chap. 1.
8. Daniel, chap. 5.

Such persons are said to serve in that they punish. Inasmuch, however, as they do not know that they are instruments of God's anger and are inflated with a wicked vanity, they receive from God only a temporal reward for their virtue, but they do not escape the punishment of their pride . . . similarly, when God decreed to punish the crime of killing Christ by means' of the Romans, they received the right to ascribe the destruction of the city and the wretched captivity of the Jewish people to their own power. And so the prophet inveighs against them, saying, "Lift up your hands against the pride of those who hate you and who have erected many spiteful monuments to their victory" (*that is, who have placed their standards and weapons in the midst of your house, that is, the temple, as a sign of your victory*).[9]

Gratian later adds:

Now when some persons are moved by a hidden instinct to persecute the wicked, just as Sennacherib and the others persecuted the sinful people although, while the hidden instinct functions, they are incited by the people's wrongs to persecute, yet, because they have a depraved intention, not of punishing the sins of the delinquents but of seizing their property or making them subject to their jurisdiction, they are not free of crime.

Therefore, although men of this type somehow serve God, yet they commit mortal sin because they wage war not with the intention of serving God but with the intention of looting and spreading their power. This is also proved, in addition to the foregoing passages, in Isaiah:

Woe to Assyria, the rod of my anger, the club brandished by me in my fury! I sent him against a godless nation; I gave him commission against a people that provokes me, to pillage and to plunder freely. . . . But he did not intend this, his heart did not plan it so. No, in his heart was to destroy.[10]

The obvious conclusion from the foregoing is, first, that at times God secretly moves wicked men and in this way uses their services for punishing sinners. Ambrose writes of this: "Because of their offense to the Divine Majesty, the Jewish people have frequently suffered at the hands of foreigners animated by a command from God."[11] Similarly,

---

9. Gloss on psalm 73. Gratian, c. 49, C. 23, q. 5, #*Hinc Notandum.*
10. 10[5, 11].
11. Quoted in Gratian, c. 49, C. 23, q. 5.

according to Augustine, God did this in order to bring forth the good he planned to glean from their evil acts.

The second conclusion is that those tyrants neither intend that to which God moves them nor will what he wills, but direct their depraved hearts only to plunder peoples and make them subject to their power.

The third conclusion is that since they do those things not from a love of virtue but from a lust for power, they commit most serious mortal sins, and at the end of their lives they must be condemned to the fires of hell. This is evident in the expression "Woe to Sennacherib," an expression that Scripture never uses, as Jerome and Chrysostom testify, except in reference to mortal sin, which must be punished in the end by everlasting damnation. God, then, used the Romans both to dispose that part of the world for his gracious and gentle coming and to symbolize the unity of the Church (that is, his holy kingdom, which would take in the entire world) through the unification of the nations.

Furthermore, he chose the Romans to be the executioners or executors of his justice in order to punish those nations whose crimes angered him. And so, just as God also permitted Nebuchadnezzar to overthrow, usurp, and dominate Egypt because Nebuchadnezzar had served God in the destruction of Tyre, he permitted Cyrus to capture Babylon and kill Belshazzar, although he subjugated all nations in war not in order to serve the Lord but because of his ambition and his lust for more power. Therefore, he finally cast them into hell because of their acts of violence and injustice. Likewise, he permitted and caused the Romans to have domination over the world as their reward for the sake of the already mentioned effects he planned to draw from their tyranny. This, then, does not enable Sepúlveda to throw up against us the tyranny of the Romans as a justification of our tyranny toward the Indians, which has been called *conquista*. For the Romans, the Persians, and the Assyrians have perished forever because their wars were not pleasing in the eyes of the Lord, as we have proved from the words of the holy Fathers and, God willing, shall make clear at greater length.

Chapter Fifty-Three

Those who defame the Indians also advance what John Major wrote on this point in his *Commentary on the Second Book of Sentences,* chapter 44, q. 3. With all due respect to him, [I note that] in one part of this writing he has spoken about all unbelievers in a very confused way, in another part he presents a mistaken opinion that is contrary to natural reason and the divine law, and in regard to this present question of the Indians he has made some statements that can be a stumbling block and obstacle to the faith. On the other hand, Durandus, a theologian of greater authority, rejects John's teaching in his [Durandus'] comments on the same distinction in the same book of the *Sentences.*

But in order that the errors of a man who is ignorant of both the law and the facts may be still clearer, I shall submit his own words:

Since the Indians did not understand the Spanish language and refused to admit the preachers of God's word except with a large army, it was necessary to build fortifications at various places in order that, with the passage of time, this unruly people would become accustomed to the practices of the Christians through mutual knowledge. And since, in all these things, there is need for great expenditures which no other king provides, it is lawful to take them by force

since the other person ought reasonably to will this. And when the people will
have become Christian, either their former king accepts the faith or he does not.
In the latter case, which can border on harm to the faith, he must be deposed.
For the sake of the freedom of the orthodox faith, he deserves to be deposed.
And if that people really accepts Christianity, they want this deposition. But
if you claim that the people still want to retain their former king despite the fact
that he remains a pagan, the main conclusion is that they have not yet accepted
the faith sincerely and then the kingdom must not be left in his hands. In fact,
it is not fitting that an unbelieving king rule a Christian people, since he can
turn them away from the faith by gifts and honors. But if he wants to accept
the faith along with the others, while at the same time paying for the expenses
which have been undertaken, I do not think that he should be deposed, as long
as he is a good king and there is no fear that he may lapse into unbelief.

First of all, when he presupposes that the Indians will not receive
preachers except with a large army, he is clearly mistaken and does not
know the real situation. For the Indians are very meek, and when the
Spaniards first penetrated their territories an enormous number of them
quickly boarded the ships of the Christians with a sincere attitude and
[later], entertaining the Spaniards in their homes, they paid them the
highest honor as godlike men sent from heaven. From this it is quite
clear that they would receive and all but worship the preachers if they
would bring the example of Christ and the Apostles in their behavior
and would be such as the heralds of the gospel truth ought to be.

Moreover, John Major is certainly wrong in saying that the kings can
be despoiled of their kingdoms until they pay the expenses incurred by
the kings of Spain in sending soldiers and preachers. Are we, under the
pretext of a security, to seize a kingdom as though it were a cloak which
is easily returned once the debt is paid? Furthermore, if a king is robbed
of his kingdom by this tyrannical pretense, how many massacres, how
many burnings, how many deplorable calamities will necessarily take
place beforehand? Where does this theologian read about securities of
this sort, which cause the loss of so many souls? Besides, what will the
kings of the Indians think when they see the Spaniards, a rough, fierce,
robust, and formidable people, build fortresses and stone houses without the kings' permission? Will these actions not make Christ's sacred
name hateful, and will there not follow from them the innumerable
evils we have just listed? Did Paul receive securities of this kind from
those to whom he preached the gospel? Or did he not rather work with
his hands in order not to hinder the gospel? "We have put up with

anything rather than obstruct the gospel of Christ."[1] Did he say this
only for himself, as if he alone were obliged to give the gospel freely?
Or did he not rather say for all what he is recorded as having said to
the Bishop and prelates at Miletus:

I have never asked anyone for money or clothes; you know for yourselves that
the work I did earned enough to meet my needs and those of my companions.
I did this to show you that this is how we must exert ourselves to support the
weak, remembering the words of the Lord Jesus, who himself said, "There is
more happiness in giving than in receiving."[2]

Why do we not imitate the generous attitude of this man? Why,
under cover of money or expenses, which he spurned, do we give the
Indians the opportunity to think that the law of the gospel is irksome
and burdensome? Let us follow the footsteps of Paul, who said that this
is how we must help the weak. The expression "must" is preceptive and
introduces the idea of necessity, as I have said before. Therefore, while
conceding that the Indians have kingdoms, John Major is wrong in
claiming that, under the pretext of a security, their kings should be
despoiled of their kingdoms in order that, after they have paid the
expenses mentioned, they should receive them back if they accept the
faith of Christ. This is hollow talk. For let us suppose that they refuse
to accept the faith of Christ and to pay the expenses. On what grounds,
I ask, can they be deprived of a kingdom? Surely not on the grounds
of business transacted to their advantage, since it cannot be called
advantageous for them inasmuch as, with the coming of the Spaniards,
they are despoiled of their own kingdoms and innumerable evils result
from the war that has to be waged if the Indian king is to be deprived
of his authority. Therefore, since the business is not transacted to [the
king's] advantage, there is no reason why they [*sic*] should bear the
expenses.[3] Since, according to the teachings of Christ, no one must be
punished on the grounds that he refuses to accept the Christian faith,
nor must anyone be forced to the faith, what example is there in depriving a ruler of his kingdom because he refuses to accept the faith, especially when it is preached by wicked men whom you would call foul

1. 1 Corinthians 9[12].
2. Acts 20[33–35].
3. Digests, 24, 3, 21.

demons, servants of Satan, and enemies of Christ's glory rather than messengers of peace and heralds of the truth?

Away, then, with John Major and his dreams! He knows neither the law nor the facts. It is ridiculous that this theologian should say that, even before a king understands the Spanish language and even before he understands the reason why the Spanish build fortifications, he should be deprived of his kingdom by reason of expenses if he does not accept the faith. If the unfortunate king does not understand the Spanish language, how will he grasp or believe Christ's truth and abandon his own religion, approved by so many centuries of acceptance? Would not the man be insane to do this? Or are Christian dogmas like the principles nature itself teaches and demonstrates by a special light implanted in every pagan and unbeliever? Who is so blind as to fail to see that to despoil an innocent and thoroughly ignorant ruler and to lead him, after he has been deprived of his property, into captivity under the pretext of expenses, are wiles of Satan? What does this have in common with the charity of Christ or with common sense? Does the Indian who has never heard the name of Christ believe any less, at least in a human way, that his religion is true than the Christian does of his religion? John Major adds that the Indian king should reasonably put up with this. I do not at all think that John Major would tolerate such evils and crudities, supposing he were an Indian. If Hungarians or Bohemians, of whose language he would be ignorant, were to despoil him of his dignity or rule if he were a king, when they first approached him, upsetting everything and terrifying his provinces with the tumult of war, even if they were motivated by a good cause, would he graciously and joyfully accept that good cause? And would he gladly pay the expenses when, after the passage of time, there would be a mutual grasp of both languages? I do not think so. What is forced faith, if not this? Nor is it simple force, but it involves massacres and the terror of war, the worst of all. In a passage cited previously, Gregory says "Preaching which exacts faith by punishment is novel and unheard of."

Chapter Fifty-Four

And so John Major teaches, in the first place, that a king must be deprived of his rule if his people are converted to the faith and he refuses to accept it. But Major mistakes the fact, because he does not know the attitude of the Indians. No one accepts the faith more willingly or quickly, if they are correctly instructed, than do the kings and rulers of those nations (whom we call *caciques* in Spanish). Similarly, John mistakes the law, since not even a king should be forced to the faith. Moreover, no one must be punished merely because he is able to do harm but has not yet sinned or done anything against his people because they have accepted the Christian religion. For innumerable things that can take place according to active and passive potency do not actually happen.[1] God never wants an innocent person to be punished. A project that is well begun may possibly be spoiled if we should tyrannically deprive a king of his kingdom because of a sin he has not committed, even if he is able to commit it.

1. See Aristotle, *Metaphysics,* Books 5 and 9.

John Major would use better judgment if he would add that this must be understood on the strong and probable presumption, not on empty conjectures, that the king would do harm to the faith and punish the people. This is hardly credible in the case of the Indian rulers because of their very mild character. But if the suspicion is strong, something must be given to compensate him for [the loss of] his rule, as Innocent teaches.[2] Speaking about pagan rulers who have seized our provinces, he teaches that they must not be deprived of or deposed from their sovereignty even if their people are converted to Christ, lest rebellion and hatred of the name Christian be implanted in the souls of the pagans. This is what Major should have taught, this theologian who spoke about the Indians he had never seen, who have not seized Christian territories or even heard the word Christian in their kingdoms, so far distant from ours.

John Major teaches, in the second place, that such a ruler should be deprived of his authority so that his subjects can freely profess the Catholic faith. But he is wrong, because the jurisdiction, even of pagan rulers, arises from the natural law, as well as from the law of nations and divine law, as we have proved elsewhere by unimpeachable arguments and the citations of divine Scripture. Surely if his subjects are converted to the faith, they owe him reverence and obedience as to their master in matters that are not contrary to God's law. Moreover, his jurisdiction lasts and taxes must be paid to him as long as he exercises his jurisdiction without harm to the faithful, even if that ruler refuses to be converted to the faith. For Truth itself has taught that the Jews must pay taxes to Tiberius Caesar, a pagan ruler: "Give back to Caesar what belongs to Caesar—and to God what belongs to God."[3] In keeping with this answer, the Apostle Paul teaches that believers should be subject to princes and authorities, etc.[4] Jerome teaches this same thing in a passage that will be cited later, where he uses these words of Romans 13:

You must all obey the governing authorities. . . . You must obey, therefore, not only because you are afraid of being punished (*that is, because of peril or in order*

2. On the Decretals, 3, 24, 8.
3. Matthew 22[21].
4. [Titus 3:1].

to avoid temporal or physical punishment), but also for conscience' sake (*that is, so that there will be no sin on your conscience*), since he who resists authority is rebelling against God's decision and such an act is bound to be punished.

Now the fact that Christians are commanded to obey their rulers, even unbelievers, is proved in the first place from the sacred doctors, who explain Paul's words in the thirteenth chapter of Romans in this way.

Second, because it is obvious both from sacred and profane accounts of history that, at the time Paul wrote this, all rulers were pagan and the Apostles and the faithful were living under them. Chrysostom also teaches this when he comments on the words "They serve God." "Now at that time, Christians belonged for the most part to the ordinary classes," according to the words of Chrysostom. Paul, then, gave the command "You must all obey" to his own subjects, that is, to the Christians, not to the pagans, who either ridiculed or refused to recognize it. Paul adds: "Pay every governmental official what he has a right to ask—whether it be direct tax or indirect, fear or honor."[5] Paul states the same teaching quite clearly in 1 Timothy: "All slaves 'under the yoke,' " (*that is, of unbelievers, according to the interlinear gloss*), "must have unqualified respect for their masters," (*that is, the unbelievers*), "so that the name of God and our teaching are not brought into disrepute."[6] Then he adds: "Slaves whose masters are believers are not to think any the less of them because they are brothers; on the contrary, they should serve" (*the unbelievers*) "all the more." Therefore, respect should be given to masters of rulers by subjects, even if the subjects are Christians but the master an unbeliever. The gloss on the words "you must all obey the governing authorities" teaches this rather explicitly: "For it seemed that unbelieving masters should be equal to the faithful. The Apostle removes even this bit of pride, since power is only from God."

Again, in connection with the words "so that the name of God and our teaching are not brought into disrepute," the interlinear gloss says: "as if he invaded what belongs to another but rather let the unbelieving masters be converted through the services of their believing slaves and let the [Christian] teaching not be brought into disrepute as being unjust

5. [Romans 13:7].
6. [6:1–2].

and preached against the law." Moreover, commenting on 1 Corinthians 6, Saint Thomas says, at the beginning of his first reading, that it is contrary to the divine law to forbid the faithful to appear before the courts of unbelieving rulers if they are summoned or before those set up by them, that is, the magistrates or judges appointed by them, since it is within the authority of a ruler to pass judgment on his subjects. Such a thing would be contrary to the subjection that is owed to rulers.

Therefore an unbelieving ruler should not be deposed and deprived of his rule for the sake of the freedom of the Catholic faith. Rather, his subjects should pay taxes to him. Durandus bolsters this conclusion with a clear argument that the conversion of the subjects of some pagan ruler to the faith does not increase his sins nor is he guilty of any new crime.[7] And so it is their good act, not his bad one. Therefore, just as he does not deserve to be deposed if his subjects do not accept the faith, much less should he be deposed if his subjects accept it. And surely the opinion of John Major smacks of the heresy of those who think that through baptism they are freed from all obedience and every obligation of paying taxes. Jerome says that these persons defend themselves with Paul's words to the Galatians: "When Christ freed us, he meant us to remain free."[8]

7. *In II Sententiarum,* d. 44, q. 3.
8. *Commentary on Titus,* chap. 3.

Chapter Fifty-Five

There is no conflict between what was said above and what Saint Thomas writes: "By reason of their lack of faith, unbelievers merit the loss of their power over the faithful who are transferred to the status of children of God."[1] This would seem to agree with the opinion of John Major. However, Thomas explains his position in the body of the question and in his reply to the second objection, where he teaches that since kingdoms come under the law of nations which is derived from the natural law, and since the distinction between believer and unbeliever is of divine law, and since the divine law does not do away with a human law that is derived from the divine law, unbelief, considered in itself, certainly does not abolish the jurisdiction of an unbelieving ruler over believing subjects.

Now in his reply to the second objection he writes that Nero's sovereignty and jurisdiction, which flourished at the time of Saint Paul, were not done away with even though persons who were subject to his rule were converted to the faith. Therefore, unless there was some new and just reason why he deserved the loss of his sovereignty and jurisdiction, Christians always remained subject to him. And so Saint Thomas's first words must necessarily be understood of a case where there is some great and probable danger to the faith if a pagan rules, for example, if he treats his subjects tyrannically and violently because they have accepted the faith, if he is blasphemous toward Christ, or if he does or says anything that would lessen Christ's glory. Saint Thomas lists these reasons in the eighth article of the same question.

We have taught in the fourth case, given above, what must be done with rulers who do such things; that is, if a ruler should directly incite his subjects to hatred of the faith, he would be automatically deprived of his rule, or at least he could be judicially deprived of it by the Church because of the power entrusted to it by God, as Saint Thomas notes in the article cited.

This case fits the argument John Major offers in proof of his second conclusion; that is, that just as a lesser noble who incites his subjects

---

1. [*Summa Theologiae,*] II–II, q. 10, a. 10c.

to rebel against their king can be lawfully deprived of his authority, so too a ruler who tries to make his subjects give up the faith of Christ, to whom all things in heaven and on earth are subject, should be deprived of his sovereignty.

However, this argument does not apply beyond this case. For what if a ruler does not prevent his people from accepting the faith of Christ? Or what if the subjects refuse to accept it? Certainly in this case the argument of John Major has no force, especially in regard to unbelievers who have never heard about Christ, the faith, or the Church. Therefore when the holy doctor said that unbelievers merit the loss of their power over the faithful because of their lack of faith, he means this on the supposition that some condition is opposed to the progress of the faith. Now since the Church, having learned from the experience of very many past centuries, presupposes the stubborn blindness of the Jews and the wicked harshness of the Saracens, who openly fight against Christ's gospel, [and counts them] among those unbelievers who are subject to the Church or its members, it will make a judgment that the slave of Jews or Moors gains freedom by acknowledging Christ's truth.[2] The reason is that the Church believes the latter will do all they can to have the slave who has been converted to the faith abandon it. The Church could make the same decision about the slaves of Jews or Saracens who are not subject to us, yet, to avoid scandal, it does not do so. Saint Thomas teaches this in the article cited.

That this is the reason for this rule is proved in [Gratian's] Decree:[3] "Lead to freedom without any dissimulation any Christian chattel which it is clear a Jew has amassed lest (God forbid!) the Christian religion should be desecrated by subjection to the Jews."[4] And since, in the case of Turks and Saracens, the Church has learned from very long experience to consider as a condition totally fulfilled the fact that they are always ready to attack the faith and unsettle the Christian people; therefore it rightly and always has the power to invade them, even if they should stop their attacks for a few years. However, wherever that situation does not apply, as in the case of unbelievers who have known neither the Church nor the Christian people and who have not heard

---

2. See Gratian, c. 13, D. 54; c. 15, D. 54. Decretals, 5, 6, 19.
3. Gratian, c. 13, D. 54.
4. The text is found in the Decretals, 3, 33, 2.

anything about Christ or the Catholic faith, as is clearly the case with our Indians, surely that law (established by the Church) does not hold at all.

All of this is confirmed by the words of Saint Thomas in the first article of the same question 10, where he writes that the lack of faith of those who have never heard of the faith and do not resist it has the quality not of guilt but of punishment, since by reason of the sin of our first parents we are ignorant of divine things. And although such unbelievers are damned for all eternity by reason of the sins they commit, which cannot be cleansed without the Christian sacraments, yet this is not because they have not believed in Christ, about whom they have never heard. Therefore in no way should it be said that by reason of their lack of faith unbelievers should lose the jurisdiction and power they have over their subjects, because the subjects accept the faith, while the former refuse to accept it. This is especially true if they refuse to accept it not with the obstinacy of a stubborn attitude but from ignorance, or because they put off embracing the faith from the desire for fuller instruction in it.

Since the merit of subjects who join the Christian army does not add a new sin to the rulers who remain in their unbelief, as we have said (for it is difficult for pagans to abandon their ancient faith, according to Chrysostom),[5] Saint Thomas should be interpreted as speaking about the rulers of the Turks and the Moors who, at his time, were known throughout the world as enemies of the Christians. For not only do they not allow their subjects to embrace the Christian faith, they also have a deep-seated wish that the whole religion of Christ had long ago been blotted out, and generally, in every locality and at all times, they do their utmost to perturb the lives of Christians. This is the true meaning of Saint Thomas's words. Otherwise he would hardly be consistent in his other writings—which is not an accusation to be made against the teaching of the holy doctor. Now in case of doubt, according to the jurists, that meaning must be accepted as genuine that removes contradictions and harmonizes positions that at first sight appear to be different.[6]

5. *Commentary on 1 Corinthians,* chap. 2, homily 7.
6. See the Decretals, 3, 42, 3; 2, 28, 54. Digests, 50, 17, 188. Our conclusion is supported specifically by Durandus, *In II Sententiarum,* d. 44, q. 3; Abulensis, *Super Matthaeum,* c. 20, q. 96; Albert of Campi, *De Ecclesiastica Hierarchia,* book 5, and the book *Controversiarum Controversia,* 16; John Driedonius, *De Libertate Ecclesiastica,* I, c. 1, and 4, at the beginning and sententia 7, and part 5, c. 2, part 2 and part 3.

Now the position of these men is much less doubtful in regard to the Indian rulers. And so it is evident that John Major fell into considerable error when he said that if the people of an unbelieving ruler are converted to the faith but he wants to remain in his unbelief, he should be deposed from his sovereignty for the sake of the freedom of the faith.

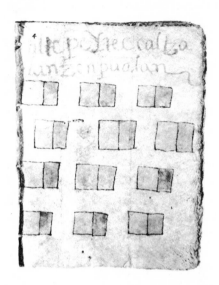

Chapter Fifty-Six

John Major teaches, in the third place, that if a people who have embraced the faith of Christ have embraced it wholeheartedly, they ought to want their ruler to be deposed if he persists in his paganism. As a matter of fact, a people naturally, or almost naturally, love their original ruler, according to Aristotle[1] and Augustine.[2] Therefore a people would admit this with as much difficulty as they would a new religion, especially if a foreigner is substituted for the deposed former lord—something that is usually disagreeable and odious to a people. For this reason Almighty God commanded the Jews that if they were to choose a king, he should be chosen from among them.[3]

[handwritten marginalia: rules / religion / ruler / resemblances / important / draw parallels]

1. *Ethics,* Book 8, chap. 7. *Politics,* Book 3, chap. 10.
2. *De Civitate Dei,* Book 19, chap. 16.
3. Deuteronomy 17. Saint Thomas gives the reason for this in his [*Summa Theologiae*], I–II, q. 105, a. 1, ad 2um.

Therefore there must be no sinister suspicion of a recently converted people just because they do not want their former ruler deposed, even if he is a pagan, since there is hope that he will eventually accept the faith. Further, one must not be astonished that a recently converted people does not have such a great evangelical strength as to enable them to strip themselves of all their feelings and hate their former ruler whom they have known through many years' habit. Therefore something must be allowed for and conceded to their feelings, although these feelings may not be purely Christian.[4] Gregory says: "Lest the good which has been planted and which still has weak roots should be pulled up. Rather, the good which has been begun should be strengthened and guarded until it becomes perfect."[5] And so John Major has gone too far in his fourth conclusion, saying that in such a case a king must be deposed.

Then John Major adds that if the Indian peoples on that island (and thus he shows how poorly he speaks about Indian affairs) are not governed by kings but their jurisdiction and rule belong to the state, the state must be deprived of its rule in order that the faith may be implanted. Here John strikes me as ridiculous, since he went through this matter quite hurriedly. For even if ruling power is left to a king once he has paid the expenses, why should John be unwilling to have this power restored to the state on the same condition? For whatever right a king has, he has by the consent of his people. If a king should die without heirs, the right of choosing a new king belongs to the people. Why, then, did John want a state, any more than a king, to be deprived of choice when the jurisdiction and power of a state are more natural than the rule of a king, which derives its origin from the consent of the state? For it is obvious that a greater injustice is committed by depriving a community or people of its right of choice without any lawful cause than by depriving a ruler of his power, since the former is more opposed to justice. And so Peter of Paulus writes, in reply to a certain argument, that if the Pope deposes a king for some just cause, he cannot substitute another in his place, for the right of choosing a king, which belongs to the people by the natural law, cannot be taken away from them.[6]

---

4. As Gregory says in his thirty-first letter, Book 13.
5. Chap. 7, sections of which are in Gratian, c. 20, C. 35, q. 2–3.
6. *De Causa Immediata Potestatis Papalis,* a. 4.

John Major goes on to speak falsely about the Indians in these words:

There is yet something else. Those people live like beasts on either side of the equator and between the poles live men like wild beasts, as Ptolemy says in his *Quadripartite.* And now this has been discovered by experience, etc.

He also brings forward the statement of the Philosopher in the first book of the *Politics,* that the Greeks should rule over barbarians. If I am not mistaken, this is where Sepúlveda gets his poisons. However, I am amazed that John Major has so easily believed those who betray the Indians—a docile, sincere, and clever people—by most shameless lies that they are stupid and bestial, so that these inhuman plunderers might act more unrestrainedly against them. Such a theologian should not have been so careless in such an important matter, especially since the bull of Alexander VI, based on the account of the Kings of Castile, relates that "Christopher Columbus recently encountered some gentle peoples, living peacefully without harming anyone and yet not completely ignorant of the name of God."

What serious man has ever taken up the pen without an exact knowledge of the facts and the law? This man, however, shows that he is totally unskilled in law, and when he directs his statements to facts, he blunders completely. What he cites as being from Ptolemy's *Quadripartite* is false, for Ptolemy wrote no such thing. He describes the world, as it was known at his time, in the second treatise of the *Tripartite,* chapter 3. But of what John Major cites, he did not write a single word, since he did not describe the provinces of the equator, which he thought were uncultivated and uninhabitable. The persons whom Ptolemy calls bestial lived in Moorish Africa, on the promontory we now call Cabo de Aguer, where the Arabs or Alarabs live. Further, since Ptolemy never had any knowledge of our Indians, how could he take note of them? What he writes—that is, that wild jungle men live on either side of the equator—is false, unless these men moved very far from the equator, so that because of the severity of the cold and the intemperate weather in that region they would almost lack human reason.[7] For the closer a

---

7. This is what the Philosopher writes in *Politics,* Book 7, as does Vegetius in his tract *De Re Militari,* Book 1, chap. 2.

Geographic Knowledge

region is to the Arctic and Antarctic zones and circles and the nearer it is to the poles, the colder it is because of the distance from the sun. Hence the inhabitants are less capable of reasoning. Now since men of this type are considered freaks of nature, they are necessarily very rare, as we have previously shown. For this reason those extremely cold zones are considered uninhabitable, not because no one lives there but because their inhabitants are few in number.

From this we conclude that what John Major cites from the Philosopher, that is, that the Greeks should rule the barbarian, does not fit here at all since, contrary to what he was thinking, the Indians are in no way barbarians, as we have taught in the second chapter. This absurd error of John Major may have been followed by one of his disciples, named Carlos. Sent in the year 1513 to be a vicar of the bishopric of Concepción, which is on the island of Española, he gave a sentence of divorce by which he dissolved a marriage between an Indian woman and her Spanish husband for this reason: that since she was an Indian, he judged she was stupid and lacking in reason. When Carlos later returned to Spain, he was permitted by the just judgment of God to fall into many errors, for which he was accused before the Holy Office of the Inquisition by my Dominican brothers. Condemned at length at Burgos, he publicly abjured those errors, to his great disgrace and shame, and he was deprived of the function of preaching and was sentenced to life imprisonment, either in a prison or a monastery designated to be his prison. Since then, nothing more has been seen of him. See what these absurd, or I might say wicked, incantations of John Major have done!

Furthermore, in order to strengthen his wicked opinion Sepúlveda says that the very learned Father Francisco de Vitoria approved the war against the Indians. Lest he should be deprived of his own glory, Sepúlveda adds that the famous and learned father did not by any means give the principal arguments that he [Sepúlveda] brings forward. However, anyone who reads the two parts of the *Prima Relectio* of that scholar [Vitoria] will easily see that, in the first part, he proposes and in a Catholic way refutes the seven headings by which war against the Indians would seem to be just. In the second part, however, he introduces eight titles by which, or by some of which, the Indians could come under the jurisdiction of the Spaniards. In these titles he presupposes, for the most part, that certain reasons for judging this war to be just are very false and that they have been appealed to by those plunderers who overflow far and wide that whole world. He is a little more careless, however, regarding some of those titles, since he wished to moderate what seemed to the Emperor's party to have been rather harshly put, although for lovers of the truth, nothing he discussed in the first part is harsh; that is, it has not merely been true in the past but is Catholic and certainly very true. He indicates this well enough by speaking conditionally, fearing that he might suppose or make false statements instead of true ones. Now since the circumstances that this learned father supposes are false, and he says some things hesitantly, surely Sepúlveda should not have thrown up against us an opinion that is based on false information.

Similarly, Brother Sepúlveda, it would have been more decent had you not cited the Reverend Father Miguel de Arcos and Masters Herrera and Esbarroya and the candidate Fray Diego de Vitoria, all learned monks of the institute of our Blessed Father Saint Dominic. You throw their names around as if they agree with you and approve your wicked opinion. But though you are not ignorant of better things, Sepúlveda, how strongly do some of those here present oppose you as you bandy these ideas. They complain that you attribute to them what they have never said. Others, furnished with false information and wicked lies, have answered conditionally that this war can be just, but only on the basis of all those criminal lies of which they were persuaded when they were consulted. They have added, however, that your work, which contains these outrages, should under no circumstances be published, so that this highly touted little book of yours should not give added encouragement to the wicked, who lack only the excuse to plunder and murder. In fact, this is what, unsolicited by any letters of mine, they have voluntarily written to me. So stop covering up your error with the names of so many men; rather you should aid the cause of Christ, as befits a scholar.

Chapter Fifty-Seven

It seems that we should not omit something that contributes to the truth of this question. In his unbelievable passion to publish the irreligious work he has written on this matter, Sepúlveda has presented it in the Supreme Council of the Indies, where, having ascertained the evil of the work and its very deadly poison, the prudent councillors rejected the work and refused to let it be printed. But again, lest his charming work should perish, Sepúlveda used amazing intrigues to tempt the supreme judges of the Royal Council [of Castile,] thinking that men ignorant of Indian affairs would not notice the poison. However, in keeping with their good judgment they deferred judgment on the work to the universities of Salamanca and Alcalá. After [the faculties] had argued about it on many occasions and had taken mature deliberation, they answered that the work was unworthy of the press, since the teaching it contained was hardly sound. Some theologians at Alcalá thought it was very dangerous.

Sepúlveda had previously sent the work to the Council of Trent, but, after having read it thoroughly and seeing that the material was scarcely Christian, some of the Council fathers refused to discuss this matter.

Undoubtedly they would have forbidden the work to be printed and would have imposed silence on its author if they knew that Sepúlveda had such a strong desire to have it published. A trustworthy man who was present at the holy Council told me this as something well known. Sepúlveda did not rest. Rather, in open contempt for the judgment of the universities and of both Royal Councils he secretly sent his work to Rome so that it might be printed there, since he knew about the freedom in that city and that there was no one there of a contrary mind who would fling back his poisoned darts. Perhaps the outcome of the affair will teach us how much damage that irreligious work will bring.

However, I do not know why an older man, who is a priest and a theologian, should want to print a work that has been condemned by so many men of such high quality in two universities, and finally by the fathers who were at the Council. Perhaps he does not want his many sleepless nights to go to waste. Instead, Sepúlveda should seek to prevent the loss of so many souls, to whose destruction he seems to have devoted himself. I beg him to form a better attitude.

He offers as a confirmation of his contagious opinion, that is, a work on Indian affairs which its author, a certain Oviedo, calls *A General History*. In book 3, chapter 6 of this work, this Oviedo writes that the people on the island of Española are undependable, idle, untruthful, inclined to evil and given over to many vices, inconstant, forgetful, cowardly, ungrateful, and hardly capable of anything. Then he says that although they are somewhat virtuous during adolescence, when they enter the age of manhood they fall into abominable vices. Then, in chapter 9 of book 6, speaking about the inhabitants of the mainland, he calls them wild, fierce, incorrigible, and unable to be corrected by severity or led to virtue by inducements or friendly warnings, that they are shameless, prone to evil, harsh, and do not know how to show mercy. He also writes that their baptized children can attain eternal happiness, but that once they become adolescents, they have little concern about the Christian religion even if they receive baptism at the same time or have received it previously, both because the Christian religion seems burdensome and bothersome to them and because, being forgetful, they immediately forget whatever is taught them. Oviedo is not shamed to write these lies, scattered in various passages of his history, from which he stupidly promises himself immortality.

Although these slanderous lies, falsely written against a sincere and decent people, have made them infamous—a people who from the very beginning were worthy of high praise for their docility, their character, and their very well-established state (as we shall indicate in the proper context)—Oviedo nonetheless has his judge. Christ lives, and holds a whip in his hand. Oviedo will give an account to him. For by his most virulent slanders, this utterly empty trifler has encouraged very wicked plunderers to destroy a nation totally undeserving of such treatment and has lessened the zeal of godly men, who thought that they were preaching the gospel, not to men, but to wild beasts. If false defamation of one person is a sin worthy of eternal death—the more serious in proportion to the loss of property or honor that results from it—and if a sin of this type is scarcely forgiven by recantation, what must one think of or who can worthily exaggerate the sin of this very unhappy man who reviles almost the entire human race and from whose sin so many massacres, so many burnings, so many bereavements, and, finally, such an ocean of evils result? How many evils extraneous to this cause has that wretched man piled up, who claims that he will write the truth but foists sheer fables on the reader? But I know that I must pardon an ignorant man who is overly busy with tracing the history of each nation.

Chapter Fifty-Eight

It is not surprising that Oviedo reviles the Indians with so many slanderous lies; and there are two reasons for this. The first is that he was one of those looters who went to the mainland in 1513 at the time of Pedrarias [Dávila]. They, before anyone else, began at the province of Darién, which stretches to the Gulf of Urabá, and laid waste to the whole mainland with completely inhuman savagery. They spared neither women, children, nor the aged, and even burned men alive so that they might steal their gold, and divided the other men among themselves, that is, enslaved them. At that time, when Oviedo was in charge of inspecting the King's accounts, his office was that of the person we call in Spanish the *veedor*. To him belonged a share of the loot that was taken during those detestable raids. The poor Indians were asleep, unsuspecting—and behold, before dawn those savage men, plunderers rather than soldiers, rushed to attack the Indian huts, which are made of straw, put them to the torch and burned men alive, together with their homes. After the flames died out they looked for the gold melted down by the fire. Not content with this, they most cruelly tortured the Indians they had captured alive so that they would tell where a greater supply of gold might be hidden.

Now all of this was done with the advice and consent of Oviedo himself and the other officials of the King, so that they might have a share of the booty proportionate to the servants and retainers they have sent to perform these heinous deeds, together with the rest of the Spaniards. Oviedo should try to make reparation by offering restitution for these detestable obscenities, rather than by his accusing slanders and shameless lies defame a gentle and decent people, redeemed by the blood of Christ. Oviedo well knows how many Indians were branded on the forehead and led into slavery as his share. He knows how many nobles and persons of the first rank they savagely destroyed and how tyrannically they divided the natives among themselves, so that the Indians would serve not one tyrant but many. He remembers how harsh and excessive were the tasks they imposed on them, to the point of death. They did not spare tender children, nor women, nor those broken by age, until they dug up gold from the bowels of the earth. He knows the truly sad outcome of this ungodliness. For how will he be ignorant of something that is known to the entire world? Those regions, so well cultivated by an immense number of natives but now devastated, destroyed, and utterly depopulated by the thousands and hundreds of thousands all the way to Nicaragua, have furnished pitiful evidence of the totally inhuman savagery of those thieves.

Oviedo played his part in all this. Without doubt, he was one of those wicked plunderers—a fact which he takes no pains to conceal. This is how he speaks in the preface to the first part of his utterly worthless history: "For the service of Your Majesty I kept busy in checking accounts whenever and to whatever extent I had to, but in such a way that I would do my duty in the war and the pacification of those people by arms." By "pacification" this sycophant means killing God's rational creatures with Turkish savagery for little or no cause, and with astounding infamy to the name Christian to sacrifice souls to hell who might have come to know Christ. Anyone must be amazed by the enormity of these crimes. But may Christ be kind to me and grant them the spirit of penance for his glory, for if these sins are true, they are light and humane in comparison with those about which I must remain silent in view of the multitude, immensity, and seriousness of the cruelties they perpetrated.

Furthermore, in chapter 8 of book 6 Oviedo tells how gold is mined in those regions. "I had gold extracted by my Indian slaves," he says. You see that he was one of those who used Indians as slaves, that he was a leader, and that he is proud of that diabolical war, and still more of the desolation and destruction of those provinces which were called *del Darién*. Therefore anyone who reads Oviedo's history knows that so many inhuman crimes were committed in that expedition that, even if the Indians were cattle, they could have moved to mercy not only decent human beings but even men with hearts of steel. But if Oviedo was a member of this wicked expedition, what will he not say about the Indians? With what vices will he not charge them in his writings? But what trust is to be given an enemy, one who has fabricated all that history from absolutely shameless lies? Because of these brutal crimes, God has blinded his eyes, along with those of the other plunderers who were infamous for their pride, greed, brutality, lust for power, and ambition, in order that he should not be allowed by God to know that those naked people were mild, simple, and meek, what wealth they had (for the plunderers did not understand the character and docility with which they were endowed), or how ready and willing they were to accept the Christian religion. And this was the second reason why Oviedo wrote so many destructive lies against those harmless peoples.

Why did he not imitate Saint Gregory, who on noticing certain Angles who had been reduced to slavery asked the name of the province from which they had been taken and was told that it was called Deira. "It is indeed rightly called Deira," the holy man said, "for they are led from anger [*de ira*] to Christ's mercy." He asked what the name of their king was and was told that he was called Adelle. "Rightly so," Gregory said, "for he will sing alleluia to the Lord." Oviedo should have done likewise. He should have thought that although the Indians were naked, they could be clothed with faith, hope, and charity. It would be right for a man who wants to be thought to have read the old histories (but which were written in Spanish!) to remember that the Persians, the Scythians, the Massagetes, the Derbices, the Tybarenes, and the Hyrcanians, as well as the Romans, the Angles, the Cantabrians, and the other peoples in Spain, far outdid the Indians (whom our opponents defame as cattle) in vices and uncivilized behavior, as is evident from Strabo, Mela, Solinus, Diodorus, Herodotus, and Jerome.[1] Yet who has read that they were crushed or despised on this pretext, that is, that they were not considered men but beasts? The gospel was preached to those peoples, but in a Christian way, with the moderation of the gospel. Egypt surpassed all other regions in the monstrous and detestable worship of demons, yet when the light of the gospel shone forth the grace of God was so abundant that the lonely places and strange deserts were inhabited by crowds of holy monks. How can Oviedo know whether or not the Indian territories would be inhabited in the same way, had they not been inhumanly devastated? For what cannot be accomplished by the word of God and the grace of baptism? If only Oviedo had applied as much diligence to questioning learned men to learn the marvelous and effective results produced by the word of God, the habit of faith, and the other supernatural virtues, which are most certainly infused into the soul in the sacrament of baptism! Similarly, if only he would busy himself in considering how sweet Christ's yoke is and how light his burden, and also in studying the pious approach and modera-

1. *Adversus Iovinianum,* Book 2.

tion the universal Church has always used in drawing to its bosom those who have not yet come through its doors! [If he had devoted himself as much to these things] as he has devoted his whole life to profane studies in order to appear learned (although he has never learned Latin!), he would immediately temper the abusive and for the most part false words he has used against poor and innocent persons.

Furthermore, in chapter 3 of book 5 Oviedo writes that the inhabitants of Española were given over to sodomy and other heinous crimes. But what he writes is false. For I am one of those who sailed to that island for the first [settlement], or at least on the second [expedition], about the year 1500, at the time the Comendador [Francisco de] Bobadilla (who sent Columbus back to Spain in chains) was there. I stayed there many years. I made a very careful investigation of this matter and learned that among them the heinous vice of sodomy does not exist at all, or very rarely. Indeed, I found that if anyone was known to be guilty of that detestable sin, he would barely escape the hands of the angry women who would rise up against him. Now at the time Oviedo came to that island the entire Indian population had already perished. And of the immense multitude of Spaniards, including those who had killed the Indians, only two or three remained. All the rest had died.

Now Oviedo fabricated his history—or better, his trifles—from stories told to him by one of [these survivors], a certain sailor named Fernando Pérez, who, while serving aboard ship, had never landed [on Española], or only at a very late date. Moreover, Pérez habitually gave an evil account of the Indians, after the manner of sailors, so that those who were more truly plunderers than soldiers might fatten the more on the labor and property of the Indians. Of this we are quite certain. God willing, I shall teach at greater length in the history I shall write about Indian affairs that all the inhabitants of Española, the islands of San Juan [Puerto Rico], Cuba, and Jamaica, as well as the other islands which are called the Lucayas [Bahamas] (which were all very well cultivated at one time but now are abandoned because of the savagery of these men), were completely free of three vices. They did not offer human sacrifice, or eat human flesh, or commit sodomy. They quickly learned very many vices from the Spaniards, however, in the belief that everything done by them was holy. Oviedo's assertion that the Indians are unteachable and incorrigible is falser than false, as will be clear from the second part of this *Defense*.

Chapter Fifty-Nine

Finally, Sepúlveda claims that the Supreme Pontiff Alexander VI advised the kings of Castile to subjugate the Indians by war and that he condoned the war by which those peoples have been brought under our rule. This is absolutely false. The Pope granted the kings of Castile the right to set themselves over the Indian rulers whom they had converted to the faith of Christ and to keep them as subjects under their protection and jurisdiction. But the Pope never commanded or permitted them to subjugate these rulers by war. For how would he permit something that conflicts with Christ's precept and instruction and produces hatred of the name of Christ in the hearts of unbelievers, and is utterly irreligious? For the will of a ruler is always judged to be in conformity with the law.[1]

Now it is unlawful to force the Indians to the faith by war, or by the misfortunes of war to make them hate the Christian religion, by

1. Gratian, c. 6, C. 25, q. 1.; c. 7, C. 25, q. 1.; c. 101, C. 11, q. 3.; c. 23, C. 1, q. 7. Decretals, 2, 13, 13; 1, 2, 7, as well as what the doctors say on this section. Innocent on the Decretals, 5, 39, 43; 1, 3, 5. And what the lawyers say on the Digests, 1, 4, 1, the Codex, 1, 14, 4 and 1, 22, at the end of the book.

whose preaching they see so many regrettable evils inflicted on them. It is beyond belief, then, that the Vicar of Christ permitted war to be waged against them, since this is against all divine and human laws, and especially as it is his concern to spread the faith.[2] Therefore we must believe that he wants what is just and in keeping with Christ's commands and example. And so this is what he ought to do.[3]

Now Christ wanted his gospel to be preached with enticements, gentleness, and all meekness and pagans to be led to the truth not by armed forces but by holy examples, Christian conduct, and the word of God, so that no opportunity would be offered for blaspheming his sacred name or hating the true religion because of the conduct of the preachers. For this is nothing else than making the coming and passion of Christ useless, as long as the truth of the gospel is hated before it is either understood or heard or as long as innumerable human beings are slaughtered in a war waged on the grounds of preaching the gospel and spreading religion. We must think that the Pope wanted the gospel to be preached with Christian meekness. That this was the Pope's intention is proved by the fact that in his bull of concession he cites the petition of the Catholic Kings, which contains the statement that the Indians are a gentle people who have some knowledge of God and are such a people that if they were instructed in the faith, there would be hope that Christ's religion would be spread far and wide. Therefore it is unthinkable that the Pope believed that a people whom the petitioners called gentle had to be overcome by war. And so Sepúlveda's assertion that Pope Alexander exhorted the kings to subjugate those peoples by war is not true.

In order that the matter may be even clearer, I submit the Pope's words:

We have learned for certain that, not long ago, you offered a plan for seeking and discovering some islands and continents which were remote, unknown, and not as yet discovered by others, in order that you might lead their natives and inhabitants to worship our Redeemer and profess the Catholic faith.

2. Gratian, c. 13, C. 24, q. 1.
3. See the Decretals, 1, 29, 2 [or possibly 11]; 1, 3, 20; 3, 6, 1; 5, 29, 21. Gratian, c. 62, C. 11, q. 3.

And a little later:

Who, finally, with God's help, have sailed the ocean with extreme care and discovered certain remote and unknown islands (and continents, too) inhabited by very many peoples living peacefully and not feeding on human flesh and, as far as your aforementioned messengers can judge, those peoples living on the aforementioned islands and continents believe that there is one God, the Creator, in heaven and they seem sufficiently capable of embracing the Catholic faith and becoming imbued with good morals and there is hope that, if they are instructed, the name of Our Lord and Savior Jesus Christ will be easily introduced into the aforementioned continents and islands. Hence, after carefully weighing all matters, especially that of the exaltation and spread of the Catholic faith (as befits Catholic kings and rulers), after the manner of your royal predecessors of honored memory, you have proposed with the help of the divine mercy to make the aforementioned continents and islands, as well as their natives and inhabitants, subject to yourselves and to lead them to the Catholic faith. Therefore, with a high commendation in the Lord for your holy and praiseworthy proposal and desiring that it may be brought to its due fulfillment and that the name of Our Savior may be introduced into those areas, we most earnestly exhort you in the Lord both by that reception of the sacred cleansing by means of which you became bound by apostolic commands and by the heart of Our Lord Jesus Christ, we attentively ask that when you set yourselves to undertake readily and carry out an expedition of this type with zeal for the orthodox faith, you see and consider it your duty to lead the peoples living on these islands and continents to accept the Christian religion. May dangers and labors never deter you at any time from your firmly conceived hope and trust that Almighty God will bring your efforts to a happy outcome.

Five points can be noted in the words of this apostolic decree.

First, the Catholic Kings conceived the plan of seeking through their messengers and discovering islands and continents that were remote, unknown, and not as yet discovered by others in order that by their labor, help, and royal ingenuity they might lead the natives of these lands to worship God and profess the Catholic faith. Here is the purpose of the whole enterprise, which the Supreme Pontiff declares to be his intention (as he ought) at the beginning of the decree cited above, when he says:

Among the other works which are well pleasing to the Divine Majesty and are our heart's desire, assuredly the greatest is that the Catholic faith and the Christian religion be exalted, especially in our times, that it increase and spread everywhere, and that the salvation of souls be attained.

Second, with God's help and with extreme care on their part, they discovered certain islands and continents in the ocean sea in which large numbers of peoples lived peacefully and, as far as their argonauts could judge, believed that there is one God, the Creator, in heaven, that they seemed sufficiently capable of embracing the Catholic faith and being imbued with good morals, and that if they were instructed, there was hope that the name of the Savior would be easily introduced into the aforementioned areas.

Third, imitating the examples of their ancestors, the Catholic Kings wanted to make that naked, simple, sincere, and meek people subject to their rule with the blessing of the Supreme Christ.

Fourth, the Pope praises the Lord for this pious purpose of our rulers and adds that he seeks in a special way that Christ's name be imprinted on their hearts and that he be worshiped by them as the true God in a Christian way.

Fifth, the Pope exhorts the Catholic Kings, by the heart of Christ, as well as by the vow taken in baptism by which they were obliged to observe the apostolic commands, to undertake the enterprise with contempt for all danger and thus for any of their private temporal goods and to have no doubt about the outcome, since they will have the blessing of the all-powerful Christ, who will make their plan succeed.

Chapter Sixty

The intention of the Pope, the plan the kings of Castile presented, and the command imposed on them to fulfill the enterprise are clear in the first and fifth points of the bull. This is why, in the fourth point, the Pope praises the Kings precisely because they wanted to seek new regions, unknown in former centuries, with the intention of spreading the Christian religion. In the bull's second point, where the Pope makes note of the meekness, sincerity, and simplicity of the Indians, as well as their capacity and receptiveness for God's word, he clearly implies the restriction that ought to be found in the third point; that is, that they subjugate (that is, dispose) them for the faith in a way in which one should subjugate a most civilized, sincere, naked, docile, decent, and peaceful people who are very ready to serve, that is, mildly, in a Christian and humane way. As a result, after they first know the true God through belief in the gospel, they may at last freely subject themselves to the king of Castile (from whom they have received such a benefit) as to their supreme prince and emperor, while the rights of their natural lords are retained.

Now the assertion that "subject" should be interpreted as "dispose" is proved from the fact that the subjection of those peoples is taken to be a means by which they may gladly listen to the preaching of the faith and freely accept it. But according to Christ's instructions, the preaching of the faith must be peaceful and loving; and the means must be proportionate to the end, according to the Philosopher.[1] Therefore "subjecting" those peoples is nothing else than peacefully and humanely disposing them to hear the gospel and accept the faith freely. And so it has to be done, according to the traditions of the Christian faith, since leading them to the faith is the purpose and joint plan of both the Pope and the king, as has been said.

Furthermore, these points are confirmed by a maxim of law: "The interpretation of what has been said must be derived from the reasons for saying it, since reality is not subject to speech but speech to reality."[2]

1. *Physics,* Book 2.
2. The rule *Intelligentia: De Regulis Juris.*

This means that words should serve the intention or understanding, since the gospel consists not of the written page but of the foundation of reason and meaning,[3] and whenever reality cannot be preserved in any other way, the words must be extended to a different meaning.[4] Therefore those peoples must be subjected with the meekness of the gospel, as Christ has taught and their nakedness and simplicity demands.

And so this is the way in which we must understand those words of the bull: "you have proposed . . . to make . . . their natives and inhabitants subject to yourselves." For it was very easy for our rulers to subject that people to their authority without the disturbances of war, which are quite foreign to what concerns the gospel. For this would be to act in reverse, that is, to make the means the end and the end the means—a procedure that the Philosopher calls a very bad error.[5] And so war would be very wrong since it would hinder the objective, that is, the spread of the Christian state and the conversion of those peoples, as we have proved above. For this reason it is quite clear that when the Vicar of Christ said "subject," he did not mean to indicate that the Indians had to be subjugated by war, since war would obviously overturn the purpose of God and his Vicar, the Pope, that is, the spread of the faith and the conversion of those peoples, contrary to the command of the Apostle: "Whatever you eat, whatever you drink, whatever you do at all, do it for the glory of God" and "Never say or do anything except in the name of the Lord Jesus."[6] Therefore Sepúlveda's claim that the Pope approved of war against the Indians and exhorted the Catholic Kings to subjugate them by war is false.

Here are the words of the bull: "We most earnestly exhort you in the Lord by the reception of the sacred cleansing . . . that . . . you see and consider it your duty to lead the peoples living on these islands and continents to accept the Christian religion." Note the words "lead to" the faith. Now does leading to the faith mean assailing peoples who are gentle, meek, peaceful, and undeserving of such treatment? Is this leading or is it not, rather, forcing them to accept the faith, not sincerely but

3. Gratian, c. 64, C. 1, q. 1.
4. Codex, 6, 38, 4; 6, 37, 23. See also the gloss on the second rule.
5. *Ethics*, Book 5.
6. Corinthians 12[31]. Colossians 3[17].

externally, as they experience the wickedness of the Christians? Far more certainly, it means driving them further away. The kings are commanded to have as their purpose leading the Indians to the faith. It is granted that subjection to their rule is fitting and helpful for attaining this purpose; still it must be proportionate and suited to that purpose, which is specifically the spread of the glory of the divine name and the conversion of those peoples. But war is not a suitable means for spreading Christ's glory and the truth of the gospel, but rather for making the Christian name hateful and detestable to those who suffer the disasters of war. So war against the Indians, which we call in Spanish *conquistas,* is evil and essentially anti-Christian. For that is not a reason why we may pursue them by war, nor have they ever, even in past centuries, committed any crime against us that would call for war. They have been totally unknown in our regions. Therefore, since war should not be waged unless there has first been a provocation by the person against whom warfare is being prepared toward the one who is waging the war, it follows that war against the Indians is unlawful.[7] This conclusion has also been proved from many arguments that have been offered previously in this work. However, war against them could be just if they committed something that is found in any of the six cases we listed above.

Again, the conclusion that war against the Indians is unjust is proved from the words of the bull, which I shall quote here.

Furthermore, we command you in virtue of holy obedience, what you also promise, and we do not doubt that, in keeping with your very great devotion and royal magnanimity, you will do this, that is, to send to the aforementioned continents and islands upright men who fear God and are learned, experienced, and expert at instructing the aforementioned natives and inhabitants in the Catholic faith and imbuing them with good morals, applying all due care in regard to the foregoing.

Note well, dear reader, the Pope's intention: that those peoples should be led to the truth by a holy and Catholic instruction. Note too what sort of soldiers he commands be sent into those provinces: upright men who fear God and are learned and expert at instructing the natives

---

7. See Saint Thomas [*Summa Theologiae*], II–II, q. 40, a. 1c. The reference from Augustine is in Gratian, c. 2, C. 23, q. 2. See what the canonists say on this passage.

in the Catholic faith and good morals. What do such soldiers have in common with armed thieves and plunderers, who with inhuman savagery overthrow everything with fire and sword? Therefore the assertion that the Pope advised the Kings of Castile to wage war against the Indians is false. It could not occur to the mind of the most holy Pontiff to adopt a means that would necessarily hinder and thoroughly destroy the purpose intended by God and by his Vicar, the Pope.

Chapter Sixty-One

The Catholic Kings understood that this was the mind of the Pope, and still more of Christ (that is, that those peoples be converted to the faith gently and with Christian kindness, not by the terrors of war). This is proved from the words of the will of the Most Serene of Spanish Ladies, Isabella, the ornament of her century, to whom, as the Queen of Castile, the concession was especially granted by the Pope. She says:

Item. Whereas, from the time when the Holy Apostolic See granted us the islands and the continent of the ocean which have been or will be discovered, our principal intention at the time when we asked Pope Alexander VI, of happy memory, to grant us the said concession, was to try to lead and draw the peoples of the said areas and convert them to our Holy Catholic Faith and to send to the said islands and continent prelates and religious and clerics and other learned and God-fearing persons to instruct the natives and inhabitants of these areas in the Catholic Faith and teach and endow them with good morals and to apply due diligence in this work, as is contained at more length in the letters of the said concession—

Therefore, I very earnestly entreat My Lord, the King, and I charge and command the said Princess, my daughter, and the said Prince, her husband, that they so act and fulfill this charge and that this be their principal aim, and that they apply much diligence to this work and neither consent nor yield to any action whereby the Indians, natives and inhabitants of the said Indies and continent, either already acquired or to be acquired, suffer any harm in their persons or goods. Rather, they should command that they be treated well and justly. And if they have suffered any harm, they should remedy and correct it in such a way that they do not exceed in any way what has been enjoined on and commanded us in the letters of the said concession.

These are the words of the solemn document.

You hear, dear reader, that the Queen understood that war against the Indians was not to be inferred from the papal bull but that it commanded that they be instructed in Christian doctrine. You see, too, that she gives the express command that both the Indians and their neighbors be protected from all injury, for it was not loot that had been seized but a land. Therefore she commands her heirs to make good every injury inflicted on the Indians and to carry out everything enjoined upon them by the Pope. And so this is how it has been expressly decreed and stated in many instructions, decrees, and mandates of our Kings.

In agreement with the foregoing is the fact that the Pope granted that the kings of Castile make those realms subject to themselves, not in order to extend the borders of their empire by the addition of so many new kingdoms but in order that those peoples might acknowledge Christ as true God and might be drawn from darkness to light and from death to life. Therefore it is undeniable that the concession of the Pope was made more in favor of the Indians than in favor of the kings. But if we cruelly afflict and completely destroy that people by war, we act most wickedly, as is clear from the rules of law: "What is granted for the sake of some person must not be twisted to his detriment"[1] and "No

1. Liber Sextus, 5, rule 61. See the Codex, 1, 14, 6.

reckoning of law or benevolence of equity allows us to turn whatever is introduced for men's advantage and utility to severity by a harsher interpretation which is to their disadvantage."[2] Therefore the Kings of Castile can neither directly nor indirectly do anything that is opposed to the spiritual or even the temporal development of those peoples.

2. Digests, 2, 3, 25.

Chapter Sixty-Two

Therefore the word "subject," as contained in the bull, has to be understood in a civilized and Christian way. This is proved not only by what has been said previously but also from the common principles of law, that any law or statute should be broadened or restricted according to the limits of the reasoning it expresses, even if the words do not allow this.[1] In the final rule of the rules of law it is said that anyone who understands the words of the law and yet works against the will of the law violates the law.[2] Moreover, the mind of the ruler must be studied,

1. See the Digests, 37, 14, 6, #2; 31, 77, #20; 32, 38, #3. And the Decretals, 3, 30, 4.
2. Liber Sextus, 5, rule 88.

observed, and carried out, even if it does not agree with the exact meaning of the words.[3] For the intention of the speaker must always be taken into consideration rather than just his words.[4] Nor should the words of the speaker be studied more than his will,[5] for the words should serve the intention, not the intention the words, as has been established above.[6] And generally the mind of the ruler must be taken into consideration in documents, as also the reason on which his commands depend.[7] The Archdeacon says that the Pope's intention must be followed completely whenever it is clear and that the Pope's words expressing his intention dispose and prove that this intention is primary.[8]

Now the Pope's intention was that those peoples be led to Christ. But it is certain that this cannot be achieved by war, which gives rise to hatred rather than love of our religion. Therefore the Indians must be led to the faith by meekness, charity, holy conduct, and the word of God, not by war, of which the Pope never dreamed—as we have often said. The kings themselves have understood the command they received from the Pope to mean that those peoples must be subjected not by war but by the word of God, as has been proved very clearly above. In agreement with this is the rule that words must be interpreted strictly in unfavorable matters, while favorable laws must be broadened and extended. "It is fitting that odious matters be restricted and that favorable ones be broadened."[9] Now war, which Homer says is sent from hell, is the most wretched and pestilential of all things under heaven and is utterly opposed to Christ's life and teaching, except when unavoidable necessity forces one to it. But inviting pagans to the faith by the

---

3. Digests, 33, 77, 20.
4. Digests, 33, 10, 7.
5. Codex, 8, 16, last law [9]. Gratian, c. 11, C. 22, q. 5. Digests, 1, 3, 17, and the two following. Digests, 2, 4, 11, and the last gloss on this passage. See Panormitanus and others. Decretals, 3, 31, 6, after John of Legnano. Decretals, 3, 30, 12.
6. Also see John of Legnano on the Decretals, 3, 30, 12.
7. Also see Liber Sextus, 1, 3, 10, as well as the comments of the doctors on this section. Ancarano in the repetition of the same chapter on rescripts, Liber Sextus, 3, 7, and Decretals, 3, 30, 3.
8. On Gratian, c. 6, C. 25, q. 2. See also Gratian, c. 10, C. 25, q. 2. Baldus cites and confirms this in the introduction to his *Liber Feudorum, #Aliqua,* at the beginning.
9. Liber Sextus, "De Regulis Iuris," #15.

word of God and living according to the gospel are holy, truly Christian, and apt for spreading and increasing Christ's glory.

Therefore let us restrict war, the plague of body and soul, and embrace the preaching of the gospel and the sword of the divine word, which are more effective than all human weapons. Close to all this is the principle that even things that should ordinarily be restricted, such as penalties, are extended if it is a question of public welfare.[10] Now it is a matter of public welfare to those peoples that they be led to the faith and to the empire of the kings of Spain, not by war, which is fatal to human beings, but by the word of God, since the result of war will be that they hate the faith rather than embrace it. Furthermore, I believe that no welfare is more public than that which provides for the salvation of so many thousands of persons, in addition to the tranquillity of so many provinces, since the soul must be preferred to all other things.[11]

Therefore let us restrict the word "subject" so that it is understood as meaning that subjection that will be born of the meek and gentle preaching of the divine word. "Subject" must be taken in this sense, even if its literal meaning be opposed to this interpretation, especially since the bull of the Roman Pontiff Paul III expressly forbids these detestable wars that are waged against the Indians under the pretext of religion. He commands that they be led to the faith not by the terror of war but by the word of God and by holy living. I have previously reported the tenor of this bull, dated in the year 1537, in chapter [12].

10. See Bartholus on the Codex, 11, 48, 7.
11. See the Decretals, 5, 38, 13, and Gratian, c. 24, C. 12, q. 1.

Chapter Sixty-Three

Again, to strengthen his error, Sepúlveda takes note of another passage in the same bull of Alexander VI in which the Pope says that he wants nothing more than the exaltation of Christ's glory and the suppression of the barbarians. Sepúlveda throws these last words against us as if they were an Achilles' argument. But if the whole text of the bull is read, the slander—I may even say the shamelessness of [Sepúlveda's] words—will be very clear. Here is the whole matter. The Pope gives high praise to the aspirations of the Catholic Kings and with an expression of great honor says that their victory over the kingdom of Granada and a fierce and barbarous enemy is very well known throughout the entire world.

Hence, when we were called forward to this See of Peter, knowing, as we always have, that as truly Catholic kings and princes (as has been shown in your splendid deeds which are already well known in almost every part of the world) you needed no exhortation to act but with full effort, zeal, and diligence, without sparing any labors ... as your recent recovery of the kingdom of Granada from the tyranny of the Saracens, with so much glory to God's name, gives witness. ...

From this quotation we infer that the words of the Pope, saying that he hoped for nothing more than to see the barbarians vanquished, referred to the Moors of Granada, who were barbarians—as I have said before—and in comparison with other barbarians were most dangerous enemies of the Christian state. Therefore those words of the bull do nothing toward strengthening Sepúlveda's wicked opinion. For how could the Roman Pontiff approve what is so far from Christ's teaching, as has been sufficiently argued above?

I have preached these things, in keeping with the measure of grace granted me, in defense of this lengthy and holy cause, bound as it is by Christian piety. As for the rest, I exhort and advise by Jesus Christ, Sepúlveda, my brother and colleague in Christ, and the other enemies of the Indians to obey the words, to heed and respect the traditions of the holy Fathers, and to fear God, who punishes perverse undertakings.

The Indians are our brothers, and Christ has given his life for them. Why, then, do we persecute them with such inhuman savagery when they do not deserve such treatment? The past, because it cannot be undone, must be attributed to our weakness, provided that what has been taken unjustly is restored.

Finally, let all savagery and apparatus of war, which are better suited to Moslems than Christians, be done away with. Let upright heralds be sent to proclaim Jesus Christ in their way of life and to convey the attitudes of Peter and Paul. [The Indians] will embrace the teaching of the gospel, as I well know, for they are not stupid or barbarous but have a native sincerity and are simple, moderate, and meek, and, finally, such that I do not know whether there is any people readier to receive the gospel. Once they have embraced it, it is marvelous with what piety, eagerness, faith, and charity they obey Christ's precepts and venerate the sacraments. For they are docile and clever, and in their diligence and gifts of nature, they excel most peoples of the known world.

The second part of this *Defense*, written in Spanish, will set all this before the eyes of everyone with very clear arguments and a true description of that world in order that the wicked plunderers who have defamed that very sincere, docile, moderate, and clever people by poisonous detractions and slanderous lies may be silenced.

THANKS BE TO GOD

Translator's Commentary

Pages 3–5 It is not certain whether Bartolomé de la Vega (or Veyga) was Spanish or Portuguese. Little is known about him except that he was the author of *Computo Eclesiastico* (1588). Cf. Jacobus Quetif-Jacobus Echard, *Scriptores Ordinis Praedicatorum* (Paris, 1719–1723), tomus 2ᵘˢ, par. 1ᵃ, A.D. 1499–1639, p. 281b.

Page 3, lines 13–14. In the Latin, "who attacked some outstanding abuse" is *"aliquod insigne facinus adorientes,"* which can also be translated as "those who undertook some outstanding deed." The first translation is more in accord with the ordinary meanings of *facinus* and *adoriri.*

Page 4, lines 17–23. These lines are slightly puzzling in their division. The arrangement given here is that of the Latin manuscript; however, it can also read: "With the greatest assurance they assert that they are battling for the truth, upholding the just cause of our Spanish people, though they are more bound to defend the cause of God and of the Indian peoples who have been redeemed by the blood of Christ. I do not doubt that many thousands of their [the Indians'] souls have been consumed by ever-lasting flames because of this widespread teaching, etc." *"Asserentes nihilo securius sese pro veritate dimicare, nostrorum Hispanorum justam causam sustinere. (Cum causam Dei potius tenerentur defendere, atque Indorum gentium, ob hoc tam impium tamque iniustum disseminatum dogma, sempiterno igne cremari non dubitem."*

Page 5, line 1. If Vega was exact, his letter was written about 1562; however, this is of small help in dating the manuscript except as it indicates the latest possible date.

Page 5, line 19. "Bring to light" in the Latin is *"in lucem sedentibus,"* which, though it comes from Luke 1:79, is meaningless in the context. It is probably a scribal error for *aedentibus,* a variant of *edentibus. In lucem edere* means "to publish," "to bring to light."

Page 5, lines 19–20. The quotation is from Ecclesiasticus 24:32 (verse 31 in some versions). The book of Ecclesiasticus (or Sirach) is included in the Apocrypha in most non-Catholic versions of the Bible. Vega does not cite the verse exactly but in its liturgical form, as used in some of the Masses of the Blessed Virgin Mary.

Page 5, line 23. "Agreement" is one translation of *"animo,"* which can also mean "with purpose" or "with enthusiasm."

Pages 7–9   *Page 7, line 9.* Valladolid in the Latin is *"Pintiae sive Valisoleti."* The present site of Valladolid is sometimes considered to have been the ancient Roman Pintia.

Page 7, line 21. The terms *encomienda* and *repartimiento* were still used indiscriminately at that time to refer to a quasi-feudal grant of land and native workers given by the Crown to *conquistadores* and deserving Spaniards in return for services rendered. Cf. Lesley Byrd Simpson, *The Encomienda in New Spain* (Berkeley, 1966), passim. The legislation referred to was New Laws of 1542.

Page 8, line 17. Marginal note: *"Guines* [sic] *de Sepúlveda."*

Page 9, lines 22–30. There are three marginal notes to this last paragraph: (1) "Condemning the conquests"; (2) "Nothing about the allotments or *repartimientos*"; and (3) concerning the statement that some of the New Laws were revoked, "He is wrong and all the ordinances were revoked, as witnessed by Zarate (?), and other historians."

For "he is wrong" the annotator uses the harsh Latin *"impie loquitur."*

This is one of the few contemporary statements about the outcome of the Valladolid dispute.

(Henceforward only those marginal notes will be mentioned that add something not already found in the text.)

Pages 11–16   *Page 11, line 15.* Gonzalo Fernández de Oviedo y Valdes (1478–1557) was a royal official and one of the earliest chroniclers of the Indies. Most of his anti-Indian prejudices, which aroused the ire of Las Casas, were embodied in his *Historia general y natural de las Indias* (Asunción, Paraguay, 1944–1945 [14 vols.]). For Oviedo and Las Casas, see Hanke's introductory volume to this translation.

Page 11, line 19. "Wiser," in this context, is the translation of the Latin *"prudens."* Because the word and the concept occur frequently throughout the *Defense* and are translated in a variety of ways, it may be well to summarize its meaning. In the sixteenth century the term still had its Aristotelian-scholastic definition and lacked the connotation of caution or care that it now seems to have. For the scholastics, prudence was defined by the almost untranslatable *recta ratio agibilium,* "the right way of doing things." It was contrasted with art (*recta ratio factibilium*), which was concerned solely with the end to be accomplished or produced, whereas prudence looked to the means, especially moral means. The prudent man was the one who knew his objective, his purpose (final cause), and used all the appropriate means to secure it.

A good descriptive definition is given by R. Trevor-Davis in his *Golden Century of Spain* (Harper, 1961): "*Prudente* in sixteenth-century Spanish often retained the force of the Latin *prudens* in the sense of *skillful* or *wise* rather than *prudent,* which suggests too much the idea of cautiousness or even timidity in modern English" (p. 255, n. 1). He also cites the definition of the dictionary of the Royal Academy: "One of the four cardinal virtues which consist of distinguishing or discerning what is good or evil in order to follow or flee it."

Page 12, line 11. Aristotle (384–322 B.C.), the greatest Greek philosopher, was one of the most profound influences on Christian theological and philosophical thought in the Medieval period and immediately after. The synthesis of his philosophy with Christian theology, especially as found in the works of Saint Thomas Aquinas (see below), was the basis on which most theologians of Las Casas's time worked. He was almost the court of last appeal for all information, especially for that which was not strictly Christian and theological.

Page 12, line 15. Thomas Aquinas (1225–1274), a Dominican, was the greatest synthesizer of Aristotle's philosophy and Christian revelation. Called the *Doctor Angelicus* (Angelic Doctor), he was, with Saint Augustine, one of the most profound influences on Catholic theology. His greatest work, frequently cited by Las Casas, is the *Summa Theologiae* (Summary of Theology).

Page 12, line 27. Saint Augustine (Aurelius Augustinus, 354–430) was Bishop of Hippo in North Africa and the foremost theologian of the early western Church. He wrote voluminously on every subject, but his greatest works are his autobiographical *Confessions* and his *De Civitate Dei* (The City of God). Together with Aquinas and Aristotle, he was the most important authority for Medieval and later theologians.

Page 13, line 21. Saint Cyprian (Caecilius Cyprianus, 200/210–258) was Bishop of Carthage in North Africa and an early Christian martyr. He was noted for having engaged in a dispute with Pope Saint Stephan over the value of heretical baptism. His major work is *De Catholicae Ecclesiae Unitate* (On the Unity of the Catholic Church).

Page 13, line 26. Cajetan (Tommaso de Vio, Cardinal Gaetano, 1468?–1534), an eminent theologian, was most famous for his classic commentary on the *Summa Theologiae* of Saint Thomas. An ardent reformer, he was the master general of the Dominicans for ten years (1508–1518) and is famous in Church history as the papal legate who interviewed Martin Luther at Augsburg in 1518.

Page 14, line 30. Saint Ambrose (339–397) was Bishop of Milan and a friend and mentor of Saint Augustine. He began his career as a Roman official, but was popularly elected to the see of Milan when he intervened to stop a quarrel over the episcopal succession. He was deeply involved in the political and religious life of his age.

Page 15, line 6. Saint Gregory the Great (540–604) was one of the outstanding figures of the early Medieval world and in a very real sense helped form it, as well as the modern papacy. As Pope, he was de facto ruler of a good part of Italy, dispatched the first missionaries to England, reformed the Church, and authored many important works. Among these is the *Moralia,* (a commentary on the book of Job), and the *Regula Pastoralis* (Pastoral Rule), which contains the earliest biography of Saint Benedict of Nursia.

Pages 17–22   *Page 21, line 25.* "Hide" is *"celare."* Perhaps the scribe intended *revelare* or *culpare.* Obviously, Las Casas did not try to conceal the crimes of his countrymen.

Page 21, line 32. Marginal note: "The answer to this will be given in chapter 1 and the following."

Page 21, line 35. Marginal note: "The answer to this will be given in chapter 6 and the following."

Page 22, line 1. Marginal note: "The answer to this will be given in chapter 24 and the following."

Page 22, line 4. Marginal note: "The answer to this will be given in chapter 39 and the following."

Chapter One   *Page 25, line 11.* The reference is to Oviedo.

Page 27, lines 33–35. This section is obscure.

Page 28, lines 1–9. This is not a complete sentence in the Latin.

Page 28, line 34. Scholastic theologians habitually referred to Aristotle as "the Philosopher."

Page 29, line 9. Boethius (Anicius Manlius Torquatus Severinus Boethius, 480?–524/526) was the foremost Roman philosopher of the early Medieval period. His most famous work is *De Consolatione Philosophiae* (The Consolation of Philosophy), which was written after he had been imprisoned by the Ostrogothic King Theodoric.

Page 29, line 14. The Second Book of Maccabees is not in non-Catholic versions of the Bible.

Page 29, line 21. "Scythian" was a global name for several nomadic tribes that lived to the north of the Black Sea several centuries before Christ. They were proverbial for their fierceness and cruelty.

Page 29, line 22. Saint Isidore of Seville (Isidorus Hispalensis, 560?–636) succeeded his brother Leander as Archbishop of Seville in 600/601. His most famous work is the *Etymologiae* or *Origines,* an encyclopedia of all the secular and religious knowledge of his time.

Chapter Two   *Pages 30–32, line 12ff.* Bede, called the Venerable (?–735), was the most notable writer and historian of the Anglo-Irish renaissance of the eighth century. His principal work, *Ecclesiastical History of the English People,* is our most important source for pre-Norman English history. It is not true, as Las Casas says, that he wrote in English (i.e., Anglo-Saxon); all his works were written in Latin. This error may have arisen from some early biographies of Bede which indicate that works on the liberal arts in both the classical languages and the vernacular survived from the pens of Archbishop Theodore and Abbot Hadrian. Cf. Migne, *PL,* 90:37, 40.

Page 31, line 2. Jean Gerson (1363–1429) was chancellor of the University of Paris and a theologian of conciliarist sympathies. His principal work was *De Unitate Ecclesiae* (On the Unity of the Church).

Page 31, line 13. John, surnamed Chrysostom ("Golden Mouth") (344?–407), was Patriarch of Constantinople and a famous doctor and theologian of the early Church. Among his other works is a series of homilies (sermon-commentaries drawn from Scripture and the liturgy), some ninety in number, on the Gospel according to Saint Matthew. They survive in two different Latin translations, one of which is complete, the other incomplete. Las Casas cites both, and usually indicates which one he means. Cf. Quasten, *Patrology,* 111:438.

Page 31, lines 24–25. "Lead a settled life" corresponds to what the Spaniards understood by living *politicamente,* i.e., living in a city under a stable government.

Page 34, line 8. On *Old Age and Youth* is a work of doubtful origin, erroneously attributed to Aristotle.

Page 34, line 17. Augustine gives a list of freaks of nature in his *De Civitate Dei,* book 15, chap. 8.

Page 34, lines 21–22. The *Book on Causes* (Liber de Causis) is a pseudo-Aristotelian work that appeared in the last half of the twelfth century and has been variously attributed to Arab and Jewish sources. Thomas Aquinas wrote a commentary on it. This citation is probably from proposition 16.

Page 34, line 28. "The Commentator on *The Soul*" was the Arab Aristotelian philosopher Averroes (Ibn Roshd, 1126–1198), whose works on Aristotle earned him the soubriquet "the Commentator." Cf. *Averrois Commentarium Magnum de Anima* (Cambridge: Medieval Academy of America, 1953). The citation is probably chap. 36, p. 502.

Chapter Three   *Page 40, line 18.* "Sacrificed lamb" in the Latin is *"Agno Theta."* The Greek letter *theta* (θ) stands for $\theta\alpha\nu\alpha\tau\text{os}$ (*thanatos,* death) and was so used in Medieval monastic necrologies, in the same way that we put a cross before a person's name to indicate the fact of his death. In ancient Rome, judges put theta before the names of those condemned to death (Juvenal, satire 4). Du Cange, *Glossarium,* 6: 573.

Page 40, line 25. "Dionysius" (or better, the pseudo Dionysius) refers to four Greek treatises on liturgy and mystical theology, dating from the early sixth century and supposedly written by Dionysius the Areopagite, who had been converted to Christianity by Saint Paul (Acts of the Apostles 17:34). They are neo-Platonic in tone.

Page 40, line 34. The *Roman Lectionary* was one of a series of liturgical books, often in the form of commentaries, that were read at Mass. They often contained information on the saint or martyr whose feast was being celebrated.

Chapter Four   *Page 43, line 5.* This is the first of several references to the second half of the *Defense.* Just what this means, or what was intended, is not clear. Later, he mentions that it was to have been written in Spanish.

Page 43, line 7. Trogus Pompey, a first-century Roman historian, was the author of the forty-four-volume *Historiae Philippicae,* which has been preserved only in an abridgment by Justinus.

Page 43, line 27. Diodorus of Sicily (Diodorus Siculus) was a Roman historian of Greek background and language who began his chief work, the *Bibliotheca Historialis* (Library of History), about 56 B.C. Of the forty books of this work, only books 1–5 survive intact.

Page 44, line 22. Prosper of Acquitaine (390?–455) was a lay theologian and papal secretary who was famous for a series of epigrams.

Page 44, lines 32–33. See 1 John 1:1. "Something which has existed since the beginning, that we have heard, and we have seen with our own eyes; that we have watched and touched with our hands."

Page 44, lines 33–34. Marginal note: "I have lived among them for thirty years and have experienced their marvelous accomplishments in every ingenious craft." Written by hand E.

Page 45, line 8. Paolo Giovio (Paulus Jovius, 1483–1552) was Bishop of Nocera in northern Italy after 1528, but he devoted most of his life to literary pursuits. He is not now highly regarded as a historian. His chief work, *Historiarum Sui Temporis Libri XLV* (The Forty-five Books of the History of His Times), covers the years 1494–1544.

Page 45, lines 24–25. Marginal note: "They write very beautifully and with great skill they print books on skins for the choirs of religious."

Page 46, lines 23–24. An antidotal obligation is one that equals the favor given and thereby cancels the debt.

Page 46, line 28. The chapter number has been left blank.

Page 48, line 22. Augustine of Ancona (Agostino Trionfo) was born of noble parents at Ancona about 1243. He became an Augustinian friar and studied at the University of Paris, where he was a fellow student of Egidio of Rome whom Las Casas cites later —see below. He died in 1328. One of his best-known works was *Summa de Potestate Ecclesiastica* (Summa on the Church's Power).

Page 49, lines 5–6. Emphasis in the original.

Page 48, n. 15. Egidio of Rome (Aegidius Romanus, Egidio Colonna, c. 1243–1316) was an Augustinian theologian. He was successive general of his order and Bishop of Bourges. He is sometimes considered to be one of the earliest disciples of Thomas Aquinas.

Chapter Five   *Page 50, line 2.* For "converts souls," cf. psalm 18 in the Vulgate.

Page 50, line 18. Lactantius (Lucius Caelius Firmianus Lactantius) was a Christian rhetorician and historian who flourished in the last part of the third and the first part of the fourth century. His *Divine Institutes* (the title was derived from the textbook of Roman law) was a refutation of paganism and a demonstration of the superiority of Christianity.

Page 51, line 26ff. Las Casas has confused the principal port of Lesbos, Mytilene, with the Latin word for Malta, *Melita.* As a result, he writes of Malta as a port of Lesbos rather than as a separate island.

Page 52, line 3. Nicholas of Lyra (1270–1340), a French Franciscan theologian and commentator on Scripture, was known as the *Doctor Planus et Utilis* (The Clear and Practical Doctor). He was the author of numerous *postillae* (a short form of *post illa verba,* after these words), which opened scriptural commentaries.

Chapter Six   This chapter may be confusing to a person with a nonscholastic background, but it will be easier to understand if one keeps in mind the basic Aristotelian distinction of potency and act. Potency refers to the capability or the ability to do or receive something, a capability that is retained even when it is not actualized. Thus a sitting man can be said to be in potency to standing. When the capability is fulfilled, it is said to be reduced to act. When Las Casas speaks of a future actual jurisdiction, he is talking about something that is only in the stage of potency at this time but, at some time in the future, is certain to be reduced to act. For example, we say that it is actually dark, but that it is day by potency. But we can also speak of the day as a future actuality because we are certain that it will come about. Las Casas uses "habitual" as synonymous with "potential."

Page 54, line 20. "Competence" is my translation for the Latin *"forum."* Originally this term meant both the public squares of Rome and the law courts. In Church law it has a somewhat wider meaning than jurisdiction, and refers to an entire area of authority or the entire area within which authority is competent to act.

Page 55, n. 2. Peter of Ancarano (1330?–1416) was a Medieval lay canonist and teacher at the University of Bologna. Little is known of his life, though his principal works, including a commentary on the Decretals, have survived. I have not been able to locate the precise rule of law referred to here.

Page 57, line 22. In Catholic theology, *"cultus"* is a generic term that includes any kind of worship, veneration, or honor, whether given to God or to civil authorities or parents. As for worship, it has numerous subdivisions, of which *"latria"* (from the Greek word for worship, which is also found in "idolatry") is the specific form of worship that is given to God alone.

Page 57, n. 9. The Athanasian Creed, a profession of faith, puts special emphasis on the mystery of the Trinity, and was long attributed to the famous Bishop of Alexandria, Saint Athanasius (295?–373). However, it seems to have originated in Gaul in the second half of the fifth century.

Page 59, line 28. "Capable of grace and glory" is a theological expression that means a rational being is capable of attaining eternal life.

Page 60, line 1. "Wayfarer" is the translation of the Latin *"viator."* A theological term, it refers to man in this present life, which is considered a transitional phase *(in via)* to the next. It considers man as striving for eternal life, not as having attained it.

Page 61, line 3. "Contentious jurisdiction" is defined as "jurisdiction in cases involving a legal controversy between the parties to the trial. It is opposed to voluntary jurisdiction, the intervention of a magistrate in matters in which there is no quarrel between the parties and the fictitious trial serves only as a way of performing certain legal acts or transitions" (Adolf Berger, *Encyclopedic Dictionary of Roman Law* [Philadelphia: American Philosophical Society, 1953], p. 524).

Chapter Seven   *Page 63, line 9.* Marginal note: "So it is now in the Council of Trent, Session 14, chapter 2." Speaking of the differences between the sacrament of baptism and the sacrament of penance, chapter 2 says: *"Cum Ecclesia in neminem iudicium exerceat qui non prius in ipsam per baptismi ianuam fuerit ingressus. Quid enim mihi, inquit Apostolus, de iis qui foris sunt iudicare?"* "Since the Church does not pass judgment on anyone who has not first entered it through the door of baptism." "For it is not my business," says the Apostle, "to pass judgment on those outside."

Page 63, line 11. Glosses of all sorts—biblical, legal, theological—were quite popular in the Medieval period. They originally consisted of words or phrases added in the margin or between the lines (interlinear) of texts to explain obscure passages, but they often reached the length of full commentaries. The earliest glosses were biblical, but the commonest ones were on civil or canon law. The earliest legal gloss has been attributed to Ioannes Teutonicus, about the year 1216. The most popular biblical gloss was the *Glossa Ordinaria,* attributed to Walafrid Strabo (d. 849) or Anselm of Laon (d. 1117). This is the one most commonly cited by Las Casas.

Page 63, line 12. Saint Jerome (Eusebius Hieronymus, 347?–420?) was one of the four great Doctors of the western church. He is most famous for his translation of the Scriptures into Latin, called the Vulgate, which is still the official Latin Bible of the Catholic Church.

Page 63, line 13. Anselm of Canterbury (1033–1109) was abbot of the monastery of Bec and later Archbishop of Canterbury (thirty years in all). He was one of the earliest scholastic philosophers. His proof for the existence of God will be treated later.

Page 63, line 20. Saint Athanasius (295?–373), Patriarch of Alexandria, was famous as the inflexible opponent of the Arian heresy.

Page 63, line 25. Theophylactus, also called Bulgarus (from his bishopric at Ocrida in ancient Bulgaria), was an early Medieval Byzantine scripture scholar (?–1107). His works can be found in *PG,* vols. 122–126.

Page 63, line 25. Nicholas of Gorran or Gorrain (Nicholas Gorranus, 1232?–1295) was a French Dominican preacher and scriptural commentator. His best-known work was a commentary on the Epistles of Saint Paul.

Page 64, line 9. Saint Bruno (1030?–1101) was an ecclesiastical writer, scriptural commentator, and the founder of the Carthusians.

Page 64, line 9. Richard of Middletown (Richard of Middleton, Richardus a Media Villa, 13th century) was the author of a commentary (c. 1281–1285) on the *Sentences* of Peter Lombard.

Page 65, line 13. The lines in italic were inserted by Las Casas.

Page 65, line 16. This line is very obscure.

Page 65, line 24. "Circumcellions." Throughout the fourth and fifth centuries North Africa was badly divided and ravaged by a heresy called Donatism. It had grown out of the persecution of Diocletian at the beginning of the fourth century, and had originally been a quarrel over whether those who had apostatized during the persecution (and especially those who had handed over the sacred books to be burned, the *traditores*) should be received back into the Church. Theologically, it became a question of the worthiness of the minister for the valid administration of the sacraments. Donatists held that Christians should freely submit to martyrdom, or even provoke it. By the time of Saint Augustine the issue had become very complicated, involving theological, social, and ethnic factors. Augustine was one of the most strenuous opponents of Donatism.

The Circumcellions were groups of armed Donatist insurgents, often runaway slaves and dispossessed peasants, who terrorized North Africa from the middle of the fourth century down to the time of Augustine. They were notorious for their fanaticism and religious frenzy.

Page 65, line 26. Mapala was a town in North Africa, the burial place of Saint Cyprian, and evidently the scene of Circumcellion disturbances.

Page 66, line 7. "Surrender the place" in the Latin is *"locum dare,"* which can also mean "to yield."

Page 66, n. 10. Hostiensis was Henry of Segusio (?–1271), a Medieval canonist and one of the foremost legal authorities of his age. He was the Cardinal-Bishop of Ostia (whence his name) and the author of the *Summa Aurea* (Golden *Summa*) or *Summa Archiepiscopi* (Archbishop's *Summa*).

Page 67, line 9. Elvira (Latin *Illiberis,* modern Granada) was the scene of a famous Church council that was held about the year 300. Las Casas was mistaken in saying that the chapter he cites refers directly to the Circumcellions, since they did not exist at that time. The problem of Christians who precipitously sought or courted martyrdom was an old one in the Church.

Page 69, line 1. "Strenuously preach" in the Latin is *"prementes maxime Christum,"* literally, those who press forward the cause of Christ very strongly." The exact translation in this context is somewhat obscure.

Page 69, line 8. William of Paris (Gulielmus Parisiensis, 1105–1202) was the French abbot of Eskill in Denmark and the author of *Tractatus de Legibus* (Treatise on Laws).

Chapter Eight *Page 73, lines 20–28.* This quotation from Dionysius is quite different from that given by Migne in *PG* (2:139), and it may be either a paraphrase or from a different version.

Page 74, line 24. "Capable of himself" means either that man is independent and autonomous (and thus the phrase is predicated of man) or that man is capable of achieving a divine destiny, that is, God himself.

Page 74, line 26. "Concupiscible" and "irascible" have been retained because they are technical terms in scholastic philosophy. A concupiscible appetite (from the Latin *concupiscere,* to desire) is attracted toward some good that is fairly easily achieved. Irascible appetite (from the Latin *ira,* wrath) is directed toward a good that is achieved only after some obstacle or difficulty has been overcome.

Page 76, line 20. A play on words, since in the Greek of the New Testament "religious" can also mean "superstitious."

Page 76, lines 21–22. Unbelief as a negation. Scholastic theology distinguishes the lack of something that is not due *(negatio)* from the lack of something that should be present *(carentia).* In English, the difference can be illustrated in the terms non-Christian and un-Christian. The former denotes the lack of Christianity without indicating that it should be present *(negatio);* the latter connotes the lack of something one would expect to find *(carentia).* To say that a person is non-Christian or that he is un-Christian is to say two entirely different things.

Page 76, lines 32–33. The argument from the removal of the genus is roughly equivalent to saying that if one removes the whole, he necessarily removes the part.

Page 77, line 8. *"Ex genere suo"* is a technical theological term that refers to a sin or crime that ordinarily would be considered serious but, because of some extrinsic circumstance (e.g., lightness of matter), can be light. Thus theft is ordinarily considered a serious sin, but if the stolen object is of slight value, the sin is not serious.

Page 77, line 32ff. This seems to be an erroneous citation.

Chapter Nine   *Page 80, lines 26–28.* This quotation was mistakenly attributed to Jerome in some early editions of Gratian. It is really from Augustine's *De Baptismo* (Book 7, chap. 51).

Page 80, lines 28–29. This quotation also was mistakenly attributed to Jerome. It is from Augustine's *Tractatus 68 in Ioannem* (chap. 14).

Page 81, lines 3–5. This quotation is from Gregory's *Moralia* (book 35, chap. 6).

Page 81, line 17. Origen (185/186–254/255) was a famous theologian and teacher of the school of Alexandria. He was one of the most prolific writers in the history of early Christianity and was very influential, despite the fact that some of his teachings were suspected of being unorthodox.

Page 81, lines 18–23. Origen, *Super Leviticum*, homily 14, on chap. 24.

Page 82, line 32. Anthony of Butrio (1338–1408) was a well-known decretalist from Bologna.

Page 83, line 3. John Anania, also known as John of Anagni (1376–1457), was a pupil of Peter of Ancarano. He became a priest after the death of his wife, and is sometimes called the Archdeacon.

Page 83, lines 33–34. Las Casas is following popular etymologies.

Page 83, n. 16. Felinus was Maria Sandeo Felina (1444–1503), Bishop of Lucca and a well-known canonist.

Page 84, lines 21–30. The paragraph in brackets has for some reason been expunged by the corrector.

Chapter Ten   *Page 86, lines 4–10.* The quotation is from *De Poenitentiae Medicina* but in a paraphrased form. It is almost verbatim with the *Glossa Ordinaria* on 1 Corinthians 5.

Page 86, lines 16–20. This quotation is taken from Augustine's *De Baptismo* (Book 6, chap. 44).

Page 89, line 6. Cf. 1 Timothy 2:4–5.

Page 89, n. 8. This is either a faulty citation or it has been incorrectly copied.

Page 90, line 2ff. The terms "should" and "must" are translations of the Latin "*oportet,*" which is used by Las Casas throughout this section.

Page 91, line 14. The words in italic were added by Las Casas.

Chapter Eleven   *Page 83, line 14.* Cf. *PL*, 15:1105.

Page 95, line 5. "Sign of the sheet." Cf. Acts of the Apostles, 10:9–16: "Peter went to the housetop at about the sixth hour to pray. He felt hungry and was looking forward to his meal, but before it was ready he fell into a trance and saw heaven thrown open and something like a big sheet being let down to earth by its four corners; it contained every possible sort of animal and bird, walking, crawling or flying ones. A voice then said to him, 'Now, Peter; kill and eat!' But Peter answered, 'Certainly not, Lord; I have never yet eaten anything profane or unclean.' Again, a second time, the voice spoke to him, 'What God has made clean, you have no right to call profane.' This was repeated three times, and then suddenly the container was drawn up to heaven again.''

Page 95, lines 16–19. This is an erroneous citation. The quotation is actually from Augustine's *De Baptismo* (Book 7, chap. 51), as cited in Gratian, c. 20, C. 24, q. 1.

Page 96, line 18. Jacques Almain (Almaynus, d. 1515) was a well-known conciliarist at the beginning of the sixteenth century. One of his most notable works was the *Liber de Potestate Ecclesiastica* (Book on the Power of the Church).

Page 96, line 24. Panormitanus was Nicholas de Tudeschis (d. 1453). He was called the *Abbas Siculus* (Sicilian Abbot) or *Abbas Junior seu Modernus* (the Younger or Recent Abbot) to distinguish him from the *Abbas Antiquus* (Ancient Abbot), and he wrote a commentary on the Decretals about the year 1275. He was Bishop of Palermo (whence his name Panormitanus) and a decretalist.

Page 97, line 17. Pope Innocent IV (Sinibaldo Fieschi, 1200?–1254) was a famous canonist. He also was the author of *Commentaria super Libros Quinque Decretalium* (Commentary on the Five Books of the Decretals).

Chapter Twelve *Page 99, line 25.* Saint Cyril of Alexandria (370/375–444) was Bishop of that city and a prolific writer of apologetical and exegetical works. The work cited by Las Casas, *Adversus Iulianum,* was directed against the Emperor Julian, called the Apostate. This quotation can be found in *PG,* 76:830.

Page 101, line 25ff. I have been unable to locate a copy of this bull to the Archbishop of Toledo.

Chapter Thirteen *Page 105, lines 19–20ff.* Throughout this section Las Casas is referring to the Old Testament practice of the ban or anathema (Hebrew: *cherem*), whereby all the living things in any city conquered from the pagans in the Promised Land were destroyed. It was for a violation of this ban that the prophet Samuel disowned King Saul. (I Samuel, 13:8–15)

Page 105, n. 4. Abulensis was Alonso Tostado, (1400?–1455) Bishop of Ávila (whence the surname) and a noted scriptural commentator.

Page 109, line 24ff. Las Casas has confused the citation. Rahab the harlot is not mentioned in the book of Numbers but in the second and sixth chapters of Joshua. The marriage of Rahab to Salmon is taken from the genealogy in Matthew 1:5.

Page 109, line 27. Serapion (?–362) was Bishop of Thmuis in Lower Egypt. Little is known of him except his chief surviving work, *Against the Manicheans.* Saint Epiphanius (315?–413) was a native of Palestine and Bishop of Constantia in Cyprus. The work cited by Las Casas is the *Anchoratus* (The Firmly Anchored Man), an exposition of Christian belief.

Page 109, line 28ff. The story of Noah is found in Genesis 9:18–29.

Page 111, line 4ff. The story of Phineas is in Numbers 25:6–15.

Page 111, line 7. See Hosea, chap. 1.

Chapter Fourteen   *Page 112, line 13ff.* Cf. *PL,* 4:658ff.

> *Page 114, line 8.* Cf. 2 Timothy 4:2.

Chapter Fifteen   *Page 118, line 12.* "Serbia" is *"Belgradum"* in the Latin.

> *Page 118, line 17.* Oldraldus of Lodi (or Laude or de Ponte, d. 1355) was a professor of law at Padua and Bologna; he died at Avignon. Alberic may be Alberico de Rosate, a native of Bergamo, who died in 1354; he wrote a commentary on the Liber Sextus.

> *Page 119, n. 10.* This is a free citation.

> *Page 119, n. 11.* This reference to Saint Thomas does not seem relevant to the subject under discussion.

> *Page 122, lines 2–3.* "The ban on first entering the Promised Land" is ambiguous. It can mean either the ban against entering the Promised Land or the anathema that the Jews had to use when they first entered it. Cf. commentary on chap. 13 above.

> *Page 122, line 3.* For the Achan incident, see Joshua 7:19–24.

> *Page 122, n. 26.* "The Master of History" is obscure, but is probably Eusebius of Caesarea (260?–339), often called the Father of Church History.

Chapter Sixteen   *Page 124, line 17.* Here, as elsewhere, Las Casas presumes that Mohammed is the object of Moslem worship.

> *Page 124, n. 1.* Bartholus is Bartolo di Sassoferrato (1313–1357), a Medieval canonist.

> *Page 125, line 8.* "Wicked communications corrupt good morals" is from 1 Corinthians 15:33.

Chapter Seventeen   *Page 127, line 3ff.* Cf. *PL,* 82:314. Isidore of Seville derives the term gentile *(gentilis, gens)* from the Latin word for "beget" *(gignere,* archaic form *geno)* and makes a Christian application.

> *Page 127, line 21.* Invincible ignorance is defined by Catholic theologians as ignorance that cannot be overcome, or only by extraordinary efforts, and that excuses a person from any sort of grave moral guilt. Ignorance is called vincible if it is such that a person is able to overcome it readily. If vincible ignorance is deliberate, it is called affected.

> *Page 127, lines 31–32.* "Voluntary" translates the Latin *"voluntarium,"* a technical theological expression that refers to an act that is freely willed and deliberate. It is an act of which man is the master and is fully responsible for.

> *Page 128, line 18.* Las Casas is arguing that pagans can be invincibly ignorant of the existence and unique character of God because these truths are not self-evident. Scholastic philosophy recognizes certain first or self-evident principles whose truth is apparent without a reasoning process and that, fundamentally, cannot be proved. Thus there is the principle of contradiction: something cannot be and not be at the same time and under the same aspect. Or: the whole is greater than any of its parts. To know the meaning of the terms is to know the truth of the proposition; and these unprovable principles are the bases for all other proofs. But, according to Las Casas, the existence of God and his unique character do not belong to this class of propositions, and so, in

line 27, when he calls this "true," he means only after revelation or a reasoning process. And in line 27, "necessary" means that the opposite cannot be true.

It should be noted that Las Casas goes somewhat beyond the Thomistic school by implying that God's existence cannot be known by reason alone. From the time of Saint Thomas, Catholic theology has been fairly unanimous in teaching that created things can give a glimpse or clue of the nature of the Creator.

Page 129, line 1ff. Las Casas is citing the ontological proof for the existence of God given by Saint Anselm in his *Monologium.* Anselm thought that instead of reasoning to the existence of God from created nature, it is possible to deduce his existence entirely within the mind, that is, from the concept of God itself. Briefly, it is this: God is that than which nothing greater can be conceived, that is, absolute perfection. But to be absolutely perfect, he must exist. Otherwise he would lack an important perfection. Therefore God must exist. Saint Thomas repudiated this argument as an unwarranted jump from the world of the mental to the world of the extramental, or from the world of concepts to the world of reality outside the mind.

Chapter Eighteen *Page 130, line 10.* Saint John Damascene (John Mansur of Damascus, 645?–750?) was an advisor to the Moslem rulers of Damascus and later became a monk. He was involved in the iconoclastic controversy of the eighth century. His best-known work is *De Fide Orthodoxa (The Orthodox Faith).*

Page 133, lines 8–15. Cf. *PL,* 26:1114.

Page 135, line 7. The words in italic were inserted by Las Casas.

Chapter Nineteen *Page 136, line 21.* John Duns Scotus (c. 1266–1308) was a Scottish Franciscan philosopher and theologian, one of the foremost in the period following Thomas Aquinas. He was called the *Doctor Subtilis* (Subtle Doctor), the *Doctor Maximus* (Greatest Doctor), and the *Doctor Marianus* (Marian Doctor). He lectured at Paris and Cologne, and was noted for the subtlety and complexity of his thought.

Page 137, lines 11–12. When Las Casas speaks of doing what lies within one he is echoing the theological principle *Facienti quidquid in se latet, Deus non denegat gratiam* (To him who does what lies within him, God does not deny grace).

Page 138, lines 30–31 to page 139, lines 1–3. PL, 44:959–992. The lines in italic were inserted by Las Casas.

Page 138, line 3. Cf. *PL,* 45:993–1034. The words in italic were inserted by Las Casas.

Page 140, n. 13. Giasone del Maino (1435–1519) was a famous jurist who taught at Pavia.

Chapter Twenty *Page 141, line 6.* The Archbishop of Florence is Saint Antoninus (1389–1459). A Dominican, he founded the famous convent of San Marco in Florence, later became Archbishop, and was famous as a reformer, theologian, historian, and pioneer sociologist. He was the author of *Summa Moralis* (1477) and the *Chronicon* (1440–1459).

Page 141, line 7. Sylvester was probably Sylvester Mazzolini, also called Mazolini or Mozolini, or Prierias from his birthplace of Priero in Piedmont. He was a Dominican theologian (1460–1523) and one of the earliest opponents of Martin Luther. He wrote the *Summa Summarum quae Sylvestrina dicitur* (1519) (The *Summa* of Summas, also called the Sylvestrine).

Page 145, lines 33–34 to page 146, lines 1–4. Cf. *PL,* 22:391–392.

Page 146, line 22. Baldus was Baldo degli Ubaldi (1320?–1400), a student of Bartolo di Sassoferrato and a Medieval authority on both civil and canon law. He wrote commentaries on both the Justinian *Corpus* and the Decretals.

Page 148, n. 29. Francesco Cardinal Zabarella (1360–1417) was a canonist and ecclesiastical diplomat. He studied at Bologna, taught at Florence and Padua, and was the author of commentaries on the Decretals and the Clementines. He was an active participant in the Council of Constance.

Chapter Twenty-One   *Page 151, lines 20–21.* The term alien has been used to translate the Latin *"gentiles,"* which has an ambiguous meaning. Originally it was a Hebrew term (translation of *ha goyyim,* the nations) that was used to designate non-Israelites. Among Christians it came to denote a pagan or heathen. Hence in ecclesiastical literature it can mean (1) a non-Jew, (2) a non-Christian or pagan, and (3) a non-Roman. In Las Casas's usage here it seems that the last two meanings are intended.

Page 151, line 21. Another case of ambiguity in the Latin. *"Imperium"* translates both as "rule" and "empire." According to Du Cange, the latter usage seems to have been more popular, if unofficial (in Las Casas's time the official title was *Sancta Respublica Romana*). Las Casas probably intends both meanings.

Page 151, lines 32–35. Cf. *PL,* 63:711. The quotation is from *In Somno Scipionis.* The words in italic have been added by Las Casas.

Page 152, line 6. The words in italic have been added by Las Casas.

Page 152, n. 4. Angelo degli Ubaldi of Perugia who taught at Perugia, Bologna, Padua, and Florence.

Page 153, line 6. Michael Ulcurrunus is Miguel Ulzurrum, the author of *De Regimine Mundi* (1525), a pro-imperial tract.

Page 153, line 10. John Andrea (Giovanni d'Andrea, 1275?–1348) was an Italian canonist and author of commentaries on Gratian, the Decretals, and the Clementines. He wrote *Additiones in Speculum Gulielmi Durantis* (Venice, 1577).

Page 153, n. 8. The Speculator was Gulielmus Durandus (1237?–1296), a Medieval canonist and liturgist. The sobriquet was derived from one of his principal works, *Speculum Iudiciale* (Mirror of Judgment), on which John Andrea wrote a commentary.

Chapter Twenty-Two   *Page 155, line 15.* Pope Evaristus was Bishop of Rome from the year 99 to about 107. He left no writings, and what Las Casas is citing is attributed to him in the pseudo-Isidorian Decretals, an early Medieval forgery.

Page 156, lines 25–26. Adrian of Florensz (1459–1523) was tutor to Charles V and later became Pope Adrian VI (1522–1523). He wrote *Quaestiones Quodlibeticae* (1515). "Quodlibet" ("whatever") can be translated as "miscellany."

Chapter Twenty-Three   *Page 160, lines 33–34.* "Both they and the Saracens ... as being long established" ("... *cum seniores sint*'") is a confusing sentence. It has been translated to agree with the virtues listed, implying that they have long been practiced among Christians. It could also refer to the Jews and Saracens themselves, or to the fact that the books and works of the Jews were older than those of the Christians. Also, *senior* could be taken in its Medieval sense of master (whence *seigneur* and *señor*), meaning that these things had been practiced among Christians when they were the masters of the Jews and Saracens. All the same, it seems a rather remarkable statement to make in a country that less than a century before had forcibly expelled all Jews and non-Christian Arabs.

Chapter Twenty-Four   *Page 163, lines 23–29.* Cf. *PL,* 34:121–172.

Page 165, line 28. "Little cake" in the Latin is *"placentulum massae."* Placentulum is the diminutive of *placentum,* which means a cake. *Massa* is used in the Vulgate for "dough," rather than the more classical *farina.* It seems probable that Las Casas was talking about a tortilla. I theorize that Las Casas used this circumlocution rather than the word tortilla or a direct Latin translation of it that would probably have been misleading to his audience.

Page 166, lines 11–12 (n. 3). Saint Paul is quoting Ezeckiel 36:20 rather freely in this passage.

Chapter Twenty-Five   *Page 169, lines 31–33.* This is taken from Chrysostom's *Homilia LXXXVIII in Ioannem, alias LXXXVII,* cap. 21, 15, *PG,* 59:478–482.

Page 170, lines 1–9. Cf. *PL,* 182:752.

Page 170, lines 10–12. This is from Leo's *Sermo de Natali Ipsius,* 4ª, *PL,* 54:149–150.

Page 171, line 12. After "centuries" there was another passage, which has been altered by the corrector. It read: "But because from the Spanish nation, so destructive to themselves and all their Indian nations, which of all peoples they rightly judge to be the most untamed and ferocious, barbarous in their fury and inhuman, since they have received from them so many fierce and absolutely unheard of troubles."

Chapter Twenty-Six   *Page 177, line 28ff.* The quotation from Saint Thomas may be generic.

Page 180, line 7. "Tecultan" in the Latin is *"Tecultanas."* It is not clear what it refers to, but it may be the closest the scribe could come to Tezulutlan, the Guatemalan province that was the original Tierra de Guerra, which was evangelized by Las Casas and his companions and later renamed Vera Paz.

Page 180, line 14. "Gently" in scholastic terminology means "in accord with their nature."

Chapter Twenty-Seven   *Page 182, line 21.* Alberto Pio, Count of Carpi, was a pupil of Aldus Manutius, the great Venetian printer. He was driven out of Carpi by Charles V in 1525, and his title was given to the Este family. He was a patron of Sepúlveda.

Chapter Twenty-Eight   *Page 186, line 23.* "In Christ's name" is the translation of the Latin *"antonomastice,"* which is very confusing in this context. As a rhetorical figure, it is the use of a title in place of a proper name, e.g., to refer to Aristotle as the Stagirite or to the Pope as the Vicar of Christ. As a legal term, the meaning is not clear, nor can it be found in most standard dictionaries of Roman law. By an extension of its rhetorical use, I have translated it to agree with the concept of vicarious power, that is, power exercised in the name of another or by reason of a title received from another. Hence it would correspond to the concept of Vicar of Christ in the same sentence.

Page 187, lines 8–9. The quotation from Ecclesiasticus is found in the original in a context of almsgiving.

Page 188, line 12. "The goddess of War" is *Bellona.*

Page 180, line 20ff. The citations from Saint Augustine present some problems in translation. Augustine used the Greek Septuagint translation (third century B.C.) of these verses from Genesis, and since they are obscure it was necessary for him to give a more or less symbolic explanation. The original text of Genesis 4:7 is corrupt. A literal translation, as given by the Jerusalem Bible, is: "If you do well, is it not elevation? And if you do not well, sin [feminine] is crouching [masculine] at your door and unto you its [masculine] desire, and you shall rule over it."

The Septuagint translators handled this as best they could, but the results are still unintelligible. Lacking the tools of modern textual criticism, the Fathers of the Church were accustomed to give such passages figurative or symbolic, or entirely moral, interpretations.

In this section I have based my translation of Augustine on that of Marcus Dods (New York: Modern Library, 1950). However, mine is more a paraphrase than a translation, because the Latin in Las Casas's version is quite cryptic.

For the original, see *PL,* 41:443.

Page 189, lines 12–13. Although the concept antedated him, the pseudo Dionysius seems to have coined the scholastic axiom that Las Casas quotes here: *Bonum ex integra causa, malum ex quovis defectu.* This means that all the circumstances that enter into human acts must be good if the act is to be morally good. One evil circumstance vitiates the goodness of the entire act. Thus to do a good deed with an evil intention or at the wrong time or to the wrong person would be immoral.

This quotation can be found in chapter 4, #30, *PG,* 3:730.

Page 189, lines 16–17. Apparently this is a free paraphrase of Aristotle. The closest parallel to it seems to be Book 2, chapter 6, in the Ross translation, p. 1106b.

Chapter Twenty-Eight [bis]   *Page 192, line 14.* "Permission" is given two definitions by Bouvier: (1) a license to do a thing, an authority to do an act which without such authority would be unlawful; (2) a negation of law, arising either from the law's silence or its express declaration.

Page 193, line 22ff. Las Casas follows a fairly standard, though incomplete, division of human acts: (1) those that are intrinsically good; (2) those that are intrinsically bad; (3) those that under ordinary circumstances would be considered bad but can be rendered moral by some circumstances; and (4) those that are indifferent, that is, neither good nor bad when considered abstractly, and that derive their morality from circumstances and from the intention of the person acting.

Page 193, n. 11. Henry of Ghent (Henricus Gandaviensis, 1217?–1293), a scholastic philosopher and theologian, was known as the *Doctor Solemnis* (Solemn Doctor) and the *Summus Doctorum* (Greatest Doctor).

Chapter Twenty-Nine *Page 195, line 3.* "Achor" for Achan, who was executed in the valley of Achor.

Page 197, lines 15–18. Cf. *PL*, 63:810.

Chapter Thirty *Page 200, line 24.* "Foreigners, merchants, and pilgrims" is ambiguous in the Latin, which is *"exteri mercatores et peregrini."* Both *exteri* and *peregrini* can mean foreigners, but I chose to translate the latter in its later meaning of "pilgrim."

Chapter Thirty-One *Page 205, line 8.* "Imprudent" is the translation of *"indiscretum."* No other meaning fits this context, even though Du Cange does not consider it a proper meaning of the Latin, which basically means "indistinguishable."

Page 205, line 30. For Raymond of Péñafort, see editor's preface. He was the compiler of the Decretals.

Page 206, line 3. Ulrich of Strasburg (?–c. 1278), a pupil of Saint Albert the Great, was a Dominican philosopher and theologian, whose *Summa Theologiae* is more commonly called the *Summa de Bono.*

Page 206, line 8. Astensano of Asta was an Italian Franciscan (died c. 1380) who wrote a *summa* that has been called the *Summa Astensana.* Little is known of his life.

Page 206, line 30. John of Tabia (Giovanni Cagnazzo of Tabia) was the author of the *Summa Tabiena.*

Chapter Thirty-Two *Page 211, line 22.* The Archdeacon was Guido di Baysio (d. 1313), a decretalist. The title is also applied on occasions to John of Anagni.

Chapter Thirty-Three *Page 212, line 7.* "Fear of invaders" is ambiguous in the Latin, meaning either fear on the part of those who are invading or on the part of those who are invaded.

Page 214, line 28ff. In general, Las Casas bases his argument on the canonical principle that no positive law binds under a grave difficulty.

Chapter Thirty-Four *Page 223, line 8.* Hesus and Teutates are known only from the writings of Lactantius.

Page 223, line 12. Marginal note: "On this, see the second book of Livy's *Decades.*

Page 224, line 18. Caius Julius Solinus, a fourth-century Roman grammarian, was the author of *Collectanea Rerum Memorabilium,* which was revised in the sixth century and renamed the *Polyhistoria.* Pomponius Mela was a first-century Roman writer, a native of Spain, and the author of *De Chorographia,* one of the earliest accounts of the ancient world.

Page 224, line 18. Diodorus of Sicily (Diodorus Siculus) was a Greek historian of Roman times. Little is known of his life, but he was the author of *The Library of History.*

Page 224, line 20. Strabo (63 B.C.–A.D. 24) was a geographer-historian; his principal work was the *Geography.*

Page 224, line 29. Polydor Vergil (1470?–1555) was a Renaissance historian, papal diplomat, and the author of *Anglicae Historiae Libri XXVII.*

Page 225. Lines in brackets have been deleted from the Latin by the corrector.

Chapter Thirty-Five *Page 226, lines 13–14.* This seems to be a paraphrase. Cf. *PG,* 94:842.

Page 227, lines 8–11. Cf. *PL,* 63:765.

Page 227, n. 2. Gregory of Nazianzen (325?–389/390) was one of the foremost theologians of the early Greek Church. The reference is probably to his *Theological Discourses.*

Page 228, line 16ff. Las Casas is speaking of the theological concept of merit and reward *de condigno* and *de congruo.* The former refers to merit that establishes a strict right, something an individual earns in the full sense of the term. Thus fulfillment of a valid contract establishes a strict right *de condigno* to the object of the contract.

Congruous merit, on the other hand, comes from a person who is not strictly obliged to reward an individual and yet does so out of a certain fittingness. Although no strict right in justice is involved, yet an individual can be said to deserve something for some other reason, e.g., because it is highly appropriate. There is a basic relationship, but it is not based on strict justice.

Chapter Thirty-Six *Page 234, line 35.* Dionysius of Halicarnassus (first century B.C.), a Greek historian, was author of *Roman Antiquities,* a history of Rome to the first Punic War. His works can be found in the Loeb Classics.

Page 236, line 15ff. Scholastic philosophy and theology accept certain truths as self-evident (*per se nota*). This means that no reasoning process is demanded in order to know that they are true: to know the terms of a proposition is to apprehend the agreement between them. The simplest form is tautology, e.g., "A mouse is a mouse." The most fundamental of these self-evident principles, the one on which all others depend, is the principle of contradiction: Something cannot be and not be at the same time and under the same aspect. The principle of affirmation and negation, mentioned by Las Casas, is derived from it: Something cannot be affirmed and denied about a subject at the same time and under the same aspect.

Page 238, line 5ff. This reflects Las Casas's principle that sovereignty resides first and foremost in the people, a principle that he elaborates more fully in chapter 56.

Chapter Thirty-Nine *Page 251, line 4ff.* These peoples all seem to have lived in the vicinity of Asia Minor and the Caspian Sea.

Page 252, line 7. Juan de Torquemada (1388–1468) was a famous Dominican theologian and anti-conciliarist.

Chapter Forty *Page 255, line 6.* A word is missing here, probably a main verb, which makes the meaning of the sentence elusive.

Page 258, lines 11–12. Las Casas is referring to the canonical and moral principle *Accessorium sequitur principale,* by which a secondary or accessory obligation or power always follows the nature of the original or principal.

Page 259, lines 25–27, page 260, lines 10–13. Cf. *PL,* 182:749.

Page 261, lines 14–16. The Roman Breviary responsory at the second nocturne of matins for the feast of Saints Peter and Paul, 29 June.

Chapter Forty-One *Page 265, line 20.* "And so men. . . . " This was originally a part of the previous sentence, but the corrector has altered the verb to a finite form from the original infinitive with subject accusative. However, he did not alter the form of "men" (*"viros"*), and so some confusion remains.

Chapter Forty-Two *Page 268, line 15.* "There was a man who gave a great banquet and he invited a large number of people. When the time for the banquet came, he sent his servant to say to those who had been invited, 'Come along; everything is ready now.' But all alike started to make excuses. The first said, 'I have bought a piece of land and must go and see it. Please accept my apologies.' Another said, 'I have bought five yoke of oxen and am on my way to try them out. Please accept my apologies.' Yet another said, 'I have just got married and so am unable to come.'

"The servant returned and reported this to his master. Then the householder, in a rage, said to his servant, 'Go out quickly into the streets and alleys of the town and bring in here the poor, the crippled, the blind, and the lame.' 'Sir,' said the servant, 'your orders have been carried out and there is still room.' Then the master said to his servant, 'Go to the open roads and the hedgerows and force people to come in to make sure my house is full; because I tell you, not one of those who were invited shall have a taste of my banquet.'" Luke 14:15–24.

Page 269, line 4. "Shape" in the Latin is *"optant,"* almost certainly a scribal error for *aptant.*

Page 269, line 8ff. A parable is usually defined as a story whose entire framework contains a particular lesson. Whole corresponds to whole, so that the parable can have details that are included merely for the sake of the story. On the other hand, an allegory is a story in which each detail has a symbolism or meaning. Thus the parable of the unjust judge, which teaches the lesson of perseverance, is pure parable, since Christ was not comparing the Father to an unjust judge in every detail. On the other hand, the parable of the weeds among the wheat, in which the farmhands represent angels, the fire hell, etc., contains many allegorical elements.

Page 271, line 9. "Nebuchadnezzar was driven from human society and fed on grass like oxen and was drenched by the dew of heaven; his hair grew as long as eagles' feathers and his nails became like birds' claws. . . . 'At that moment my reason returned and, to the glory of my royal state, my majesty and splendor returned also.'" Daniel 4:30 ff.

Page 273, line 11. Cardinal Hugo is possibly Hugh of Saint-Cher, a thirteenth-century Dominican scriptural commentator.

Chapter Forty-Three   *Page 277, line 26.* "Special [bestial]"; the original is ambiguous.

Chapter Forty-Eight   *Page 299, line 6.* "Spiritual father" is translated from *spiritualis compater,* a phrase whose precise meaning is obscure.

Page 300, n. 1. Paul the Deacon (730?–799?), a Carolingian historian, was the author of *Historia Langobardorum* (History of the Lombards).

Chapter Fifty   *Page 309, lines 11–12.* This line is obscure. "The first obedience" refers to the citation from Saint Paul quoted previously.

Page 310, lines 15–16. The reference to law and "their books" may refer to the law of the Jews (the Torah) and the books of the Old Testament.

Page 312, line 8. Arius was a fourth-century priest of Alexandria who denied the divinity of Christ. His heresy spread rapidly throughout the east and was condemned by the first Council of Nicea (325).

Page 312, line 13. "Actively working" in the Latin is *"perduelliones,"* an abstract verb referring to the general act of working against one's own side in favor of the enemy. It is probably a mistake for *perduellis,* which refers to the person who so works.

Page 312, line 28. "Prejudiced pleading" in the Latin is *"praevaricatio,"* which in Roman law refers to a lawyer's knowingly pleading what is false or misleading.

Chapter Fifty-One   *Page 314, lines 4–9.* It is difficult to determine the correct form of this quotation. The words in italic are not in Gratian's citation, but they are in *PL,* 77:530. According to Migne's note for *Daticii* (*Daticiorum*), some read *Datitiis* and others *Daratitiis.* All of these are obscure. The Dacians were a Danubian people and had nothing to do with North Africa.

Page 314, line 8. "The patrimony" was the Patrimony of Peter, a collective name for all the estates, holdings, and property of the Church of Rome.

Page 314, line 25. Eutropius, a fourth-century Roman historian, was the author of *Breviarium ab Urbe Condita* (*Summary from the Founding of the City*), a popular historical textbook that was expanded by later authors.

Page 315, line 10. "Jesus" is the Greek form of Joshua. "Nava" is the latinized form of Naue, which in turn is based on a misreading by the Greek Septuagint of the original Nun.

Page 316, lines 20 and 22. The words in italic were inserted by Las Casas.

Page 318, line 26ff. Las Casas here follows many early Christian authors who mistakenly attributed an anti-pagan religious policy to Constantine.

Page 318, line 29. Hugh of Fleury (d. circa 1118) was a Benedictine monk and Medieval historian.

Chapter Fifty-Two   *Page 324, lines 9–11.* These lines, inserted by Las Casas, paraphrase Psalms 74:8.

Chapter Fifty-Three   *Page 326, line 1.* John Major (or Mayr) was a Scottish theologian, and one of the first to address himself to the theological-juridical problems of the Indies. At the age of twenty-three he was at the college of Santa Barbara, and later at Monteagudo, where he received his doctorate in 1505. Vitoria appears to have known him and perhaps was his pupil, or at least may have attended some of his lectures as an occasional student, though he quotes him but rarely and shows no definite sign of having been influenced by the Scotsman. Major seems to have considered the questions of the Indies in marginal fashion. See also Lewis Hanke's comments on Major in the introductory volume to this translation, *All Mankind is One* (De Kalb: Northern Illinois University Press, 1974).

Chapter Fifty-Four   *Page 331, line 33, page 332, lines 1–2.* The words in italic were inserted by Las Casas.

Chapter Fifty-Six   *Page 338, line 22ff.* Like many Spanish scholastics of the sixteenth century, Las Casas believed that sovereignty resides in the people. Suarez and Mariana taught the same thing. Part of this may be traced to the constitutionalism of the Medieval period or to the influence of the various Spanish *fueros*.

Page 340, f. line 7. Due to translator's error the following paragraph was omitted from the text:

"What has this to do with the Indians of the New World who live very close to the equator? All of their provinces are twenty or twenty-five or thirty degrees distant from the Arctic and a little more from the Antarctic, both to the north and to the south. Now since the days and nights on the equator are equal in length, it is very temperate. From this we infer that the Indians live in the most favorable regions of the whole world— a fact which we not only know theoretically but have experienced in practice. Consequently, according to the ideas of Aristotle, Vegetius, and Ptolemy, the Indians are clever and most capable of reasoning. We ourselves are witnesses to this fact for we have traveled for very many years through those regions, thoroughly observed those peoples, have considerable information about their practices and capacities, and know far more than what John Major foolishly writes in his ignorance about the happy nature of the people and of the equator. If he knew only this, it would be enough to make him reject the slanders and lies of those who, on invading those provinces, did most monstrous damage to a gentle, sincere, and decent people—something which can hardly be told without tears."

Page 341, lines 2–4. This is capable of another translation: "since he wished to moderate the rather harsh things he seems to have said to (or about) the Emperor's men." Though there is only a shade of difference in meaning, the translation chosen in the text seems to fit the context better.

Page 341, line 6. "Speaking conditionally"; that is, on the hypothesis or supposition that the submitted information is accurate.

Page 341, lines 12–13. Miguel de Arcos was a native of Córdoba. Almost nothing is known of his life except that he was the author of *Collationes de Quindecim Virtutibus Beatae Mariae Virginis* (Quetif-Echard, *Scriptores,* part 2, p. 824).

Master Herrera was probably Alfonso de Herrera (Quetif-Echard, part 1, p. 165), though the authors say that he never advanced beyond the bachelor's degree. He was

Court preacher to Charles V and had studied at the University of Paris. His principal work was *De Valore Bonorum Operum adversus Lutheranos Disceptatio* (Paris, 1540). He died about 1558.

Agustín de Esbarroya, of noble lineage, was a native of Córdoba who studied at Seville. Soto, on hearing him dispute, exclaimed *"O felix ingenium, infeliciter natum,"* referring to the fact that as a *cordobés* he had studied in Andalusía rather than Salamanca or Alcalá and so fell short of greatness (Quetif-Echard, Pars Ia, p. 152). He died in 1554.

In the *Democrates,* Sepúlveda claims that Esbarroya agreed with his position: *"Item nobis suffragantur magno consensus Hispalenses theologi, qui nuper summa quaestionis diligenter perlegerunt. . . . Augustinus Esbarroia, monachus Dominicanus, qui theologiam ex cathedra in suorum collegio docet."* (We are likewise supported by the agreement of the theologians of Seville, who recently read over the summary of this question very carefully and diligently. . . . [including] Agustín Esbarroya, a Dominican monk, who holds the chair of theology in their college.)

Diego de Vitoria, the younger brother of Francisco, was famous as a preacher and teacher. He was Court preacher to Charles V (Quetif-Echard, *Scriptores,* p. 107). Las Casas refers to him as a *"presentatus,"* though no mention of this is found in Quetif-Echard. It is difficult to say exactly what the term means in this context.

It should be noted that the names of Vitoria and Arcos are attached to *Democrates* as having given it their approval.

Chapter Fifty-Seven   *Page 342, line 16ff.* Sepúlveda's appeal to the Council of Trent does not seem to be mentioned elsewhere. The first session of the Council met from December 1545 to the spring of 1547, when part of it moved to Bologna because of the plague. It accomplished little there and adjourned in September 1549.

Page 343, line 5ff. According to Hanke (*Spanish Struggle,* p. 114), what Sepúlveda sent to Rome and had printed there was an apology or defense of his original work, directed against Bishop Ramirez of Segovia. It is quite clear that the original *Democrates Alter* was never printed in the lifetime of either antagonist. Sepúlveda evidently thought that he would have a better chance at Rome, which at that time was still very much a Renaissance city.

Page 344, line 19. The translation is obscured by the meaning of *"stemma."* Originally it meant crest or crown (as in the modern Italian), but it also has the meaning of genealogy. Because of this I have given it the extended meaning of history. There is also the possibility that it is a form of *estema,* the Medieval Latin for mutilation or destruction.

Chapter Fifty-Eight   *Page 345, line 4.* Pedrarias Dávila (Pedro Arias de Ávila, 1440?–1531?) served against the Moors in Spain and Africa. As governor of Darién after 1514, he was responsible for the execution of Balboa (1517). He founded Panama City in 1519 and in 1526 was made governor of Nicaragua. He was one of the least admirable personalities involved in the Spanish conquest.

Page 345, line 5. "Darién" is present-day Panama.

Page 345, line 11. *"Veedor"* (literally, one who sees) was a Spanish official in charge of inspecting or checking on various affairs, especially financial ones.

Page 346, line 17ff. This is a complicated but not obscure section. In customary fashion, Las Casas begins by asking for divine mercy for himself at the same time that he asks it for others, so as not to appear to judge others rather than himself. Then he twists the sentence to indicate that what they must do penance for is far worse than anything he has thus far mentioned.

Page 347, lines 5–11. The famous story of Gregory and his puns can be found in Bede's *Ecclesiastical History* (book 2, chap. 1). For "Adelle" read Aella.

Chapter Fifty-Nine *Page 352, line 3.* The irony of "argonaut" may be deliberate.

Chapter Sixty-Two *Page 359, line 8.* The Archdeacon could be either John Anania (see commentary on chapter 9) or Guido de Baysio (see commentary on chapter 32). Probably it is the former who is cited here since the subject under discussion is a canon from Gratian (Baysio was a decretalist).